Professional Refactorin

MW01221675

Professional
Refactoring in C# & ASP.NET

Danijel Arsenovski

WILEY

Wiley Publishing, Inc.

Professional Refactoring in C# & ASP.NET

Published by
Wiley Publishing, Inc.
10475 Crosspoint Boulevard
Indianapolis, IN 46256
www.wiley.com

Copyright © 2009 by Wiley Publishing, Inc., Indianapolis, Indiana

Published simultaneously in Canada

ISBN: 978-0-470-43452-9

Manufactured in the United States of America

10 9 8 7 6 5 4 3 2 1

Library of Congress Cataloging-in-Publication Data is available from the publisher.

About the Author

Danijel Arsenovski is an author, software architect, and agile coach. Currently, he works as Product and Solutions Architect at Excelsys S.A., designing web 2.0 banking solutions for numerous clients in the region. He started experimenting with refactoring while overhauling a huge banking system, and he hasn't lost interest in refactoring ever since. He is known for evangelizing about refactoring on the .NET platform. Arsenovski is a contributing author for *Visual Studio Magazine, .NET Developers Journal*, and *Visual Systems Journal*. He holds the Microsoft Certified Solution Developer (MCSD) certification, and was named Microsoft MVP in 2005. You can reach him at danijel.arsenovski@empoweragile.com, and feel free to drop by at his blog at `http://blog.refactoring.net`.

Credits

Acquisitions Editor
Katie Mohr

Development Editor
Julie M. Smith

Technical Editor
Vojislav Stojkovic

Production Editor
Angela Smith

Copy Editor
Luann Rouff

Editorial Manager
Mary Beth Wakefield

Production Manager
Tim Tate

Vice President and Executive Group Publisher
Richard Swadley

Vice President and Executive Publisher
Barry Pruett

Associate Publisher
Jim Minatel

Project Coordinator, Cover
Lynsey Stanford

Proofreader
Jen Larsen, Word One

Indexer
Johnna VanHoose Dinse

Acknowledgments

Writing a book requires a lot of dedication and hard work. It is also an opportunity to learn and it is generally a lot of fun. Several people helped to keep the writing of this book on a fun side while still making sure I did a good job.

Vojislav Stojković showed special dedication while reviewing this book, much surpassing his role of a technical editor. Many of his smart suggestions found their way into the manuscript. It is great to write knowing that you have such a knowledgeable developer overlooking your efforts.

Julie Smith, my development editor, made sure I stayed on the right track and was always available to answer my doubts and queries. I would like to thank Katie Mohr, the acquisition editor, for her support, professionalism, and openness.

I would like to thank my coworkers at Excelsys S.A. for their support, their understanding, and the interest they have shown in my work.

Finally, I want to thank Dusan Miloradović for his review and excellent feedback. Other people that provided feedback and made me believe I was on the right track are Dan Mabbutt, Sandeep Joshi, Anthony Williams, Rod Stephens, Mark Miller from Developer Express, and others.

Thanks to Vukan Djurović for convincing me that you can always improve the way you write code, and to Diego Dagum for his interest in my work.

Contents

Contents

Contents

Contents

Contents

Introduction

Thank you for choosing this book and welcome to the fabulous world of refactoring. I hope you will find this book useful as you go about your daily programming chores, as you discuss different design solutions with your peers, when you are getting ready to attack some obscure legacy code, and even as you are going over some lines in your mind that are keeping you awake at night. If this is your first encounter with refactoring, I expect this book to profoundly change the way you program and think about code. This is not an easy task to learn, and, ultimately, you will be the judge of how successful a teacher I was.

I adopted refactoring in a systematic manner after I read the book *Refactoring: Improving the Design of Existing Code* by Martin Fowler (Addison-Wesley, 1999). This book proved to be both down-to-earth and practical, helping me learn some indispensable techniques that I could apply in real-life projects right away. The book is not based on some complex theory, nor does it contain any complex mathematical formulas.

It speaks in a language immediately understandable by anyone writing the code. Soon after I read the book, I noticed a number of changes in the way I program:

- ❑   I was able to detect with much greater certainty problematic code and design flaws.
- ❑   I was able to think of solutions for those problems and resolve them effectively through refactoring.
- ❑   When talking to my peers, I was able to explain my decisions in a clear and concise manner.

I stopped looking at code as some solid structure constant in time, and started viewing it as a plastic, moldable form that I can fashion at any moment to my liking and in accordance with my needs. This provoked a fundamental change in the way I treat code. I realized that there is a way to modify and extend code in an efficient, predictable manner and improve its design in the process.

Soon, the word about refactoring started to spread inside the team I worked with, and I saw more and more of my coworkers taking the book from the shelf. A few even got their own copies. I was able to speak with them using refactoring terminology and introduce refactoring as an integral part of the software construction process. Even management proved to be forward-looking in this respect.

Partly because of my own interest in learning different languages and technologies, and partly because of the necessities that I am often presented with at my workplace, I get to work with different teams and program in different languages. I tried disseminating refactoring when working with teams that program in C# in a similar manner to how I did it with Java teams. This proved to not go that smoothly. Soon I realized there is very little information on refactoring available for .NET programmers. While most of the refactorings can be applied in a similar manner in any object-oriented programming language, there are some subtle differences. There is no reason why programmers should not learn to refactor by looking at code examples written in their language of preference.

This inspired me to first write a book about refactoring in Visual Basic .NET and finally to write this book about refactoring in C# and in ASP.NET. I am convinced that there is a real need for such a text and that this book will be of practical use to many who program in C#.

Whom This Book Is For

This book is intended for experienced (intermediate to advanced) C# developers who wish to be introduced to the world of refactoring. To get the most out of the book, you should have a reasonable command of the C# programming language and especially object-oriented programming principles.

If you are a beginning programmer, you will not be able to use this book as your primary source. This book will not teach you the basics of programming in C#. There is no reason, however, not to get acquainted with refactoring as early in your career as possible. As you learn to program your first classes, you can use this book to learn how to design them properly and how to correct any mistakes you might have introduced into your design.

You might find this book useful if you are coming to C# from other programming languages such as C++, Java, or VB.NET. For a transitioning programmer, a new language syntax is generally easy to pick up, but the spirit of a programming language is something much more difficult to grasp. This book can help you learn to program "in the spirit of C#."

This book makes no assumptions about the type or domain of your application. It can be a typical web application, a web service, a framework, a component, a shopping cart application, a new Facebook widget, or a shooter game; but whatever it is, as long there is some C# code in it, you will find the techniques explained in this book valuable.

The book also deals with some ASP.NET-related refactorings. These will be of primary interest to you if you are creating web applications in .NET and write HTML and ASP.NET code. Here, the book ventures beyond pure C# code and deals with code and technologies such as HTML, HXTML, CSS, HTTP, and similar. While chapters dealing with ASP.NET can be read by any ASP.NET developer, ASP.NET code examples are written in C#.

Most of the refactorings I deal with in this book are standard refactorings applicable in any fully object-oriented language. This means that if you program in some other object-oriented language, such as C++, as long as you are familiar with C# syntax and you are able to read code examples, you will be able to use and apply the information provided in this book.

What This Book Covers

I have tried to make this book a thorough introduction to refactoring in C# and some refactoring concepts specific to ASP.NET.

This book covers the following basic refactoring concepts:

❑   Code smells

❑   Refactoring code transformations

❑ Some basic object-oriented principles

❑ Using a refactoring tool to automate the refactoring process

The book uses a single case study, relatively large in size for a book case study, to demonstrate the practical, real-life application of refactoring over a realistically large code base.

In addition to standard refactorings applicable to any object-oriented language, this book teaches some C#-specific refactorings. It also demonstrates some special uses of refactoring. For example, you will learn how to convert classic C# code to LINQ, and how to use extension methods. Also included is the subject of design patterns.

This book contains a large number of important smells and refactorings. However, it does not represent a complete refactoring catalog; because of time and space limitations, some important refactorings had to be excluded. For example, it does not deal with refactorings such as Simplify Conditional or Reverse Conditional, already available for automation in the Refactor! for ASP add-in from Developer Express.

Nor does it deal with many "reverse" refactorings, such as Inline Class. This book is intended first of all to be an introduction to refactoring. My experience has shown me that the first problem that programmers deal with when starting out on the refactoring path is poorly structured code, and refactorings such as Extract Method or Extract Class deal with this problem. Their opposites, Inline Method and Inline Class refactorings, help you deal with excessively structured code. They will aid you in eliminating constructs (methods or classes, for example) that are not needed anymore. This often happens after extensive refactoring is applied to the code base.

This does not mean that "reverse" refactorings are less important. The need for them is more likely to appear later on in the refactoring acquisition, once you have already grasped the basics of refactoring. Part of the learning process is understanding that the knowledge acquisition process never really ends. For example, with each new version of the Refactor! add-in, new refactorings are added to the battery of supported refactorings.

People invent and devise new refactorings continuously. As you become proficient in the technique, you will invent your own refactorings and might eventually decide to share them with others. I invite you to go beyond this book; don't feel limited by the refactorings covered here. Look for and try to invent new refactorings. This way, you will truly master the art of continuous code improvement.

How This Book Is Structured

Because this is the first book that deals exclusively with refactoring in C# and ASP.NET and will probably be the first book on refactoring for the reader, I hope this book functions on multiple levels:

❑ A thorough introduction to refactoring in C#

❑ A thorough reference on refactoring techniques and code smells that can be consulted during everyday programming sessions

❑ A demonstration of how refactoring techniques can be applied in a real-world scenario, by means of single case study, the Rent-a-Wheels application, which is analyzed and modified at the end of each chapter throughout the book

Introduction

In order to accomplish that, the main book narrative reads just like those of any other technical books. New concepts are introduced and elaborated in logical progression from more basic to more complex. Simplified, illustrational code examples are given for each concept. This way, you can read this book in logical order from beginning to end. This is something that you should probably do once or twice after you acquire this book and open it for the first time.

In addition to this main narrative, you will see that the book is sprinkled with so called "definition boxes" of smells, refactorings, and object-oriented design principles. The purpose of these definitions is to give a condensed overview of the subject. In the case of smells, for example, the definition contains heuristics on how the smell can be discovered. In the case of refactorings, there is a section called "Mechanics" that contains a type of recipe describing the steps you need to perform in order to execute the refactoring effectively. You should be able to consult these during your everyday work, to remind yourself how the refactoring is performed, how a smell is discovered, what refactoring can be used to eliminate it, and so on.

At the end of most chapters is a discussion of how the refactorings, smells, and principles covered in the chapter are reflected in the case study included with the book. You can download the code for the chapter and browse it as you read about what happened to the case study in the current chapter. The purpose of the case study is to present you with a realistic application of refactoring. Often in technical books you will find a selection of code samples that have been unrealistically simplified in order to prove a point. While this makes the examples clearer and easier for the writer to demonstrate, it often means the reader will later confront much more complex situations in real life, with many unexpected obstacles appearing if certain techniques are to be applied to production code. In this book, I tried to present readers with a much more realistic scenario by means of the "Rent-a-Wheels" study case.

The book is divided into five major parts that lead the reader from more basic concepts to more complex concepts in a logical, easy to follow progression:

- ❏ Chapters 1 to 4 are meant to lay the foundation for the book. For example, in Chapter 1 I talk about refactoring in general terms. This chapter also dispels some common myths about refactoring. Chapter 2 gives you a taste of refactoring in practice right away, and then Chapter 3 goes over the tools that you will find indispensable in order to automate your refactoring work. Chapter 4 presents you with the case study used throughout the book.

- ❏ Chapters 5 to 8 deal with some standard, core refactorings. You learn about the importance of choosing names for your code constructs and about the devastating effects of duplicated code. You deal with standard refactorings such as Extract Method and go into the details of code structuring on a method level.

- ❏ Chapters 9 to 11 cover some more advanced refactorings that enable you to obtain the most from the object-oriented capabilities of your programming environment. Good object-oriented skills are essential for this part of the book. You will learn how to discover classes, create inheritance hierarchies, and reorganize your code on a large scale.

- ❏ Chapters 12 and 13 show you how refactoring can be successfully applied in order to reach a more specific goal. For example, you will see how refactoring can be paired with design patterns to produce even more sophisticated designs. You will see some of the new features that come with the Visual Studio 2008 version of C# and how refactoring can be used to get the most out of them. In Chapter 13 I talk about leveraging LINQ, extension methods, and other C# 3.0 features. I even go back to the example from Chapter 2 and give it another go with the sample application, this time from a C# 3.0 perspective.

❑ Chapters 14 and 15 deal with ASP.NET-specific refactorings. Chapter 14 lays the foundation for refactorings in the following chapter. It begins by describing the Refactor! for ASP.NET Visual Studio add-in, and then explains the historical background for many of the smells associated with web applications and HTML. In Chapter 15 you will learn how you can make your code compliant with newer web standards such as XHTML and CSS and how you can benefit from ASP.NET code reuse mechanisms such as master pages and user controls.

What You Need to Use This Book

In order to successfully use this book, you will need the following software:

❑ **Visual Studio .NET 2008:** You need at least the Professional Edition in order to be able to use the Refactor! for ASP add-in. You will still be able to debug, execute code, and perform refactorings manually in the free Visual C# 2008 Express Edition. If you use Visual Studio 2005, you will also find most of the book useful, except for Chapter 13, which deals exclusively with features available in C# 3.0 and Visual Studio 2008 only.

❑ **Refactor! for ASP.NET add-in from Developer Express:** Download the latest version of this free Visual Studio add-in from the Developer Express site at www.devexpress.com/Products/VisualStudioAdd-in/RefactorASP/.

❑ **Microsoft SQL Server:** You need this in order to run the sample case study included in the book. This can be MS SQL Server 2000, 2005, or 2008, and the Express edition will suffice for the application that comes with this book.

❑ **Operating system:** You can use any operating system, such as Windows XP, Windows Server 2003 or 2008, or Windows Vista, that can run the software listed above.

Conventions

To help you get the most from the text and keep track of what's happening, a number of conventions are used throughout the book.

Tips, hints, tricks, and asides to the current discussion are offset and placed in italics like this.

As for styles in the text:

❑ New terms and important words are *highlighted with italics* when introduced.

❑ Keyboard strokes look like this: Ctrl+A.

❑ Filenames, URLs, and code within the text look like this: persistence.properties.

❑ Code is presented in two different ways:

❑ Monofont type with no highlighting is used for most code examples.

❑ Gray highlighting is used to emphasize code that's particularly important in the present context.

❑ Also, **bold** is occasionally used within code listings to emphasize parts of code.

Smell, Refactoring, and Object-Oriented Design Principle Boxes

In addition to the conventions just mentioned, throughout the course of this book you will come across three other types of boxed text: Smells, Refactorings, and Object-Oriented Design Principles.

Smells

These boxes contain condensed definitions of code smells. A code smell is an important refactoring concept, and each box contains three sections:

❑ **Thumbnail diagram:** While loosely based on UML static class diagrams, these illustrations are by no means strict in UML language sense. These diagrams should visualize the transformation that the refactoring in question is performing on the code. Not all refactorings carry thumbnail diagrams; some small-scale, method-level refactorings are not well suited for this kind of illustrations. When creating these diagrams, I was inspired by the work done by Sven Gorts on his "Refactoring Thumbnails". For more information about his diagrams, take a look at his page at www.refactoring.be/thumbnails.html.

❑ **Detecting the Smell:** This describes some simple heuristic about how to detect the code smell in your code.

❑ **Related Refactorings:** This lists the refactorings you can use in order to eliminate the smell.

❑ **Rationale:** This explains the negative effect of the code smell in more theoretical terms.

Refactorings

These boxes provide the bare basics of the refactoring. Each box contains the following sections:

❑ **Motivation:** This explains the beneficial effect this refactoring has on code and how the design is improved with its application.

❑ **Related Smells:** This lists the smells this refactoring can help you eliminate.

❑ **Mechanics:** This gives a step-by-step recipe for how to perform the refactoring.

Object-Oriented Design Principles

In these boxes I define some of the crucial object-oriented design principles and often use some short code samples to illustrate them.

Index of Smells

For ease of reference, the following table indicates what smells are included in the book and the page number where the box dealing with that specific smell can be found.

Index of Refactorings

The following table indicates what refactorings are included in the book and the page number where the box dealing with that specific refactoring can be found.

Introduction

Index of Object-Oriented Design Principles

The following table indicates the object-oriented design principles that are included in the book and the page number where the box dealing with that specific principle can be found.

Source Code

As you work through the examples in this book, you may choose either to type in all the code manually or to use the source code files that accompany the book. All of the source code used in this book is available for download at www.wrox.com. Once at the site, simply locate the book's title (either by using the Search box or by using one of the title lists) and click the Download Code link on the book's detail page to obtain all the source code for the book.

>   *Because many books have similar titles, you may find it easiest to search by ISBN; this book's ISBN is 978-0-470-43452-9.*

Once you download the code, just decompress it with your favorite compression tool. Alternately, you can go to the main Wrox code download page at `www.wrox.com/dynamic/books/download.aspx` to see the code available for this book and all other Wrox books.

Errata

We make every effort to ensure that there are no errors in the text or in the code. However, no one is perfect, and mistakes do occur. If you find an error in one of our books, such as a spelling mistake or a faulty piece of code, we would be very grateful for your feedback. By sending in errata, you may save another reader hours of frustration, and at the same time you will be helping us provide even higher quality information.

To find the errata page for this book, go to `www.wrox.com` and locate the title using the Search box or one of the title lists. Then, on the book details page, click the Book Errata link. On this page you can view all errata that has been submitted for this book and posted by Wrox editors. A complete book list, including links to each book's errata, is also available at `www.wrox.com/misc-pages/booklist.shtml`. If you don't spot "your" error on the Book Errata page, go to `www.wrox.com/contact/techsupport.shtml` and complete the form there to send us the error you have found. We'll check the information and, if appropriate, post a message to the book's errata page and fix the problem in subsequent editions of the book.

Refactoring: What's All the Fuss About?

Take a look at any major integrated development environment (IDE) today and you are bound to discover refactoring options somewhere at the tips of your fingers; and if you are following developments in the programming community, you have surely come across a number of articles and books on the subject. For some programmers, it has become the most important development in the way they code since the inception of design patterns.

Unlike some other trends, refactoring is being embraced and spread eagerly by programmers and coders themselves, because it helps them do their work better and enables them to be more productive. Without a doubt, applying refactoring has become an important part of programmers' day-to-day labor no matter the tools, programming language, or type of program being developed. C# is a part of this; currently, a great number of developers are performing refactoring in C#, and a number of good and mature tools are available that you can use to automate refactoring process.

This chapter covers the following topics:

- ❑ What refactoring is and why it is important

- ❑ The benefits that refactoring delivers

- ❑ Common misconceptions about refactoring

- ❑ Specifics of C# as a programming language and how it relates to refactoring

First, however, let's start with some background on refactoring in general.

A Quick Refactoring Overview

When approaching some programming task, you have a number of ways in which you can go about it. You start off with one idea, but as you go along and get into more detail, you inevitably question your work along these lines: "Should I place this method in this class or maybe in this other class? Do I need a class to represent this data as a type or am I better off using the primitive? Should I break this class into more than one? Is there an inheritance relationship between these two classes or should I just use composition?"

If you share your thoughts with some of your peers, you are bound to hear even more options for designing your system. However, once you commit yourself to one approach, it may seem very costly to change these initial decisions later. Refactoring teaches you how to efficiently modify your code in such a way that the impact of those modifications is kept to a minimum. It also helps you think about the design as something that can be dealt with at any stage of the project, not at all cast in stone by initial decisions. Design, in fact, can be treated in a very flexible way.

> **Definition:** *Refactoring* is a set of techniques used to identify the design flow and to modify the internal structure of code in order to improve the design without changing the code's visible behavior.

All design decisions are the result of your knowledge, experience, and creativity. However, programming is a vast playfield, and weighing the pros and cons of your design can be daunting. In C# you are, first and foremost, guided by object-oriented principles and rules. Unfortunately, very often it is not so clear how these rules work out in practice. Refactoring teaches you some simple heuristics that can help improve your design by inspecting some of the visible characteristics of your code. These guidelines that refactoring provides will set you on the right path toward improving the design of your code.

The Refactoring Process

Refactoring is an important programming practice that has been around for some time. Pioneered by the Smalltalk community, it has been applied in a great number of programming languages, and it has taken its place in many programmers' bags of tricks. It will help you write your code in such a way that you will not dread code revision. As a programmer myself, I know this is no small feat!

The refactoring process is fairly simple and consists of three basic steps:

1. **Identify code smells:** You'll learn what *code smell* means very soon, but, in short, this first step is concerned with identifying possible pitfalls in your code, and code smells are very helpful in identifying those pitfalls.

2. **Apply the appropriate refactoring:** This step is dedicated to changing the structure of your code by means of refactoring transformations. These transformations can often be automated and performed by a refactoring tool.

3. **Execute unit tests:** This step helps you rectify the state of your code after the transformations. Refactoring is not meant to change any behavior of your code observable from the "outside." This step generally consists of executing appropriate unit tests to ensure that the behavior of your code didn't change after performing refactoring.

You might have noticed the word *design* used in the refactoring definition earlier in the chapter. This is a broad term that can assume very different meanings depending on your background, programming style, and knowledge. Design in this sense simply means that refactoring builds upon object-oriented theory, with the addition of some very simple heuristics dedicated to identifying shortcomings and weak spots in your code. These anti-patterns are generally referred to as *code smells*; a great part of refactoring can be seen simply as an attempt to eliminate code smells.

> **Definition:** *Code smell* **is a sense you develop that tells you there might be a flaw in your code.**

The code smell can be something as simple as a very large method, a very large class, or a class consisting only of data and with no behavior. I'll dedicate a lot of time to code smells in the book, because improving your sense of code smell can be very important in a successful refactoring process.

The aim of refactoring is to improve the design of your code, which is generally achieved by applying modifications to it. The refactoring methodology and its techniques help you in this task by making it easier to perform and even automate such modifications.

A Look at the Software Situation

As a software developer, your success depends on being able to fulfill different types of expectations. You have to keep in mind many different aspects of your development work, including the following concerns:

- ❑ **User requirements:** This generally means that you should create software that does what the client paid for.

- ❑ **Quality:** To guarantee the quality of your product, you should strive to reduce defects and to release a program that has the minimum number of bugs.

- ❑ **Usability:** This includes making programs that are easy to understand and use.

- ❑ **Performance and efficiency:** As you develop, you want to find new ways to minimize memory usage and the number of cycles needed in order to solve the given problem.

- ❑ **Timeliness:** In order to achieve all of this in a timely manner, you should always be looking for ways to augment productivity.

These goals cause us to focus, and rightly so, on the final product (also known as the *binary*) and how it will behave for the final user. However, in the process of producing the binary, you actually work with source code. You create classes, add properties and methods, organize them into the namespaces, write logic using loops and conditions, and so on. This source code, at a click of a button, is then transformed, compiled, or built into a deliverable, a component, an executable, or something similar. However, there is an inevitable gap between the artifacts you work on — the *source* — and the artifacts you are producing — the *binary*.

This gap between the creation process and the finished product is not typical in other areas of human activity. Consider stonemasonry, for example. While the mason chips away pieces of stone and polishes the edges, he or she can see the desired result slowly appearing under the effort. With software, the process is not at all as direct. You write source code that is then transformed into the desired piece of software. Even with the visual tools, such as Windows Forms Designer inside Visual Studio for example, which largely bridges this gap between source and binary, all you do in the end is create the source that is later processed and turned into a compiled unit.

What's more, there are many ways to write the source that will produce essentially the same resulting binary. This can easily lead you to forget or sacrifice some qualities inherent to the source code itself, because the source code can be considered just a secondary artifact. While these qualities are not directly transformed into a final product, they have an immense impact on the whole process of creation and maintenance.

This leads to the following question: Can you distinguish between well-written and poorly written code, even if the final result is the same? In addition, if the final result, the binary, is performing well from user's point of view, is it at all important how the source code is written? The following sections explore these questions, and you'll see how refactoring can clarify any doubts you might have in this respect.

Refactoring Encourages Solid Design

Regardless of your previous programming experience, I am certain you will agree that you can indeed distinguish between good and bad code. Assessing code may begin on a visual level. Even with a simple glance you can see whether a bit of code is indented and formatted in a pleasing manner, whether the standard naming conventions are used, and so on.

At a less superficial level, you start to analyze code according to principles and techniques of software design. In C#, you first and foremost follow the object-oriented software paradigm. You look into how well classes are structured and encapsulated, what their responsibilities are, and how they collaborate. You use language building blocks such as classes and interfaces, and features such as encapsulation, inheritance, and polymorphism to build a cohesive structure that describes the problem domain well. In a certain sense, you build your own ad hoc language on top of a common language — one that will communicate your intentions and design decisions.

There are a number of sophisticated principles you need to follow in order to achieve a solid design. When you create software that is reusable, extendable, and reliable, and that communicates its purpose well, you can say you have reached your goal of creating well-designed code.

Refactoring provides you with a number of recipes to ensure that your software conforms to the principles of well-designed code — and when you stray from your path, it helps you reorganize and impose the best design decisions with ease.

Refactoring Accommodates Change

Popular software design techniques such as object-oriented analysis and design, UML diagramming, use-case analysis, and others often overlook one very important aspect of the software creation process: constant change. From the first moment it is conceived, software is in continuous flux. In some cases, requirements will change even before the first release, new features will be added, defects will be corrected, and even some planned design decisions, when confronted with real-world demands, will be overruled.

Software construction is a very complex activity, and it is futile to try to come up with a perfect solution up front. Even if you're using some sophisticated techniques such as modeling, you'll still come up short of thinking of every detail and every possible scenario. It is often this state of flux that presents the biggest challenge in the process of making software. You have no choice but to count on change, be ready to adapt, and react readily when it happens. If you are not ready to react, the design decisions you made are soon obsolete, and the dangerous malaise of rotting design settles in.

Refactoring is a relatively simple way to prepare for change, implement change, and control the adverse effects any changes can have on your original design.

Refactoring Prevents Design Rot

Software is definitely one of the more ephemeral human creations. Driven by new advances and technologies, software creations are soon replaced with revised or entirely new versions. Even so, during its lifetime, software will journey through a number of reincarnations. It is constantly modified and updated, new features are added and old ones are removed, defects are resolved and adaptations are performed. It is quite common to find more than one person putting their hands on the same piece of software, each with his or her own style and preferences. Rarely will the same team of people see the software process from the beginning to the end.

Go back for a moment to the stonemason example. Now imagine that there is more than one person working on the same stone, that these people can change during the collaboration, and that the original plan is often itself changed, with new shapes added or removed and different materials used. That may be a task for somebody of Michelangelo's stature, but it's definitely not for the ordinary craftsman.

No wonder, then, that initial ideas are soon forgotten, a well-thought-out structure is superseded by a new solution, and the original design is diluted. The initial intentions become less pronounced and the metaphors more difficult to comprehend; the source is closer and closer to a meaningless cluster of symbols that still, but a lot less reliably, perform the intended function. This ailment steals in quietly, step by step, often unnoticed, until you end up with source code that is difficult to maintain, modify, or upgrade.

What I've just described are the symptoms of *rotting design*, something that can occur even before the first release lives to see the light of a day. Refactoring helps you prevent design rot.

This brief survey of the software landscape has pointed out several challenges that developers face. In order to understand how refactoring can help, the next section describes refactoring in more detail.

The Refactoring Process: A Closer Look

The previous section described a few key areas of software development that can often lead to poor code. Obviously, you need to stand guard over the quality of your code. In effect, you need to have the design quality of your code in mind at all times.

While this sounds sensible, thinking continuously about design and code quality can be costly and quite complicated. The refactoring methodology and its techniques help you in this task by making it easier to perform and even automate modifications that will keep the design active.

In this section, you'll learn about the refactoring activities you would typically complete during a software development cycle.

Using Code Smells

As a first step in your refactoring activity, you'll take a look at the code in order to assess its design qualities. Refactoring teaches you a set of relatively simple heuristics called code smells, which can help you with this task (along with the well-known notions and principles of object-oriented design). Programming, being as varied and complex as it is, makes it difficult to impose precise rules or metrics, so these smells should be used as general guidelines only. Susceptible to taste and interpretation, they have to be applied using your own judgment in accordance with each specific situation.

Coding schools that promote strict coding guidelines, along with strict usage of static code analysis tools, might see this as unnecessary flexibility, but such a relatively liberal approach actually promotes programmer creativity and freedom, resulting in quality code that does not inhibit originality and innovation. Creative programmers thrive in an environment where refactoring is promoted as a first-class practice. In this sense, refactoring promotes programming excellence.

Therefore, in addition to gaining more experience and knowledge, you develop more expertise in identifying and eliminating bad smells in your code.

Transforming the Code

The next step leads you to modifying the code's internal structure. Here, refactoring theory has developed a set of formal rules that enable you to execute these transformations in such a way that, from a client's standpoint, the modifications are transparent. To make use of refactoring, you do not have to tackle the theory behind these rules. The toolmakers use these rules to ensure that refactoring modifies the code in a predictable way, so you can rely on your tool to perform a transformation without breaking the code.

To illustrate how refactoring preserves the original behavior of the code, let's look at an example. Using the contents of Table 1-1, imagine you transformed the code on the left side into the code on the right side.

All you did here was to replace the literal value 1.5m with a constant OvertimeIndex. Executing the code on both sides provides identical results, but the one on the right is a lot easier to maintain or modify. In case you use OvertimeIndex again, the value will be specified in a single place and not scattered around in your code.

What's more, the code on the right side of the table is definitely easier to understand. Once you understand that the literal 1.5m has a special meaning, you can easily relate its value to the business rules that govern your code.

Automating Refactoring Transformations

Refactoring rules have one great consequence: It is possible to automate a large number of these transformations. Automation is really the key to letting refactoring put its best foot forward. Refactoring tools will check for the validity of what you are trying to perform, and then enable you to apply a transformation only if it doesn't break the code. Even without a tool, refactoring is worthwhile; however, manual refactoring can be slow and tedious.

Figure 1-1 shows extract method refactoring in progress in Visual Studio 2008.

Table 1-1: Two Ways of Writing Code That Execute in the Same Way

Free Literal Value	Literal as Constant

<pre>public class Employee
{
 	
    private int hoursWorked;
 	
    private int overtimeHoursWorked;
 	
    private decimal hourlyWage;
 	
    public decimal GetWage()
    {
        return (hoursWorked *
        hourlyWage) +
            (overtimeHoursWorked *
            hourlyWage * 1.5m);
    }
}</pre>
	<pre>public class Employee
	    {
	        public const decimal
	    OvertimeIndex = 1.5m;
	
	        private int hoursWorked;
	
	        private int overtimeHoursWorked;
	
	        private decimal hourlyWage;
	
	        public decimal GetWage()
	        {
	            return (hoursWorked *
	            hourlyWage) +
	                (overtimeHoursWorked
	                * hourlyWage
	                * OvertimeIndex);
	        }
	    }</pre>

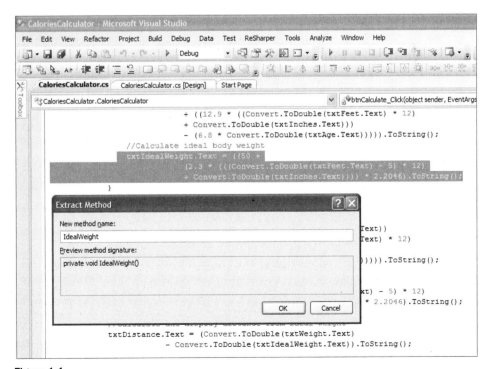

Figure 1-1

The Benefits of Refactoring

In light of all the rules and techniques associated with refactoring, it is pertinent to ask what benefits refactoring offers. After all, it does not add new features or resolve bugs, and you end up with code that basically does what it used to, so why should you invest the time and money to perform this activity? What are the benefits of keeping your design optimal at all times? How does refactoring pay off?

Keeping the Code Simple

Because software development is a continuous, evolving process, refactoring can simplify the numerous aspects you need to juggle as a developer, streamlining your work and providing important qualities to your code. Keeping your code lean at all times can be challenging, especially when you're under pressure to deliver the results quickly. Code can become overly complex in several ways:

❑   **Adding new features:** In one typical scenario, you have to add some functionality to your application. You add a function here, a property there, another condition crops up, and so on. This will soon produce a situation in which classes and methods have grown and ultimately exceeded their original purpose. They have too many responsibilities, communicate with many other elements, and are prone to change for many different reasons. This also becomes a breeding ground for duplicated code.

❑   **Big design up front:** In another scenario, you start off with a very thorough design that proves to be more than you really need. Simple code does only what it is supposed to do; you need not be concerned with trying to have your solution anticipate and respond to every possible scenario before it even happens. You can easily develop a tendency to over-engineer your code, using complex structures when simple ones will suffice. (You can easily identify this tendency by how often "what if" statements are used in discussions of the code.) This situation is motivated by an urge to anticipate future requirements even before they are expressed by the client.

❑   **Premature optimization:** Performance has proved to be a lure for generations of programmers. You might spend numerous hours in order to obtain nanosecond gains in execution time. Without trying to lessen the importance of this key quality of software, you should bear in mind the right moment to deal with it. It can be very difficult to find the critical line you need to change in order to improve performance even for systems already in production; there is even less of a probability that you can find it while the system is in plain development and you are not sure what the rest of the pieces will end up looking like. Using the IDE as the performance-testing environment can be equally misleading.

How can you avoid such pitfalls? Once you become aware of them, you should deal with them quickly. Keeping things on the simple side will be greatly rewarded each time you need to add a feature, resolve a bug, or perform some optimization. Let me show you a few examples:

❑   If you see that a method has grown out of proportion, then it is time to add a new method, or methods, that will relieve some of the burden.

❑   If a class has too many members, maybe it can be restructured into a group of collaborating classes or a class hierarchy.

❑   If a modification left some code without any use and you are certain that it will never be executed, then there's no need to keep it; it should be eliminated.

All these solutions represent typical refactorings. After a smell is discovered, the solution is a restructuring of the problematic code.

When code is simple, it is easy to navigate — you don't lose time in long debugging sessions in order to find the right spot. The names of classes, methods, and properties are meaningful; code purpose is easy to grasp. Such code follows the *rule of least surprise* and it is written in a uniform manner. This type of code won't have you reaching for documentation or desperately searching through the comments. Even after a short amount of time is spent with such code, you feel it does not hide any major mysteries. In simple words, you are in control.

Keeping the Code Readable

Programming is intellectually a very intense activity. You are often so immersed in your work that you tend to have a deep and detailed understanding of your creation in order to maintain complete control over it. You may try to memorize every single detail of the code. You feel proud when you are able to immediately correct a bug or change some behavior. After all, it is what makes you good at the work you perform. As you become more productive, you develop strategies and gain your own programming style. There is nothing wrong with being expert with the code you create, unless that expertise becomes the only weapon you have in your arsenal.

Unfortunately, sometimes you can forget one important fact: When developing software, you seldom work alone — and in order to be able to work in a team, you must write code so it is easily understood by others, who might need to modify, maintain, or optimize the code. In that case, when confronted with cryptic or hermetic code, other team members could lose numerous hours attempting to understand the code. Sooner or later you'll have a computer to do all your bidding, but until then, writing source in such way that it is easy for others to understand can prove to be a very difficult task. Ironically, you can find yourself in the "other person" role even with your own code. Your memory has its limits, and after a while you may not be able to remember every detail of code you wrote yourself.

Readability can depend on different factors. Visual disposition is easily corrected and standardized with the IDE. Other factors, such as the choice of identifier names, require a carefully thought-out approach. Because programmers come from different backgrounds and have different experiences, the best bet is relying on natural language itself. You have to translate your decisions into code so they are easily understandable from a reading of the code, not only visible as a consequence of code execution. Code becomes truly meaningful when a relation between it and a problem domain is correctly established.

As a programmer, you continuously develop your vocabulary. Using well-known idioms, patterns, and accepted conventions can increase the clarity of your code.

Reliance on comments and documentation can also affect the capacity of code to communicate with the reader. Because these artifacts are never executed, they are the first to suffer from obsolescence. In addition, they are notorious for containing superfluous information.

I will try to illustrate this with two code snippets that perform equally during execution. Using the contents of Table 1-2, try reading the snippet on the left side first and then the one on the right.

Table 1-2: Difficult to Read Code vs. More Readable Code

Difficult to Read Code	More Readable Code
```XmlDocument oXMLDom = new XmlDocument(); //loads the file into XMLDom object oXMLDom.Load(strAppPath + "\\ pfl.xml"); XmlNodeList oNodes = oXMLDom.SelectNodes("//stocks[1]/*");```	```XmlDocument portfolio = new XmlDocument(); portfolio.Load(ApplicationPath + "\\ portfolio.xml"); XmlNodeList stocks = XMLDom.SelectNodes("//stocks[1]/*");```

If I have proved my point, you will find the second snippet more to your liking. In case you still are not convinced, as an interesting experiment, you can try obfuscating your code with an obfuscation tool and then trying to find your way around it. Even with the smallest code base, it soon becomes impossible to understand the code. No wonder, because obfuscation is a process completely opposite to refactoring.

Refactoring tools can help you improve readability by enabling you to rename identifiers in your code in a safe and systematic way and by transforming your code along well-known patterns and idioms — you use comments in a more profound manner. Strong structure in the code gives you confidence that the information you obtain from reading the code relates well to execution time.

All this sounds very good. However, you can often hear arguments against refactoring. While some of those arguments are well founded, let's first look at some baseless objections.

Debunking Common Misconceptions

Like any topic that creates a huge amount of interest among developers, refactoring has produced an avalanche of opinions and contributions, some of more value and others of less value. In certain cases, I find the opinions so unfounded that I call them misconceptions. I feel it is worthwhile taking some time to debunk them, because they can add doubt and confusion, and lead you astray from a quest to adopt this valuable technique.

"If It Ain't Broke, Don't Fix It"

Often portrayed as longstanding engineering wisdom, the "if it ain't broke, don't fix it" posture only promotes complacency. Refactoring teaches against it, and for a good reason.

Early in your programming life you learn how failure to pay attention to even a minuscule detail in code can make huge difference, often paying dearly for this knowledge. A small change can provoke software to break in a surprising manner and at the worst time. Once you have burned your hands, you can become reluctant to make any change that is not absolutely necessary. This can work well for a while. Inevitably, however, a situation comes along whereby bugs have to be resolved and petitions for new features cannot be evaded anymore. You are faced with the same code you tried so hard not to confront.

Those who adopt the "if it ain't broke, don't fix it" position look upon refactoring as unnecessary meddling with something that already serves its purpose. Actually, this conformist posture, which tries to maintain the "status quo," often results from rationalizing the fear of confronting the code and the fact that you do not have control over it.

Many experienced programmers adopt this posture out of a legitimate intent to minimize any effort that is not truly necessary. For example, if the application is doing fine in terms of performance, then there is no need to squeeze that last processor cycle out for the sake of performance. The same is true for speculative design, often argued with "prophetic" programmer talk such as "we might need that feature one day."

In that sense, refactoring is pretty much on the same wavelength. When you refactor, you should eliminate dead code and avoid speculative design or premature optimization. However, for refactoring adepts, software can also be broken "on the inside." If the design is flawed, or the code poorly written and badly structured, then even if the application is serving users correctly at the moment and is not broken visibly "on the outside," it should still be refactored and have its design "fixed." In that sense, refactoring insists on some less tangible but decisive characteristics of software, such as design, simplicity, improved source code comprehension, readability, and the like.

Refactoring will help you win back your command over your code. While this is hardly an easy task with a code base that has grown out of control, without refactoring the only solution you have left is the complete rewrite.

"Refactoring Is Nothing New"

This misconception could be restated as "refactoring is just another word for what we all know already." In other words, you might think this means you have mastered good code practices, object-oriented design, style, good coding, and so on, and refactoring is just another buzzword that someone invented to sell some books.

Refactoring does not pretend to impose radically new paradigms such as object-oriented or aspect-oriented programming when they appeared for the first time. What it does do is radically change the way you program: It defines rules that make it possible to apply complex transformations to code at the click of a button. Rather than see your code as some frozen construct that is not susceptible to change, you instead see yourself as capable of maintaining the code in optimum shape, responding efficiently to new challenges and changing the code without fear.

"Refactoring Is Rocket Science"

Programming is hard. It's a complex activity that requires a lot of intellectual effort, and some of the knowledge can be very difficult to grasp. With C#, programmers had to first acquire the ability to work in a fully capable object-oriented language. Nowadays, C# is being enriched by elements of functional and even dynamic language capabilities. For many, this can be baffling. Fortunately, learning new skills definitely pays off.

The great thing about refactoring is how simple it can be. It equips you with a very small set of simple rules to begin with. This, coupled with a good tool, makes first steps in refactoring a breeze. Compared to other techniques an advanced programmer should know nowadays, such as UML or design patterns, I'd say that refactoring has the easiest learning curve.

Very soon, the time spent in learning refactoring will start to reap rewards. Of course, as with anything else in life, gaining mastery requires a lot of time and effort.

"Refactoring Causes Poor Performance"

This objection is really suggesting that because after refactoring you usually end up with a larger number of fine-grained elements, such as methods and classes, a new design with so much indirection must incur some performance cost.

If you go back in time a little, however, you'll discover that this argument sounds curiously similar to the one used to voice initial skepticism about object-oriented programming languages, as compared to procedural programming languages, such as comparing C with C++.

The truth is that the differences in performance between refactored and unstructured code are, at best, minimal. Except in some very specialized systems, this is not a real concern.

IO-intensive Code vs. Computation-intensive Code

The majority of typical enterprise applications are distributed, layered applications that involve a lot of input-output operations. This is especially true under today's prevailing architectural paradigm of service-oriented applications. These I/O operations can be network communication, inter-process communication, file I/O, and so on. For example, from an architectural point of view, an ASP.NET application's execution stack might look like this:

❑   IIS receives petition from browser (network I/O)

❑   ASP page communicates with remote COM+ component (network I/O)

❑   COM+ component communicates with several other remote components (network I/O)

❑   Next COM+ component communicates with remote web service (network I/O)

❑   Next COM+ component writes to log (file I/O)

❑   Next COM+ component communicates with database (network I/O)

Generally, I/O operation is by magnitudes slower than internal, computational operations. In such applications, the biggest performance gains are obtained by optimizing I/O operations. Such optimizations might include tactics such as connection pooling, optimizing database query performance, and filtering data in the database versus filtering data in the client, and so on. This leads you to the next premise related to refactoring and performance.

Application Performance Is Defined by Performance Bottlenecks, Not by Absolute Performance

Once you have committed yourself to a certain platform, you should try exploit all the benefits it provides. You could write a procedural program in C#, but it doesn't make sense. Aggressively structuring your code might produce some small overhead, but such overhead is well compensated by the benefits that refactored code provides.

When code is refactored and well structured, it is much easier to optimize it. Because there is less duplication, there is only a single place where such optimization needs to be performed. Even the computational part of your code will reap the same benefits from well-organized code. The alternative — not structuring your code in order to avoid method lookup overhead or applying similar optimization strategies — will confer only insignificant benefits. One of the reasons for this is the intelligence that the .NET platform has been bestowed with.

Compiler, Optimizations, and JIT

Compilers today are mature and extremely sophisticated pieces of technology. They are a critical piece in any software platform, so it is no surprise that so much time and so many resources have been put into them. .NET is by no means an exception. In contrast to other managed environments .NET produces a native code that makes no performance-related concessions. As a comparison, Java code is compiled to bytecode and then executed inside the Java Virtual Machine.

Just-in-Time (JIT) compilation is a technique used to improve the performance of programs by compiling the code (in the case of .NET Common Intermediate Language, or CIL) to native and executable binary file.

Even so, the .NET JIT compiler is capable of producing many very sophisticated optimizations. Moreover, code can be optimized for a specific platform, as it is compiled on the same machine on which it is executed, dead code can be eliminated, methods can be inlined, and so on. Theoretically, even runtime profiling data can be used to optimize code even further, but at this point we are entering a territory that is covered with the veil of secrecy. No wonder, as these technologies are critical for the platform's success and can represent an important competitive advantage.

This means that a lot of the overhead that aggressively structured, refactored code can introduce will be eliminated by the .NET runtime itself — and by the looks of it, it does a pretty good job of doing so. In the next section I plan to prove it.

Experimenting with Performance

Experience shows that performance flows are generally afflicted by some precise spots in the code. Fixing those during an optimization phase will enable you to reach the required levels of performance. Being able to easily identify the critical pieces of code can prove to be very valuable. By producing understandable code in which duplication and total size is minimized, and by enabling changes to be performed in a single place, refactoring greatly aids the process of optimization.

These days, as CPU horsepower is constantly incremented, other aspects of code, such as maintainability, quality, scalability, and reliability, are forcing performance out of the top-priority code features. Now, don't use hardware speed as a pretext to write code that performs lousy, just don't go overboard with optimizing your code.

Just in case you would like to see some numbers here, I have prepared a small experiment. I will use two code samples. The first is an example of poorly structured code and has single `Main` method. The second example has a `Main` method inside a `Module` and a class `Circle` with a number of fine-grained methods. I originally used these samples to illustrate unstructured versus structured code style, so all it lacks is some measurement code.

I will measure the time it takes to execute a simple geometrical formula (circle circumference length); in order not to make this code computation-intensive, I will add some database query code. To even out the measurement, I will repeat execution inside a loop 10,000 times. Since I don't mean to make this an extremely precise experiment, I will use the `System.Diagnostics.Stopwatch` class to capture the interval; the precision of `Stopwatch` will suffice in this case.

In Listing 1-1 you can see an example of deliberately unstructured code.

Listing 1-1: Unstructured Code

```
using System;
using System.Data;
using System.Data.SqlClient;
using System.Diagnostics;

namespace RefactoringInCSharp.Chapter1
{
    struct Point
    {
        public double X;
        public double Y;
    }

    class CircleCircumferenceLength
    {

        public void Main()
        {
            Point center;
            Point pointOnCircumference;
            //read center coordinates
            Console.WriteLine("Enter X coordinate" +
                "of circle center");
            center.X = Double.Parse(Console.In.ReadLine());
            Console.WriteLine("Enter Y coordinate" +
                "of circle center");
            center.Y = Double.Parse(Console.In.ReadLine());
            //read some point on circumference coordinates
            Console.WriteLine("Enter X coordinate" +
                "of some point on circumference");
            pointOnCircumference.X = Double.Parse(Console.In.ReadLine());
            Console.WriteLine("Enter Y coordinate" +
                "of some point on circumference");
            pointOnCircumference.Y = Double.Parse(Console.In.ReadLine());
            //calculate and display the length of circumference
            Console.WriteLine("The length of circle" +
                "circumference is:");
            //calculate the length of circumference
            double radius;
            double lengthOfCircumference = 0;
            int i;
            //use stopWatch to measure transcurred time
            Stopwatch stopWatch = new Stopwatch();
            stopWatch.Start();
            //repeat calculation for more precise measurement
            for (i = 1; i <= 10000; i++)
            {
                //add some IO
                IDbConnection connection =
                    new SqlConnection("Data Source=TESLATEAM;" +
                        "Initial Catalog=RENTAWHEELS;" +
```

```
                    "User ID=RENTAWHEELS_LOGIN;"
                    + "Password=RENTAWHEELS_PASSWORD_123");
                connection.Open();
                IDbCommand command = new SqlCommand("SELECT GETDATE()");
                command.Connection = connection;
                IDataReader reader = command.ExecuteReader();
                reader.Read();
                reader.Close();
                connection.Close();
                radius = Math.Pow((Math.Pow((pointOnCircumference.X -
                    center.X), 2) +
                    Math.Pow((pointOnCircumference.Y - center.Y), 2)),
                    (1 / 2));
                lengthOfCircumference = 2 * 3.1415 * radius;
            }
            stopWatch.Stop();
            Console.WriteLine(stopWatch.Elapsed);
            Console.WriteLine(lengthOfCircumference);
            Console.Read();
        }
    }
}
```

Listing 1-2 shows the structured version, which will perform exactly the same operation as the code in Listing 1-1.

Listing 1-2: Structured Code

```
using System;
using System.Data;
using System.Data.SqlClient;
using System.Diagnostics;

namespace RefactoringInCSharp.Chapter1
{
    public struct Point
    {
        public double X;
        public double Y;
    }

    class CircleCircumferenceLength
    {

        public void Main()
        {
            Circle circle = new Circle();
            circle.Center = InputPoint("circle center");
            circle.PointOnCircumference =
                InputPoint("point on circumference");
            Console.WriteLine("The length of circle "
                + "circumference is:");
```

Continued

Listing 1-2: Structured Code (continued)

```
            double circumference = 0;
            int i;
            //use stopWatch to measure transcurred time
            Stopwatch stopWatch = new Stopwatch();
            stopWatch.Start();
            //repeat calculation for more precise measurement
            for (i = 1; i <= 10000; i++)
            {
                circumference =
                    circle.CalculateCircumferenceLength();
            }
            stopWatch.Stop();
            Console.WriteLine(stopWatch.Elapsed);
            Console.WriteLine(circumference);
            WaitForUserToClose();
        }

        public Point InputPoint(string pointName)
        {
            Point point;
            Console.WriteLine("Enter X coordinate "
                + "of " + pointName);
            point.X = Double.Parse(Console.In.ReadLine());
            Console.WriteLine("Enter Y coordinate "
                + "of " + pointName);
            point.Y = Double.Parse(Console.In.ReadLine());
            return point;
        }

        private void WaitForUserToClose()
        {
            Console.Read();
        }
    }
    public class Circle
    {
        private Point centerValue;
        private Point pointOnCircumferenceValue;
        public Point Center
        {
            get { return centerValue; }
            set { centerValue = value; }
        }
        public Point PointOnCircumference
        {
            get { return pointOnCircumferenceValue; }
            set { pointOnCircumferenceValue = value; }
        }

        public double CalculateCircumferenceLength()
        {
            QueryDatabase();
```

```
            return 2 * 3.1415 * CalculateRadius();
        }

        private double CalculateRadius()
        {
            return Math.Pow((Math.Pow((this.PointOnCircumference.X
                - this.Center.X), 2) +
                Math.Pow((this.PointOnCircumference.Y - this.Center.Y),
                2)), (1 / 2));
        }

        private void QueryDatabase()
        {
            IDbConnection connection =
                new SqlConnection("Data Source=TESLATEAM;" +
                    "Initial Catalog=RENTAWHEELS;"
                    + "User ID=RENTAWHEELS_LOGIN;"
                    + "Password=RENTAWHEELS_PASSWORD_123");
            connection.Open();
            IDbCommand command = new SqlCommand("SELECT GETDATE()");
            command.Connection = connection;
            IDataReader reader = command.ExecuteReader();
            reader.Read();
            reader.Close();
            connection.Close();
        }
    }
}
```

After a few executions, you can see that the times for both samples are pretty close. On my machine, these values are in the neighborhood of 2.2 to 2.4 seconds. One small difference I could discern is that the best time for the unstructured sample was 1.9114800, whereas for the structured sample it was 2.0398497.

"Refactoring Breaks Good Object-Oriented Design"

Well-structured and refactored code can look awkward to an untrained eye. Methods are so short that they often seem without substance. Classes also seem without enough weight, consisting of only a few members. It seems as if nothing ever happens in your code.

Having to manage a greater number of elements such as classes and methods can imply that there is more complexity to deal with. This argument is actually misleading. The truth is that the same complexity was always present. In refactored code, however, it is expressed in a much cleaner, more structured manner.

"Refactoring Offers No Short-Term Benefits"

There is overwhelming consensus among refactoring converts that refactoring actually makes you program faster. So far, I do not know of any study that I could call upon in order to prove this, but my own experience tells me this is the case. It is only logical that this is so. Because you have a smaller quantity of code overall, less duplication, and a clearer picture, unless you are dealing with some trivial and unrealistically small-scale code, refactoring benefits become apparent very soon.

"Refactoring Works Only for Agile Teams"

Because it's often mentioned as one of the pillar techniques in agile methodologies, refactoring is interpreted as working only for teams adhering to these principles.

Refactoring is indispensable for agile teams. Even if your team has a different methodology, most of the time you are the one in charge of the way you code, and this is where refactoring enters the picture. Other team members or management might even be oblivious to the fact that from time to time you reach for the "refactor" option inside your IDE. There is nothing to prevent you from refactoring your code, regardless of the methodology your team might subscribe to.

The best results in refactoring are achieved if you adopt it in small steps, performing it regularly while you code. Some practices, such as strict code ownership or a waterfall process, can work against refactoring. If you can prove that refactoring makes sense from a programming point of view, you can start building your support base, first with your peers and then by spreading the word to the rest of your team.

"Refactoring Can Be Applied As a Separate Stage in the Development Process and Performed by a Separate Team"

This one is generally favored by managers. Being able to look at refactoring as a separate stage and placing it somewhere between the implementation and testing phases can suggest a false sense of control from a managerial point of view, where tasks and resources are often seen as bars on some Gantt chart that can be easily squeezed or moved around.

The truth is that in order to perform refactoring successfully, you should have a full understanding of the problem domain, and be aware of requirements, the design, and even implementation details. If you are not part of the team from the beginning — that is, you did not spend time working with clients, analyzing requirements, and thinking about the design — then you will have a hard time improving something constructed by the original team.

Following the model in which code can be refined *a posteriori*, akin to some substance in an industrial process, will generally bring few benefits. Without a good understanding of what the code is actually doing, refactoring that you can really perform with confidence will bring only small improvements. If you try to make any substantial change in such circumstances, the results will likely be quite the opposite of what is supposed to be achieved. Instead of making code relate better to the problem domain, you will probably make things worse and end up introducing bugs into your application.

Refactoring Can Work Just As Well Without Unit Tests

I imagine some simple refactorings can be performed even without unit testing in place. Refactoring tools and the compiler itself can offer a limited safety net that you can count on to catch some simple human mistakes. You can also test the code in traditional ways, using a debugger or performing functional tests, although these manual testing methods tend to be tedious and unreliable. Moreover, with refactoring, your code is more amenable to change than ever.

Avoid unnecessary problems by adding some NUnit tests to your project, and you will be able to test for errors with each small step you make. You will learn more about unit tests in Chapter 3. In the next section, you'll see how refactoring can be an indispensable tool in a team environment.

No Programmer Is an Island

A lot of the motivation for refactoring comes from one simple fact: Programmers work in teams. Programming in a team environment requires a major paradigm shift; not only does your code have to tell a computer what to do, it has to communicate your intentions to other members of your team.

Not every person in your organization will look inside source code, but a number of those will do so. Consider the typical programming ecosystem that revolves around source code, as shown in Figure 1-2:

❑ **Client programmer:** In today's modular and layered architectures, there is a good chance that you will work on a library that another programmer will (re)use in his or her project. For a client programmer, it is of paramount importance that your classes are designed and written so that they can be employed easily. They should be clearly related to the problem domain they were created to deal with. Simplicity and good naming strategies are critical for a client programmer. You will learn all the details about code naming strategies in Chapter 6.

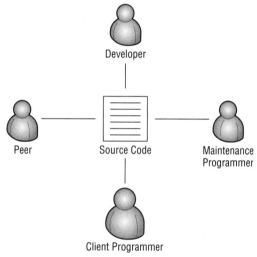

Figure 1-2

❑ **Maintenance programmer:** This is the person who will have to dig inside the internals of your code. To make this person's life easier, your code should be well structured, with small and simple methods and classes. The maintenance programmer also benefits from good naming strategies, and clean and well-formatted code.

❑ **Peer programmer:** Whether you work with a partner or go over your code with your peers in a code review session, it is your code that reflects your skills and professionalism. Good code earns you the respect of your colleagues.

Always keep others in mind when you write your code. This is not really altruism; it is a reciprocal interest for anyone who writes code. As you write code, you will use code written by others. The chances are good that you will have to modify code that you didn't create or review code that someone else has written.

Any organization involved with software will also employ people that do not write code. In the next section I will address some reasoning strategies that can be used to justify refactoring to managers and others.

Refactoring for Business People

Programming teams today have more and more liberty to organize themselves as they see fit, as long as this results in good productivity and a quality product. Such an approach is especially common in an agile software culture.

In a way, this is contradictory to a traditional approach to organization, whereby managers are not just enablers, but are also responsible for internal team organization and low-level task management. In such a more traditional environment, you might find yourself in a situation where you have to justify the work you put into refactoring your code. Remember that for someone not dealing with code, it might be quite difficult to grasp what benefits refactoring offers.

For the purpose of explaining the benefits of refactored code to a nontechnical audience, managers, and the like, you might find the following formula, which some authors use to represent the cost of software, useful:

$$Cost(total) = Cost(develop) + Cost(maintain\ and\ evolve)$$

According to many studies, and likely reflecting your own daily experience, the cost to maintain and evolve a system surpasses the cost to initially develop the system. Many times, for a programmer, there is no such thing as a clear line separating the development phase and the maintenance or evolution phase. For managers, release is more than an important milestone; after the release, the software is expected to start bringing in revenue. Therefore, bearing in mind that the benefits of refactoring are especially visible in the maintenance/evolution phase, the cost related to this phase can be further expressed as follows:

$$Cost(maintain\ and\ evolve) = Cost(understand) + Cost(change) + Cost(test) + Cost(deploy)$$

Refactoring will help you cut time and effort from each of these phases:

- ❑ Refactored code is written is such a manner that it is easier to understand, as it is written for comprehension. In addition, improved reuse will reduce the overall size of the code-base.

- ❑ Refactored code is easier to change. Less duplication means it is easier to discover the right place to make a change. Again, improved reuse reduces the overall size of the code-base, making this task easier to perform.

- ❑ Refactored code is easier to test thanks to readable code. Refactored code often includes ready unit tests that bring their own benefits to the refactoring process.

- ❑ Applications for which refactoring is put into practice often have better handled component-level dependencies, making them easier to deploy.

Now let's take a look at C# and how its modern language characteristics are well suited for the refactoring process.

C# and Refactoring

With the advent of the .NET platform, Microsoft decided it was time to begin with a clean slate — a new programming language. Created especially for .NET, C# is becoming the most popular language on the platform and today is in many cases the best choice for programming in .NET. C# has all the characteristics of a modern object-oriented programming language. Following are some of the reasons why C# is so popular:

❑ C-inspired syntax is immediately familiar to anyone with previous programming experience in C++, Java, C, or another language from the "curly braces" family.

❑ C# has an automatic memory management facility known as *garbage collector* that hugely simplifies the programming process and eliminates one of most problematic tasks in programming: reclaiming memory.

❑ C# is a strongly and statically typed language, meaning that a number of programming errors can be successfully detected during compilation.

❑ The inheritance hierarchy has a root class, `Object`, from which all classes are inherited.

❑ It has multiple-interface inheritance, meaning that a class can implement many interfaces, and it has single-implementation inheritance, meaning it can inherit only a single class.

❑ C# attributes can add powerful declarative capabilities to C# code.

Less than 10 years since it has appeared, C# has evolved significantly compared to its first version. While the language is still relatively simple and consistent, it has successfully integrated elements of other programming paradigms, such as functional, declarative, and dynamic programming. Here are some of the advances that C# has been endowed with:

❑ C# generics have further improved the C# type system.

❑ Extension methods offer an additional level of flexibility to programming in C#.

❑ Language Integrated Query (LINQ) enables you to query different sources of data in a uniform manner.

No wonder than that C# was the first language to obtain refactoring support in .NET. C# is still the only programming language with out-of-the-box support for refactoring in Visual Studio. There is also a healthy third-party refactoring tools market for C#, as you will see in Chapter 3.

C# is a code-loving programmer's language of choice for the .NET platform. The fundamental philosophy of power and simplicity that is characteristic of C# is naturally complemented with a refactoring approach to programming. Refactoring will sharpen your programming skills and help you climb another step on the skills ladder of the expert programmer.

Summary

This introductory chapter has given you a brief overview of refactoring, explaining its relevance and benefits. You have seen how refactoring helps you design your applications and prevent design rot, and at the same time accommodate any change that your software might be exposed to.

You have learned the three important stages in each cycle of the refactoring process: smell identification, refactoring, and testing. These three stages are mandatory for successful refactoring. In order to make this process even more productive, you can rely on automated refactoring tools that remove a lot of the drudgery and complexity from refactoring, making it easily accessible and applicable.

You have also been presented with some of the most common misconceptions about refactoring, just so you won't be surprised by the diversity of opinions on the subject and can make your own informed choices.

Refactoring has a special significance in a team environment. Programming as an act of communication with other programmers instead of a programmer-to-computer monologue will require significant changes in the way you work and write code.

C# is a powerful, consistent language with an expressive syntax. Code written in such a language can especially benefit from refactoring, helping a programmer exploit the language and platform capabilities to their fullest extent.

Now it's time to see some of this in practice. In the next chapter you are going to see refactoring at work.

2

A First Taste of Refactoring

Before getting into the details of refactoring procedures, including the theory and mechanics behind them, it's a good idea to start with a very simple, yet complete application. Looking at a simple application first will enable you to gain a perspective on the process being described. This way, you'll have a better sense of where each of the elements of the refactoring process fits and the purpose behind it as we get into the specifics of refactoring or code smells.

This chapter presents a simple application that consists of a single form and a single event-handling procedure, in its first incarnation. Soon, however, the requirements will start to grow, and as the application responds to these, flaws and imperfections in the design will materialize. As an example, I will identify the code smells and eliminate them as we progress. I'll also follow the refactoring process as I perform these modifications. As you have already seen, the refactoring process consists of three steps:

1. Identifying the smell.
2. Using specific refactoring techniques to eliminate the smell.
3. Executing tests to validate the changes.

We'll focus on the refactoring process, but I'll also explain and develop the complete application as we go along. Of course, because the main purpose of this chapter is give you just a first taste of refactoring, the application is moderate in size and detail.

Sample Application: Calories Calculator

The application we are going to develop in this chapter starts out as an application for calculating the recommended daily intake of calories. My client, a doctor, needed an application that could perform a recommended daily amount of calories calculation quickly so that he could pass the information along to his patients. Using a simple calculator and pen and paper is tedious and error prone.

In order to implement this first requirement, I wrote a single event-handling routine. However, as new requirements are added and the application continues to grow, a series of refactorings will have to take place. As you'll see later in the chapter, in its final stage the application consists of five classes, with three of them organized as part of a small inheritance hierarchy.

It is important to note that the more complex solutions and refined structures appear only after the requirements and corresponding code increase. In fact, it's this observation that promotes the principle of making the application's simplicity its most important characteristic. With this application, almost all of the refactorings we'll perform will be initiated only after a code smell is detected. While we eliminate a code smell, I'll show you how some underlying abstractions appear related to the domain we are working on, such as Patient, Male Patient, Female Patient, and so on. Ultimately, you'll see how work on both the design and the elimination of code smells, when based on object-oriented principles, converge to create an efficient and robust solution.

Keep in mind that more complex, large-scale systems might benefit from a more elaborately designed solution right from the outset. In the example presented here, the application is so simple that any complex design up front would suggest an over-engineered solution.

The Calories Calculator application is developed using mostly C# 2.0 (Visual Studio 2005) syntax. Later in the book, we will come back to this application and modify it in order to illustrate the new features available in C# 3.0 (Visual Studio 2008). If you're the impatient type, feel free to jump to Chapter 13 to see the Calories Calculator C# 3.0 makeover right after reading this chapter.

Calories Calculator Application with Recommended Daily Calories Amount Calculation

My client has the formula for calculating daily recommended calories and can perform the calculation manually, but he finds that using a calculator is too tedious and error prone. The calculation is based on the patient's personal data and it varies according to the patient's gender. Here are the formulas:

- ❑ **Male:** 66 + (6.3 × body weight in lbs.) + (12.9 × height in inches) − (6.8 × age in years)
- ❑ **Female:** 655 + (4.3 × weight in lbs.) + (4.7 × height in inches) − (4.7 × age in years)

These formulas seem pretty straightforward, so I opened Visual Studio and designed the Calories Calculator form shown in Figure 2-1.

This single form contains patient data input controls and displays the recommended daily amount of calories in the Recommended Daily Amount read-only text box.

The code to calculate Recommended Daily Amount isn't very complicated either. All that is required of the user is the ability to click the Calculate button, which can be accomplished by writing the event-handling code shown in Listing 2-1.

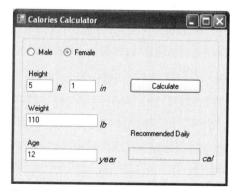

Figure 2-1

Listing 2-1: The btnCalculate_Click Code

```
private void btnCalculate_Click(object sender, EventArgs e)
{
    if (rbtnMale.Checked)
    {
        txtCalories.Text = (66
                    + (6.3 * Convert.ToDouble(txtWeight.Text))
                    + (12.9 * ((Convert.ToDouble(txtFeet.Text) * 12)
                            + Convert.ToDouble(txtInches.Text)))
                    - (6.8 * Convert.ToDouble(txtAge.Text))).ToString();
    }
    else
    {
        txtCalories.Text = (655
                    + (4.3 * Convert.ToDouble(txtWeight.Text))
                    + (4.7 * ((Convert.ToDouble(txtFeet.Text) * 12)
                            + Convert.ToDouble(txtInches.Text)))
                    - (4.7 * Convert.ToDouble(txtAge.Text))).ToString();
    }
}
```

I experimented with the form for a while and it proved to work reasonably well. However, I noticed that I needed to add some user input-verification routines — otherwise, the program might display some unpleasant error messages and exit. Listing 2-2 shows the code for the first version of the application.

Listing 2-2: Calories Calculator First Try

```
private void btnCalculate_Click(object sender, EventArgs e)
{

    /* Validate User Input: */
    //Validate height (feet) is numeric value
```

Continued

Listing 2-2: Calories Calculator First Try *(continued)*

```
        double result;
        if (!double.TryParse(txtFeet.Text, out result))
        {
            MessageBox.Show("Feet must be a numeric value.");
            txtFeet.Select();
            return;
        }
        //Validate height (inches) is numeric value
        if (!double.TryParse(txtInches.Text, out result))
        {
            MessageBox.Show("Inches must be a numeric value.");
            txtInches.Select();
            return;
        }
        //Validate weight is numeric value
        if (!double.TryParse(txtWeight.Text, out result))
        {
            MessageBox.Show("Weight must be a numeric value.");
            txtWeight.Select();
            return;
        }
        //Validate age is numeric value
        if (!double.TryParse(txtAge.Text, out result))
        {
            MessageBox.Show("Age must be a numeric value.");
            txtAge.Select();
            return;
        }
        /*End validation*/
        if (rbtnMale.Checked)
        {
            txtCalories.Text = (66
                    + (6.3 * Convert.ToDouble(txtWeight.Text))
                    + (12.9 * ((Convert.ToDouble(txtFeet.Text) * 12)
                        + Convert.ToDouble(txtInches.Text)))
                    - (6.8 * Convert.ToDouble(txtAge.Text))).ToString();
        }
        else
        {
            txtCalories.Text = (655
                    + (4.3 * Convert.ToDouble(txtWeight.Text))
                    + (4.7 * ((Convert.ToDouble(txtFeet.Text) * 12)
                        + Convert.ToDouble(txtInches.Text)))
                    - (4.7 * Convert.ToDouble(txtAge.Text))).ToString();
        }
    }
```

I have used the `double.TryParse` function in order to validate that values entered by the user are numeric. If users input any invalid characters, then a message box will appear informing them of the mistake, and the method will exit.

So far, the application is so simple that it doesn't require any more effort; but you can already see that there is a lot of code mixed up in this single method, meaning that if the application starts to grow, we would probably need to restructure it in order to make it smaller and more manageable.

At this point the initial requirements of the application were met, and I sent the executable to my client.

Growing Requirements: Calculating Ideal Weight

Not surprisingly, some time after submitting the application, I received an e-mail from my client asking me to add more features to the Calories Calculator. The new required feature requested by the client was an ideal-weight calculation. The idea was for the application to be able to calculate a patient's ideal weight based on height, along with calculating daily calories. As before, the calculation depends on gender, so there are separate formulas for men and women.

Here are the formulas:

❑ **Male**: 50 + 2.3 kg per inch over 5 feet

❑ **Female**: 45.5 + 2.3 kg per inch over 5 feet

At this point, I decided to implement the requested functionality by modifying the existing form. I added a few controls, as shown in Figure 2-2.

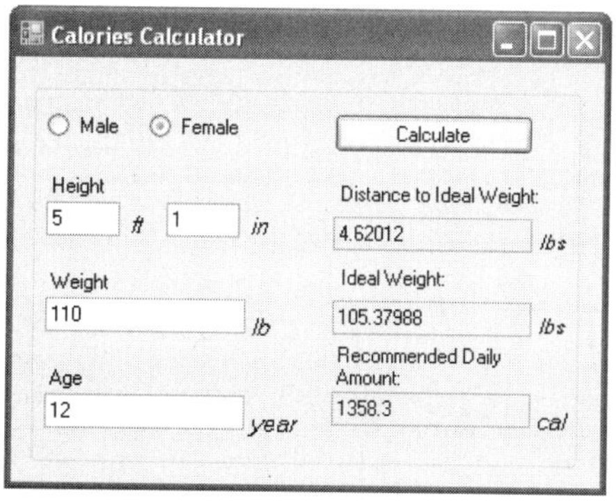

Figure 2-2

As I programmed the formula for calculating ideal weight, I made some changes to my initial formula. For one thing, I noticed that the application currently only applied to people standing at or above five feet tall. In order to take this limitation into account, I added the verification code for the patient's height. If the entered height value is less than five feet, then a message box with information on the height limit will be displayed, and the method will exit.

I also noticed that old results needed to be cleared before each calculation, because otherwise they might confuse the user. I added a few lines of code that clean text boxes each time the Calculate button is pressed. This way, even when invalid data is entered, results will be cleared before the user is informed of erroneous input.

Listing 2-3 shows how to implement the new feature.

Listing 2-3: Calories Calculator with Ideal-Body-Weight Calculation

```
private void btnCalculate_Click(object sender, EventArgs e)
{
    //Clear old results
    txtDistance.Text = "";
    txtIdealWeight.Text = "";
    txtCalories.Text = "";

    /* Validate User Input: */
    //Validate height (feet) is numeric value
    double result;
    if (!double.TryParse(txtFeet.Text, out result))
    {
        MessageBox.Show("Feet must be a numeric value.");
        txtFeet.Select();
        return;
    }
    //Validate height (inches) is numeric value
    if (!double.TryParse(txtInches.Text, out result))
    {
        MessageBox.Show("Inches must be a numeric value.");
        txtInches.Select();
        return;
    }
    //Validate weight is numeric value
    if (!double.TryParse(txtWeight.Text, out result))
    {
        MessageBox.Show("Weight must be a numeric value.");
        txtWeight.Select();
        return;
    }
    //Validate age is numeric value
    if (!double.TryParse(txtAge.Text, out result))
    {
        MessageBox.Show("Age must be a numeric value.");
        txtAge.Select();
        return;
    }

    if(!(Convert.ToDouble(txtFeet.Text) >= 5)){
        MessageBox.Show("Height has to be equal to or greater than 5 feet!");
        txtFeet.Select();
        return;
    }
    /*End validation*/
    if (rbtnMale.Checked)
    {
        txtCalories.Text = (66
                + (6.3 * Convert.ToDouble(txtWeight.Text))
                + (12.9 * ((Convert.ToDouble(txtFeet.Text) * 12)
```

```
                                + Convert.ToDouble(txtInches.Text)))
                    - (6.8 * Convert.ToDouble(txtAge.Text))).ToString();
         //Calculate ideal body weight
         txtIdealWeight.Text = ((50 +
                    (2.3 * (((Convert.ToDouble(txtFeet.Text) - 5) * 12)
                    + Convert.ToDouble(txtInches.Text)))) * 2.2046).ToString();
    }
    else
    {
         txtCalories.Text = (655
                    + (4.3 * Convert.ToDouble(txtWeight.Text))
                    + (4.7 * ((Convert.ToDouble(txtFeet.Text) * 12)
                        + Convert.ToDouble(txtInches.Text)))
                    - (4.7 * Convert.ToDouble(txtAge.Text))).ToString();
         //Calculate ideal body weight
         txtIdealWeight.Text = ((45.5 +
                    (2.3 * (((Convert.ToDouble(txtFeet.Text) - 5) * 12)
                    + Convert.ToDouble(txtInches.Text)))) * 2.2046).ToString();
    }

    //Calculate and display distance from ideal weight
    txtDistance.Text = (Convert.ToDouble(txtWeight.Text)
                - Convert.ToDouble(txtIdealWeight.Text)).ToString();

}
```

Changing the application to meet the new requirement isn't very difficult. Actually, all you need to do is go into the old code and add new code to fulfill the new requirement of calculating ideal weight. Here is a step-by-step explanation of what needs to be done:

1. When applying the formula, subtract five feet from the feet value and then convert the resulting height into inches:

   ```
   (((Convert.ToDouble(txtFeet.Text) - 5) * 12)
    + Convert.ToDouble(txtInches.Text))
   ```

2. Apply the formula by multiplying the height in inches by 2.3 and then add 50 to that result in the case of a male patient and 45.5 in the case of a female patient.

3. Because the result obtained this way represents the value in kilograms, multiply it by 2.2046 in order to convert it to pounds.

You may have noticed that the sole method in the application, btnCalculate_Click, has become alarmingly long, making the ideal body weight calculation difficult to understand.

Adding the necessary code to existing classes and methods is a very typical way to add new requirements to applications, but over time this can easily lead to poorly structured and tangled code. While even this short sample could benefit from refactoring at this point, I decided in this case that I wasn't going to spend any more time on improving the application unless I was asked to implement more functionality, and I sent the application to my client. Somehow, I had a feeling that this would not be the end of the story!

Growing Requirements: Persisting Patient Data

The next requirement that my client asked for confirmed that the application had demonstrated its value and that it was being used. The doctor now expressed a need to save patient historical data so that he could easily track his patients' progress.

At this point I want to stop a moment and analyze this latest requirement. If you take a look at the existing form, you'll notice that it provides no means of identifying the patient for whom the calculation is being performed. Therefore, for this requirement, I needed to capture some data that could be used to identify the patient. I also needed to persist the data and display it.

These conclusions told me that the Calories Calculator application now needed to provide the following functionality:

❑ **Identification of the patient**: I decided to use patient names and social security numbers (SSNs). Using names would make it easy for the doctor to identify the patient, and the SSN would prevent any possible mix-up concerning patients with the same or similar names.

❑ **Separation of the calculation operation and the operation of persisting patient data**: At first I was tempted to add some code to the existing btnCalculate_Click event-handling routine and use it to save patient data; but looking at it from the users' perspective, I decided that these two actions should be separated. This way, users would be able to perform some ad hoc calculations without having to input a patient's name and SSN. In addition, users could save the data only when they were sure that all the entries were correct.

❑ **Presentation of a patient's history**: Users need an easy way to display the patient's history.

All of this functionality requires additional changes to the form. After adding a few controls (for patient data and history capability), the form ended up looking like the one shown in Figure 2-3.

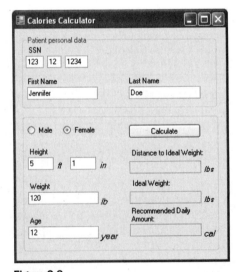

Figure 2-3

After making the changes, the Patient personal data section holds the data necessary to identify and differentiate patients, the Save and View buttons enable users to persist patient data or display patient history, and the Calculate button maintains its original function.

For implementing persistence of a patient's history, a few alternatives are available, such as a flat file, a database (e.g., Access), or even a spreadsheet. The simplest solution is probably to use an XML file, so I decided to do that. Before I dedicated myself to implementing any new requirements, however, I decided it was time to look at the code produced so far and deal with any outstanding issues.

I had been postponing this up until this point, simply adding more code to the existing method, mostly because I wasn't sure I was going to continue to work on the application. However, now that the application had grown and more complex requirements were being implemented, I needed to restructure the existing code. The first and very obvious problem with the code as it is now stood was that I had a single method implementing the entire functionality of the application. The method had grown out of proportion, and long methods are difficult to understand and reuse.

I'll return to the issue of persisting patient data later in the chapter, but first I want to deal with the outstanding issues that can stand in the way of implementing the new functionality, which requires some refactoring. You can see that although we haven't really gone very far with implementation, some smells have already managed to creep inside the code. We'll deal with these smells before going any further.

Refactoring in Action

So far, I haven't been paying too much attention to the way I programmed the Calories Calculator application. It was rather simple initially and a straightforward approach worked well. With new requirements, things get more complicated; bearing in mind the interest the application created, it is an auspicious moment to give it some more thought.

If we continue to simply add new functionality, the application will soon grow out of control and become impossible to maintain, so I am going to reorganize the code so that its internal structure is improved. We can do that without changing its behavior; the calorie calculation will happen just as it did before. If you remember the definition of refactoring (discussed thoroughly in Chapter 1), you'll see that this is exactly what I plan to do with the Calories Calculator.

> **Unit Testing:** Since I am now starting to change the code in ways that can have adverse effects (and even introduce bugs), I need to make sure that application consistency is maintained at all times. I can do this by developing a set of tests. I will write down data for a few imaginary patients and the results of the calculations that the application is performing. I will then run the application each time I make a change to it and execute all those tests, making sure correct results are returned. I will also test for invalid data. This sounds tedious, but it's necessary. Fortunately, there is a much better way to do this — as you'll learn in Chapter 3, which covers unit testing.

This section begins by looking into the code created so far. The only routine, `btnCalculate_Click`, looks alarmingly long. I used comments in order to separate it into several parts, but even when commented, long methods are much more difficult to understand. In refactoring terminology, this method displays a "long method smell." The solution is to split it into several shorter methods.

Decomposing the btnCalculate_Click Method

One very natural way of dealing with a long method is to separate it into multiple shorter methods. Doing this with btnCalculate_Click is really rather obvious. If you refer to Listing 2-3, you'll see that the code comments essentially segment the code into modules that indicate where you should extract the code into the new methods. This will not change the behavior of the code; it will make the code better organized and make the btnCalculate_Click method easier to read. I will move the code into the new method and make btnCalculate_Click call the new method. The following sections demonstrate how to take each segment from the method and make that segment its own method.

The Clear Old Results Segment

This segment is transformed into the clearResults private method:

```
private void ClearResults()
{
    txtDistance.Text = "";
    txtIdealWeight.Text = "";
    txtCalories.Text = "";
}
```

The Validate User Input Segment

This segment is transformed into the userInputValid private method:

```
private bool UserInputValid() {
    double result;
    if (!double.TryParse(txtFeet.Text, out result))
    {
        MessageBox.Show("Feet must be a numeric value.");
        txtFeet.Select();
        return false;
    }
    if (!double.TryParse(txtInches.Text, out result))
    {
        MessageBox.Show("Inches must be a numeric value.");
        txtInches.Select();
        return false;
    }
    if (!double.TryParse(txtWeight.Text, out result))
    {
        MessageBox.Show("Weight must be a numeric value.");
        txtWeight.Select();
        return false;
    }
    if (!double.TryParse(txtAge.Text, out result))
    {
        MessageBox.Show("Age must be a numeric value.");
        txtAge.Select();
        return false;
```

```
    }
    if (!(Convert.ToDouble(txtFeet.Text) >= 5))
    {
        MessageBox.Show("Height has to be equals or greater than 5 feet!");
        txtFeet.Select();
        return false;
    }
    return true;
}
```

This method needs to return the result of user input verification. In case the data is not valid, I need to interrupt the execution of the btnCalculate_Click method. You will see that approach when you take a look at the refactored btnCalculate_Click method.

The Calculate and Display Distance from Ideal Weight Segment

This segment can be transformed into the DistanceFromIdealWeight private method, so it receives two parameters, actual weight and ideal weight:

```
private double DistanceFromIdealWeight(double actualWeightInPounds,
    double idealWeightInPounds)
{
    return actualWeightInPounds - idealWeightInPounds;
}
```

Notice that in order to avoid any confusion in regard to measurements used, I added the name of the measurement to the parameter names: actualWeightInPounds and idealWeightInPounds.

Calculating Calories and Ideal Weight by Gender

The last remaining section is a little less self-explanatory than the others. The application will still calculate calories or ideal weight, but it does so according to gender. The easiest way to approach this issue is to transform the section into four private methods:

```
private double DailyCaloriesRecommendedMale(double weightInPounds,
    double heightInInches, double age)
{
    return 66 + (6.3 * weightInPounds) + (12.9 * heightInInches) - (6.8 * age);

}

private double DailyCaloriesRecommendedFemale(double weightInPounds,
    double heightInInches, double age)
{
    return 655 + (4.3 * weightInPounds) + (4.7 * heightInInches) - (4.7 * age);

}

private double IdealBodyWeightMale(double heightInInches)
{
```

```
        return (50 + (2.3 * (heightInInches - 60))) * 2.2046;
    }

    private double IdealBodyWeightFemale(double heightInInches)
    {
        return (45.5 + (2.3 * (heightInInches - 60))) * 2.2046;
    }
```

Instead of using code comments to indicate the intention behind a few lines of code, I now use a method to achieve the same goal. Method names clearly describe their purpose. This way, the code is a lot easier to understand and reuse. As I move code to new methods, I eliminate the comments.

The technique of decomposing large methods by extracting pieces of the method into new methods is called *extract method refactoring*. You'll learn about this refactoring detail in detail in Chapters 9 and 10.

The btnCalculate_Click Method after Method Extraction

What does the btnCalculate_Click routine look like now? You can see the code I ended up with in Listing 2-4.

Listing 2-4: The btnCalculate_Click Method after Decomposition

```
private void btnCalculate_Click(object sender, EventArgs e)
{
    ClearResults();
    if (!UserInputValid())
    {
        return;
    }
    if (rbtnMale.Checked)
    {
        txtCalories.Text = DailyCaloriesRecommendedMale(
            Convert.ToDouble(txtWeight.Text),
            (Convert.ToDouble(txtFeet.Text) * 12)
            + Convert.ToDouble(txtInches.Text),
            Convert.ToDouble(txtAge.Text)).ToString();

        txtIdealWeight.Text = IdealBodyWeightMale((
            Convert.ToDouble(txtFeet.Text) * 12)
            + Convert.ToDouble(txtInches.Text)).ToString();
    }
    else
    {
        txtCalories.Text = DailyCaloriesRecommendedMale(
            Convert.ToDouble(txtWeight.Text),
            (Convert.ToDouble(txtFeet.Text) * 12)
            + Convert.ToDouble(txtInches.Text),
            Convert.ToDouble(txtAge.Text)).ToString();

        txtIdealWeight.Text = IdealBodyWeightFemale(
            (Convert.ToDouble(txtFeet.Text) * 12)
            + Convert.ToDouble(txtInches.Text)).ToString();
    }
```

```
    txtDistance.Text = DistanceFromIdealWeight(
        Convert.ToDouble(txtWeight.Text),
        Convert.ToDouble(txtIdealWeight.Text)).ToString();
}
```

The method is definitely a lot shorter now. In addition, the comments are gone, as they are no longer relevant. The new method names are equally expressive.

The result of this transformation is multiple, shorter methods that do exactly what the original single method did. The benefits of more granular code are improved clarity and greater possibility for reuse of the new, shorter methods.

Discovering New Classes

In object-oriented programming you often use classes to establish links in code with real-world phenomena. This mapping between elements in the code and domain entities can greatly improve readability and comprehension of code. So far, I haven't even attempted to model the application code according to object-oriented principles. Instead, I have a single class inheriting `System.Windows.Forms.Form`, a base class for a basic GUI element. This class now sports a few methods I created by decomposing the event-handling method.

If you analyze for a moment the code created so far, you can see that the newly created methods can be divided into two distinct groups:

❑   Methods that are related to the behavior of the visual elements, and the GUI, such as the `ClearResults` method
❑   Methods that embed the medical formulas that perform the calculations, such as `IdealBodyWeightMale` and `DailyCaloriesRecommendedFemale`

So far, the CaloriesCalculator class is the only one in the project. It extends the Form class, a base class for windows or dialog boxes, which is a fundamental building block for the desktop interface. This class works well for our first group of methods, but the second group of methods, concerned with medical calculations, clearly does not belong to it.

By running the Calories Calculator application, you can observe that its purpose is collecting and computing certain data. This data represents human characteristics. In this case, as you can observe on the form itself, this data refers to patients.

Defining the Patient Class

Because this application deals with a medical issue, it makes sense to structure the data inside a new class called `Patient`. Listing 2-5 shows the class definition.

Listing 2-5: The New Patient Data Class

```
public class Patient

{
    private string ssn;
```

Continued

Listing 2-5: The New Patient Data Class *(continued)*

```
private string firstName;
private string lastName;
private double heightInInches;
private double weightInPounds;
private double age;
public string SSN {
    get { return ssn; }
    set { ssn = value; }
}
public string FirstName {
    get { return firstName; }
    set { firstName = value; }
}
public string LastName {
    get { return lastName; }
    set { lastName = value; }
}
public double HeightInInches {
    get { return heightInInches; }
    set { heightInInches = value; }
}
public double WeightInPounds {
    get { return weightInPounds; }
    set { weightInPounds = value; }
}
public double Age {
    get { return age; }
    set { age = value; }
}
}
```

So far, this class is a simple data structure, consisting only of properties. While grouping the data inside a new data type is definitely a step forward in attempting to improve the design of the application, having a class that has only data and no behavior is another hint that I need to continue improving the design of the program. A class with only data and no behavior is referred to as a *data class* and it is generally considered a code smell.

Moving Methods to the Patient Class

If you now return to the second group of methods, the ones performing medical computations, you can see that they operate on exactly the same patient data that the Patient class is used to describe.

Therefore, according to basic object-oriented principles, we should keep operations close to the data to which they refer. That means doing the following:

1. Move the DailyCaloriesRecommendedMale, DailyCaloriesRecommendedFemale, IdealBodyWeightMale, and IdealBodyWeightFemale methods to the Patient class.

2. Because methods have access to private variables for the class, we can make these four methods use Patient class properties instead of receiving parameters. We can also eliminate

parameters from the method declaration because the body of the method refers to the same names given to properties in the Patient class. It's just the matter of adjusting the case of letters. For example, the code

```
private double DailyCaloriesRecommendedFemale(double weightInPounds,
    double heightInInches, double age)
{
    return 655 + (4.3 * weightInPounds)
        + (4.7 * heightInInches) - (4.7 * age);

}
```

is transformed into the following:

```
public double DailyCaloriesRecommendedFemale()
{
    return 655 + (4.3 * WeightInPounds)
        + (4.7 * HeightInInches) - (4.7 * Age);
}
```

WeightInPounds, HeightInInches, and Age all now refer to properties of the Patient class. In this case, parameter and property names coincided by chance. The only detail that needs to be taken care of is the case of property names, because they start with capital letters. You can see how this works out in a more graphic way in Figure 2-4, where the DailyCaloriesRecommendedFemale method references the HeightInInches property in the same Patient class.

```
public class Patient
{
    //...
    private double heightInInches;

    public double HeightInInches
    {
        get { return heightInInches; }
        set { heightInInches = value; }
    }
    public double WeightInPounds

    public double DailyCaloriesRecommendedFemale()
    {
        return 655 + (4.3 * WeightInPounds)
            + (4.7 * HeightInInches) - (4.7 * Age);
    }
    //...
}
```

Figure 2-4

The Patient class is now a fully fledged class consisting of properties and methods, grouping the data and related behavior inside a cohesive whole. The Extract class and Move Method refactoring are described in detail in Chapter 9.

Narrowing the Patient Class Interface

If you have been paying attention so far, then you might have noticed that I didn't treat a very important piece of patient data in any special way. I am referring to gender, of course. Unless I have this information available inside the Patient class along with the rest of the patient data, I will not be able to move the last function left, DistanceFromIdealWeight, to make it a method in the Patient class. The method needs to know both the actual and the ideal body weight in order to perform the calculation; but after the latest refactorings, I have two methods that can give me ideal body weight: IdealBodyWeightMale and IdealBodyWeightFemale. Which one of the two should the DistanceFromIdealWeight method call?

Creating the Gender Enum

I'll set up the Patient class with another property, Gender. In this case, gender can have one of two values: male or female. To express this, it would be better to add another element to the project: the enumerator Gender. This way, DistanceFromIdealWeight can check the patient's gender and call the correct calculation method for ideal body weight:

```
public enum Gender {
    Male,
    Female
}
```

Adding a Gender Property to the Patient Class

It is quite easy now to add a Gender property to the Patient class that is typed as enum Gender. It will help discern a gender for each patient instance. Do what you usually do when you add a new property to a class:

```
private Gender gender;
// ...
public Gender Gender
{
    get { return gender; }
    set { gender = value; }
}
```

Moving the DistanceFromIdealWeight Method to the Patient Class

Now that the Gender enumerator is created and the Gender property is added, we can move the DistanceFromIdealWeight method to the Patient class. Again, we eliminate parameters and add a simple condition that uses the Gender property so that it works correctly:

```
public double DistanceFromIdealWeight()
{
    if (this.Gender == Gender.Female)
    {
        return WeightInPounds - IdealBodyWeightFemale();
    }
    else
    {
```

```
        return WeightInPounds - IdealBodyWeightMale();
```

" "

The method now works fine.

At this point, we have succeeded in moving all the relevant logic to the `Patient` class. This is a great feat, as the potential reusability of the code has improved greatly. You can now easily imagine the `Patient` class being used in another module someone might develop, or even in another application altogether. This was not at all the case with a sole `CaloriesCalculator` class.

Now, before we modify `CaloriesCalculator` so that it uses the `Patient` class, let's take another look at the methods in the new class. You might suspect there's more refactoring that can be performed here before moving on. Since we now have gender data available to code in the class, is it really necessary to have different methods for the male and female patients? Maybe we could move the gender logic inside the class somehow and release the client from the burden of tracking the gender information. Shouldn't the `Gender` class be able to manage gender-related logic on its own?

Putting Conditional Logic in the Patient Class

A lot of method names in the `Patient` class, such as `DailyCaloriesRecommendedMale` and `IdealBodyWeightFemale`, terminate with the word Male or Female, indicating that the method is applicable to patients of a certain gender only. This will result in clients (and by "clients" here I mean anyone using the class) having to think about this condition and having to write code akin to this:

```
if (myPatient.Gender == Gender.Female)
{
    idealWeight = myPatient.IdealBodyWeightFemale();
}
else {
    idealWeight = myPatient. IdealBodyWeightMale();
}
```

If you compare this to the `DistanceFromIdealWeight` method, you can see quite a different approach there. The method itself contains gender-related conditional logic, because gender data is already available in the Patient class. There are two obvious benefits to moving this conditional logic into the Patient class itself, as with the `DistanceFromIdealWeight` method:

❑   There are fewer publicly visible methods in the `Patient` class, so the code is a lot simpler for anyone using this class.

❑   Because classes are generally referenced from more than one place, moving conditional code inside the method prevents a lot of duplication in the client code. Probably anywhere the `Patient` class is used, the code would contain a lot of Ifs and end up looking like this:

```
if (myPatient.Gender == Gender.Female)
{
    //female patient related code
}
```

```
        else {
            //male patient related code
        }
```

In short, we would be better off transforming all the methods along the same lines as DistanceFrom IdealWeight. That entails adding a few new methods to the Patient class. The next couple of subsections show you how to do that.

Encapsulating DailyCaloriesRecommendedMale and DailyCaloriesRecommendedFemale

First, make the methods DailyCaloriesRecommendedMale and DailyCaloriesRecommendedFemale visible through a single method, DailyCaloriesRecommended:

```
public double DailyCaloriesRecommended()
{
    if (this.Gender == Gender.Female)
    {
        return DailyCaloriesRecommendedFemale();
    }
    else {
        return DailyCaloriesRecommendedMale();
    }
}
```

Encapsulating Ideal-Body-Weight Calculation

The same fate awaits the ideal body weight methods. Methods IdealBodyWeightMale and IdealBodyWeightFemale are now visible through a single method, IdealBodyWeight:

```
public double IdealBodyWeight()
{
    if (this.Gender == Gender.Female)
    {
        return IdealBodyWeightFemale();
    }
    else
    {
        return IdealBodyWeightMale();
    }
}
```

Making Encapsulated Methods Private

Finally, we can't forget to reduce the visibility of all the SomeMethodMale and SomeMethodFemale methods to private. The declarations now look like this:

```
private double DailyCaloriesRecommendedFemale()
private double DailyCaloriesRecommendedMale()
private double IdealBodyWeightMale()
private double IdealBodyWeightFemale()
```

With those declarations in place, we have managed to further encapsulate the logic inside the Patient class. This way, no unnecessary logic is exposed to the Patient class client. As you know, encapsulation is one of the pillars of object orientation, and taking this step will make your code more robust.

Restructuring the DistanceFromIdealWeight Method

We still have one more method to deal with. The `DistanceFromIdealWeight` code can be written in a more expressive manner that makes it easier to read and understand. While containing the same condition, and in that sense being similar to other methods, `DistanceFromIdealWeight` does not yet use private methods. The following code adds two private methods, `DistanceFromIdealWeightMale` and `DistanceFromIdealWeightFemale`, structured just like the methods `DailyCaloriesRecommended` and `IdealBodyWeight`:

```
private double DistanceFromIdealWeightMale()
{
    return WeightInPounds - IdealBodyWeightMale();
}

private double DistanceFromIdealWeightFemale()
{
    return WeightInPounds - IdealBodyWeightFemale();
}
```

`DistanceFromIdealWeight` now looks like this:

```
public double DistanceFromIdealWeight()
{
    if (this.Gender == Gender.Female)
    {
        return DistanceFromIdealWeightFemale();
    }
    else
    {
        return DistanceFromIdealWeightMale();
    }
}
```

Again, we performed method extraction. This way, the method is structured along the same lines as other methods. You will see the benefits of this modification later in the chapter, when we create the `Patient` class hierarchy.

In short, we have simplified the class for any client. In fact, you could say that the class interface has been reduced, thereby simplifying use of the classes. (Here, "interface" refers to all public elements in the class.)

Making CaloriesCalculator Use the Patient Class

Now we can modify the `CaloriesCalculator` class and make it use the `Patient` class for all related calculations. The following code adds a `Patient` property to the class:

```
public partial class CaloriesCalculator : Form
{
    private Patient patient;
```

```
        public Patient Patient {
            get { return patient; }
            set { patient = value; }
        }
// ...
    }
```

This instance is created in the `btnCalculate_Click` event-handling routine. Add the following line to it:

```
patient = new Patient();
```

Now we need to set `Patient`'s properties:

```
if (rbtnFemale.Checked) {
    patient.Gender = Gender.Female;
}else{
    patient.Gender = Gender.Male;
}
patient.HeightInInches = (Convert.ToDouble(txtFeet.Text) * 12)
    + Convert.ToDouble(txtInches.Text);
patient.WeightInPounds = Convert.ToDouble(txtWeight.Text);
patient.Age = Convert.ToDouble(txtAge.Text);
```

Next, the `Patient` instance is used to perform the required calculations:

```
txtCalories.Text = patient.DailyCaloriesRecommended().ToString();
txtIdealWeight.Text = patient.IdealBodyWeight().ToString();
txtDistance.Text = patient.DistanceFromIdealWeight().ToString();
```

Finally, to see how `btnCalculate_Click` ends up, take a look at Listing 2-6.

Listing 2-6: The btnCalculate_Click Method After Creating the New Patient Class

```
private void btnCalculate_Click(object sender, EventArgs e)
{
    ClearResults();
    if (!UserInputValid())
    {
        return;
    }
    //Creating new instance of Patient class
    patient = new Patient();
    //Setting patient properties with data from form
    if (rbtnFemale.Checked) {
        patient.Gender = Gender.Female;
    }else{
        patient.Gender = Gender.Male;
    }
    patient.HeightInInches = (Convert.ToDouble(txtFeet.Text) * 12)
        + Convert.ToDouble(txtInches.Text);
    patient.WeightInPounds = Convert.ToDouble(txtWeight.Text);
    patient.Age = Convert.ToDouble(txtAge.Text);
    txtCalories.Text = patient.DailyCaloriesRecommended().ToString();
```

```
        txtIdealWeight.Text = patient.IdealBodyWeight().ToString();
        txtDistance.Text = patient.DistanceFromIdealWeight().ToString();
    }
```

By extracting the `Patient` class and moving the logic related to medical calculation to this newly created class, we have laid the foundations of object-oriented design in the application, moving from an exclusively event-driven paradigm to an object-oriented paradigm. While solely event-driven programming can be effective on a small scale, it has to be coupled with object-oriented design to be as effective for more complex applications.

Creating the Patient Class Hierarchy

Now that we have taken all the preceding important steps in redesigning the application, it is time to take another look at the code I ended up with. After the latest changes, certain uniformity in all of the methods is becoming apparent. They all contain the same conditional code shown here:

```
if (this.Gender == Gender.Female)
{
    //some code
}
else
{
    //some code
}
```

In effect, this code — condition tests for a very specific attribute of `Patient`, the gender — has been duplicated. I might as well have used copy and paste to create it. This is a very good indication that some further refinements are required — in other words, I have just identified another major code smell. Code duplication generally indicates a serious flaw in your design: When you write the same code more than once, if you need to modify this logic, then you need to find all occurrences of it in your code. It is all too easy to miss other occurrences when the section that is currently of interest has been modified. It also means that you have more code than necessary to worry about.

There is a way to go about fixing this problem. In this case, we can create two new classes: `MalePatient` and `FemalePatient`. They will inherit the `Patient` class. Then we can move all gender-specific code to either `MalePatient` or `FemalePatient`, as appropriate. (Chapter 10 covers Extract Super Class and other inheritance-related refactorings.)

The mechanics for this transformation are a bit more complicated. The steps are as follows:

1. Add two new classes that inherit the `Patient` class:

```
public class FemalePatient:Patient
```

and

```
public class MalePatient:Patient
```

2. Move private methods with names ending with Male to the `MalePatient` class, and private methods with names ending with Female to the `FemalePatient` class. This is an example of *pull-down method refactoring*. Pulling down refers to moving a method from a class in the hierarchy to another class lower in the inheritance hierarchy.

3.   The `Patient` class declares methods that will have their implementation in its subclasses, `MalePatient` and `FemalePatient`. Since only some of the `Patient` class members are implemented, this class is abstract and must be marked by the `abstract` keyword:

```
public abstract class Patient
```

4.   Methods in the `Patient` class that are implemented in `MalePatient` and `FemalePatient` need to be marked as abstract by means of the abstract keyword. Once these methods are marked as abstract, their bodies have to be removed. `DistanceFromIdealWeight`, `DailyCaloriesRecommended`, and `IdealBodyWeight` in the `Patient` class now look like this:

```
public abstract double DailyCaloriesRecommended();

public abstract double IdealBodyWeight();

public abstract double DistanceFromIdealWeight();
```

Now we have the two new classes we need, `MalePatient` and `FemalePatient`, each containing the code specific to the appropriate gender.

Dealing with Gender-Specific Methods

Next, in the `MalePatient` and `FemalePatient` subclasses, we still have methods — methods that provide implementation for abstract methods in the `Patient` class — ending with the words Male and Female. It is time to change this, eliminating "Male" from method names in the `MalePatient` class and "Female" from method names in the `FemalePatient` class. This way, the names of the methods in `MalePatient` and `FemalePatient` will coincide with method names in the `Patient` class. We'll also change the visibility of the methods to public; and at this point, we are getting a timely reminder from our IDE, visible in the Task List window:

```
'CaloriesCalculator.MalePatient' does not implement inherited abstract member
'CaloriesCalculator.Patient.DailyCaloriesRecommended()'
```

Visual Studio will also display a helpful compiler warning:

```
'CaloriesCalculator.MalePatient.DailyCaloriesRecommended()' hides inherited member
'CaloriesCalculator.Patient.DailyCaloriesRecommended()'. To make the current member
override that implementation, add the override keyword. Otherwise add the new keyword.
```

The same error is present for the `FemalePatient` class. Just one thing missing: We need to add the `override` keyword to method declarations in the `MalePatient` and `FemalePatient` classes.

As you can see, I started with some conditional code that was gender-specific and managed to replace it with an inheritance hierarchy. This kind of refactoring replaces conditional logic with polymorphism. See Chapter 10 for more information on polymorphism.

Removing Gender-Specific Code from the DistanceFromIdealWeight Method

The `DistanceFromIdealWeight` method refers to `IdealBodyWeightMale` in the `MalePatient` class and to `IdealBodyWeightFemale` in the `FemalePatient` class, so it has to be changed so that it refers to the `IdealBodyWeight` method. The previous section eliminated gender-specific methods; now, in both classes, we modify the method `DistanceFromIdealWeight` so it looks the same:

```
public override double DistanceFromIdealWeight()
{
    return WeightInPounds - IdealBodyWeight();
}
```

Looking at the Patient Classes Hierarchy

Now it's time to have a look at the complete classes hierarchy. We end up with classes that look like the code shown in Listing 2-7.

Listing 2-7: Patient Classes Hierarchy

```
public class FemalePatient:Patient
{
    public override double DailyCaloriesRecommended()
    {
        return 655 + (4.3 * WeightInPounds)
            + (4.7 * HeightInInches) - (4.7 * Age);
    }

    public override double IdealBodyWeight()
    {
        return (45.5 + (2.3 * (HeightInInches - 60))) * 2.2046;
    }

    public override double DistanceFromIdealWeight()
    {
        return WeightInPounds - IdealBodyWeight();
    }
}

public class MalePatient:Patient
{
    public override double DailyCaloriesRecommended()
    {
        return 66 + (6.3 * WeightInPounds)
            + (12.9 * HeightInInches) - (6.8 * Age);
    }

    public override double IdealBodyWeight()
```

Continued

Listing 2-7: Patient Classes Hierarchy *(continued)*

```
    {
        return (50 + (2.3 * (HeightInInches - 60))) * 2.2046;
    }

    public override double DistanceFromIdealWeight()
    {
        return WeightInPounds - IdealBodyWeight();
    }
}

public abstract class Patient
{
    private string ssn;
    private string firstName;
    private string lastName;
    private double heightInInches;
    private double weightInPounds;
    private double age;
    private Gender gender;
    public string SSN
    {
        get { return ssn; }
        set { ssn = value; }
    }
    public string FirstName
    {
        get { return firstName; }
        set { firstName = value; }
    }
    public string LastName
    {
        get { return lastName; }
        set { lastName = value; }
    }
    public double HeightInInches
    {
        get { return heightInInches; }
        set { heightInInches = value; }
    }
    public double WeightInPounds
    {
        get { return weightInPounds; }
        set { weightInPounds = value; }
    }
    public double Age
    {
        get { return age; }
        set { age = value; }
    }
    public Gender Gender
```

```
        {
            get { return gender; }
            set { gender = value; }
        }


        public abstract double DailyCaloriesRecommended();

        public abstract double IdealBodyWeight();

        public abstract double DistanceFromIdealWeight();

    }
```

This is a long listing, but notice that no comments are really necessary. The design is simple and the intent is understandable from the names used for the class methods and properties. Now it's time to go back to the CaloriesCalculator class and make use of the newly created classes.

The btnCalculate_Click Method Using a Patient Classes Hierarchy

To complete the latest changes, we now need to modify the client, the CaloriesCalculator class. In the btnCalculate_Click method, we should create the correct subclass of the Patient hierarchy, based on user input and the value of the Gender radio button. This is demonstrated in Listing 2-8.

Listing 2-8: The btnCalculate_Click Method, After the MalePatient and FemalePatient

```
private void btnCalculate_Click(object sender, EventArgs e)
{
    ClearResults();
    if (!UserInputValid())
    {
        return;
    }

    //Creating instance of Patient subclass
    if (rbtnFemale.Checked) {
        patient = new FemalePatient();
    }else{
        patient = new MalePatient();
    }
    //Setting patient properties with data from form
    patient.HeightInInches = (Convert.ToDouble(txtFeet.Text) * 12)
        + Convert.ToDouble(txtInches.Text);
    patient.WeightInPounds = Convert.ToDouble(txtWeight.Text);
    patient.Age = Convert.ToDouble(txtAge.Text);
    txtCalories.Text = patient.DailyCaloriesRecommended().ToString();
    txtIdealWeight.Text = patient.IdealBodyWeight().ToString();
    txtDistance.Text = patient.DistanceFromIdealWeight().ToString();
}
```

This looks a lot better. I'd say we're almost done, but before calling it a day, notice two details.

Because gender information is now represented by subclasses, we have no need for a `Gender` property in the `Patient` class. If you look carefully, you'll see it is not used in any of the other classes. We can eliminate it. This means the `Gender` enumeration is redundant. Dead code is yet another smell you want to remedy, so we'll eliminate the `Gender` enumerator in addition to the Gender property. I call this eliminating dead code refactoring. Eliminating dead code is discussed in more detail in Chapter 5.

Pulling Up the DistanceFromIdealWeight Method

When I made modifications to the body of the `DistanceFromIdealWeight` method in the `FemalePatient` and `MalePatient` classes, I realized one detail. Both methods ended up looking the same:

```
public override double DistanceFromIdealWeight()
{
    return WeightInPounds - IdealBodyWeight();
}
```

This is actually duplicate code, a smell we must try to eliminate. The solution is to move the method implementation back to the `Patient` class. Eliminate the method from the `FemalePatient` and `MalePatient` classes and copy it back to the `Patient` class:

```
public double DistanceFromIdealWeight() {
    return WeightInPounds - IdealBodyWeight();
}
```

Pulling methods and properties up in the hierarchy is another type of refactoring that is very useful in eliminating duplicated code. It's generally referred to as pull-up method or pull-up property refactoring. I deal with these refactorings in detail in Chapter 10.

This has created an object-oriented structure for the domain-related logic, and separated it from the GUI-related logic. We have also grouped patient data inside a single structure, and this is exactly the data we need to persist. Therefore, all this work has established a good starting point for the implementation of persistence functionality in the application, which is the subject of the next section.

Implementing the Persistence Functionality

Generally, when I program I refactor all the time. Each time I add a method or a property, or resolve a bug, I take a look at the code, searching for the code smells. In this specific case, the application was very simple and I postponed refactoring for a while. Therefore, the smells accumulated, so I had to dedicate more time to refactoring procedures in a single go. Normally, refactoring is an integral part of the coding process.

By any accounting, the time used to refactor the application was well spent. Now the code is better organized and a lot easier to read, comprehend, and maintain. Because it is more modular, any changes applied from now on will be more isolated and therefore have a more limited effect. In addition, this code manages to group and gather the data related to the patient — again, exactly the data we need to persist — into a single structure, simplifying the job of implementing this functionality.

Because I was given a blank slate regarding how to implement the persistence functionality, there are a number of ways I could go about saving patient history: a database such as Access, a textual file, or even an Excel worksheet. Because .NET has very good support for XML, I decided to save patient history into an XML file. This will save me some work during the implementation, and given that XML is also easily readable by humans, it can save me even more work in implementing GUI elements for viewing the data.

Saving the Data

As usual, we begin by filling in the event-handling methods. Remembering the recent experience I had with the application, I decided to put data-validation code in a separate `ValidatePatientPersonalData` private method, much like the existing `ValidateUserInput` method.

Validating a Patient's Personal Data

This `ValidatePatientPersonalData` method is called from the `btnSave_Click` method, and it checks that a valid social security number and last and first name are entered. It looks just as you would expect:

```
private bool ValidatePatientPersonalData()
{
    int result;
    if ((!int.TryParse(txtSSNFirstPart.Text, out result)) |
        (!int.TryParse(txtSSNSecondPart.Text, out result)) |
        (!int.TryParse(txtSSNThirdPart.Text, out result)))
    {
        MessageBox.Show("You must enter valid SSN.");
        txtSSNFirstPart.Select();
        return false;

    }
    if (txtFirstName.Text.Trim().Length < 1) {
        MessageBox.Show("You must enter patient's first name.");
        txtFirstName.Select();
        return false;
    }
    if (txtLastName.Text.Trim().Length < 1)
    {
        MessageBox.Show("You must enter patient's last name.");
        txtLastName.Select();
        return false;
    }
    return true;

}
```

Next, we must make sure that the calculation has been performed before saving the measurement. For that purpose it's easiest to directly call the `btnCalculate_Click` method. It will check the validity of the data, create a patient instance, perform the calculation, and display it on the form.

Creating the XML File Used for Patient Data Persistence

Now it's time to take care of persisting the measurement to the file. Because we are not going to distribute a separate XML file, we must create the file programmatically. Therefore, when saving the data, we must check for the existence of the XML file. If it exists, then the data must be appended so that the existing history is not lost. In this case, we also need to look for the previous measurements by the same patient. It is best to structure the XML so that all measurements by one patient are under the same patient element.

49

For that purpose, we define the format of the XML file as shown in Listing 2-9.

Listing 2-9: The Patient History XML File Format

```xml
<?xml version="1.0" encoding="utf-8" ?>
<PatientsHistory>
        <patient ssn="33-333-3333" firstName="John" lastName="Doe">
            <measurement date="05/27/2006">
                <height>72</height>
                <weight>210</weight>
                <age>23</age>
                <dailyCaloriesRecommended>1043.4</dailyCaloriesRecommended>
                <idealBodyWeight>205.37988</idealBodyWeight>
                <distanceFromIdealWeight>4.62012</distanceFromIdealWeight>
                <!--Another measurement -->
            </measurement>
        </patient>
        <!--Another patient -->
</PatientsHistory>
```

The XML file is saved in the same place as the executable.

Now it's time to churn out the code. Listing 2-10 shows the code created to persist patient data.

Listing 2-10: The btnSave_Click Method Containing Persistence-Related Code

```csharp
private void btnSave_Click(object sender, EventArgs e)
{
    if ((!ValidatePatientPersonalData()) || (!UserInputValid()))
    {
        return;
    }
    //make sure to perform fresh calculation
    btnCalculate_Click(null, null);

    bool fileCreated = true;
    XmlDocument document = new XmlDocument();
    try
    {
        document.Load(System.Reflection.Assembly.
            GetExecutingAssembly().Location.
            Replace("CaloriesCalculator.exe", "PatientsHistory.xml"));

    }
    catch (FileNotFoundException)
    {
        //If file not found, set fileCreated to false and continue
        fileCreated = false;
    }
    if (!fileCreated)
    {
        document.LoadXml(
        "<PatientsHistory>" +
            "<patient ssn=\"" + patient.SSN + "\"" +
```

```
                " firstName=\"" + patient.FirstName + "\"" +
                " lastName=\"" + patient.LastName + "\"" + ">" +
                    "<measurement date=\"" + DateTime.Now + "\"" + ">" +
                        "<height>" + patient.HeightInInches + "</height>" +
                        "<weight>" + patient.WeightInPounds + "</weight>" +
                        "<age>" + patient.Age + "</age>" +
                        "<dailyCaloriesRecommended>" +
                        patient.DailyCaloriesRecommended() +
                        "</dailyCaloriesRecommended>" +
                        "<idealBodyWeight>" +
                        patient.IdealBodyWeight() +
                        "</idealBodyWeight>" +
                        "<distanceFromIdealWeight>" +
                        patient.DistanceFromIdealWeight() +
                        "</distanceFromIdealWeight>" +
                    "</measurement>" +
                "</patient>" +
            "</PatientsHistory>");
    }
    else
    {
        //Search for existing node for this patient
        XmlNode patientNode = null;
        foreach (XmlNode node in document.FirstChild.ChildNodes)
        {
            foreach (XmlAttribute attrib in node.Attributes)
            {
                //We will use SSN to uniquely identify patient
                if ((attrib.Name == "ssn") & (attrib.Value == patient.SSN))
                {
                    patientNode = node;
                }
            }
        }
        if (patientNode == null)
        {
            //just clone any patient node and use it for the new patient node
            XmlNode thisPatient =
                document.DocumentElement.FirstChild.CloneNode(false);
            thisPatient.Attributes["ssn"].Value =
                patient.SSN;
            thisPatient.Attributes["firstName"].Value =
                patient.FirstName;
            thisPatient.Attributes["lastName"].Value =
                patient.LastName;
            XmlNode measurement =
                document.DocumentElement.FirstChild["measurement"].CloneNode(true);
            measurement.Attributes["date"].Value =
                DateTime.Now.ToString();
            measurement["height"].FirstChild.Value =
                patient.HeightInInches.ToString();
            measurement["weight"].FirstChild.Value =
                patient.WeightInPounds.ToString();
            measurement["age"].FirstChild.Value =
```

Continued

Listing 2-10: The btnSave_Click Method Containing Persistence-Related Code *(continued)*

```
                    patient.Age.ToString();
            measurement["dailyCaloriesRecommended"].FirstChild.Value =
                patient.DailyCaloriesRecommended().ToString();
            measurement["idealBodyWeight"].FirstChild.Value =
                patient.IdealBodyWeight().ToString();
            measurement["distanceFromIdealWeight"].FirstChild.Value =
                patient.DistanceFromIdealWeight().ToString();
            thisPatient.AppendChild(measurement);
            document.FirstChild.AppendChild(thisPatient);
        }
        else
        {
            //If patient node found just clone any measurement
            //and use it for the new measurement
            XmlNode measurement = patientNode.FirstChild.CloneNode(true);
            measurement.Attributes["date"].Value = DateTime.Now.ToString();
            measurement["height"].FirstChild.Value =
                patient.HeightInInches.ToString();
            measurement["weight"].FirstChild.Value =
                patient.WeightInPounds.ToString();
            measurement["age"].FirstChild.Value = patient.Age.ToString();
            measurement["dailyCaloriesRecommended"].FirstChild.Value =
                patient.DailyCaloriesRecommended().ToString();
            measurement["idealBodyWeight"].FirstChild.Value =
                patient.IdealBodyWeight().ToString();
            measurement["distanceFromIdealWeight"].FirstChild.Value =
                patient.DistanceFromIdealWeight().ToString();
            patientNode.AppendChild(measurement);
        }
    }
    //Finally, save the xml to file
    document.Save(System.Reflection.Assembly.
    GetExecutingAssembly().Location.Replace(
        "CaloriesCalculator.exe", "PatientsHistory.xml"));
}
```

This method is quite long, but the code doesn't look that complicated. Nevertheless, a few explanatory notes are in place. The btnSave_Click method never checks for file existence explicitly. Instead, a FileNotFoundException is caught and a flag is set indicating that this is probably the first time a patient history is to be saved. In that case, the XML structure is created by concatenating and loading a string representing the XML structure as a way to get around the rather verbose DOM API.

In the event that the file exists, the code searches for this specific patient entry by comparing social security numbers. If the patient entry is not present, it is created by the cloning of any patient's node, thus saving the trouble of using the DOM API to create it. Because the file exists, we can assume that at least one entry exists.

If the patient is found, then a new measurement entry is created by the cloning of the measurement node. Because the patient node is found, it is safe to assume that at least one measurement was saved.

Although this time I was careful to place data-validation code in a separate function, I still ended up with a very, very long method. I dare say this is an excellent specimen of what is generally known as *spaghetti code*. Therefore, before I am told to change my career in the direction of Italian cuisine, I had better do something about refactoring this method.

Method Decomposition Revisited

In studying the method, one thing that might really bother you is that there are two completely identical pieces of code involved in setting measurement values to XmlNode. This code can be moved into a new method called SetMeasurementValues:

```
private XmlNode SetMeasurementValues(XmlNode measurement)
{
    measurement.Attributes["date"].Value =
        DateTime.Now.ToString();
    measurement["height"].FirstChild.Value =
        patient.HeightInInches.ToString();
    measurement["weight"].FirstChild.Value =
        patient.WeightInPounds.ToString();
    measurement["age"].FirstChild.Value =
        patient.Age.ToString();
    measurement["dailyCaloriesRecommended"].FirstChild.Value =
        patient.DailyCaloriesRecommended().ToString();
    measurement["idealBodyWeight"].FirstChild.Value =
        patient.IdealBodyWeight().ToString();
    measurement["distanceFromIdealWeight"].FirstChild.Value =
        patient.DistanceFromIdealWeight().ToString();
    return measurement;
}
```

We can further decompose the btnSave_Click method, much as we did btnCalculate_Click. The new methods that are created — LoadPatientHistoryFile, CreatePatientsHistoryXmlFirstTime, FindPatientNode, and AddNewPatient — are shown in Listing 2-11.

Listing 2-11: Decomposing the btnSave_Click Method

```
private XmlDocument LoadPatientsHistoryFile()
{
    XmlDocument document = new XmlDocument();
    document.Load(System.Reflection.Assembly.
        GetExecutingAssembly().Location.
        Replace("CaloriesCalculator.exe", "PatientsHistory.xml"));
    return document;
}

private XmlDocument CreatePatientsHistoryXmlFirstTime()
{
    XmlDocument document = new XmlDocument();
    document.LoadXml(
    "<PatientsHistory>" +
```

Continued

53

Listing 2-11: Decomposing the btnSave_Click Method *(continued)*

```
                "<patient ssn=\"" + patient.SSN + "\"" +
                " firstName=\"" + patient.FirstName + "\"" +
                " lastName=\"" + patient.LastName + "\"" + ">" +
                    "<measurement date=\"" + DateTime.Now + "\"" + ">" +
                        "<height>" + patient.HeightInInches + "</height>" +
                        "<weight>" + patient.WeightInPounds + "</weight>" +
                        "<age>" + patient.Age + "</age>" +
                        "<dailyCaloriesRecommended>" +
                        patient.DailyCaloriesRecommended() +
                        "</dailyCaloriesRecommended>" +
                        "<idealBodyWeight>" +
                        patient.IdealBodyWeight() +
                        "</idealBodyWeight>" +
                        "<distanceFromIdealWeight>" +
                        patient.DistanceFromIdealWeight() +
                        "</distanceFromIdealWeight>" +
                    "</measurement>" +
                "</patient>" +
        "</PatientsHistory>");
        return document;
}

private XmlNode FindPatientNode(XmlDocument document)
{
    XmlNode patientNode = null;
    foreach (XmlNode node in document.FirstChild.ChildNodes)
    {
        foreach (XmlAttribute attrib in node.Attributes)
        {
            //We will use SSN to uniquely identify patient
            if ((attrib.Name == "ssn") & (attrib.Value == patient.SSN))
            {
                patientNode = node;
            }
        }
    }
    return patientNode;
}

private void AddNewPatient(XmlDocument document)
{
    XmlNode thisPatient =
        document.DocumentElement.FirstChild.CloneNode(false);
    thisPatient.Attributes["ssn"].Value =
        patient.SSN;
    thisPatient.Attributes["firstName"].Value =
        patient.FirstName;
    thisPatient.Attributes["lastName"].Value =
        patient.LastName;
    XmlNode measurement =
        document.DocumentElement.FirstChild["measurement"].CloneNode(true);
```

```
        measurement = SetMeasurementValues(measurement);
        thisPatient.AppendChild(measurement);
        document.FirstChild.AppendChild(thisPatient);
    }
```

You have just witnessed a very immediate benefit of method extraction. Because we are able to extract two identical pieces of code into the method `SetMeasurementValues`, we have managed to eliminate duplication in the code and reduce total line count significantly.

Finding the Right Place for Methods

As in the aftermath of the `btnCalculate_Click` method decomposition, I'm getting the feeling that these data-persistence methods do not really belong to the `CaloriesCalculator` class. Rather, they are related to patient data, so at this point I am tempted to move them to a `Patient` class. What do you think — is that the right move at this moment? Or are there arguments against moving newly created `LoadPatientHistoryFile`, `CreateXmlDocumentFirstTime`, `FindPatientNode`, and `AddNewPatient` methods to the `Patient` class?

The `Patient` class is performing medical calculations. So far, it has nothing to do with managing the measurements of different patients. If we were to move these new methods to the `Patient` class, it would unnecessarily encumber this class with persistence code. Some future client of our `Patient` class, who is interested in the calculation that this class provides, might prefer persisting data in some other form — a database, for example. If we were to move XML persistence methods to the `Patient` class, we would be obliged to deliver this functionality as well.

Now imagine we discover a bug in our persistence code. We would need to distribute a new version to the client just in case that client uses XML persistence.

> *The reasoning I have just used is expressed in more generic terms as the single responsibility principle (SRP); I discuss this design principle in Chapter 9.*

Extracting a New Persistence Class

As the arguments in the previous section show, we need a new class in the project. We can call it `PatientHistoryXMLStorage`, and move all the new persistence-related methods from `CaloriesCalculator` to this class. This is another example of move method refactoring, and it is an integral part of the more complex extract class refactoring discussed in Chapter 9.

Once we have all those methods in `PatientHistoryXMLStorage`, it is apparent that they all reference a patient instance. To make the code compile, the methods need to somehow obtain a patient object.

There are two possible ways to do this:

❑   Add a parameter to each and every method except `LoadPatientHistoryFile`

❑   Add a field named `patient` to the class

As you can guess, the second option requires writing a lot less code. That way, a field `patient` will form part of the `PatientHistoryXMLStorage` state. Therefore, we'll go for that solution.

While we're at it, there is another parameter that is repeated in quite a few methods: the document parameter. Again, we can make this parameter a field of the `PatientHistoryXMLStorage` class.

In addition to this change, `LoadPatientHistoryFile` and `CreateXmlDocumentFirstTime` are not returning values anymore. Their declaration is changed and now has a `void` return type:

```
private void LoadPatientsHistoryFile()
private void AddNewPatient()
private void CreatePatientsHistoryXmlFirstTime()
```

Fields in the `PatientHistoryXMLStorage` class look like this:

```
private XmlDocument document;
private Patient patient;
```

All that is needed at this point is the public method in the `PatientHistoryXMLStorage` class that the client code could use. Now `LoadPatientsHistoryFile` and `CreatePatientsHistoryXmlFirstTime` methods will use `XmlDocument` declared in the class as the field.

Going back to `CaloriesCalculator` form class, you can see that the `btnSave_Click` event handler contains exactly the code needed. The following code extracts the `Save` method from this routine and moves it to `PatientHistoryXMLStorage`:

```
public void Save(Patient patient)
{
    this.patient = patient;
    bool fileCreated = true;
    try
    {
        LoadPatientsHistoryFile();
    }
    catch (FileNotFoundException)
    {
        fileCreated = false;
    }
    if (!fileCreated)
    {
        CreatePatientsHistoryXmlFirstTime();
    }
    else
    {
        XmlNode patientNode = FindPatientNode();
        if (patientNode == null)
        {
            AddNewPatient();
        }
        else
        {
            XmlNode measurement = patientNode.FirstChild.CloneNode(true);
            measurement = SetMeasurementValues(measurement);
```

```
                patientNode.AppendChild(measurement);
            }
    }
    document.Save(System.Reflection.Assembly.
    GetExecutingAssembly().Location.Replace(
        "CaloriesCalculator.exe", "PatientsHistory.xml"));
}
```

This leaves the `btnSave_Click` event handler looking like this:

```
private void btnSave_Click(object sender, EventArgs e)
{
    if ((!ValidatePatientPersonalData()) || (!UserInputValid()))
    {
        return;
    }
    //make sure to perform fresh calculation
    btnCalculate_Click(null, null);
    storage.Save(this.patient);
}
```

In case you are wondering where the storage variable came from, it is now another field in the `CaloriesCalculator` form class, and its declaration looks like this:

```
private PatientHistoryXMLStorage storage;
```

It is initialized in the constructor method of the `CaloriesCalculator` form class:

```
public CaloriesCalculator()
{
    InitializeComponent();
    this.storage = new PatientHistoryXMLStorage();
}
```

This effectively implements persistence functionality in a separate, persistence-dedicated class.

Implementing Patient-History Display Functionality

At this point, only one functionality is pending: to somehow visualize patient data. Internet Explorer does a pretty good job at visualizing XML data, so instead of adding a new form to my project, we can simply open the Internet Explorer instance, pass the location of the `patientHistory.xml` file to it, and let it display the file contents. If we wanted to improve on this, we could write our own XSL template and visualize the data by using Internet Explorer's built-in XSL engine, but at this point we'll stick with IE's default XML stylesheet.

Calling upon Internet Explorer is easily done through the `Start` method's `System.Diagnostics.Process` class. All we need now is the location of the file. In the `Save` method of the `PatientHistoryXMLStorage` class, I programmed the application so it saves the XML file next to a `Calories Calculator` .exe. We could easily copy and paste this line, but that would mean creating a duplicate entry in our code. As a matter of fact, we already have duplicated code because we used the same line in the `LoadPatientHistoryFile` method.

Instead of copying the code — and you can read about all the headaches duplicated code can create for you in Chapter 7 — we can add a public property to the `PatientHistoryXMLStorage` class. Since we need to access it easily from another class, make this field static. Here is the code:

```
public static string PatientsHistoryFileLocation
{
    get
    {
        return System.Reflection.Assembly.
        GetExecutingAssembly().Location.Replace(
            "CaloriesCalculator.exe", "PatientsHistory.xml");
    }
    private set { }
}
```

This also manages to simplify `LoadPatientHistoryFile`. Now it looks like this:

```
private void LoadPatientsHistoryFile()
{
    document.Load(PatientsHistoryFileLocation);
}
```

In addition, the related line in the `Save` method now looks like the following:

```
document.Save(PatientsHistoryFileLocation);
```

Finally, the `btnView_Click` method looks like this:

```
private void btnView_Click(object sender, EventArgs e)
{
    Process.Start("IExplore.exe",
        PatientHistoryXMLStorage.PatientsHistoryFileLocation);
}
```

Listing 2-12 shows the final code for the `PatientHistoryXMLStorage` class.

Listing 2-12: Final Version of the PatientHistoryXMLStorage Class

```
using System;
using System.Xml;
using System.IO;

namespace CaloriesCalculator
{
    class PatientHistoryXMLStorage
    {
        public static string PatientsHistoryFileLocation
        {
            get
            {
                return System.Reflection.Assembly.
                GetExecutingAssembly().Location.Replace(
```

```
                "CaloriesCalculator.exe", "PatientsHistory.xml");
        }
        private set { }
    }

    private XmlDocument document;
    private Patient patient;

    public PatientHistoryXMLStorage()
    {
        this.document = new XmlDocument();
    }

    public void Save(Patient patient)
    {
        this.patient = patient;
        bool fileCreated = true;
        try
        {
            LoadPatientsHistoryFile();
        }
        catch (FileNotFoundException)
        {
            fileCreated = false;
        }
        if (!fileCreated)
        {
            CreatePatientsHistoryXmlFirstTime();
        }
        else
        {
            XmlNode patientNode = FindPatientNode();
            if (patientNode == null)
            {
                AddNewPatient();
            }
            else
            {
                XmlNode measurement = patientNode.FirstChild.CloneNode(true);
                measurement = SetMeasurementValues(measurement);
                patientNode.AppendChild(measurement);
            }
        }
        document.Save(PatientsHistoryFileLocation);
    }

    private void CreatePatientsHistoryXmlFirstTime()
    {
        document.LoadXml(
        "<PatientsHistory>" +
            "<patient ssn=\"" + patient.SSN + "\"" +
            " firstName=\"" + patient.FirstName + "\"" +
            " lastName=\"" + patient.LastName + "\"" + ">" +
```

Continued

```
                "<measurement date=\"" + DateTime.Now + "\"" + ">" +
                    "<height>" + patient.HeightInInches + "</height>" +
                    "<weight>" + patient.WeightInPounds + "</weight>" +
                    "<age>" + patient.Age + "</age>" +
                    "<dailyCaloriesRecommended>" +
                    patient.DailyCaloriesRecommended() +
                    "</dailyCaloriesRecommended>" +
                    "<idealBodyWeight>" +
                    patient.IdealBodyWeight() +
                    "</idealBodyWeight>" +
                    "<distanceFromIdealWeight>" +
                    patient.DistanceFromIdealWeight() +
                    "</distanceFromIdealWeight>" +
                "</measurement>" +
            "</patient>" +
        "</PatientsHistory>");
    }

    private void LoadPatientsHistoryFile()
    {
        document.Load(PatientsHistoryFileLocation);
    }

    private void AddNewPatient()
    {
        XmlNode thisPatient =
            document.DocumentElement.FirstChild.CloneNode(false);
        thisPatient.Attributes["ssn"].Value =
            patient.SSN;
        thisPatient.Attributes["firstName"].Value =
            patient.FirstName;
        thisPatient.Attributes["lastName"].Value =
            patient.LastName;
        XmlNode measurement =
            document.DocumentElement.FirstChild["measurement"].CloneNode(true);
        measurement = SetMeasurementValues(measurement);
        thisPatient.AppendChild(measurement);
        document.FirstChild.AppendChild(thisPatient);
    }

    private XmlNode SetMeasurementValues(XmlNode measurement)
    {
        measurement.Attributes["date"].Value =
            DateTime.Now.ToString();
        measurement["height"].FirstChild.Value =
            patient.HeightInInches.ToString();
        measurement["weight"].FirstChild.Value =
            patient.WeightInPounds.ToString();
        measurement["age"].FirstChild.Value =
            patient.Age.ToString();
```

```
        measurement["dailyCaloriesRecommended"].FirstChild.Value =
            patient.DailyCaloriesRecommended().ToString();
        measurement["idealBodyWeight"].FirstChild.Value =
            patient.IdealBodyWeight().ToString();
        measurement["distanceFromIdealWeight"].FirstChild.Value =
            patient.DistanceFromIdealWeight().ToString();
        return measurement;
    }

    private XmlNode FindPatientNode()
    {
        XmlNode patientNode = null;

        foreach (XmlNode node in document.FirstChild.ChildNodes)
        {
            foreach (XmlAttribute attrib in node.Attributes)
            {
                if ((attrib.Name == "ssn") & (attrib.Value == patient.SSN))
                {
                    patientNode = node;
                }
            }
        }
        return patientNode;
    }
}
}
```

It's a rather long listing, but it is here for a purpose. Before this book ends, we will have another go at this code from the C# 2008 perspective. (If you can't wait to see what happens to this code in the C# 2008 version, take a look at Chapter 13.) With this piece of code, we have concluded implementing the latest requirements of the Calories Calculator application.

Calories Calculator, Refactored Version

Now it's time to take a look at the new structure of the application. A class diagram (see Figure 2-5) provides a good overview of the code we ended up with.

Despite the fact that the code now contains a lot more classes and methods than it did initially, it is clearly more balanced and better organized, with each class dedicated to a single and specific purpose. It also uses inheritance, possibly opening the door for future extensions.

What does this tell you? What did you observe during the process of developing this sample application? Have we managed to improve the code as the requirements were implemented? What are the benefits of all this?

Table 2-1 summarizes some of the answers to these questions.

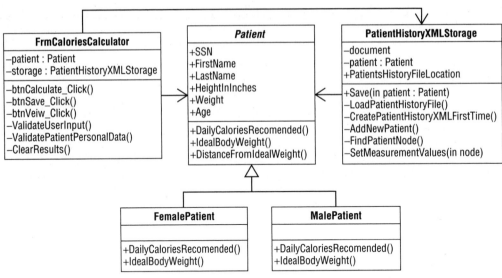

Figure 2-5

Table 2-1: Refactoring Techniques Applied and Benefits Gained

Refactoring Technique	Benefit
Extract method	Atomic, more reusable methods with a clear purpose
Extract class	Single-purpose classes improve reuse, maintainability, and readability of code
Move method	Better structured code, used in conjunction with "Extract class"
Reduce method visibility	Improves encapsulation, thus making code simpler and clear cut
Replace conditional logic with polymorphism	Reduces duplication in the code, improving maintainability and extensibility
Pull-up method	Reduced duplication in code
Eliminate dead code	Simplifies code and makes it easier to read

The following list summarizes the refactoring process performed and the logic applied on Calories Calculator:

❑ Decomposing the long methods improved the code in several ways. By giving explicit names to pieces of code, you improve the readability of the code and make it simpler. It is easier to understand the purpose of each method; the intent is explicitly stated, so the maintainability of the code is improved. Any new programmer starting out on the code will need less time to get acquainted with it. Even experienced programmers can forget a specific detail of the code they developed, so everyone benefits from improved comprehensibility.

❑ Making the code more granular and structured improved the reuse potential of the code. This simplifies the code by making the code-base smaller. You end up with less code.

❑ Reuse potential was also improved by extracting the `SetMeasurementValues` method. This immediately resulted in another benefit. We replaced another piece of code with the call to this method, thus eliminating duplication in the code. This improves the maintainability of the code — if we ever need to modify some behavior, we only need to perform the modification in a single place. This results in code less prone to bugs, since you are less likely to encounter a situation in which you modified behavior in one place but failed to modify it in another place that contained the same duplicated code.

❑ By eliminating code that ended up unused, we made the application easier to read and to debug, improving the code's simplicity. This refactoring has reduced the overall quantity of code.

❑ Maintainability is improved by replacing literals scattered throughout the code with a constant. This way, if a value ever needs to be changed, the change can be performed in a single place.

❑ Extracting new classes also improves code reuse, and organizing classes in a hierarchy helps to avoid duplication, but on a different scale. At the same time, extensibility of the code was enhanced. Now that the application's `MalePatient` class and `FemalePatient` class extend the `Patient` class, it is not so far-fetched to imagine, for example, `ChildPatient` as an addition to the hierarchy. This means you can add more behavior without modifying existing code — which translates into less code to test, recompile, or redeploy.

This list wraps it up for the demonstration in this chapter. In the following chapters, you'll study refactoring techniques in greater detail.

Summary

RAD programmers typically like to dip into the code right from the project's outset. This no-nonsense, goal-oriented approach can have a lot of benefits, allowing for early prototyping and increased early productivity. However, as an application progresses and new requirements appear, it becomes necessary to restructure the code so that the optimum design is maintained.

The example in this chapter followed this typical approach. I first constructed a simple application that could perform some medical calculations, such as estimating ideal body weight and the recommended daily amount of calories to intake. Initially, I didn't put too much emphasis on the design or the quality of the code. However, in response to growing requirements from the client, it was necessary to spend some time refactoring the code in order to keep it in shape (and to prove how it pays off).

This example has shown the ways in which refactoring improves the design and makes code simpler and easier to understand. Making methods more granular improved code reusability. The same was achieved by making classes responsible for a single task. Eliminating duplications in the code made it smaller and easier to modify. Organizing classes into a logical hierarchy also dealt with duplicate code and made the code more extensible. Refactored source is easier to reuse, extend, and maintain. It is less prone to bugs and easier to optimize.

With the example in this chapter, I tried to provide insight into how individual refactoring techniques work together to improve the design of the code. By providing this practical demonstration, a general context for individual refactoring techniques should become apparent. This should help you understand where each of these refactoring techniques fits inside the big picture and should prepare you for examining each of these techniques in detail.

Although some of the refactoring techniques demonstrated here can be performed much more efficiently by using an automated refactoring tool, they were performed manually in this chapter in order to focus on the code and how the refactoring techniques are actually applied. In the next chapter, you'll learn about the tools that can help you refactor much more efficiently and securely, including a refactoring toolkit and an automated refactoring tool.

3

Assembling a
Refactoring Toolkit

Many techniques and methodologies make you produce and maintain artifacts, in addition to source code, as an integral part of the project — things such as documentation, diagrams, and so on. Some approaches are very strict in controlling the way you code, imposing rules and guidelines that confine the way you program in order to make your code more uniform. In these cases, you may often feel that an additional burden has encumbered this already demanding line of work. It can easily make you reluctant to adopt new techniques.

With refactoring, the rules are not cast in stone, nor do you have to deal with any additional baggage. On the contrary, the more expert you become in refactoring techniques, the more confident you are with the code. Refactoring makes you feel like you are in charge. The productivity gain and coding proficiency that come from refactoring are further enhanced by the right set of tools.

When I talk about assembling a refactoring toolkit, which is the topic of this chapter, I consider the following three pieces of software mandatory, no matter the size of your team or project, your methodology, or the type of software you are making:

- ❑   An automated refactoring tool

- ❑   A unit-testing framework

- ❑   A source-code version-control system

Only the first item is directly related to performing refactoring transformations, while the other two are, in my opinion, indispensable for any type of serious refactoring work. The refactoring tool can automate certain refactorings, but only when it is used together with unit testing and source-code control will you have the freedom and security to perform refactoring continuously and on a large scale.

This chapter discusses the first two items in detail. I haven't met many teams that don't use some kind of version-control system, so I will not go into any great detail about it other than to dedicate just enough space to treat version-control issues relevant to refactoring.

While Visual Studio Team System Edition provides some refactoring capabilities and supports unit testing, it is a top-of-the-line product, priced accordingly. Since I would like to reach the widest audience possible, I have opted to use the open-source unit testing framework called NUnit, which can be used with any edition of Visual Studio. This solution is much more cost effective but by no means less useful.

If you would like to learn about refactoring techniques right away, you can skip this chapter and come back to this discussion of tools later, after you have read about each individual refactoring technique.

Using an Automated Refactoring Tool

Wider adoption of refactoring in any programming language has generally been influenced by the availability of an automated refactoring tool. It is one thing to understand the theory, the pros and cons, and even to be an eager devotee of the technique, and quite another to start meddling with your code in the face of an ever-closer deadline. Even the smallest change to your code can break it, so you need a really cool head and audacity to vouch for some intangible characteristic like design and code quality when pending requirements are waiting to be implemented.

Wouldn't it be great if you had a tool with enough intelligence to know how to perform changes in your code without breaking it? For example, if you renamed a method, the tool would search for all the client code that calls this method and replace its name in the client code. Or if you extracted a piece of code and put it into a new method, the tool would ensure that all the necessary parameters were included in the method declaration.

With Visual Studio 2008, a number of such tools are available for C# programmers. Some basic refactoring capabilities come with Visual Studio out of the box; but if you want some advanced refactoring support, you will have to opt for a commercial third-party solution that generally comes in the form of a Visual Studio add-in. All of these tools allow you to download a demo version before you make the purchase. Choosing the right tool is often a matter of taste and personal preferences. If you consider purchasing a third-party refactoring tool, I suggest you download it and give it a test ride before you buy it. The following section takes a look at some of these tools.

ReSharper from JetBrains

JetBrains (www.jetbrains.com) made its name with the excellent IntelliJ IDEA Java IDE, which brought a new level of productivity to often nonresponsive Java IDEs and pioneered comprehensive refactoring support for Java. Its first venture into the .NET arena is ReSharper, a refactoring and developer productivity add-in for Visual Studio. It originally supported C#, hence the name, but ReSharper is now a cross-language tool that supports Visual Basic XML, XAML, and ASP.NET.

ReSharper sports a number of useful refactoring transformations. I will mention only a few:

- ❑ Comprehensive, project-wide Rename refactoring
- ❑ Extract Method with dialog window preview
- ❑ Move Class refactoring
- ❑ Use Base Type Where Possible refactoring
- ❑ Convert Extension Method to Plain Static

- ❏ Convert Static to Extension Method
- ❏ Convert Property to Auto-Property
- ❏ Convert Interface to Abstract Class
- ❏ Inline Method
- ❏ Move Type to Another File or Namespace
- ❏ Pull Members Up
- ❏ Push Members Down
- ❏ Replace Constructor with Factory Method
- ❏ Change Scope

It has an integrated NUnit test runner, advanced navigation and formatting capabilities, code analysis features, MSBuild and NAnt integration, coding assistance, C# 3.0 and LINQ support, and a lot of other interesting features that will make your programming life a lot easier.

Refactor! Pro from Developer Express

Developer Express is well known for its GUI ASP and Windows components and for a Visual Studio productivity add-in Code Rush (which includes the Refactor! Pro refactoring add-in).

Refactor! Pro includes over 150 refactorings (according to official documentation) and supports C#, VB, ASP.NET, C++, JavaScript, and more. It also works with previous editions of Visual Studio — namely, 2002 and 2003. Furthermore, it enables you to customize the way refactorings are performed and even extend the tool by programming your own refactorings.

Some of the interesting refactorings that Refactor! Pro supports include the following:

- ❏ Extract Interface
- ❏ Expand Lambda Expression
- ❏ Compress to Lambda Expression
- ❏ Extract Method
- ❏ Extract to XAML Resource
- ❏ Move Type to Namespace
- ❏ Safe Rename
- ❏ Use StringBuilder

The latest version of Refactor! Pro has also been updated to work with Visual Studio 2008 and supports the latest addition to C# syntax in version 3.0, such as LINQ and lambda expressions.

If you search the Internet, you will find other third-party refactoring tools for C#, but the two just described seem to be the most popular and the most actively maintained. Both can integrate with the 2008 version of Visual Studio and support the latest additions to C# syntax from version 3.0.

Refactor! for ASP from Developer Express

Refactor! for ASP is a free, scaled-down version of Refactor! Pro. Refactor! for ASP features a number of specific refactorings for C#, HTML/CSS, and ASP .NET. Among the more interesting refactorings it provides are the following:

- ❑ Extract Method
- ❑ Encapsulate Field
- ❑ Extract Property
- ❑ Inline Temp
- ❑ Introduce Constant
- ❑ Replace Temp with Query
- ❑ Move Declaration near Reference
- ❑ Move Initialization to Declaration
- ❑ Extract Style
- ❑ Rename Style
- ❑ Move to Code-behind
- ❑ Extract ContentPlaceHolder (Create Master)
- ❑ Extract to UserControl

I talk about Refactor! for ASP at length in Chapter 14, and deal in detail with HTML/CSS and ASP .NET refactorings. In Chapter 15 I mention some other tools useful for refactoring web applications, such as HTML Tidy and Fiddler Debugging Proxy.

Visual Studio Refactoring Features

Visual Studio, since the 2005 version and including the 2008 version, provides some basic refactoring features for C# developers. While these features are not many in number, they are still highly valuable because they include some of the most common refactorings, such as Rename and Extract Method refactoring.

You can access refactoring features through the Refactor option in the main Visual Studio menu. This menu item becomes visible once you open and put into focus the C# editor window. Alternatively, you can access refactoring options through an item in the context menu that becomes visible after you right-click on the C# editor window.

A few refactoring options are well hidden inside the Edit ➤ IntelliSense ➤ Organize Using menu item. These refactorings will help you reorganize the Using section.

Refactorings can also be invoked by means of shortcut key combinations. Once you become more familiar with these features, you will probably use shortcuts to invoke them, as shortcuts are the fastest way to do so when you code.

Figure 3-1 shows the Refactor menu, with the shortcut key combinations for each type.

Another alternative to invoking refactoring features in Visual Studio is the class diagram. Start by adding a class diagram to your project and then visualize the type of class diagram (by dragging and dropping a class from Solution Explorer to class diagram, for example). Next, you will be able to invoke refactoring features through the context menu after clicking the desired element (class, method, field, and so on) with the right mouse button. Figure 3-2 illustrates how to invoke refactoring features from a class diagram in Visual Studio.

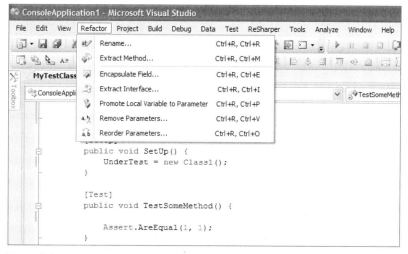

Figure 3-1

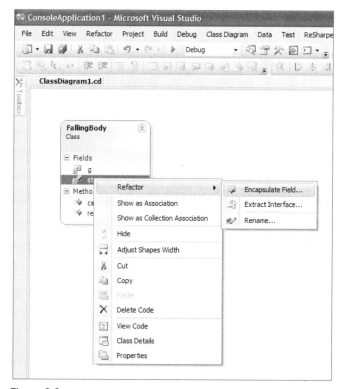

Figure 3-2

You will take a detailed look at each refactoring feature in Visual Studio later in the book. Table 3-1 shows a list of the refactoring supported by Visual Studio and where you can find those refactorings covered in the book.

Table 3-1: Refactorings Supported by Visual Studio

Refactoring Name	Purpose	Used in Chapter
Rename	Renames the identifier	6
Extract Method	Extracts a block of code into a new method	7
Encapsulate Field	Transforms a field into a property	9
Extract Interface	Creates a new interface that declares public members of a class and has the class implement this newly created interface	10
Promote Local Variable to Parameter	Promote local variable declaration to a parameter in method signature	Relevant for Chapter 8
Remove Parameters	Remove unused parameter from method signature	Relevant for Chapter 8
Reorder Parameters	Change order of parameters in method signature	Relevant for Chapter 8
Remove Unused Usings	Removes unused using directives from using section	5
Sort Usings	Orders using directives in using section alphabetically	5
Remove and Sort (Usings)	Both removes unused usings and sorts the remaining ones in a single operation	5

Unit-Testing Basics: The Testing Harness

Refactoring can be addictive. Once you start, it's difficult to stop! However, one step too far and you won't be able to find your way back. That is, make one simple mistake, and suddenly the program is not doing what it was supposed to do. You try reversing the latest changes but to no avail. You made a mistake somewhere along the way, and you just can't figure out where. The only solution is to go all the way back to the beginning. The scenario I just described is not uncommon for a refactoring novice. Refactoring has to be performed in a disciplined manner, but that alone will often not suffice.

Refactoring has to be performed carefully, step by step, and each step has to be followed by verification. You have to ensure that your changes do not influence the behavior of your program. Remember the definition of refactoring? You are improving the design without changing the behavior. How can you verify the behavior in a simple yet efficient way? The solution is unit testing.

As some of you might already know, Visual Studio Team System comes with integrated unit-testing support. At this point, you might be wondering why I chose to talk about NUnit instead. First, as a top-of-the-line Visual Studio product, Team System is not inexpensive. If I had used it, this section would have had a smaller audience. Second, NUnit is more applicable to a test-driven development style (something a lot of you might decide to pursue). At any rate, exposure to NUnit is also a good starting point for unit testing with Visual Studio. NUnit is less integrated with Visual Studio and less GUI-based than Microsoft's tool, so by learning unit testing with NUnit, you will acquire a generic and more universal understanding of the unit-testing process. As a side note, there are other alternatives to unit testing in .NET. For example, two other accomplished open-source unit-testing frameworks are MbUnit (`www.mbunit.com`) and csUnit (`www.csunit.org`).

In this section you will learn more about unit testing in general and the benefits it brings. You'll explore in more detail one open-source unit-testing framework, NUnit. You will learn how to install it and use it and how to write unit tests with its help. Finally, you'll return to the Calories Calculator application and write tests for some of the classes in the application so you can see unit testing in practice. We'll begin by taking a look at how unit testing as a discipline came about.

Why a Unit Testing Framework?

One of the ways you deal with software complexity is through testing. Testing is your attempt to discover bugs and errors in the software you are creating before it reaches a final user. In an attempt to ensure software quality, companies often have teams, even departments, dedicated to different forms of testing. The types of tests these teams perform vary and can be geared toward ensuring different qualities of the software. They might perform functional, usability, integration, load, stress, and other types of tests. All of these are important parts of the software development process.

Manual Data Entry

In order to perform any type of test thoroughly, a lot of time and resources are needed. It might take days, even weeks, before results are obtained and feedback ends up in the hands of a programmer; but it is of utmost importance that the coder be able to test the code every step of the way during the development process.

Each time the most minimum functionality is added, changed, or removed, programmers have a natural tendency to want to assure themselves that the software still works correctly and that no fresh bugs have been introduced. The most obvious way to go about this is for the programmers themselves to simulate users. An IDE makes it easy to start the execution, enter the desired data, and verify the result. In case anything unexpected occurs, the process can be repeated and followed through with a debugger, enabling you to observe the execution depicted in the source code, line by line, and to interactively review and change variable data states. This makes the task of identifying the offending bug a lot easier. At this point, you might remember that this is exactly the approach used to test the Calories Calculator application in Chapter 2.

With all these capabilities and tools, programmers still produce very costly and difficult-to-identify bugs. Why does this happen? Partly because the type of ad hoc testing I just described, performed by programmers manually, has some very serious drawbacks:

❑ It requires a lot of manual data input, making the whole process very tedious. (This drawback is directly related to the next one.)

❑ Because it is tedious and time-consuming, coders limit their testing exploits to scenarios most directly related to their current tasks. However, there is no guarantee that only the tested functionality has been affected by the current changes.

❑ For the same reason, the pool of test data is often insufficient, failing to test for invalid and limit values.

❑ Because they are not automated, the tests are difficult to repeat in a reliable manner. In one sweep you might test for some important values and in the next those values are forgotten or misspelled.

❑ Because of the large amount of time associated with this type of testing, testing frequency is low, leading to situations in which a lot of changes are introduced without test assurance in between. If a bug is identified after substantial changes have been applied, it is a lot more difficult to locate it. This leads to a vicious circle wherein more and more time is lost because of an unreliable development process, while the lack of time discourages a systematic approach to testing.

A lot of programmers have identified the drawbacks I just mentioned and reached the following conclusion: Automating the tests would greatly improve their quality and make them less costly and easier to perform. Therefore, the logical question to ask is whether there is anything you can do about it.

A First Attempt at Automated Unit Testing: Ad Hoc Unit Testing

The easiest and the most direct way to test a piece of code in an automated and repeatable manner is to write a program to exercise the targeted code. For example, if you write a dynamic link library, you can program an executable that will consume the functionality offered by the DLL and ensure that the DLL behaves according to the specification.

While this approach to automating testing is a great improvement over manual testing, a number of problems still become apparent once you adopt it:

❑ It offers no way to write tests in a systematic and standardized way, making it difficult for you to maintain the quality of tests and promote their teamwide adoption. There are no real guidelines for programming the tests.

❑ If you do not perform the testing in a focused way, by isolating one piece of code from the rest of the application state, it may still be possible to discover the bug, but it can be very difficult to pin down the offending line of code. This approach to test automation is similar to the recording of user interaction: It is based on a surface view of tested code.

❑ In certain setups, you might want unit testing to play an integral part in a wider and automated development process. This would require better tools integration, standardized output, reports, and the like.

No wonder programmers tried to find a solution to all these problems. Programmers needed the ability to write their own tests, counting on detailed knowledge of tested code. These tests would have to be executed and repeated at will. They would have to exercise small modules of code in isolation so no time would be lost searching for the source of the bug. Finally, the solution needed to encompass standardized means of capturing and displaying results.

Voilà! Unit-Testing Frameworks

All of this led to the appearance of unit testing frameworks, which granted programmers new levels of freedom and productivity. While solving many of the previously mentioned problems, the tests written in this manner had another very interesting side effect.

It became apparent that these tests could serve as a very good tool for expressing user requirements in an explicit, unambiguous manner. Diagrams, storyboards, use cases, and the rest of the traditional requirements-taking tools are all subject to human interpretation. Because unit tests are written in code and then executed as a program, it is the computer that decides whether a requirement has been satisfied — that is, whether the test has failed or not. Of course, it is still programmers who have to write the right test, one embodying the right requirement.

This style simplifies the development in another way: It eliminates the constant need to decide what exactly should be implemented, what methods and classes are actually needed. Programmers often speculate about the scope of a program, wondering whether they might need a feature in the future, or what if the customer needs to solve the same problem later. If you actually write each test before you implement the code, then these questions disappear. You implement only the code that makes all the tests execute successfully, and nothing more. If you don't have the test that uses it, then you don't need the code. This approach to programming is known as *test-driven development*.

Next, I am going to help you examine a popular unit-testing framework in more detail. This framework is arguably one of the most popular in the .NET world. However, we will only be able to scratch the surface. Indeed, entire books have been dedicated to unit-testing test-driven development in .NET exclusively, so you can consider the following paragraphs as encouragement and an invitation to dip into this practice further.

Your First Taste of NUnit

The NUnit framework is an open-source unit-testing framework for .NET. Thanks to the language neutrality of .NET programming languages, NUnit can be as easily used in C# as in Visual Basic .NET, managed C++, or any other .NET language. NUnit was developed as a part of the JUnit framework, written by Erich Gamma and Kent Beck for unit testing in Java. JUnit sparked a wave of tools and frameworks that resulted in the porting of JUnit to a variety of languages, and in the development of various types of extensions that facilitate testing in diverse environments: web applications, mock-object development (see the section "Open-Mocking Frameworks" later in this chapter), GUI testing tools, and others. The sheer size of the response this framework provoked in the developer community is a testimony to its success and usefulness.

As with any framework, NUnit provides a lot of features that can be reused. This streamlines the test implementation and its execution. When you write tests with NUnit, you program plain, old C# classes. The first version of NUnit required you to extend (inherit) classes provided within the framework, but since version 2.0, an approach more in line with .NET programming style has been adopted. You need to apply different attributes provided by NUnit to the classes and methods, so that NUnit knows that these contain unit tests. When you use NUnit to run your tests, it searches for classes and methods marked with the NUnit attributes to execute them and report the results.

Before getting into the details of implementing tests with NUnit, however, I want to dedicate a few lines to installation procedures.

Installing NUnit

NUnit is available free from the NUnit site, www.nunit.com. It is distributed under an open-source license, and installation comes in different flavors, with the source code available for download in addition to the standard Windows installation package. Because work on NUnit is permanent, you should always download the most recent stable version. On the web site, this version is generally marked as "Recommended."

After the installation, NUnit will place an item in your Start menu. One of the menu sub-items is called NUnit-GUI and is used to activate the NUnit graphical interface. The NUnit GUI is used to run tests: it's one of NUnit's test runners. There is also a console test runner available, which is recommended for more advanced and integrated build setups.

As a first step after the installation, I recommend you open the NUnit GUI and execute the sample tests provided with the NUnit installation. By running these samples, you can achieve two objectives:

- ❑ **Verify that installation of NUnit went smoothly**: One possible issue you might face is the version of the .NET framework you have installed. With .NET Framework 3.5 and Visual Studio 2008, you should use NUnit version 2.5 or later.

- ❑ **Familiarize yourself with NUnit's GUI**: While there are other ways to run NUnit, this is the most common place to start.

Working with the Samples

Now take a look at the GUI after the successful installation of NUnit. In order to get things going, you can try running some of the samples that come with it. C# samples are placed in the Samples/C# folder inside the NUnit installation folder. These tests are distributed as source code, so you should build the samples first with the Visual Studio IDE. Don't worry about the code for the moment; you will get to that later. For now, just build the DLL. After that, using the File ➤ Open option in the NUnit GUI, locate the DLL you just created and select Run. Figure 3-3 shows the NUnit GUI after the execution of a sample C# project.

On the left side of the window you can see a tree view representing all the available tests. Once you begin writing tests, you will see that nodes represent a hierarchical organization of assemblies, namespaces, classes, and methods and properties in your test project. By selecting a certain node in the tree, you can choose to run only a selected test or a group of tests. This is a useful feature after the number of tests grows such that it would take too long to execute all the tests each step of the way.

On the right side of the window are two buttons, Run and Stop. After selecting Run, you can use the Stop button to interrupt the execution of tests at any time. Below the buttons is the progress bar, which indicates the state of test execution.

Under the area with the Run and Stop buttons and the progress bar is a set of tabs displaying different information related to test execution. These can be configured in the Options section to your liking, but the defaults are as follows:

- ❑ **Errors and Failures**: Lists all the tests where an error was encountered

- ❑ **Tests Not Run**: Lists all tests that were not executed. These can be tests that are marked with the Ignore attribute or, for example, nonpublic test fixture classes. If a test is marked with the

Ignore attribute, it will not be taken into account by the test runner — for example, if you didn't finish a particular test yet and you'd rather skip it. (I'll get into the details of attribute use with NUnit once you start implementing your own tests.)

❑ **Text Output**: Displays the following types of output in single tab by default:

    ❑ **Standard Output** displays console output from the program. Generally, this is the debug information left in the code by Console.WriteLine.

    ❑ **Error Output** displays all unhandled exceptions encountered during the test execution.

    ❑ **Trace Output** displays trace output written by your tests using the Trace class from the System.Diagnostics namespace.

    ❑ **Log Output** displays NUnit internal log messages.

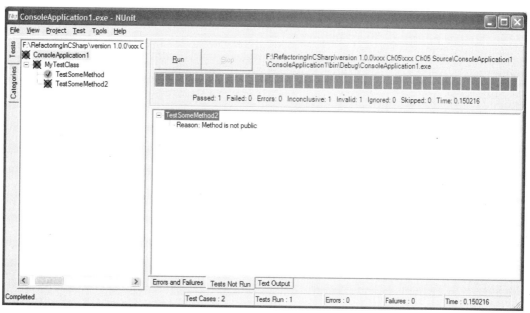

Figure 3-3

Finally, the area below the tabs displays a summary of execution, providing statistics such as number of test cases, tests run, errors, failures, and how long it took to execute the tests. Color plays an important part in communicating the success or failure of test execution. Nodes in the tree are displayed in different colors depending on the execution's success or failure. In order to make working with NUnit available to people with color-vision deficiencies (color blindness and similar), each type of test is marked with a corresponding symbol in the test tree after the test has been executed.

Table 3-2 shows the meaning of each color and symbol.

The progress bar is rendered similarly. There is one difference, however: Failure of even one test will cause the progress bar to turn red.

Table 3-2: NUnit Color Legend

Color	Meaning	Symbol
Green	Success	Tick
Yellow	Ignored	?
Red	Failure	X
Gray	Test not executed yet	None

Implementing Your First Test

In order to implement your first test, let's return for a moment to the application we refactored in Chapter 2, the Calories Calculator. As you might remember, the core logic ended up in three classes: `Patient`, `MalePatient`, and `FemalePatient`. You'll use the `Patient` and `FemalePatient` classes for the NUnit demo, writing NUnit tests that can verify the behavior of these two classes. After you implement the tests, each time you modify one of these classes — to change or add functionality, to resolve a bug, or to refactor it — you will be able to confirm that no undesired effect has been produced by the changes and that the code still behaves as intended.

Creating the Test Project

Begin by creating a new project for your tests. This is because you do not want to distribute any of the tests with the production code. You'll use the existing Class Library Visual Studio template to create your new project. That means you'll end up with a dynamic link library once you build the project. You have already seen how you can use the NUnit GUI application to execute tests in such a library. Figure 3-4 shows the Visual Studio New Project dialog window.

Now add a reference to the NUnit dynamic link library to your project. The name of the DLL is `nunit.framework`, and you can locate it on the .NET tab in the Add Reference dialog, shown in Figure 3-5. You can open the Add Reference dialog by selecting Project ➤ Add Reference.

Add the existing `Patient`, `MalePatient`, and `FemalePatient` classes to the project by selecting Project ➤ Add ➤ Existing Item. Once the Add Existing Item dialog opens, you need to locate the .cs source files containing the classes you want to test. The Add Existing Item dialog is shown in Figure 3-6.

You need to repeat this step for each class, because each class resides in its own .cs file. Now that you have access to all the classes you are going to test, it's time to add a first test class to the project.

Creating a Test Fixture

As mentioned earlier, writing unit tests is akin to any other type of programming. As always, the first step is adding a new class to the project. Call it `TestFemalePatient`. This class needs to be marked with a NUnit attribute: `TestFixture`. By marking the class with the `TestFixture` attribute, you are telling the NUnit test runner that the class contains tests that need to be executed. You can group different tests in the same class if they share runtime resources. This often means that you'll end up having one `TestFixture` per tested class.

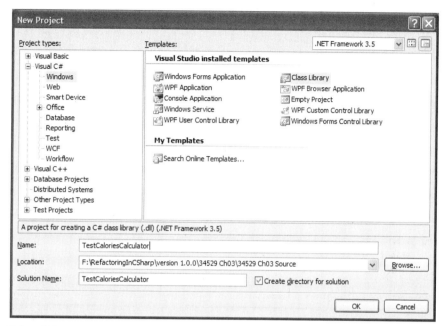

Figure 3-4

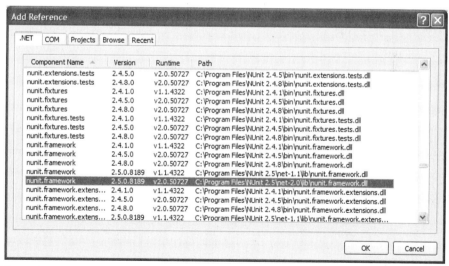

Figure 3-5

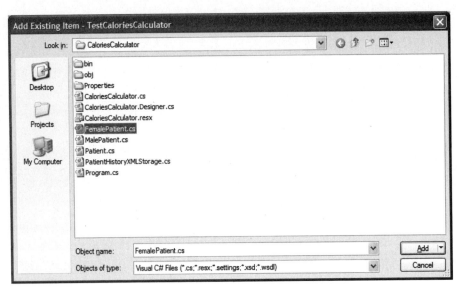

Figure 3-6

Take a quick look at the class declaration:

```
using NUnit.Framework;

namespace TestCaloriesCalculator
{
    [TestFixture]
    public class TestFemalePatient
    {
    }
}
```

You can see how the NUnit.Framework namespace is imported through the using directive and how the TestFixture attribute is applied to the TestFemalePatient class. If you build the project now and open the DLL using the NUnit GUI, you will see the class in the test tree view. You can even run the tests. Because the class is still empty, the progress bar and test tree are yellow: The test runner wasn't able to find any test methods yet.

Writing a Test

You have now prepared the first class that will become part of your test suite. In NUnit, each test is written in the form of a method. This method has to be public. It has no parameters and does not return any values. In order to be identified as a test method to be executed by the test runner, it has to be marked with another NUnit attribute: Test. For this example, you are going to add such a method to your class and call it IdealBodyWeight. In other words, you are going to test the IdealBodyWeight functionality offered by the FemalePatient class. In this particular case, you are going to test the method for the most common situation, wherein valid parameters are provided for the calculation. (Just to remind you, the formula provided for the ideal weight calculation is not suitable for persons shorter than five feet.)

The mechanics for writing tests are as follows:

- ❑ Prepare all parameters and property values the object needs for execution.
- ❑ Create an instance of the tested class and set all the necessary properties of the instance.
- ❑ Execute the tested method with parameters that were already created.
- ❑ Compare the effect or value returned by the tested method to an expected value or effect.

In the case of FemalePatient, you need to set the Age, Height, and Weight properties of the FemalePatient instance. Then you need to call the IdealBodyWeight method of an object. This method expects no parameters, but it does return the Decimal type value. As a last step, you will tell NUnit to assume that the expected result and real result are equal. If they are not equal, NUnit will report the error in test execution. Listing 3-1 shows the code for the process just described.

Listing 3-1: Testing the IdealBodyWeight Method

```
//NUnit Test attribute applied to a test method
[Test()]
public void TestIdealBodyWeight()
{
    //Instance of object under test created and properties set
    FemalePatient femalePatient = new FemalePatient();
    femalePatient.HeightInInches = 72;
    femalePatient.WeightInPounds = 110;
    femalePatient.Age = 30;
    double expectedResult = 161.15626;
    double realResult = femalePatient.IdealBodyWeight();
    //Result of test defined through NUnit assertion
    //by comparing that expected and returned result are equal
    Assert.AreEqual(expectedResult, realResult);
}
```

This code listing should not raise any eyebrows, except maybe for the last line, where the Assert class of the NUnit framework is used. The next section takes a look at it in detail, as it is the crucial line in the listing.

Using Asserts

NUnit includes a class, Assert, which provides a number of shared methods. These methods are used to communicate to NUnit how you expect the program to behave. By asserting, you are making an assumption or claim about something. This assumption can prove to be true, in which case a green progress bar is displayed; or it can fail, resulting in a red node and progress bar in the NUnit GUI.

In this specific case, here is what I did:

1. I used a formula for the ideal weight calculation to obtain the expected value.
2. I wrote down this literal value in the test code by assigning it to a local variable called expectedResult.

3. I used an instance of `FemalePatient` to obtain the result of a calculation performed in the program and stored it in the local variable `realResult`.

4. I established that these two values are equal.

Now it's time to run NUnit again. Because the code is behaving as expected, you should see green in the NUnit GUI.

The `Assert` class contains a number of methods. They all do more or less similar things. If you think about it, you only need one method to verify any type of assertion you might think of — a method to check whether a certain Boolean statement is true. Unsurprisingly, there is exactly such a method in the `Assert` class. It is called `IsTrue`.

Another method, similar to `AreEqual`, is `AreSame`. This method is used to assert that two references are pointing to the same instance. The following code snippet illustrates its use:

```
FemalePatient femalePatient1 = new FemalePatient();
FemalePatient femalePatient2 = new FemalePatient();
FemalePatient femalePatient3 = femalePatient1;

Assert.AreSame(femalePatient1, femalePatient2);
Assert.AreSame(femalePatient1, femalePatient3);
```

Have you guessed already? In this case, the first assert will fail, whereas the second will pass. I have initialized `femalePatient3` with a reference to `femalePatient1`. Both variables point to the same object, and ultimately to the same memory space. This is why the second assert passes the test. In the first assert, I am comparing two completely different objects. This results in the `AreSame` method returning a value of `False`, making the first assert fail the test.

If you want more information about the results of the `Assert.AreSame` test shown in the code illustration, see Chapter 9, which covers in more detail object identity and the differences between value and reference types.

Yet another method available in the `Assert` class is the method `IsNull`. This method enables you to assert that a certain variable does not refer to any instance.

A number of other methods are added to the class for your convenience. A lot of them are negative forms of methods you have already seen — for example, `AreNotEqual`, `AreNotSame`, `IsFalse`, `IsNotNull`, and so on. It's worth exploring the available methods in the `Assert` class further yourself. For now you need to continue writing tests for the `FemalePatient` class.

You need to test another method in your application. This method is called `DailyCaloriesRecommended`. To test it, you can repeat the steps you took to test `IdealBodyWeight`. The method I came up with is shown in Listing 3-2.

Listing 3-2: Testing the DailyCaloriesRecommended Method

```
[Test()]
public void TestDailyCaloriesRecommended()
{
```

```
    FemalePatient femalePatient = new FemalePatient();
    femalePatient.HeightInInches = 72;
    femalePatient.WeightInPounds = 110;
    femalePatient.Age = 30;
    double expectedResult = 1325.4;
    double realResult = femalePatient.DailyCaloriesRecommended();
    Assert.AreEqual(expectedResult, realResult);
}
```

You can now run the NUnit GUI again and see both of the methods pass. It means that the second test method was written well also.

Still, there is one detail that is not to my liking. Both methods have large portions of code that are completely identical. You are better off writing that code in only one place. The next section shows how you can do that.

Using SetUp and TearDown

In the NUnit framework it is possible to mark a method with a SetUp attribute. This signals to NUnit that the method should be executed before any of the test methods are run. You can use this attribute to mark a method that contains code common to both test methods, and to create objects that represent the test fixture.

In order to do this, you need to perform two modifications to the code:

1. Add a new method and mark it with the SetUp attribute. The method creates an instance of the FemalePatient class and assigns valid values to its properties. The code you need is already contained in both test methods, so you can move it to the new CreateFemalePatientInstance method.

2. Promote the femalePatient local variable to an instance variable.

Remember that TestFixture is just another C# class, so you can add instance variables and methods at will. Listing 3-3 shows the test class TestFemalePatient.

Listing 3-3: An Example of SetUp Usage

```
using NUnit.Framework;
using CaloriesCalculator;

namespace TestCaloriesCalculator
{
    [TestFixture]
    public class TestFemalePatient
    {
        private FemalePatient femalePatient;

        [Test()]
        public void TestIdealBodyWeight()
        {
            double expectedResult = 161.15626;
```

Continued

Listing 3-3: An Example of SetUp Usage *(continued)*

```
            double realResult = femalePatient.IdealBodyWeight();
            Assert.AreEqual(expectedResult, realResult);
    }

    [Test()]
    public void TestDailyCaloriesRecommended()
    {
        double expectedResult = 1325.4;
        double realResult = femalePatient.DailyCaloriesRecommended();
        Assert.AreEqual(expectedResult, realResult);
    }

    [SetUp()]
    public void CreateFemalePatientInstance()
    {
        femalePatient = new FemalePatient();
        femalePatient.HeightInInches = 72;
        femalePatient.WeightInPounds = 110;
        femalePatient.Age = 30;
    }
  }
}
```

At this point you are probably thinking that the last step is quite familiar, similar to some transformations you saw in Chapter 2. You've guessed it. When you created the `CreateFemalePatientInstance` method you refactored the `TestFemalePatient` class. You extracted one method and promoted one local variable to an instance variable. Unit tests are an integral part of your code base, so you need to maintain them in optimal shape. Therefore, they are also subjected to refactoring.

One of biggest objections to unit testing is that it means writing a lot of code that is never exploited in production. It's just another artifact that you use to improve your procedures and protect yourself from your own mistakes. This might be true, but the benefits of unit testing greatly outweigh any drawbacks. However, in order to keep those shortcomings to a minimum, it is very important to maintain and refactor your test code.

Going back to the `SetUp` method, you have seen that it is executed before each method marked with the `Test` attribute is called. Following simple logic, you might ask for a way to write a method that is executed after each test method is performed. NUnit provides for such a case. If a method is to be executed after each test method, it should be marked by the `TearDown` attribute.

Similar to the `SetUp` and `TearDown` attributes are the `SetUpFixture` and `TearDownFixture` attributes. If you mark a method with `SetUpFixture`, that method is executed once the test class or fixture is created. A method marked with `TearDownFixture` is the last method that will be executed in the test class, after the execution of all test methods.

Dealing with Exceptions: the ExpectedException Attribute

As mentioned earlier in this chapter, you have now tested a few methods of the class in the most common situations. However, you have also seen that some of the formulas are not applicable to people whose height is less than five feet. If someone tries to use the class to calculate ideal body weight for such a person, you would expect it to throw an exception.

Testing your code for boundary and exceptional circumstances is a very important part of your testing methodology. You cannot write tests for every possible value, so you need to try to exercise the code for the most sensitive values. These are generally boundary and invalid values. Experience has shown that bugs are especially common in such situations. Programmers often fail to take into account less common values.

In the case of the Patient class, the most logical place to control for invalid height value is the Height property of the Patient class. Because FemalePatient inherits Patient, for demonstration purposes you can use the same FemalePatient instance to test whether an exception is thrown.

The way to tell NUnit that you expect an exception to occur is to mark the test method with another attribute, ExpectedException, in addition to Test. The ExpectedException attribute needs a single parameter, a type name of the exception you expect. Once the test runner executes the method marked with ExpectedException, a check is performed to determine whether the exception is thrown. If the exception is thrown, then everything went as expected, and the green light is shown in the NUnit GUI. However, if no exception is thrown or the exception thrown is of a different type than the one specified in the ExpectedException attribute, the test has failed, and the signal shows red.

You can expect an ArgumentOutOfRangeException to be thrown if you try to assign a value of less than 5 feet (equals 60 inches).to the Height property:

```
[Test(), ExpectedException(typeof(ArgumentOutOfRangeException))]
public void HeightLessThan5Ft()
{
    femalePatient.HeightInInches = 59;
}
```

After adding this method, execute the tests again. The HeightLessThan5Ft test fails. If you now take a look at the set part of the Height property in the Patient class, sure enough, we forgot to limit the value of height in code. We now have to modify the Height property in the Patient class. It ends up looking like this:

```
public double HeightInInches
{
    get { return heightInInches; }
    set {
        if (value <= 60)
        {
            throw new ArgumentOutOfRangeException(
                "Height has to be greater " +
                "than five feet (60 inches)");
        }
        heightInInches = value;
    }
}
```

If you select the Run button in NUnit again, everything's green.

This sums up the basic usage of NUnit, but you have a few more important details regarding unit testing to cover before you're done with this chapter.

The Test-Driven Approach

The simple test class illustrates the basic concepts behind unit testing and the NUnit framework well. You used familiar code and provided a testing harness that can verify its correctness. However, this is a rather rudimentary approach to unit testing.

With the wider acceptance of unit testing by developers, a very important change in the "chicken or egg" dilemma in software testing occurred. Programmers note that they often lack explicit means to define requirements. Requirements are often ambiguous, expressed in text in the form of storyboards, diagrams, and so on. Even more often, in an attempt to produce more complete solutions that can also resolve any future requirements, programmers go to great lengths to produce code that ultimately is never used. This is a great loss of time and resources.

Unit tests are quite useful in resolving these problems. There isn't too much competition when it comes to explicitly defining the behavior of your code. The code itself is as explicit as it gets. In addition, if you write the test, it must be because there is a requirement for your code to behave in a certain way. You won't waste your time testing the code for behavior that is not required.

Wouldn't be nice if you could have tests for your code even before you wrote it? All you would need to do is program the classes in such a way that none of the test fails, and you would be done. If there is no test for certain functionality, it must be because that functionality is not really needed.

In test-driven development, you actually start out by writing tests first. Because no code exists to implement the tested functionality at this point, the test will obviously fail on the first run. You can then write code to make the first test execute without error. You continue by adding the next test and then the code to make that test pass, and so on. Guided by requirements embodied explicitly in test code, you keep your code lean, relevant, and clear of bugs.

How does this work in practice? Go back to the Calories Calculator application for the moment. Imagine there is another method you would like to add to the FemalePatient class. This method is called BodyFatContent, and all needed data is already available in the FemalePatient class in the form of properties. You are going to start by adding a Test method to the TestFemalePatient class.

Call it TestBodyFatContent, and mark it with the Test attribute. In the body of the method, you are going to call the BodyFatContent method on the femalePatient instance. Because this method does not exist in the FemalePatient class, Visual Studio reports an error.

In C#, Visual Studio 2008 has a Smart Tag feature that can generate a new method stub in the FemalePatient class automatically, saving you a few keyboard strokes. It's a nice feature, and helpful for writing tests in a test-driven way:

Take a look at the code you have so far:

```
[Test()] public void TestBodyFatContent(){
    decimal expectedResult = 36;
    decimal realResult = femalePatient.BodyFatContent();
    Assert.AreEqual(expectedResult, realResult);
}
```

Figure 3-7 shows the Smart Tag feature in the Visual Studio editor.

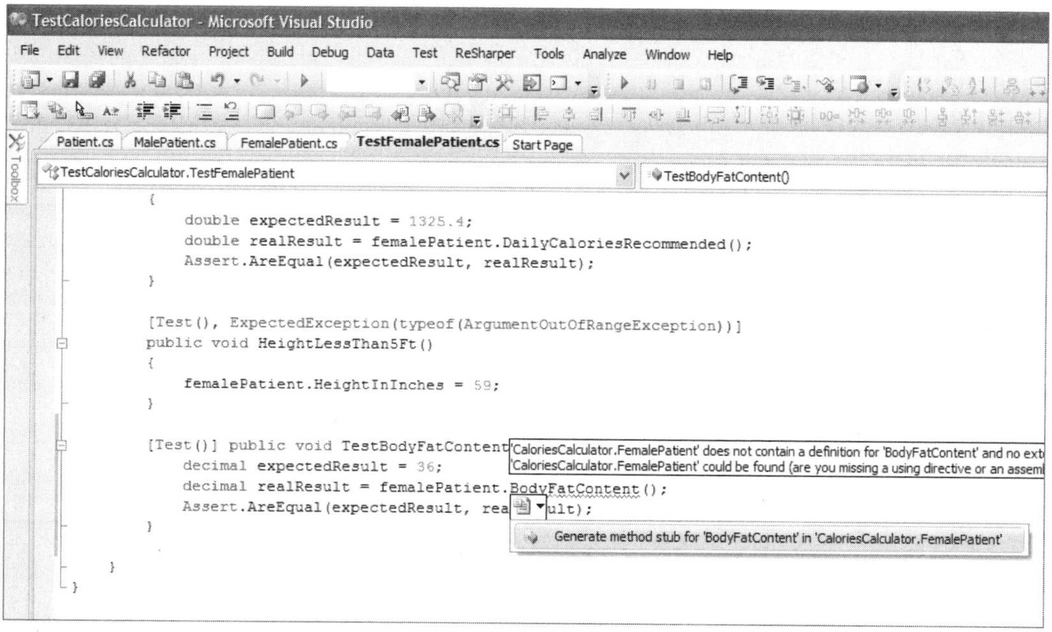

Figure 3-7

Use the Visual Studio Smart Tag feature to have it create a method stub in the `FemalePatient` class. Now when you build the project it will compile successfully. You can implement the body of the method, replacing the provisory implementation provided by Visual Studio that only throws `NotImplementedException` like this: `throw new NotImplementedException();`

Test-driven development is an important practice in agile teams. It goes hand-in-hand with refactoring as a means to achieve new levels of productivity and software quality. There is much more to test-driven development than what has been covered here, but if you are not practicing it already, it is hoped that I have managed to at least awaken your interest.

Other Test Tools to Consider

There are a plethora of other tools that you might find useful when writing unit tests. Unfortunately, there isn't enough space in this chapter to cover all these tools exhaustively. Instead, this section describes a handful of tools that I have found to nicely complement my refactoring efforts.

The TestDriven.NET Visual Studio Add-In

You can get a much better integration between NUnit and Visual Studio if you install the TestDriven.NET Visual Studio add-in. It will enable you to run and stop tests directly from Visual Studio, and it displays the test results inside the Visual Studio window. This way, you do not need to switch between the NUnit test runner and Visual Studio while you program.

You can download this add-in from www.testdriven.net. Note that the free personal license is intended for trial users, students, and open-source developers.

The NUnitForms GUI-Testing Framework

When testing parts of the GUI, you need an approach that's a bit different from the one you take in testing plain, old C# classes. You need to simulate user interaction with the program. This is not so easy to do with NUnit. NUnitForms is an extension of NUnit that was created to facilitate the task of testing GUIs made with Windows Forms. It can clean forms, detect and manipulate dialog windows, and more.

While NUnitForms can help you in your task of creating standard unit tests, this framework can also be helpful in producing another type of test. NUnitForms can be used to simulate user interaction or even to record it and replay it later. If you run these tests not against a single GUI class but against the complete application, you can create a sort of integration or acceptance test.

I found this approach very useful when faced with a completed application that doesn't include any unit tests. You cannot always dedicate the time necessary to introduce unit tests *a posteriori*. However, in the process of maintenance, you may need to refactor an application, and in those cases this type of test is the next best thing. NUnitForms can be downloaded from SourceForge.net at `http://nunitforms.sourceforge.net`. While this project hasn't seen a tremendous amount of activity, it fulfills its purpose well.

Object-Mocking Frameworks

As mentioned earlier, when you write unit tests you need to test objects in isolation. This is a very important feature of unit testing because it can help you test exactly the desired functionality and pin down a failure to an exact method or property. However, not all the code you will need to test will be as simple as the example shown in this chapter. Your code might use some very complex classes, and depend on them to behave properly. This makes writing unit tests much more difficult to accomplish.

Mock objects to the rescue! Instead of using real objects, you can use substitute objects that take on the interface of a real object. This substitute, a mock object, can verify the way the object being tested is interacting with it. If the interaction is not as expected, then the test will fail. A mock object can also provide the object being tested with expected return values. For more information on the subject and for an open-source mock-objects framework, check out the following frameworks:

- ❑ NMock (`http://nmock.org`)
- ❑ Rhino Mocks (`www.ayende.com/projects/rhino-mocks.aspx`)
- ❑ TypeMock (`http://typemock.com`)

The NCover Test Coverage Tool

Always attempt to write your tests as thoroughly and with as broad a focus as possible. During the execution of the complete suite of unit tests for your application, you should strive to get every single line of your code exercised. Sometimes, however, you cannot always be as systematic as you would like to be. For those cases, instead of leaving the quality of your tests in human hands, you can use a tool such as NCover that reports in detail which lines of your code were executed and which lines you failed to test. NCover is available at `http://ncover.org`. It can be a great help in completing your suite of tests with all relevant cases.

About Version Control

Whereas unit testing is not so widespread, source-code version control is today universally accepted. I don't know of a team or company that doesn't use some type of version control, which is why I will not dedicate much space to the subject, except to discuss how it relates to refactoring.

From the refactoring perspective, the importance of version-control systems is two-fold: protection and collision.

Version Control As a Backup System

First of all, version control provides another level of protection. No matter how disciplined you are in refactoring gradually, applying small changes and then verifying correctness with test execution, sooner or later you are bound to go one step too far. An error is introduced, and it's just too costly to debug your way out of it. In that case, you can count on version control to provide a backup. That way, in the worst-case scenario, you can start all over again — fortunately, not from the beginning, but from the last snapshot of the code you took. If you version code regularly, such a setback will probably not be catastrophic.

Version Control and Concurrency

Another way in which version-control systems affect refactoring has to do with code ownership. A lot of teams, as the first step out of the primordial chaos of team development, choose to implement individual code ownership. In this model, programmers have their own classes, components, or other code units that belong only to them; no other programmer is authorized to change them. Some version-control systems, such as SourceSafe (but not Visual Studio Team System), promote this model by default. When one programmer checks out a file, no other programmer is allowed to edit it. The idea behind this form of team organization is to promote order and field expertise. Programmers can become experts in their own area, thus being more efficient and productive. They can be sure that nobody will meddle with their code, which gives them a feeling of control and confidence. For new and inexperienced teams, this form of concurrent version control is definitely a step forward.

However, it also has various drawbacks that become more apparent as refactoring practices are adopted. With focused expertise, the phenomenon of programmer-owners can appear. The code is written in such a manner that it is very difficult for other programmers to take over. This leads to the proliferation of diverse, often cryptic, coding styles and standards. Because you are allowed to change only code you reserved for yourself at each moment in time, this model can cause stagnation, which in turn works directly against refactoring.

Some refactoring techniques require widespread changes to source code. These changes are not limited to a single method or class. In this case, individual code ownership can work against you. For example, how can you rename a class if you are not allowed to change all the code that is making use of that class? For that reason, agile teams tend to adopt *collective code ownership*. In this model, any member of a team is allowed to modify any project item. This model also enables more than one programmer to work on a single file simultaneously. When this happens, if conflicting changes are discovered at the moment of check-in, they are resolved by merger.

Summary

Effective tools are very important for the successful adoption of refactoring practices. These tools can greatly improve your productivity. The most important tool from a refactoring perspective is one that you can use to automate the application of refactoring transformations.

With Visual Studio 2008, C# programmers can make use of basic refactoring features implemented by the IDE itself. Alternately, if you are looking for a more powerful refactoring tool, you can find a number of third-party add-ins that integrate seamlessly with Visual Studio and offer numerous productivity enhancements at a reasonable price.

Another programming practice that almost always goes hand-in-hand with refactoring is unit testing. By unit testing your code, you can easily verify its correctness after any modification is applied to the code base. This chapter demonstrated NUnit, an open-source unit-testing framework that can help you streamline test creation and execution. Using familiar code from the sample application in the previous chapter, you provided it with simple unit tests. You also learned how to install and run NUnit.

This chapter also covered a few other open-source tools that can help you in your refactoring tasks, and you learned about a very popular practice among agile teams often referred to as test-driven development.

Finally, I reserved a few lines for source-code version control and its role in the refactoring process. These tools can be used to promote some form of code ownership, and with agile teams the preferred form is collective code ownership. After this chapter, you are armed with all the necessary tools for your refactoring process. In the next chapter you will read about the refactoring playground you will use throughout this book: the Rent-a-Wheels application.

Application Prototype: Rent-a-Wheels

Refactoring is a very practical, hands-on type of art. That makes it difficult to talk about the mechanics, motivation, and benefits of refactoring unless it is accompanied by a good, illustrative example. While small snippets of code serve well to prove a specific point, you might be left wanting a look at the bigger picture, or an example of refactoring in a real-world situation.

This chapter provides that real-world scenario with a working example application to which refactoring will be applied. Along the way, I will explain the logic behind the refactoring process in detail. That way, not only will each refactoring technique be illustrated with code samples, but you will see the refactoring process applied throughout the lifetime of this sample application.

Like each chapter in this book, this chapter concludes with a demonstration of refactoring in practice; I use the Rent-a-Wheels application for this purpose in Chapter 4. Throughout the book, you will witness the progress of the application from a simple but fully functional GUI-based prototype to a full-blown tiered enterprise application.

Because I will refer to the Rent-a-Wheels application in almost every chapter that is to follow, you should try to analyze the application while reading this chapter and think of possible weaknesses in the design and implementation. This way, as you progress with the book, you will be able to compare your initial judgment with the weaknesses and smells I will expose and deal with later.

My intention is to present you with a realistic scenario. I have even written down a few conversations with the client so you can put yourself in the same situation — that of analyzing and distilling raw information from typical laypeople who might want to use your product.

I also introduce another character toward the end of this chapter: Tim, a typical apprentice programmer. Tim is already in command of basic C# programming techniques, but not at all familiar with refactoring or some of the more complex design principles. He will eagerly get the job done, but, as you will see throughout the book, this is not sufficient for well-designed, refined, industrial-strength applications. In this chapter, I will let Tim explain the work he has performed on the Rent-a-Wheels prototype implementation.

I suggest you download the complete project from www.wrox.com *and use the IDE to follow along. A lot of code listings are included in the text, but you'll have an easier time finding your way around if you use Visual Studio with the complete source code at hand.*

I'll start presenting the application right from the inception. This way, you can see the business case for the application and observe work on the application in progress. Bear in mind that this chapter is not meant to teach you software design or analysis. While you are reading it, I hope this chapter accomplishes two things for you:

❑　It helps you feel as if you're having a typical day in the office and using some very familiar techniques and styles.

❑　I hope to use this familiarity as an entry point to discuss some typical .NET approaches to programming and how they relate to refactoring and software design in general.

Interviewing the Client

The client in question is a vehicle rental company that needs to automate and computerize its operation to make its process more efficient. It needs to cut the time it takes to serve each client, speed up the vehicle reception process, and get rid of unnecessary paperwork.

The first task I undertook was to speak to different people employed at the company in order to gather the information I need to define the requirement and start the project. The next sections show the transcripts of my conversations with Rent-a-Wheels employees.

Interviewing the Manager

My first meeting was with the manager. His opinion has the most weight on the project because he will make all the final decisions regarding the application. Here is what he had to say:

"Rent-a-Wheels is a successful car rental company. We have been in the market for more than 10 years and have managed to position ourselves well. Our biggest strength is a loyal clientele and a new fleet, as we had a big investment come in earlier this year. At the same time, we started another location; we opened up the airport branch.

"This challenged our operations in a new way. You see, there is a lot of competition at the airport and more than a few rental desks are placed next to one another. We have noticed that as soon as a line forms at our desk, potential clients start going over to the competition. The time we take to serve a single client is just too long. I spoke to our staff and they tell me that our existing system, based on pen and paper, is just too tedious. The competition does everything on the computer. One company recently acquired big, flat-panel monitors. The airport offers a free, wireless Internet connection, so we can rely on that for connectivity.

"We also waste time in reception. The desk is informed that a vehicle is available only after the inspection and cleaning of that vehicle is done. It doesn't take long, but we still lose customers in the process. We need to do something about it; we need to rent more!"

This talk with the manager provided some insight into the task I was facing:

❏　　The company needs an efficient system to manage the fleet, keep track of the availability of the vehicles, and present this information at the reception desk.

❏　　The company has multiple branches. The system will have to consider that also.

Although talking to the manager gave me more insight into my objectives, it failed to provide detailed information on the way business is conducted. Therefore, the next person I had to interview was the receptionist.

Interviewing the Desk Receptionist

The desk receptionist works with clients directly. She gave me more information about the business process.

> Me: I guess the first thing you look at is which vehicles are available when clients call or come over?
>
> Desk Receptionist: Yes, we have all vehicles divided into different categories. Clients generally ask for a category or specific model — that's what the price depends on. Other details, like color, come up less frequently. I maintain a list of all the vehicles in Excel and I mark them as they are rented or returned. The problem is that clients can return their vehicles to any branch they want, so I end up updating the list all the time.
>
> Me: Okay, great, let me make a note of that. I understand you have a lot of paperwork?
>
> Desk Receptionist: Oh, yes. You mean you want to know more about the receipts?
>
> Me: Yes, right, what kind of receipts?
>
> Desk Receptionist: When I finish taking all the data from the clients, I issue them a receipt that they have to deliver to our people at the parking lot in order to get the car. When they return the car, they use the same receipt to write down additional charges that might apply, like empty tank, mileage, et cetera. I guess that's about it.
>
> Me: That was very helpful. Thanks a lot!

I have even more material to work with now:

❏　　I need to manage vehicles and mark when they are rented or returned.

❏　　I need to maintain vehicle information, such as model and color.

❏　　All vehicles belong to a certain category that determines the price of the rental.

If PCs are available in all the right places, the application I provide should be able to eliminate a lot of paperwork. Next, I've determined that I need to talk to another party intimately involved with this process: one of the parking lot attendants.

Interviewing the Parking Lot Attendant

It is sometimes the case that no single employee is familiar with the whole business process in detail. Sometimes the best way to collect requirements is to hear the facts from different sources in order to piece together the whole story. This is the reason I decided to speak to employees in any position that might benefit from the application. A parking lot attendant should provide some insight into the way the lot is operated.

Me: The customers pick up the cars here?

Lot Attendant: Yes, my duty is to hand over the car to the customer and to receive it from them when they bring it back. When they are first picking up the car, customers have to give me a receipt so that I know they finished all the paperwork at the reception desk. I then write down the mileage and put the receipt in the Rented Vehicles folder. When the customer returns the vehicle, I check the mileage and the tank and write the numbers on the receipt. We give customers a bonus if they return the car with the tank full.

Me: And what happens if the tank is not full?

Lot Attendant: The maintenance guy has to fill up the tank, and this is charged in addition to other items. No bonus in that case, of course. Plus, customers have to wait if they are not satisfied with my estimate. I can only choose full, three-quarters, one-half, one-quarter, or empty from looking at the indicator. If customers think this isn't correct, they have to wait for the maintenance guy to come back with the receipt from the filling station. After that, the vehicle has to pass through a regular maintenance inspection. I can check for any obvious damage when the vehicle is returned, but I'm not in charge of the maintenance.

The story seems to be more complete now:

❑   The application needs to keep information on mileage for each rental.

❑   The application needs to keep information on the tank level after the vehicle is returned.

My conversation with the parking lot attendant has made me realize that in order to get the *complete* story I must speak to still another party: a member of the maintenance personnel.

Interviewing Maintenance Personnel

This is the last employee I need to speak with. By talking with this employee, I hope to learn more about the vehicle inspection and maintenance procedures.

Me: Your job is to inspect vehicles when they are returned?

Maintenance Worker: Yes. I have to check for any damage and ensure that the tank is full. I also keep records on regular maintenance that is performed after a certain number of miles. When the time is up, I have to take the car to the service center. I have to let the people at the desk know so they are aware that that particular car is no longer available. Since we let our customers return the vehicle to any branch they like, sometimes at the end of the day I have to take cars back to the branch they came from.

Me: Okay, thank you for your time.

From this final conversation two additional points become clear:

❑   Vehicles are regularly removed from the fleet in order to receive routine maintenance.

❑   The inspection performed after the customer returns the vehicle is mandatory.

Now it is time to compile all the information I have gathered and to prepare the proposal I am going to present to the folks back in my office.

Taking the Initial Steps in the Rent-a-Wheels Project

I decided to start the work by identifying the principal use cases. This will serve as a starting point for the prototype that I will use to obtain the final go-ahead from the client. While I am at it, I might as well sketch a few diagrams — it always adds an air of professionalism.

Actors and Use Cases

The first step is to identify all the future users of the system, or the actors. This is not so difficult. All I need to do is follow the "paper trail" I discovered in my interviews. The receipt travels from the reception desk to the parking lot and back. Additionally, the maintenance personnel has to make a report specifying whether the car has to be filled up or sent to a service center. I decided to depict actors and principal use cases with a diagram. Figure 4-1 shows the Rent-a-Wheels use case diagram I came up with.

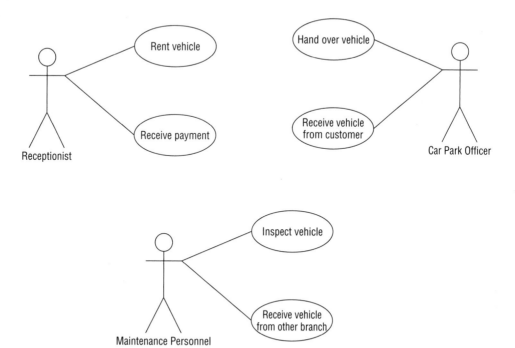

Figure 4-1

After I identified the principal use cases, I decided to write down all the steps the actors have to perform while interacting with the application in order to reach the final goal. This will provide a good breakdown of the functionality that the Rent-a-Wheels application will provide.

Rent Vehicle

1. The receptionist selects the vehicle from the list of available vehicles.
2. The receptionist inputs the customer data: ID type and number.
3. The receptionist marks the vehicle as ready to be handed over.

Receive Payment

1. The receptionist selects the vehicle from the list of all payment-pending vehicles.
2. The system displays the charges.
3. After the payment has been made, the receptionist marks the vehicle as available.

   Precondition: The customer has to return the vehicle to the parking lot first. (See the use case "Receive Vehicle from Customer.")

Hand Over Vehicle to Customer

1. The parking lot attendant finds the vehicle marked as ready to be handed over, which matches the customer's ID.
2. The parking lot attendant marks the vehicle as rented.

   Precondition: The customer has to finish all formalities at the reception desk first. (See the use case "Rent Vehicle.")

Receive Vehicle from Customer

1. The lot attendant searches for the rented vehicle in the vehicle list.
2. The lot attendant inputs mileage, tank level, and any additional comments.
3. The lot attendant marks the vehicle as "payment pending."

Inspect Vehicle

1. The maintenance personnel select the vehicle being inspected from the list.
2. The maintenance personnel mark the vehicle as "in operation."

   Alternative:

2a. If maintenance is due, the vehicle is marked as "in maintenance."

Receive Vehicle from Other Branch

1. The lot attendant searches the list of vehicles for the vehicle coming from another branch.
2. The lot attendant marks the vehicle as stationed in the receiving branch.

Receive Vehicle from Service Center

1. When the vehicle is returned from the service center, it is marked as "in operation."

These use cases give a pretty good overview both of the business process at the company and of the way in which users should interact with the future system.

One thing became rather obvious after all this: The word vehicle was present in all the use cases. Understandably, most of the business in the Rent-a-Wheels company revolves around this entity. The vehicle has characteristics such as license plate number, category, make, model, and color. As part of their work, employees have to maintain information about each vehicle and, especially important, mark the vehicle as available, handed over, payment pending, or in maintenance as it goes through various business processes. Because this state of the vehicle is at the center of the business process I am analyzing, I have decided to investigate it a little bit further.

Vehicle States

As a vehicle is selected and becomes involved in the business flow, it passes through a few states in a well-defined order. As you analyze those states, you can see that their nature is twofold: Some states associated with the vehicle are related to its customer rental status, while other states are related to its maintenance status. I decided to use two diagrams to represent these states and transitions. Figure 4-2 shows the states the vehicle goes through during a normal rental process.

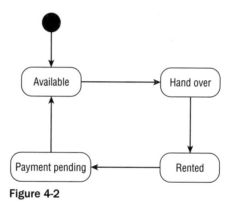

Figure 4-2

Rules related to vehicle states and state transitions embody the core of the business process in the Rent-a-Wheels company. The following list explains these states and the transitions related to normal vehicle use in more detail:

❑ The receptionist can rent only available vehicles.

❑ The parking lot attendant can hand over to customers only the vehicles marked ready for hand over.

❑ The parking lot attendant can receive only rented vehicles.

❑ The receptionist can charge for payment-pending vehicles only.

Figure 4-3 shows the states related to vehicle maintenance.

States and transitions describing the maintenance process represent another important set of business rules. The following list explains states related to the maintenance operation in more detail:

❑   The receptionist can rent only vehicles marked in operation.

❑   If a vehicle is due for maintenance or presents problems, the maintenance personnel mark it as in maintenance.

❑   Once the vehicle is back from maintenance, it is marked as in operation.

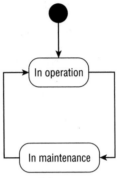

Figure 4-3

Is there any relation between these two sets of states and transitions? Naturally, only operational vehicles can be rented, handed over to customers, received, and charged for. In other words, available, hand over, rented, and payment pending are inner states of the *in operation* state. Or, to put it differently, in operation is a *super state*, and this can be represented with a single state diagram using nested states. The single state diagram is presented in Figure 4-4.

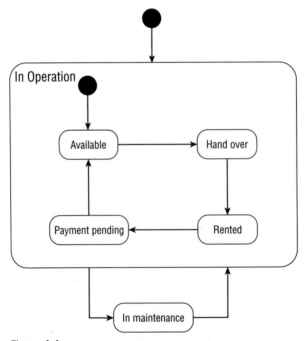

Figure 4-4

Now that the actors and use case diagrams were completed, I knew it would be good to finalize the work I had done by materializing all these ideas into some sort of user interface prototype.

First Sketch of the Main Application Window

With all this information in hand, it's time to take a shot at drawing the main application window. The central point of the application is the fleet and the different states of the vehicles. I can show vehicles in a certain amount of detail in a grid, and enable users to operate on a specific vehicle by selecting a single row in the grid. Each row represents a single vehicle. The user will be able to perform actions on the vehicle by selecting it on the grid and then pressing the appropriate button: Rent, Hand Over, Charge, or similar.

I also need to provide for filtering of the vehicles in the list. That will make jobs a lot easier for the users, as they will be able to restrict the display to vehicles they are interested in, based on vehicle state or some other characteristic. Figure 4-5 represents the main application window.

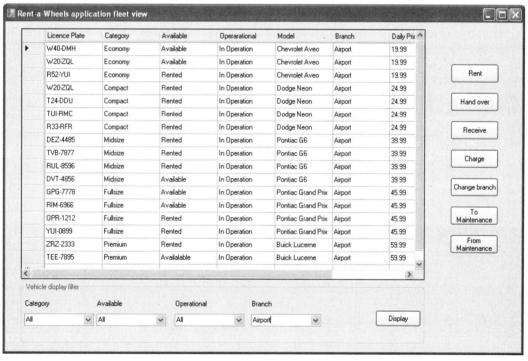

Figure 4-5

I decided that use cases, state diagrams, and a main window prototype provided a good starting point for the application I was about to build, so for the next step I presented these artifacts at the team meeting.

Rent-a-Wheels Team Meeting

The Rent-a-Wheels team at this stage consisted of three members:

❑ **Developer:** Me, of course.

❑ **Project manager:** In this case, he was not dedicated full-time to the project.

❑ **C# programmer:** Tim, a novice C# programmer, but one quite up to the task, and very efficient as a coder.

I started the meeting by presenting the information gathered so far. I first gave them some background information about the company, the meetings I had, and the people I had met. Then I presented the work I did on the analysis; I showed them the diagrams and talked about use cases. I even presented my first try at a main application window.

Because I was about to go on my vacation, we agreed that Tim should take over the application. He would continue to work on the analysis and take a first shot at the prototype. When I got back, I would join the team again and act as lead programmer.

Upon my return, I got back to working on the Rent-a-Wheels application. During my absence, the prototype was completed, presented to the client, and initial approval was received. While assembling the prototype, Tim went on to implement most of the functionality initially described. Tim's idea was to try to reuse the code from the prototype in order to cut implementation time. This is fine, of course, as long as the code is up to standards and well designed. To make sure, I have to take a detailed look at the application.

Making the Prototype Work

To begin, I asked Tim to fill me in on the progress he had made while I was away. Tim said, "I used the information you prepared during the analysis to build the prototype. I built a standalone application that connects to a Microsoft SQL database over ADO.NET. I decided not to use data binding; I had enough time to go for a more robust solution. Basically, there is one central window, based on the drawing you made, but I guess you are really interested in the database model. We had better start off there."

Examining the Database Model

Tim continued to fill me in. "The database engine is MS SQL 2005. The database name is RENTAWHEELS. It has the following tables: Vehicle, Category, Model, and Branch. I chose to use the license plate number for the primary key in the Vehicle table. The rest of the tables have an automatic, auto-incrementing primary key. That way, the relationships are easier to observe in the diagram. (See Figure 4-6.)

"Each vehicle pertains to a single branch. Each vehicle model is placed under a certain category. Category has attributes that contain the vehicle's price information: daily, weekly, and monthly. You can find the rental price for a certain vehicle by looking at its model — Model belongs to a category and Category has the price information. When writing SQL code, this translates into an inner join of the Vehicle table with the Model table and an inner join of the Model table with the Category table.

"The Vehicle table also contains information related to the rental state of the vehicle: it's the column named Available. Information related to the operational state of the vehicle is held in the column named Operational. I used the tinyint SQL Server data type for these two columns. In the case of Available, the meaning of the data is shown in this table." Tim showed me Table 4-1.

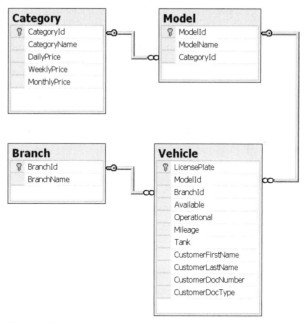

Figure 4-6

Table 4-1: Connotation of Column "Available" tinyint Values in the Vehicle Table

Column "Available" tinyint Value	Meaning
0	Available
1	Hand Over
2	Rented
3	Charge

Tim said, "You will notice that I decided to use a more compact name for the Payment Pending state. Charge fits better on the fleet display grid on the Fleet View form."

He continued, "The Operational column can have only two values." Then he showed me Table 4-2.

Tim then said, "Other attributes of the vehicle are related to information about the customer currently renting the vehicle: name, document type, and numbers. These are used by the parking lot attendant to identify the customer at the moment when the vehicle is handed over. When the vehicle is returned, tank level and mileage are saved in the Tank and Mileage columns. Of course, this data is related to a single rental, and the current customer has to be deleted once the vehicle is paid for.

"Like the Available and Operational columns, the Tank column uses different tinyint values with special meanings." Tim then showed me Table 4-3.

Table 4-2: Connotation of Column "Operational" tinyint Values in the Vehicle Table

Column "Operational" tinyint Value	Meaning
0	In Operation
1	In Maintenance

Table 4-3: Connotation of Column "Tank" tinyint Values in the Vehicle Table

Column "Tank" tinyint Value	Meaning
0	Empty
1	$1/4$ Full
2	$1/2$ Full
3	$3/4$ Full
4	Full

Tim concluded, "Those were the most important facts in regard to the database." I asked, "What about other database objects? Did you use any stored procedures, views, or triggers?" Tim said, "No, this is it. I spoke to the client and he was adamant about keeping the application as database independent as possible. They still have to buy software licenses and they want to be able to look for the best price on the market. I figured that minimizing the code on the database side will help us avoid dependence on any particular database model. That's why I put all the SQL code inside the Windows Forms app."

With all that clear, I could then examine the C# code.

Examining the C# Code

Tim explained, "There are a few forms in the project, but the main form is the one with the Fleet view, which enables users to monitor vehicles and select them in order to perform the most important operations for the business. It is the same form you designed in the analysis phase of the project. The only new functionality I added is the administration menu. It is used to invoke forms that serve to administer different tables in the database. This way, the user can add a vehicle, delete it, or edit existing vehicles. The same goes for categories, models, and branches. Let me show you the menu." Tim opened the Visual Studio IDE, ran the application, and showed me the Fleet view with the data administration menu he had added, shown in Figure 4-7.

Tim continued, "On the right side are the buttons that employees will use to perform their everyday work: a Rent button, a Hand Over button, and so on. When they press the button, in some cases the operation is directly performed; in other cases, when additional information is needed, a new form is displayed. For example, we can take a look at the code being executed when the user presses the Rent button."

100

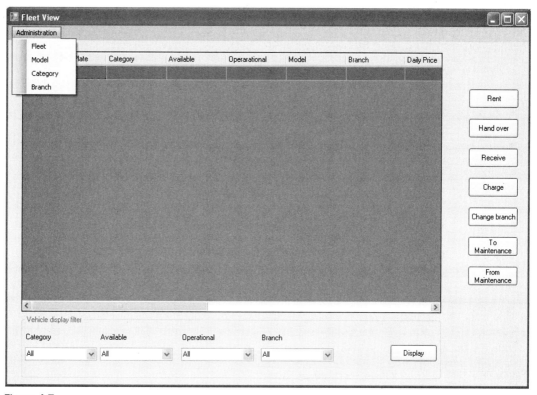

Figure 4-7

The code that handles the Rent button click event is presented in Listing 4-1.

Listing 4-1: btnRent_Click from Fleet View Event-Handling Routine

```
private void btnRent_Click(object sender, EventArgs e)
{
    //Check that user has made a selection
    if (dGridFleetView.SelectedRows.Count > 0)
    {
        //Read value from first cell as Vehicle Id
        string selectedLP =
        dGridFleetView.SelectedRows[0].
        Cells[0].Value.ToString();
        frmRent.txtLP.Text = selectedLP;
        frmRent.ShowDialog();
    }
    else
    {
        //Warn user if no selection made in table and exit
        MessageBox.Show("Please select vehicle first!");
    }
}
```

Tim said, "It is easy to follow the code because I spent a lot of time commenting on it in detail. First, a check is made in order to ensure that the user has selected a vehicle in the grid. Then, a license plate number from the first cell in the selected row is assigned to a text box in the FrmRt form, and this form is displayed. And just in case the user didn't make the selection before pressing the button, a message box with a reminder is displayed. Take a look at the FrmRt form."

He showed me the rental form he had created, named FrmRt, which is shown in Figure 4-8.

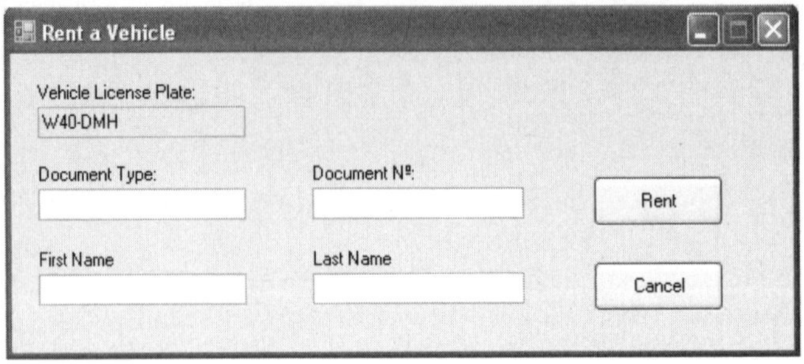

Figure 4-8

Tim said, "After entering the required data, the user performs the operation by pressing the Rent button." Listing 4-2 shows the code for handling the button click from this form.

Listing 4-2: Event-Handling Routine for btnRent_Click from the Rent Form

```
private void btnRent_Click(object sender, EventArgs e)
{
    if (MessageBox.Show("Are you sure?", "Confirm",
    MessageBoxButtons.OKCancel) == DialogResult.OK)
    {
        SqlConnection oCn = new SqlConnection(
           "Data Source=TESLATEAM;" +
           "Initial Catalog=RENTAWHEELS;" +
           "User ID=RENTAWHEELS_LOGIN;" +
           "Password=RENTAWHEELS_PASSWORD_123");
        SqlCommand oCmd;
        string strSql = "Update Vehicle " +
                "Set Available = 1," +
                "CustomerFirstName = @CustomerFirstName," +
                "CustomerLastName = @CustomerLastName," +
                "CustomerDocNumber = @CustomerDocNumber," +
                "CustomerDocType = @CustomerDocType " +
                "WHERE LicensePlate = @SelectedLP";
        oCmd = new SqlCommand();
        try
        {//open connection
            oCn.Open();
            //Set connection to command
            oCmd.Connection = oCn;
            //set Sql string to command object
            oCmd.CommandText = strSql;
            //Add parameter to command
```

```
            oCmd.Parameters.AddWithValue(
                "@CustomerFirstName", txtFirstName.Text);
            oCmd.Parameters.AddWithValue(
                "@CustomerLastName", txtLastName.Text);
            oCmd.Parameters.AddWithValue(
                "@CustomerDocNumber", txtDocumentNo.Text);
            oCmd.Parameters.AddWithValue(
                "@CustomerDocType", txtDocumentType.Text);
            oCmd.Parameters.AddWithValue(
                "@SelectedLP", txtLP.Text);
            //execute command
            oCmd.ExecuteNonQuery();
            //close connection
            oCn.Close();
        }
        catch
        {
            MessageBox.Show("A problem occurred" +
            "and the application cannot recover! " +
            "Please contact the technical support.");
        }
        this.Close();
    }
}
```

Tim explained his approach in this code: "As a first step, I give users a chance to change their mind, just in case they pressed the button by mistake. Then I initialize the connection. I am using a .NET Framework DataProvider for SQL Server to connect to the database; since the company has Microsoft SQL Server 2005, this is the most efficient provider. After that I build SQL code as a string and assign it to a command. Then the data is recollected from the form, and values entered by the user are added as command parameters. Finally, the query is executed. At the end, I close the connection."

When I asked Tim about exception handling, he said, "In the catch block you can see the code that is executed in case the error occurs. This can happen if the database server is down, if there is a connectivity problem with the database, or something like that. Basically, users are informed that an error has occurred and that they should contact technical support. The whole method is quite straightforward really, just a SQL query executed against the database.

"So, basically, that's it. If you look at the rest of the code, it pretty much follows the same pattern."

I said, "Yes, thanks, Tim. I'll take another look at the code later, but I think I have a pretty good idea of what is going on in the application. Good job!"

With that, my initial conversation with Tim about Rent-a-Wheels ended; and at this point you, too, should have a pretty good idea of what is going on in the application that I will use as an example throughout the book.

If you are interested in digging further into the example application at this point, more conversations with Tim about the details of the code can be found in Appendix A. Of course, the source code for the application is available for download at www.wrox.com, and I again encourage you to download it if you haven't already. However, for the purposes of using this example as a real-world scenario for discussion, this is enough to start with.

The next section looks at what this example demonstrates and how it applies to the topic of refactoring. I list only a few typical pitfalls C# programmers can be dragged into with their desire to get results immediately. While I have great respect for pragmatic programmers and I am not keen on wasting my time on some vague philosophical discussions, I am very interested in producing the best possible code. For that purpose, it is crucial to understand the fundamental principles behind object-oriented programming and why sometimes the fastest approach is not the best approach, nor even the most simple.

Fast and Furious Approach to Programming

In many respects, the application shown so far is a very typical .NET application. Not too much time has been spent on formally designing the application before, during, or after construction. Most of the design time was invested in blueprinting the database. In this case, you can assume from the lack of any other design-related artifacts that programmers embarked upon coding from the outset. This is not necessarily a mistake if it is followed by design-related improvements during the development process; otherwise, you can end up with some serious pitfalls in your code. This section outlines some typical approaches to Rent-a-Wheels that can lead to drawbacks in your code if not counteracted by the application of object-oriented design principles.

Database-Driven Design

Because the database was the first component of the application to be given definite shape, the rest of the code had to comply with the decisions Tim made in constructing the database. The bulk of C# code is, in fact, interested only in interacting with the data store. I call this a database-driven design.

Relational database design is governed by a different set of principles than object-oriented design. When designing databases, a designer is concerned with providing efficient data storage and retrieval, enforcing data integrity, providing transactional consistency, and so on. By putting effort into database design without structuring your C# code according to object-oriented principles, and being driven by data design instead, you will end up with poorly designed C# code. Often it is SQL code that is used to express business logic. Such a design can have an efficient data backend, but your C# code will be inefficient and difficult to maintain.

Modern applications use an object-oriented layer as the core layer for implementing business logic. Object-oriented code is much more powerful and efficient for expressing business rules. Later in this book you will see how you can express business logic in object-oriented terms and use the database layer only for data storage and retrieval, the area in which databases are on their own turf.

GUI-Based Application

In essence, this application is a standalone executable connecting to a remote database. It is a typical client-server application. The .NET platform provides a toolkit called Windows Forms for writing elements of the user interface, and it is exactly this toolkit that Tim used to construct the user interface for this application. As a matter of fact, the GUI was probably the only other part of the application besides the database to go through a more elaborate design process. You can see that most of the administration forms are very similar in appearance, because they follow the same pattern.

Another interesting detail crops up if you look at the type of classes used in the application. All classes that were created to extend the Form class (extends System.Windows.Forms.Form), are part of the user interface, and have been designed in Windows Forms Designer. This is apparent when you open the code generated by Windows Forms Designer by clicking the class name in the Class View window. Windows Forms Designer generates partial classes, and all code generated by the tool is in a separate file.

All the code programmed was added to `Form` classes; no other classes or structures were added. That is why we can say that this application is GUI-based.

Modern applications are often tiered and component-based. Such a modular design is a vast improvement over the legacy client-server design. You will benefit from improved reuse, simplified maintenance, simplified distribution, application modularization, and even shorter testing and compilation time.

In order for you to be able to construct applications in a modular manner, the typical approach is to divide an application physically in the form of components or dynamically linked libraries across tiers. When you are depending only on GUI classes produced by Windows Forms or some other visual designer, such organization is not possible.

Event-Driven Programming

Because Visual Basic programmers are very familiar with the concept of event-driven programming, this item is especially important for C# programmers with a VB background. This style was present in VB long before the .NET platform appeared. In essence, the tool is capable of generating a *hook*, an empty event-handling routine declaration. It is up to a programmer to fill in the body with the code that is executed when a certain event, a consequence of user interaction with the application, occurs.

This is exactly the approach taken in constructing the Rent-a-Wheels application. Most of the code is placed inside event-handling routines, in most cases a Click event of some button. Rent-a-Wheels is typical of event-driven programming. Problems arise when the programmer does not go beyond the routines generated by the tool. If you are not structuring code further, into separate methods and classes, then there is bound to be a lot of repetitive and duplicated code. Such code will make maintenance much more difficult, and your design bloated and inefficient. Again, the solution is to use the object-oriented approach and restructure your code in keeping with object-oriented principles.

Rapid Application Development (RAD)

The *rapid application development (RAD)* approach is meant to empower the programmer with tools and techniques that can radically cut development time. This is possible thanks to visual designers, wizards, and code generators. Another benefit is the capability to create prototypes early in the development cycle.

You have seen this approach at work with the Rent-a-Wheels application. Tim was able to construct a fully functional prototype in a short time. This prototype will be reused to create a final version for production.

While this approach is very suitable for constructing quick-and-dirty prototypes and some very simple applications, it shows weaknesses at different scales when you are working with more complex applications. This is because of the code proliferation and reduced code reuse often found in RAD code: These weaknesses can easily outweigh the benefits of RAD if they are not mitigated with thoughtful, object-oriented design.

Copy and Paste As a Code Reuse Mechanism

As you gain more experience, you soon begin identifying the repetitious patterns and recurring problems you deal with while you program. Naturally, you soon start developing techniques that can help improve your productivity and avoid repetition. One of the first techniques you adopt for this purpose is copying and reusing sections of code that can be adapted to a new use with a minimum of modifications. This can be a great productivity booster and is an important confidence-builder for a novice programmer. There is nothing quite as satisfying to an inexperienced programmer as being able to finish a new task quickly by reusing work done on some other project, done in some other part of the application, or simply found on the Internet.

While this is an important improvement in programming technique and productivity for an aspiring programmer, it has serious downsides. Copy and paste as a reuse mechanism leads to code proliferation and duplication that can soon turn into a real maintenance nightmare. It is considered a first step on a programmer's path to advanced skill acquisition.

The same capacity for pattern recognition can lead to more advanced reuse mechanisms. Instead of copying a code section, a programmer can extract a method and call it from multiple locations. An object can be instantiated and used, a class inherited, and so on. Standard object-oriented reuse mechanisms are more powerful and bring greater benefits than simple code copying. Refactoring deals with this issue and teaches you how to use your pattern-recognition skills in a more powerful way.

From Prototype to Delivery Through the Refactoring Process

All in all, the prototype was fully functional and had already received user approval. This means that the important work was already completed successfully. The prototype represented a valuable base for the final delivery. However, at this stage it was important to address the design issues that this application presented. It needed to be refactored. You will see the results of that refactoring work as we return to the Rent-a-Wheels example throughout the book.

Summary

C# programmers often create prototypes very early in the development phase. They are able to materialize the application early on and present it to the client. This way a lot of risk regarding requirements fulfillment can be mitigated quickly.

This chapter presented a real-life scenario that will serve as an example application for the book. It showed how the prototype for the Rent-a-Wheels application was created. First, requirements-gathering included interviewing company employees. A manager, receptionist, parking lot attendant, and maintenance worker all had their say about the work they perform and the most important issues they expect the future application to resolve.

Facts gathered from the interviews were formalized into the most relevant use cases. The vehicle was determined to be a central entity in the business process. The vehicle's different states result from the operations that employees perform.

Based on the analysis performed, a prototype for the Rent-a-Wheels application was created, addressing most of the functionality needed. The application was implemented as a standalone executable that connects to a Microsoft SQL database. Upon examination, it became obvious that the prototype was constructed in line with the tradition of RAD programming. The database was designed up front, the GUI was then designed with the Windows Forms Designer in Visual Studio, and the coding was performed by filling in the event-handling routines generated by the tool.

While the work performed is valuable and the prototype resolved most of the business-related problems the application was meant to address, it nevertheless has numerous flaws. It will have to be refactored before it can reach the final phase.

As you move forward in this book and learn new refactoring techniques and code smells, we'll revisit the Rent-a-Wheels code created in this chapter and apply your newly acquired refactoring knowledge to this close-to-real-life sample application.

5

Basic Hygiene

In this chapter you'll investigate preliminary C# refactorings. You can generally perform these refactorings without any deeper understanding of the application problem domain, and they are mostly performed on the syntactic level. You'll use them to prepare the code for more complex restructuring where application domain knowledge is indispensable. This chapter covers the following main topics:

- ❑ **Dead code:** Dead code comprises those sections of code that are left unused after some modification has been performed: a new feature is implemented, a bug is resolved, or some refactoring is performed. Dead code can have very negative effects on maintainability, and you will learn the reasons why it should be eliminated.

- ❑ **Well-encapsulated code:** You'll be reminded of the importance of well encapsulated code. Encapsulation is a pillar of well-constructed object-oriented code. You will take a look at element scope and access level as mechanisms for hiding information and implementation details in your code.

- ❑ **Explicit imports:** You can reference elements from other namespaces by using fully qualified names in code or by using the `using` directive. I will compare both styles and explain why I prefer making use of the `using` directive.

- ❑ **Unused assembly references:** It is a good practice to eliminate these unused references as they appear, and you will see how the Visual Studio can help you do it.

With this chapter, you finish the exploration of preliminary refactorings. I hope that after you finish reading this chapter you will have a clear picture of clean code and code hygiene, and of how to perform transformations to bring into shape any code that does not respect the rules.

Eliminating Dead Code

In the first chapter I mentioned that code simplicity is one of most valuable qualities your code can possess. Each additional symbol in the source means additional effort that has to be spent on code assimilation. Programmers often have the attitude that more cannot hurt, and they keep the code somewhere inside the current code base just in case. However, code that is never executed can be the biggest riddle for a programmer who didn't author that code. He or she may reason that because the code exists, it must serve some purpose; but because no purpose is evident, the programmer assumes that full code comprehension has not been reached yet. Therefore, the programmer ends up spending more effort on testing, debugging, and profiling in an attempt to discover the lost meaning of the code.

Smell: Dead Code

Detecting the Smell

Use a compiler to find unused code. You do this by commenting suspicious code and rebuilding the project. If no new errors are reported by the compiler, then you have potentially discovered a new case of dead code. Now you need to inspect the use at runtime of this possibly dead code.

Use a code coverage tool (some of these are mentioned in Chapter 3) to find potentially dead code. Execute a comprehensive suite of tests with the coverage tool activated. Analyze coverage tool results and look for sections of code that were never executed. If the code that wasn't executed is the same as the code that was not reported missing by the compiler, it is quite probable that you have discovered dead code. The accuracy of this methodology depends heavily on the level of coverage your tests provide.

Use a simple text search to find commented blocks of code. Commented code is never executed; the information it contains is generally historic and should not form part of the code base. Such information is best kept by your source-code repository.

Related Refactoring

Use Eliminate Dead Code refactoring to eliminate this smell.

Rationale

Dead code increases the complexity of your code. It makes your code more difficult to understand and maintain; furthermore, this code has no value. Since it is never used, it is never executed. Dead code can result in unnecessary effort and can obscure the original intent and design of your code.

The most common sources of dead code are maintenance work and design changes. Maybe you have deleted a line or two, and before you know it, somewhere an entire method is left unused. Or you may have added a certain condition during debugging in order to test a specific block of code, and forgotten to remove the condition before going into production. Maybe you copied the method and then commented a version of the method you changed, instead of removing the unused method. Whatever the origin of dead code, keeping it inside your code base is counterproductive, and such historic information should be left for the version-control system to keep.

Definition: *Dead code* is redundant, inoperative code that is not executed under any circumstances.

Types of Dead Code

You can distinguish the following types of dead code:

❑ **Unreachable code:** This is the code that you know with absolute certainty will never be executed. It is still considered by the compiler, which reports any syntax error or the like. Your first instinct is to resolve the compiler error, but in this case that's a complete waste of time and effort.

❑ **Commented code:** This is ignored by the compiler but it can still cloud the programmer's vision. If a bug is present in code related to the commented code, the programmer will inevitably start to search for a solution in the commented section, looking for the reason why the code was commented and not removed. Comments can negatively affect the visual layout of the code, making it harder to read and follow.

❑ **Unused code:** This code is present if you are dealing with some type of reusable library — for example, you have a method or a class that you suspect is never used. You cannot be sure of this because you don't have the complete code base inside your IDE. In such a case, the element should be phased out gradually. In the first version, make your clients aware that in future versions this element will be eliminated by marking it with `ObsoleteAttribute`.

Listing 5-1 shows some examples of the different flavors of dead code.

Listing 5-1: Flavors of Dead Code

```
using System;
using System.Windows.Forms;
using System.Xml; //System.Xml never referenced


public class DeadCodeDemo
{
    public static void Main()
    {
        int number = 5;
        //Never evaluates to True, following line is never reached
        if (number < 4)
        {
            MessageBox.Show("Destined never to show, unreachable");
        }
        //Redundant code, "number" variable value already 5
        number = 5;
        // Exits the method, following line is never reached
        return;
        //following line detected by compiler
        MessageBox.Show("Destined never to show, unreachable");
    }

    // Method is private and never used in the class it belongs to - unreachable
    private void NotUsedInClassItBelongsTo()
    {
        MessageBox.Show("Destined never to show, unreachable");
    }
```

Continued

Listing 5-1: Flavors of Dead Code *(continued)*

```
// Public method is never used
public void NotUsed()
{
    MessageBox.Show("Destined never to show, unused");
}

//Commented method is never used
//public void Commented()
//{
//      MessageBox.Show("Destined never to show, commented"
//}
}
```

Common Sources of Dead Code

The cycle of life and death is the fundamental principle of nature. In that respect, code resembles a living thing. It is born, it grows, and finally it dies. Once it's dead, it should leave this world. Sometimes, however, code stays in this plane longer than it should. You will now see some common sources of dead code that was not eliminated in a timely manner.

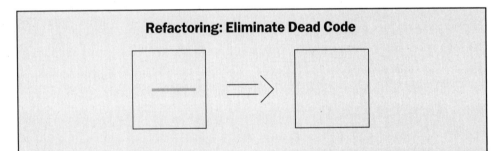

Refactoring: Eliminate Dead Code

Motivation

More code means more complexity. By eliminating unnecessary code from your code base, you are making it easier to read, comprehend, and maintain.

Related Smells

Use this refactoring to eliminate dead code smell.

Mechanics

Refer to the Dead Code Smell definition earlier in the chapter to learn how to locate occurrences of dead code. After you have identified dead code, eliminate it. Commit the eliminated version to a version control system so your latest action can be easily traced and a backup preserved.

In case you are working with reusable code such as library or component code and you suspect that some code element is unused, start by marking this element with ObsoleteAttribute. Remove it completely in the new version.

Before

```
//Import obsolete, since ToXml method commented
using System.Xml;

public class Customer
{
    private string firstName;
    private string lastName;
    private string sSN;

    public string FirstName
    {
        get { return firstName; }
        set { firstName = value; }
    }

    public string LastName
    {
        get { return lastName; }
        set { lastName = value; }
    }

    public string SSN
    {
        get { return sSN; }
        set { sSN = value; }
    }

    //public XmlDocument ToXml()
    //{
    //    XmlDocument doc = new XmlDocument();
    //    string xml;
    //    xml = "<Customer>" +
    //        "<FirstName>" + FirstName + "</FirstName>" +
    //        "<LastName>" + LastName + "</LastName>" +
    //        "<SSN>" + SSN + "</SSN>" +
    //    "</Customer>";
    //    doc.LoadXml(xml);
    //    return doc;
    //}
}
```

After

```
public class Customer
{
    private string firstName;
    private string lastName;
    private string sSN;
```

Continued

```
        public string FirstName
        {
            get { return firstName; }
            set { firstName = value; }
        }

        public string LastName
        {
            get { return lastName; }
            set { lastName = value; }
        }

        public string SSN
        {
            get { return sSN; }
            set { sSN = value; }
        }
    }
```

There are a number of ways you can end up with some dead code inside your code base. The following sections describe some of the most common sources so you can be prepared to look for them.

Detached Event Handler

The event is never fired, but the event code is still present. This happens very often if you decide to eliminate from the form a control that previously served some purpose. All related event-handling code is still preserved and needs to be removed manually.

Invisible Control

Sometimes you place control on the form and it is covered by another control, or it is resized in such a way that it is not visible anymore. In other cases, maybe it is set invisible or disabled right from the beginning and is never used. Eliminate such controls and all related event-handling code.

Using Section Importing Unused Elements

I often come across obsolete elements in using sections. Once you eliminate a property or a method, or move some code between classes, it is only too easy to forget to remove using directives that were made redundant by these changes. It may seem innocuous, but this code can have some far-reaching consequences. When you are performing large-scale refactoring, it is very important to understand how dependencies work in your code. When you are performing some fast code browsing, you often base your conclusions on the content of the "using" section. A few redundant using statements and you can be completely misled.

Fortunately, Visual Studio can help you with this task. You can invoke the Remove Unused Usings feature in Visual Studio by selecting Edit ➤ IntelliSense ➤ Organize Usings ➤ Remove Unused Usings, as shown in Figure 5-1. While you are at it, you might just as well sort using directives. You can perform both at a single click by selecting Remove and Sort in the menu. The Organize Usings option is also available through the context menu (invoked by right-clicking somewhere over the code editor in Visual Studio).

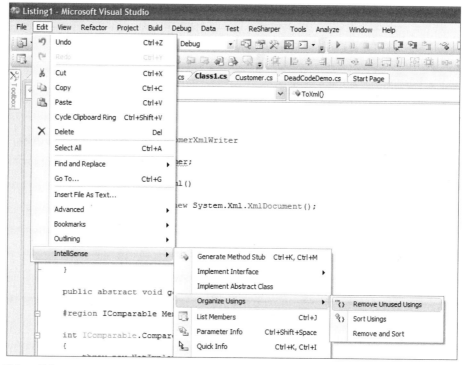

Figure 5-1

Ignored Procedure Return Value

This happens when the return value is ignored when the function is called. It means that the clients are not really interested in the information the return value provides. This function return value should be transformed to void, and code in charge of returning the value should be eliminated. If the return value is used only occasionally, then you should rethink the way the function is written.

Ignored Procedure Return Parameter

When the function is called, the return (reference and output) parameter value is ignored. Again, if this is the case with all function clients, then the ignored return parameter and related code should be eliminated.

Local Variable Is Not Read

The variable can be assigned, but if it is not read, then there is no use for it. In fact, it is just another case of dead code. Eliminate the variable in question.

Read-Only or Write-Only Property Containing Both Get and Set Property Procedures

After you write down the property declaration, Visual Studio will automatically create both get and set property procedure stubs. Very often programmers, from force of habit, will leave and implement both procedures, even though the property is supposed to be read- or write-only.

Obsolete Elements

With time, as more and more changes are applied, some bigger elements in your code can be left unreachable or unused. Such elements can be classes, enumerators, interfaces, modules, and even whole namespaces. These elements should be eliminated.

Don't have any mercy on dead code. Be sure to use some versioning system as a backup and eliminate dead code without fear. If you don't eliminate dead code, the compiler will most often do it for you anyway. After removing dead code, you will soon feel as if you have left some burden from the past behind. Your code base will become much clearer, and easier to comprehend and maintain.

Reducing the Scope and Access Level of Unduly Exposed Elements

You have often heard that encapsulation is the first pillar of object orientation. Encapsulation is applied to conceal the internal details of our code from the public eye. This is generally referred to as *information and implementation hiding*. In order to reduce the complexity of systems, you often resort to decomposing the system into different units. When you are following the "divide and conquer" principle, it is very important to hide as much internal information and implementation detail of an individual module as possible.

Smell: Overexposure

Detecting the Smell
If you suspect that a certain element has an unnecessarily broad access level, reduce the access level by one degree and then build the project. If no error is reported by the compiler, then you have found an overexposed element. The element can be any of the following: interface, module, class, structure, structure member, procedure, property, member variable, constant, enumeration, event, external declaration, or delegate.

Similarly, if you suspect that a certain element has too broad a scope, even when the minimum access level is specified, move that element to a more enclosed region and build the project. If no error is reported by the compiler, then you have successfully identified an element with unnecessarily broad scope.

Related Refactoring
Use Reduce Access Level and Reduce Scope refactoring in order to eliminate this smell.

Rationale
Unnecessary exposure of internal and implementation details goes against basic principles of encapsulation and data and information hiding. It makes your code less modular, more complex, and difficult to use and maintain. Dependencies can freely spawn in such a system, making it in fact monolithic. An unnecessary level of detail is exposed in such a way that it complicates usage of the code units.

In C#, the largest organizational unit is the assembly. In order to use the services that some assembly provides, you need only the compiled binary. You interact with the assembly through its interface — a set of publicly visible elements. Having this interface as simple and thin as possible greatly simplifies your interaction with the assembly. You need not have any notion of the internal workings of the assembly.

How does this work out in practice? I will try to illustrate this with an example. Consider Figure 5-2. The difference in size between the ShippingCost and CartPersistence interfaces can be observed visually.

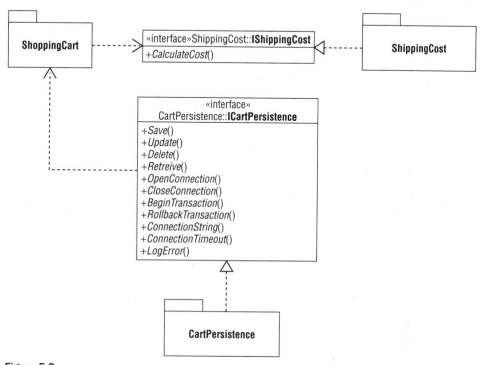

Figure 5-2

Imagine you have a system consisting of three assemblies: ShoppingCart, ShippingCost, and CartPersistence. You are working on the ShoppingCart assembly, and you are using the ShippingCost assembly services to calculate the cost of shipping for items in the cart. Using the ShippingCost assembly proves to be quite simple: A single interface and a single operation are exposed to you as a client.

Now you need to write some test code in which you use CartPersistence services also. However, this is proving to be much more complex. The CartPersistence interface exposes a myriad of implementation details related to database communication, transaction management, logging, and so on — a number of details that any client using this interface should not have to worry about. As a matter of fact, there is no reason why you should have any notion of the underlying persistence mechanism, which could just as easily use a simple file, an Excel spreadsheet, or whatever. There is no reason why any CartPersistence client should be aware of its inner workings. In this case, while interacting with CartPersistence, you are unnecessarily bogged down with overexposure of assembly internals.

As a rule of thumb, maintain a scope and an access level for programming elements that's as restricted as possible.

The benefits of encapsulation and information and data hiding are easily appreciated. Even comparing the size of the two interfaces shown in Figure 5-2 visually gives us a lot to talk about. Well-encapsulated units are easy to use and interact with, eliminating unnecessary complexity and providing good system modularity.

In C#, you can use scope and access level to control the degree of exposure of programming elements. By minimizing the exposure of programming elements, you will successfully encapsulate and hide implementation details of your code.

Scope and Access Level

The scope (or visibility) of a declared element is the region of code that can access that element without fully qualifying it. It means that for the element, this region is its closest neighborhood, where everyone is known by their first name. It also has one very practical consequence: Such elements are readily displayed by IntelliSense. Elements out of scope have to be imported in order to be displayed by IntelliSense directly. If you do not import the element, IntelliSense will still help you find it, but only if you follow the whole path of the fully qualified name. In Figure 5-3 you can see how IntelliSense helps you reference an out-of-scope element if you use the element's fully qualified name.

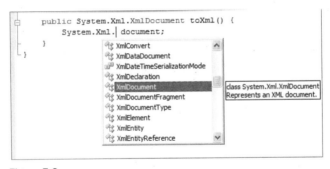

Figure 5-3

Scope

In C#, you differentiate four levels of scope:

❑ Block scope

❑ Procedure scope

❑ Module scope

❑ Namespace scope

First and foremost, scope depends on the enclosing region in which you declared the element — meaning the block, procedure, class, and structure. For example, if you declare a variable inside the method, then it will be available throughout that same method, but it will not be available from any other method in that or any other class. In case that element is declared on the module level (class or structure), element scope is further affected by access level. If a variable is declared as private, then it will have module scope, whereas if the default or public access level is used, the element will be visible throughout the namespace (namespace scope).

Access Level

Access level controls which code can access (read or write) a declared element. In C#, you differentiate the following access levels:

- Public
- Protected
- Internal
- Protected internal
- Private

Access level is controlled by corresponding access modifiers when the element is declared: `public`, `protected`, `internal`, or `private`. In some cases, the access level of an element also depends on the access level of the containing structure. For example, you will not be able to access a method declared as public from another assembly if the method containing the class is marked as internal.

Common Sources of Overexposure

As is common with many smells, change is the easiest path to overexposure. After some reshuffling of code, you might be in a situation where the scope and access level of some elements should be reduced because they are now referenced from a more enclosed area. Unfortunately, this step is frequently omitted.

Refactoring: Reduce Access Level

Motivation

Well-encapsulated code maintains internal and implementation detail well hidden from outside view. This way, thanks to a modular approach, the complexity of the system as a whole is reduced. Well-encapsulated code also helps to control dependencies in the system. Other benefits of reduced access level include less potential for name clashes and simplified security management.

Related Smells

Use this refactoring to eliminate Overexposure smell.

Mechanics

Start by reducing access level by one degree and build the project. If the compile is successful, repeat this step until an error is reported by the compiler or the private access level is reached. In case of error, return to the most reduced access level under which the project still compiles successfully.

Continued

Before

```
public class Customer
{
    public string firstName;

    public string FirstName
    {
        get { return firstName; }
        set { firstName = value; }
    }
}
```

After

```
public class Customer
{
    private string firstName;

    public string FirstName
    {
        get { return firstName; }
        set { firstName = value; }
    }
}
```

Conversely, overexposure can be the result of simple oversight. The benefits of encapsulation and data and information hiding are not easy to see in the short term or on a small scale, and programmers often don't give them due attention.

Quick Fix for Design Errors

In some situations, a quick solution to some design-related problems can lead to intentional exposure of some private element. While this can provide some fast, short-term results, a hefty price will almost certainly be paid later. Take a look at the code in Listing 5-2.

Listing 5-2: Quick Fix Requires the Exposure of a Private Connection Object

```
using System;
using System.Data.SqlClient;

public class ProductDetailPersistence
{

    private SqlConnection connection;
    //...
    public void Delete()
    {
        //...
    }
    //...
}
```

The class `ProductDetailPersistence` is, as the name suggests, responsible for the persistence of product detail. At some point during development, the developers realize that a very important omission occurred. No provision was made for transactional behavior of the class. Some operations — for example, product elimination — have to be performed under the same transaction as product-detail elimination. The quick fix is to expose the connection object by making it public, thus providing a common transactional context for both operations.

Naturally, this presents a problem, because low-level persistence implementation details are exposed to a client. Therefore, if at some point the decision is made to change the underlying data store, the changes cannot be isolated to a persistence class only. Because all clients have knowledge of SqlConnection, any attempt to replace the underlying data store with some other type of persistence mechanism or some other database would cause a chain reaction of changes in all client code.

Refactoring: Move Element to a More Enclosing Region

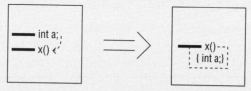

Motivation

Keeping the scope of elements at a minimum helps make your programs better encapsulated, more modular, more robust, and easier to maintain, read, and use. Other benefits are optimized memory management, simplified security, and so on.

Related Smells

Use this refactoring to eliminate Overexposure smell.

Mechanics

This refactoring should be preceded by Reduce Access Level refactoring, where applicable. Select the element for scope reduction and move its declaration to a more enclosing region.

Before

```
using System.Xml;

public class CustomerXmlWriter
{
    private Customer customer;
    //Variable doc declared on class level,
    //but used in ToXml method only
    private XmlDocument doc = new XmlDocument();
    //...
    public XmlDocument ToXml()
    {
        string xml;
        xml = "<Customer>" +
                "<FirstName>" + customer.FirstName + "</FirstName>" +
                "<LastName>" + customer.LastName + "</LastName>" +
```

Continued

```
                    "<SSN>" + customer.SSN + "</SSN>" +
                "</Customer>";
            doc.LoadXml(xml);
            return doc;
        }
    }
```

After

```
using System.Xml;

public class CustomerXmlWriter
{
    private Customer customer;
    //...
    public XmlDocument ToXml()
    {
        XmlDocument doc = new XmlDocument();
        string xml;
        xml = "<Customer>" +
                "<FirstName>" + customer.FirstName + "</FirstName>" +
                "<LastName>" + customer.LastName + "</LastName>" +
                "<SSN>" + customer.SSN + "</SSN>" +
            "</Customer>";
        doc.LoadXml(xml);
        return doc;
    }
}
```

Dealing with Overexposure

Once you have identified an overexposed element, dealing with overexposure is relatively simple. The first step should be access-level reduction. Reduction should be performed gradually: You should rebuild the project after each reduction until a compiler error is produced or you reach the private access level. If a compiler error is produced, the latest reduction should be undone. Table 5-1 shows the gradual path of access-level reduction.

Table 5-1: Gradual Access Level Reduction

Current	Reduce to
Public	Protected or Internal
Protected	Protected Internal
Internal	Protected internal
Protected internal	Private

A similar pattern can be applied to scope reduction. This step should follow access-level reduction. Here, the location of the element declaration is changed in such a way that scope is reduced to the minimal level necessary. Table 5-2 illustrates the scope-reduction path.

Table 5-2: Gradual Scope Reduction

Current	Reduce to
No namespace	Namespace
Namespace	Module (class, structure)
Module (class, Structure)	Procedure
Procedure	Block

When you are talking about access level and scope, less is truly more. If you are writing code, it pays to be secretive. Make a habit of declaring all your elements under the minimum scope and access level. This can often result in better-designed and better-encapsulated code.

Using Explicit Imports

The issue of explicit imports might not seem major at first. After all, imports are there only to help you write less, so you can reference an element (namespace, interface, module, class, structure, and so on) using its simple name instead of its fully qualified name. It will not absolve you from adding references to a project, so why attach any importance to it? If the effect is the same, why shouldn't a programmer use fully qualified names inside the body of an element? I will try to answer these questions in the next section.

Smell: Using Fully Qualified Names Outside "Using" Section

Detecting the Smell
Unfortunately, you need to resort to scanning the source visually in order to detect this smell. There is, however, a step you can perform in order to speed up the search. Remove temporarily all project references. In addition, comment the "using" section temporarily so it is not marked with an error sign by the compiler. The compiler will now mark all the declarations where types from external assemblies were used. All that is left is to review each declaration in a search for fully qualified names in the body of the code.

Related Refactoring
Use Explicit Imports refactoring in order to eliminate this smell.

Rationale
Using fully qualified names in the body of the module (class, structure, interface, and so on) will make your code more difficult to read and write. Fully qualified names can

Continued

---

be very long, and using them is just tedious. It is much better to have them imported in a single place.

The "using" section is a very good place to look when trying to understand large-scale design and system dependencies. Making use of the "using" section inconsistently and resorting to fully qualified names in the body of the module can give a false impression when you are inspecting the dependencies in your code.

Using Section Depicts Dependencies in Your System

As projects grow in size and more people take part in development, large-scale issues such as dependencies grow in importance and become more apparent. The natural way to deal with large-scale projects is to organize software into separate pieces. This way, smaller groups of programmers can dedicate themselves to constructing a single piece of a puzzle. Because you generally start out with the blueprint showing how these pieces should fit in, construction of the final product is just a matter of putting them together. In .NET, these largest organizational units are identified as assemblies.

Refactoring: Replace Fully Qualified Names with Explicit Imports

Motivation

By adding a `using` directive you reduce the quantity of code you have to write. Using imports is much more efficient than repeatedly writing fully qualified names in your code.

By consistently utilizing a "using" section, you will provide easy to find, reliable information related to dependencies in your code.

Related Smells

Use this refactoring to eliminate Using Fully Qualified Names Outside "Using" Section smell.

Mechanics

1. After identifying the fully qualified name in the body of the module, add the `using` statement for this particular name, if not already present in the Imports section.

2. Replace the recently identified fully qualified name in the body of the module with a simple named version.

Before

```
public class CustomerXmlWriter
{
    private Customer customer;
    //...
    public System.Xml.XmlDocument ToXml()
    {
```

```
                System.Xml.XmlDocument doc = new System.Xml.XmlDocument();
                string xml;
                xml = "<Customer>" +
                        "<FirstName>" + customer.FirstName + "</FirstName>" +
                        "<LastName>" + customer.LastName + "</LastName>" +
                        "<SSN>" + customer.SSN + "</SSN>" + "</Customer>";
                doc.LoadXml(xml);
                return doc;
        }
    }
```

After

```
    using System.Xml;

    public class CustomerXmlWriter
    {
        private Customer customer;
        //...
        public XmlDocument ToXml()
        {
            XmlDocument doc = new XmlDocument();
            string xml;
            xml = "<Customer>" +
                    "<FirstName>" + customer.FirstName + "</FirstName>" +
                    "<LastName>" + customer.LastName + "</LastName>" +
                    "<SSN>" + customer.SSN + "</SSN>" + "</Customer>";
            doc.LoadXml(xml);
            return doc;
        }
    }
```

However, if special care is not taken, these pieces start to develop unpredicted and undesired dependencies between each other. Growing new dependencies is as easy as adding one project reference and one using statement in your code.

Definition: One module (module Y) is dependent on another (module X) if a change in that other module (X) can provoke changes in the first (Y).

Imagine you have finished working on your class. The morning after, you find out it's not working anymore because a class you depend upon has unexpectedly changed. The other programmer was not aware that your class depends on his or her class, and decided to apply changes as he or she deemed necessary.

Imagine another scenario. Your assembly deals with a business domain but is also concerned with data persistence. For that purpose, it uses different assemblies for XML or database-type persistence. However, in this specific application, you have reused your assembly for its business-domain functionality, even though you do not need any persistence functionality. Nevertheless, XML and database-persistence assemblies still have to be deployed to go along with your assembly because your assembly depends on them.

This is just the tip of the iceberg of dependency-related problems. You will see more of them as you plunge into other more complex issues related to large-scale design later in the book. Even with this short introduction, the significance of correct dependency management should be apparent.

When trying to identify dependencies in their code, programmers have a natural tendency to visually scan the "using" sections of source-code files. In some large-scale projects, however, scanning the whole code base is not only impractical but can be close to impossible. Moreover, available documentation and diagrams can often be out of sync with the real world — more often showing good intentions than really representing the current state of affairs.

Tale from the Trenches

Consider the following anecdote: An acquaintance of mine had to perform a lot of large-scale refactoring work in order to reorganize a system and eliminate some dependencies from certain assemblies. After he thought he had finished the task, he triumphantly removed the external assembly reference from the project and pressed the Build button. As a result, a list of compiler errors appeared in the IDE, and he discovered several places where external assembly types were referenced by means of fully qualified names. He based his assumptions on the Imports section. He found that because of the free use of fully qualified names throughout the code, many places where external types were referenced were not identified from the start.

While there are tools that can help you with the task of comprehending dependencies in your code, they are not always available. That's why maintaining a current "using" section and avoiding the use of fully qualified names in the body of the modules is very important in your quest to ensure that your code is readable and easy to maintain.

Removing Unused Assembly References

While the C# compiler is intelligent enough not to include unused references in the assembly manifest, maintaining unused assembly references in your project still has a serious downside. Adding a reference to an external assembly is a significant decision from a large-scale design viewpoint and should be made with great care.

Smell: Unused References

Detecting the Smell

You should check for the presence of unused references after any major and large-scale refactorings. Remove the suspicious assembly reference and rebuild the project. If the build is performed without error, you have successfully removed the unused reference. Conversely, if the reference was used and shouldn't have been removed, the compiler will notify you with the following error message: *The type or namespace name 'SomeType' could not be found (are you missing a using directive or an assembly reference?)*.

Related Refactoring

Use Remove Unused References refactoring in order to eliminate this smell.

Rationale

An unused reference is a breeding ground for unnecessary dependencies. Dependencies greatly influence the design of your system from a large-scale "bird's eye" viewpoint. A reference is a signal to programmers that they can use services that a certain assembly provides, thereby establishing an otherwise unnecessary dependency.

Having a dependency set in your project is a kind of green light telling developers that they are free to use the services that the referenced assembly provides. In some cases, especially after some large-scale changes to the code base, the reference is made obsolete, and dependencies on the referenced assembly have to go somewhere else. The design has changed, and the project should not depend on the referenced assembly anymore.

However, if the reference from the project properties is not removed also, there is a good chance that this assembly will be used again at some point. In a way, it is only logical. "Why do we have a reference to an assembly if we are not meant to use it?" any developer might rightfully ask. In order to avoid this kind of confusion, avoid unused references and remove them as soon as they appear.

Refactoring: Remove Unused References

Motivation

Having strict policies for controlling references and removing unused references in a timely manner will help keep dependencies at bay in your project.

Related Smells

Use this refactoring to eliminate Unused References smell.

Mechanics

Make sure that the assembly is not being used in the project, using the mechanics described in Unused References smell. In Solution Explorer, select the unused reference and select the Remove option in the context menu. Build the project to ensure that the reference was unused.

Basic Hygiene in the Rent-a-Wheels Application

Thanks to the early age of the Rent-a-Wheels application, the smells described in this chapter were not rife. The changes we made amounted to removing a few commented methods and a few detached event handlers. Listing 5-3 shows one detached event handler that was eliminated after we performed basic hygiene refactorings on the Rent-a-Wheels application.

Listing 5-3: Detached Event Handler Eliminated from the Rent-a-Wheels Application

```
private void button1_Click(object sender, EventArgs e)
{
    //Test SqlConnection
    SqlConnection oCn = new SqlConnection(
        "Data Source=TESLATEAM;" +
        "Initial Catalog=RENTAWHEELS;" +
        "User ID=RENTAWHEELS_LOGIN;" +
        "Password=RENTAWHEELS_PASSWORD_123");
    oCn.Open();
}
```

Summary

This chapter showed some very common cases of poorly maintained, unhygienic code. In such cases rot will easily take hold, so you need effective methods to identify and eliminate it.

Dead code can often be a source of confusion and additional complexity. There are different ways for dead code to appear — as commented sections, unused event handlers, removed controls, ignored method parameters or return values, and so on. Whatever the form, dead and redundant code should be eliminated without exception.

Very often programmers unintentionally give unnecessarily broad scope and visibility to certain pro-gramming elements. To construct well-encapsulated code, it is important that you adhere to the prin-ciples of information/implementation hiding. Exposing unnecessary internal detail goes against this principle, and in such cases you can improve encapsulation by reducing the scope and access level of overexposed elements.

Often, when reading the code, you rely on the Imports section to understand dependencies in your code. Using fully qualified names instead of relying on the Imports section can make comprehending the dependencies in your code much more difficult. Performing imports explicitly should be favored over using fully qualified names in the body of the code. Each existing reference will tell the programmer that a referenced library is meant to be used from the current library. Problems occur when obsolete references are not removed, because such references encourage programmers to freely make use of the referenced libraries. It is a good practice to remove unused references.

The next chapter deals with standard refactoring techniques. These refactorings cannot be performed without a good understanding of code and problem domain. They can have a profound impact on the way your code is designed; dealing with them means dealing with core issues related to code quality. I hope that the preliminary refactoring in this chapter served as a good warm-up for the more complex work that lies ahead.

6

From Problem Domain to Code: Closing the Gap

It is the programmer's job to analyze and understand the business of others. Unfortunately, they often gloat over speed and algorithm effectiveness, forgetting that a program is only as good as the extent to which it fulfills its requirements and the client's needs. Unless you are one of those programmers who prefers counting processor cycles to making your software purposeful and useful to others, you will agree that understanding the problem domain of your application is the first and most critical step in the process of software development.

This step is by no means trivial. You have to guide your clients in discerning the essential requirements from those that are superficial, in defining the rules of the business, and sometimes even in educating your clients about proven solutions in software design. While you are at it, you have to learn, yourself; you need to accumulate a compendium of knowledge on the problem domain you are dealing with. Finally, you use this knowledge not only to make your application work properly and fulfill user requirements, but also to make your code meaningful: establishing the links connecting the problem domain, the design, and the source code.

In this chapter you will see how these links are established by looking at the following concepts:

❑   **Object-oriented analysis and design**: You will explore a few analysis methods, such as use cases and textual analysis, and then see how these techniques can help you define the requirements your software must meet.

  These are all very important concepts on their own, and this chapter will only tell you what you need to understand for our discussion of refactoring. So don't take this chapter as a comprehensive guide on the subject.

❑   **Naming guidelines**: You will learn why they are important and how refactoring can help. (You'll even revisit a naming convention well known to veteran programmers: Hungarian notation.)

❑ **Closing the gap between code and problem domain**: You will see some refactorings that can help you close this gap, such as the Rename and Safe Rename refactorings, which can help you eliminate smells such as Unrevealing Names and Long Method.

❑ **Published and public interfaces**: The chapter ends with a discussion of the difference between published and public interfaces. This difference is purely conceptual, meaning that you will not be able to use code to enforce it, but it has a great impact on the level and kind of refactorings you are allowed to perform on the code.

By the end of this chapter, you will be much more aware of good practices that make your code readable to other people. Taking into account that other people will work on your code is not merely altruistic; it's an important part of what being a good programmer is all about.

Understanding the Problem Domain

There are many approaches to creating software. Some developers are happy to dip into the code right from the project's outset, while others prefer to have everything laid down, described, and modeled in documents and diagrams, thoroughly worked out before even the first line of code is written. Wherever your style happens to fall, and most likely it is somewhere in the middle, you need to — without exception — spend a significant amount of effort on understanding the requirements, the problem domain, and the general context for your software.

> **Definition:** A *problem domain* is a term that refers to all real-world concepts, entities, and processes that are part of the problem to be resolved by the system you are constructing.

Personally, I am not very keen on separating the roles of analyst and programmer into two narrowly specialized individuals, something that is common practice in larger teams that adhere to some of the more traditional and formal software-development methodologies. The problem with this approach is that it introduces another "level of indirection" between the user and the developer; and if another step in communication is established on the customer's side, in the form of someone delegated to represent all the interested parties (such as final users and domain experts), a lot of disruptive noise is introduced during the requirements-gathering process.

You will generally start out by both trying to become informed about the problem domain and trying to understand the client's needs. These initial activities on the project can take the form of meetings, interviews, correspondence, and/or document exchange. Your interlocutor can be any interested party — the final user, a manager, a domain expert, or someone else. This process will typically go through certain phases of knowledge acquisition and structuring, which I describe in the next section.

At the first step, you will probably be confronted with a wealth of information that you understand only partially, and your reaction will be to try to understand and organize this information. Bear in mind that the steps described in this chapter are performed iteratively with an evolutionary approach in mind.

Let's begin our look at this typical cycle of software analysis.

Step One: Gathering the Information

When you get started, unless you have previously made a system that caters to the same business domain, you'll inevitably end up with that "first day at work" feeling. A lot of unfamiliar jargon will likely be used at the first meetings, making it difficult for you to understand the complete meaning of the conversation. At this point it is important to gather as much information as possible, to start to organize it, and to carefully take note of all the doubts you might have and all the facts and terms you need to further clarify or have explained to you.

In order for this process to be effective, you should hear the opinions of as many interested parties as possible, such as managers, final users, domain experts, contractors, and so on. They all almost certainly have their own unique views of the project, the business, the requirements, and the priorities of those requirements. It's your task to serve as a sort of mediator, reconciling different views and making sure that all legitimate concerns are met.

Tale from the Trenches

On one project that I participated in for a major bank, an IT head manager was very keen on exploiting the benefits of browser-based, thin-client architecture: lower administration costs, ease of distribution, simple hardware upgrade path, and so on. One part of the application would cater to cashiers, a typical teller front end. They were still using a standard application made in Visual Basic 6, which had a DOS-like character-based interface. After spending some time with them, I realized that they needed an extremely responsive user interface that would operate without a glitch or a pause, and one with options that were easily accessible through different keyboard shortcuts.

I decided to make a very simple browser-based prototype that cashiers could try out. It wasn't long before the solution's shortcomings in these particular circumstances became apparent. The system's lack of responsiveness, and the inability to use standard key combinations (the mouse was used for those instead) were described as "torture" by one of the employees. It was obvious that in this case that particular technology was not applicable, and the IT department was swayed toward a compromise solution: a browser-distributed standalone .NET managed executable.

Unless you are able to communicate well, you have no use for the information that you have gathered during this first step. Therefore, the next step involves developing a common vocabulary.

Step Two: Agreeing on the Vocabulary

After the initiation, you need to ensure that all the information you have gathered is as precise as possible. In order to do that, you must first ensure that everybody participating in the project speaks the same language. As you can imagine, I am not referring to English, German, or some other natural language. Every line of business has its own specific language, with precise meanings that are not immediately apparent to laypeople (or developers, in this case). This language can even have different flavors in different departments within the same organization.

In order to enable meaningful communication, it is crucial that the precise and consistent meaning of terms is agreed upon in the early phase of the project. While this process sometimes occurs naturally, it is best to tackle it directly and systematically. After all participants agree on consistent and precise meanings, the vocabulary can later be expanded and new terms added or even invented as the project progresses.

While developers must carry the brunt of the process of vocabulary acquisition, other participants might need to cope with understanding some technical terms. For example, when you're discussing usability with final users, those users should have a clear understanding of terms such as *shortcut key* and *access key* and how they differ. These terms can also become part of the common vocabulary.

A *vocabulary document* can prove to be quite useful for the purpose of formalizing and disseminating the common vocabulary. This document can also make the process of integration a lot easier for newcomers.

The interviews recounted in Chapter 4 showed that the Rent-a-Wheels employees I spoke with had developed their own vocabulary. While the conversations described there were easy to understand, there are some subtle differences between the meanings of the words as used by the employees and the common meanings of those words. For example, the word "renting" for Rent-a-Wheels employees describes the process of vehicle selection and the issuance of the receipt. A vehicle is given to a customer only after it is "handed over." The "branch" is an internal organizational unit that is defined not by the location of the reception desk but by the presence of its own parking lot.

The following list describes a small section of the vocabulary document developed for the purpose of the Rent-a-Wheels application.

Rent-a-Wheels Vocabulary

- **Vehicle**: Any vehicle, such as a car, motorcycle, SUV, truck, and so on, that a customer can rent. Each vehicle belongs to a single branch and can be found in its parking lot.

- **Renting a vehicle**: A process whereby a customer selects a vehicle at the reception desk and the receptionist issues the receipt that is used to pick up the vehicle at the parking lot.

- **Handing over a vehicle**: A process whereby the parking lot attendant hands over the rented vehicle to a customer.

- **Branch**: A Rent-a-Wheels rental company office that has its own parking lot. This is an internal organizational unit that can have multiple reception desks but always has a single parking lot.

After you have analyzed the business and agreed on the vocabulary, it's time to think about the requirements that need to be fulfilled by the system you are constructing. Requirements are best described in the form of *usage scenarios*, often called *use cases*. You'll learn more about that in the next step.

Step Three: Describing the Interactions

Now that you understand the problem domain and the purpose of the software you are creating, it is time to portray the requirements in a more structured way. You can do this by describing the series of interactions between the user and the system that results in something useful for the user. Two of the most common ways to manage requirements are through use cases and user stories.

Use Cases

A standard way to describe interactions between the system and the users is by means of use cases. A *use case* is a description of an interaction between the user and the system that results in the goal desired by the user. While use cases may differ in format and level of detail, they focus on the system's behavior as perceived from the outside; they do not involve any assumptions about the way the system will be implemented.

Chapter 4 contains descriptions of the most important use cases for the Rent-a-Wheels application.

User Stories

A less formal way to manage requirements involves user stories. *User stories* are generally more condensed and less structured than use cases, and they are written by customers in their own language. They typically do not convey enough information to implement the functionality required of the application, so if you use them you should also have a client involved throughout the project. This form of managing requirements is popular with the Agile software development community.

After you have structured the requirements, you can test your understanding by providing the client with the prototype of the software you are about to build.

Step Four: Building the Prototype

With use cases at hand, you are ready to start the implementation. While prototypes can be throw-away, the best value is obtained by those that are evolutionary. They validate your understanding of the requirements with the customer, both functional requirements and those that are not functional. There are a number of other uses for which prototypes can be employed, such as testing some design and architectural decisions, providing the customer with proof of progress, checking interface design details, and so on.

In previous chapters of this book, you started to witness how the initial Rent-a-Wheels prototype is being transformed from the initial prototype into a fully functional application.

Once you start to code, the first thing you need to decide is the names you are going to use in your code. You need to name classes, methods, variables, namespaces, and so on, in such way that they are both understandable and consistent.

Naming Guidelines

In order to write maintainable and readable code, you need to choose the names you employ very carefully. Good naming is probably one of hardest skills you need to learn as a programmer. The names you choose need to be concise and consistent, and they need to communicate well with any programmers who will be reading the code. On the surface, this may seem a rather simple issue, but it can prove to be extremely daunting, even for the experienced programmer.

Keep in mind that perfection need not be reached in the first attempt; as you proceed you can simply rename the identifiers you need to improve. Later in the chapter you will see how this refactoring is performed. You can count on tools to help you with this task, so you shouldn't find it too time-consuming.

Smell: Unrevealing Names

Detecting the Smell

Look for identifiers that have no clear or immediately obvious meaning. This is apparent when you need to look inside the code in order to know a certain element's purpose. For example, if you need to look inside the method's body in order to understand what the method is doing, then that method's name is not conveying its intent and should be changed. Alternatively, comments might explain a certain code element's purpose better than its name, forcing you to rely on them when reading the code.

Also poor choices are words that are not part of the project's common vocabulary, do not relate well to the problem domain, do not belong to the vocabulary of software development, and/or fit poorly into the project's general context.

Other more obvious signs of less than perfect names are abbreviations, unfamiliar acronyms, or capitalization styles that are not in line with the general .NET framework or C# case guidelines.

Related Refactoring

Use Rename or Symbolic Rename refactoring to eliminate this smell.

Rationale

Programmers use the names of methods, properties, classes, variables, parameters, namespaces, and so on in order to discern the purpose of some piece of source code. When these names are badly chosen, code fails in communicating its purpose. Code that does not communicate is the essence of code that is difficult to maintain.

Because this is a rather tricky issue, it might be best to start by exploring some of the guidelines that are easiest to follow, such as capitalization styles.

Capitalization Styles

C# should respect the capitalization style in general use in .NET framework libraries. Three styles are in use, with each applicable to a certain type of identifier:

- ❑ **Camel case** (also known as *camelCase*) is a capitalization style wherein the first word in the identifier is written in lowercase, and each subsequent word in compound identifiers has its first letter capitalized. Words are joined without the use of spaces, underscores, or any other special characters. For example: `corporateAccount`.

- ❑ **Pascal case** is a capitalization style wherein the first letter in the identifier and in each subsequent word in compound identifiers is capitalized. Words are joined without the use of spaces, underscores, or any other special characters. For example: `MonetaryTransaction`.

- ❑ **Uppercase** is a capitalization style wherein all letters in the identifier are capitalized. For example: `System.IO` or `System.Web.UI`. This capitalization style is less common and is used for two-letter acronyms.

Table 6-1 shows how these capitalization styles are used correctly in C#.

Table 6-1: Identifiers and Capitalization Styles in C#

Identifier	Capitalization Style
Class	Pascal case
Method	Pascal case
Property	Pascal case
Parameter	Camel case
Protected or private instance field	Camel case
Local variable	Camel case
Static or instance public field	Pascal case
Namespace	Pascal case
Enum	Pascal case
Interface	Pascal case (starting with capital I, as in IDisposable)
Event	Pascal case

Simple Naming Guidelines

Here are some fairly simple naming guidelines that are part of the .NET framework naming conventions and should be followed by all .NET languages. They consist of some simple rules that can be enforced without a lot of intellectual effort, but should be respected for consistency, readability, and aesthetic reasons.

- ❑ Suffix any exception class with `Exception`, as in `InsufficientFundsException`.
- ❑ Suffix any attribute class with `Attribute`, as in `SerializableAttribute`.
- ❑ Suffix any event handler with `EventHandler`, as in `AlarmEventHandler`.
- ❑ Suffix any event arguments class with `EventArgs`, as in `UnhandledExceptionEventArgs`.
- ❑ Prefix any interface identifier with capital "`I`," as in `IDisposable` or `ISerializable`. (At least that's what official guidelines are saying, but some say this is an old COM style convention that found its way into .NET).
- ❑ Avoid the ALL_UPPER_UNDERSCORE_DELIMITED style of declaring constants.
- ❑ Avoid misspelling words. In fact, you should be able to check your code with a spell-check tool such as Word after compound names are broken apart.
- ❑ Avoid using abbreviations and acronyms unless they are widely used and understood. For example, naming a method `ToXmlNode()` is fine — no need to use the excessively long `ToExtensibleMarkupLanguageNode()`. However, don't use `CalcFedTx()` or anything of that sort; use `CalculateFederalTax()` instead.

❑   Finally, avoid Hungarian notation (see sidebar). Because this technology has been rendered obsolete by modern tools, stick with easily pronounced and easily memorized names, and rely on Visual Studio to provide type safety and type information.

Hungarian Notation

Hungarian notation was invented by Charles Simonyi, a distinguished programmer of Hungarian origin, at Microsoft. In Hungarian notation, a variable name is used to indicate variable type, intended use, or even scope. The variable name is composed of a prefix containing additional type information and a variable name as such — for example, strName, meaning a string variable containing the name information.

An elaborate list of abbreviations had to be developed and documented for this purpose. These abbreviations were then combined to make identifier prefixes for names. For example, piszMessage is assembled from p-i-sz-Message and means a (p) pointer to an (i) index into an array of (sz) null-terminated strings (Message) containing message information.

In pre-.NET Microsoft tools such as Visual C++ or Visual Basic, Hungarian notation was a part of Microsoft's official programming guidelines and was considered a good practice by the general programming community. You typically saw a lot of variables named things like lblName or btnSave, where the lbl prefix stood for "label" and btn stood for "button."

When Hungarian notation was invented, programmers had to worry about type safety because operations performed on incompatible types were a major source of bugs. Type information contained in the variable name helped programmers with type safety.

However, this approach also had a number of drawbacks. The list of abbreviations soon grew unmanageable, and the abbreviations were often difficult to memorize and pronounce. Because the logical letter combination was often already taken, some other combination, poorly associated with the term it represented, had to be used. Furthermore, if the underlying type changed, unless the name changed also, the type information conveyed would be false.

Today, Hungarian notation is widely considered obsolete. Compilers check type compatibility and ensure type safety; IDEs with IntelliSense and other Visual Studio capabilities are much more powerful for conveying type information and providing type safety. (The exception, of course, is unsafe code in C#. When using pointer arithmetic, you cannot count on a compiler safety net.)

Good Communication: Choosing the Right Words

When choosing names, always bear in mind one thing: The code you are writing is to be read by other people. It has to be easy to understand, informative, simple, and consistent, and it should follow the rule of least surprise. This way, another person will easily be able to change the code, understand it, and become a part of the team. In addition, unless you have infinite memory, you will find that good naming practices pay off even with code that you wrote yourself. This section discusses some guidelines for making your source code informative.

Using the Problem Domain Vocabulary As a Source for Identifier Names

Try to use the words from the problem domain that are already part of the common vocabulary on the project as a basis for naming the elements in your code. This way, a more direct link between the source code and the requirements is established, and the purpose of certain elements in your code is easily understood.

If you go back to Chapter 2 and the Calories Calculator sample application, you can see that single words like `Patient`, and compound words like `WeightInPounds` and `DailyCaloriesRecommended`, are used. These are all terms that are clearly and easily related to the specific issue addressed by this application: recommending a daily caloric intake.

As your code evolves, more complex design is introduced, and terms from the problem domain might not suffice to explain your intent. However, there is one more domain that is easily understood by anyone who needs to read or change the source, and this is the solution domain.

Using the Solution Domain Vocabulary As a Source for Identifier Names

A typical programmer understands common programming terms and paradigms from computer science and software development, so algorithms, patterns, some mathematical terms, and common programming idioms won't raise any eyebrows when used in your code. There is no more than a slim chance that anyone but professional programmers will ever look inside the code. Even so, it is quite possible that you will have more than one layer of design in your code, and internal implementation details can often be easily explained in solution domain terms.

Choosing One Word to Represent One Meaning in a Consistent Manner

Another important characteristic of well-written source code is consistently applied names. While a rich vocabulary can enhance the creations of a poet, in software you have different values. A single name should be employed to indicate a single concept. Even if the same name can serve well for some other concept, choose another word, because any ambiguity in your code adversely affects its ability to communicate. When applying this guideline, you have to be much stricter than any natural language.

Choosing Words That You Can Easily Pronounce and Memorize

You will often discuss your code with your teammates, so make life easy for everyone and choose names that are easy to pronounce. This guideline is related to the one that recommends avoiding Hungarian notation and abbreviations, and the acronyms this notation is so keen on: Those are naturally more difficult to pronounce. Conversely, excessively long names are more difficult to memorize. You no longer face the problem programmers used to have when different environments limited the number of characters they could use to name a variable, or when long names had a visible impact on memory consumption, but try to avoid excessively long names for simplicity's sake.

Using Nouns and Verbs Consistently

Words have a specific role in any natural language. For example, you use nouns to denote a person, place, or thing, whereas you use verbs to express action or occurrence. The role of words in natural language can be compared to role of elements in programming language. You generally use methods to express actions, and classes and properties to indicate someone or something performing the action.

As a general rule, use nouns for object and class names, and use verbs to name methods. You can use nouns or adjectives to name properties.

Express Intent, Not Implementation

When I informally polled my colleagues, most of them identified information and implementation hiding as the direct benefits of encapsulation. Take a look at this class, for example:

```
public class FallingBody
{
    private const double  g = 9.8;

    private DateTime start;

    public void Release() {
        start = DateTime.Now;
    }

    public double CalculateDistance() {
        TimeSpan duration = DateTime.Now - start;
        double t = duration.Seconds;
        return 0.5 * g * Math.Pow(t, 2);
    }
}
```

If I choose to change the start variable's DateTime type to some other type for some reason, I can do so freely without worrying about existing clients, as they will not be affected. Nor do they depend on the constant g; as a matter of fact, they can be oblivious of its existence.

You will learn about encapsulation as a basic characteristic of object-oriented programming in Chapter 7.

Mentioned less frequently, though, is the effect that encapsulation has on wider development and even mental processes. When you program, you often use classes from libraries and components that someone else programmed. While doing so, you assume the role of a *client*, meaning you interact with the visible surface (or *interface*) of the class in question. You generally won't look into the internals of the class you are using.

When debugging, for example, you generally avoid "stepping into" the code of the class you are using even if you have the source code at your disposal. This is only practical; someone else is providing the class, so they should be responsible for it. Of course, in some more difficult (not to say desperate) situations, while chasing some elusive bug, you might actually start debugging provider class code, but this is generally an unpleasant exception to the rule.

Further benefits from encapsulation are obtained from the effect it has on your mental process. For a given method, you may not know the algorithm used or the implementation details, but you will still be able to invoke it and use it correctly. For example when you write

```
image.Rotate(180);
```

you can pretty much immediately visualize in your mind the effect this line will have. Were you to replace this single line with several lines of code used to implement it, code would immediately become more complex to use, to change, and even to think about.

In order to benefit the most from encapsulation, you should consider all of these aforementioned arguments. Going back to our `FallingBody` example, imagine you have named `calculateDistance` method like this:

```
CalculateDistanceWithClassicEquationUsingDateTimeForTimespanMeasurementAnd9pt8asgValue
```

Such a name would open up a wealth of internal implementation details to client programmers, but would they really benefit from it? I'd say that the effect is hardly positive. Now, what used to be a simple calculation behind a method call has suddenly become a complex issue provoking a number of questions:

- ❏   What is a Classic Equation?
- ❏   What is the precision of time measurements with the `DateTime` class?
- ❏   Is 9.8 the right value of the gravitational acceleration constant?

If you are working for NASA, then all of these questions are valid, but then you are not likely to use the code in this example. Even then, the implementation information belongs to class or library documentation and not to a method name.

Implementation details as a part of public names become even less purposeful when you put polymorphism into a picture. Imagine that a system also contemplates a `FallingBodyWithParachute` class that inherits `FallingBody` class and overrides the `CalculateDistanceWithClassicEquation` method with behavior that `FallingBodyWithParachute` would display. How do you express implementation details in the `calculateDistance` method name of the `FallingBodyWithParachute` class and preserve polymorphic behavior? In order for this class to be used polymorphically, method names and signatures of polymorphic methods in both the parent and child class have to be the same. Simple `CalculateDistance` suddenly seems to be a much better choice of name for the method.

You should spare the client programmer all internal implementation details and use names to communicate your intent. This simplifies the client programmer's job and makes your code readable and enjoyable to use.

Choosing Names in Inheritance Hierarchies

When working with class inheritance hierarchies, you will often come across a pattern: an interface at the root of the hierarchy implemented by an abstract class, which provides some basic implementation at the same time.

The benefit of such a pattern is that you have managed to preserve full flexibility and at the same time obtain optimum reuse. In case you are not happy with the functionality the abstract class provides, you are free to provide a completely new implementation by writing your own class that implements the root interface. If, however, that abstract class provides some useful behavior, your implementation can extend the abstract class.

Some hierarchies in the .NET framework are constructed in this way. Take a look at the interface `IStream`, the abstract `Stream` class, and implementing the `BufferedStream`, `MemoryStream`, or `FileStream` classes from the `System.IO` namespace shown in Figure 6-1.

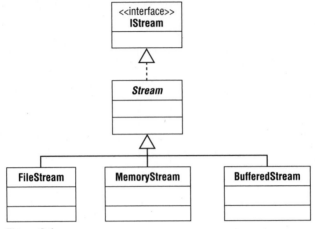

Figure 6-1

There is one lucky consequence of prefixing interfaces with "I" in .NET. When choosing names in such hierarchies, you can have both the root interface and the abstract root class share the same name, with the interface prefixed with "I," as in IStream and Stream. For classes further down in the hierarchy, you should qualify each class with its distinctive role, which expresses how the class specializes the superclass, and how it can be differentiated from the rest of its siblings (just like the File, Memory, and Buffered prefixes in the example). Avoid using names that do not help in differentiating implementing classes, such as ConcreteStream or StreamImpl.

You should follow this rule in any inheritance hierarchy, not only those with an interface and abstract class at the top. Finding good class names is far from easy, and you may not find the best solution right at the outset. That is why the next refactoring solution I am going to talk about is so important.

Rename Refactoring

In a perfect world you would get these things right the first time. However, you often won't choose the best names for your code the first time around; and if you come up with a better name, there is no reason not to change it.

Since the advent of refactoring tools, the once tedious task of searching for all the invocations of a piece of code in order to replace an old name with a new name has been reduced to only a few clicks of the mouse.

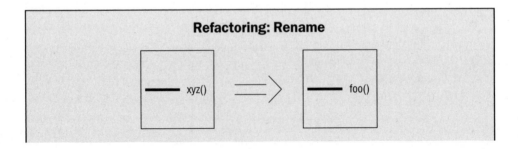

Motivation

Poorly chosen names prevent the code from communicating with the programmer. It makes it difficult to understand the purpose of the code and to establish the link between the problem domain and the code. This makes maintenance work a lot more difficult, as it is hard to find the spot in the code that needs to be modified. It can even result in code duplication and poor reuse, as the purpose of the existing code was not clear. In order to avoid these code shortcomings, you can use Rename refactoring.

Related Smells

Use Rename refactoring to eliminate the Unrevealing Names smell or to rename elements that do not comply with general naming guidelines.

Mechanics

Change the name of the element that suffers from Unrevealing Name smell. Then search for all the code that invokes the recently changed element and rename it as well. When using tools, this step is automated.

Before

```
public class FemalePatient:Patient{

    // ...

    //The name DailyCalRec uses abbreviations
    //and does not communicate very well
    public decimal DailyCalRec(){
        return 655 + (4.3 * WeightInPounds) +
        (4.7 * HeightInInches) - (4.7 * Age);
    }
}

[TestFixture]
public class TestFemalePatient{
    // ...
    [Test]
    public void TestDailyCaloriesRecommended(){
        FemalePatient femalePatient = new  FemalePatient();
        femalePatient.Height = 72;
        femalePatient.Weight = 110;
        femalePatient.Age = 30;
        decimal expectedResult = 1015.2;
        //The method DailyCalRec is invoked here
        decimal realResult =  femalePatient.DailyCalRec();
        Assert.AreEqual(expectedResult, realResult);
    }
}
```

After

```
public class FemalePatient:Patient{
```

Continued

```
// ...

    public decimal DailyCaloriesRecommended(){
        return 655 + (4.3 * WeightInPounds) +
        (4.7 * HeightInInches) - (4.7 * Age);
    }
}

[TestFixture]
public class TestFemalePatient{
    // ...
    [Test]
    public void TestDailyCaloriesRecommended(){
        FemalePatient femalePatient = new  FemalePatient();
        femalePatient.Height = 72;
        femalePatient.Weight = 110;
        femalePatient.Age = 30;
        decimal expectedResult = 1015.2;
        //The method DailyCalRec is invoked here
        decimal realResult =  femalePatient.DailyCaloriesRecommended();
        Assert.AreEqual(expectedResult, realResult);
    }
}
```

Rename Refactoring in Visual Studio

You can perform Rename refactoring on any identifier in your code. You select the identifier either by placing the cursor over it or by selecting it in the source code editor. In the class view, you select the identifier to be renamed in the same way; the selected element in the diagram will be marked by a blue color in the case of class member and by a gray frame in the case of type (class, interface, and so on). Then, you can select Rename Refactoring from the context menu or from the Refactoring main menu item in Visual Studio. Figure 6-2 illustrates Rename refactoring selected in the context menu using the calculateDistance method, and changing its name to the correct Pascal case naming convention.

Once you click the Rename menu item, you are presented with the dialog in which you can enter a new name for an identifier and select some of the Rename refactoring options. Figure 6-3 shows the Rename dialog.

Here is what each of the offered options means:

❑ **Preview reference changes**: If you select this option, Visual Studio will next display the refactoring preview window. In this window you will be able to preview all changes in all the files that Rename refactoring will provoke.

❑ **Search in comments**: If you select this option, Rename refactoring will search comments for the identifier in question and rename the identifier inside comments as well. Be careful when using this feature, as the search performed is a simple text search, so you will be better off confirming these renames in the preview window.

❑ **Search in strings**: When this option is selected, Visual Studio will also search string literals in code inside your project for a match. Again, because search is textual, a preview is advised.

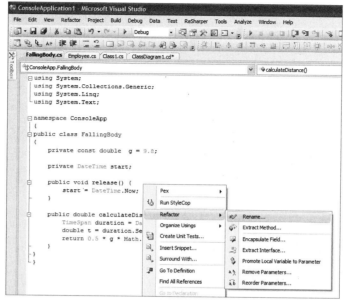

Figure 6-2

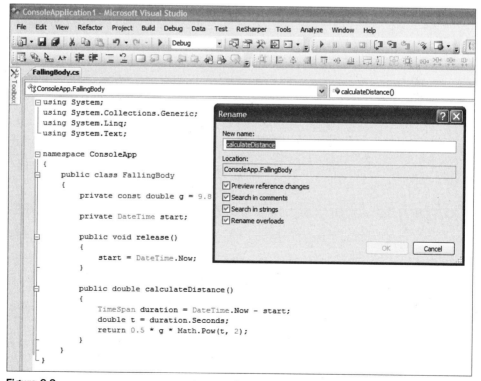

Figure 6-3

❏ **Rename overloads**: This option is displayed when renaming methods only. If you select this option, Visual Studio will rename all overrides and all overloads of the method you are renaming.

If you choose to preview changes, you are presented with the Preview Changes dialog, shown in Figure 6-4.

Rename refactoring is fairly intelligent. It will warn you of possible conflicts the rename might provoke. It is also intelligent enough to rename overrides and overloads when renaming methods. However, it is not perfect. Dialog windows can, for example, be tedious. At least in the beginning and until you get the hang of it (and always when in doubt), it is advisable to go through the Preview Changes dialog.

Published and Public Interfaces

One of the reasons for the great popularity of COM-based tools and technologies was the component paradigm. *Components* are reusable binaries with well-defined interfaces. C++ and Visual Basic programmers quickly learned how to make use of the ready-made COM components, which provided an enormous productivity boost. The components also provided new opportunities for reuse and encapsulation, which raised programming in VB to a new level of rapid application development (RAD). Two great features of COM technology were the ability to create custom components in C++ and VB and to develop and use components across languages, which enabled VB programmers to use components developed in C++, and vice versa.

While component technology in COM was a great advancement, programmers had to treat some issues with care when using or creating components. For example, if the interface of a component was replaced with a new version, the compatibility between the component and the client would break, and replacing the old version with the new version of the component would result in an application breaking down.

At the base of any component technology are the interfaces. Here I define the word *interface* in broad terms as anything exposed by the component to the outside world. Interfaces help you define the contract specifying how you can communicate with a certain component. C# also supports an interface as a language construct, wherein the contract is explicitly defined and separate from the implementation. While you can change the interface in a self-contained application with minimum consequences, the same operation with reusable modules can have far-reaching effects.

Self-Contained Applications versus Reusable Modules

When programming, you can roughly categorize the project you're working on into one of two groups, based on the reach of your code:

❏ **Self-contained applications** use code only in the context of the current application, nowhere else. It also means that you have in reach the client code of any class or other construct used in the code. For example, if you need to modify a method's signature, you can find all invocations of the method and change them accordingly so the code does not break.

❏ **Reusable modules** are components and libraries that were created to be used by others in many different projects. In this case, you generally do not have any idea of the client code that is using your component or library; and it isn't possible for you to modify it. When releasing new versions of these components or libraries, you have to act with utmost care in order not to break the compatibility of existing applications. When breaking compatibility with previous versions cannot be avoided, because ultimately all projects have to evolve, a clear upgrade path and versioning policy must be provided.

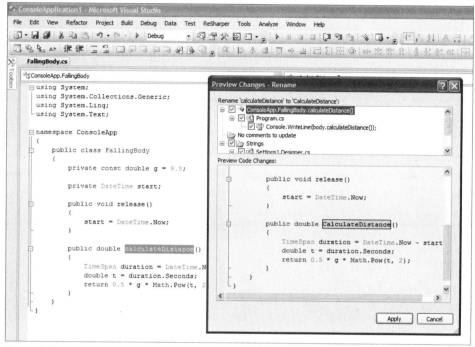

Figure 6-4

You can observe the difference between the two categories by comparing the direction of dependencies between the assemblies depicted in Figure 6-5.

When you deal with any private element, such as a field or a method, you can be sure that any changes you perform are not far-reaching. You can easily find any invocation or reference to a private method or field and fix the problem that this change has caused.

Even when changing a public element in a self-contained application, you can be confident that in the end you'll be able to fix any problem caused by the change. However, when changing public elements in reusable modules, you can't anticipate the cascading effect of change you might provoke. This means you have to develop a good versioning plan and a clear versioning policy for your product. Failure to do so can place clients in a very frustrating position.

> **Definition:** A *published interface* consists of all public elements from your reusable assembly whose changes can provoke effects you are not able to control, because you do not have access to the client code making use of the assembly.

Imagine that in order to add some new functionality, you are shipping a new version that has fixed a few bugs but has also broken the backward compatibility of your reusable component. A few clients will make use of the new functionality offered in a new version and will modify their code, rebuilding their projects in order to do so. So far, so good. However, although all your clients will probably try to make use of the new version in order to resolve the bugs you have fixed, some will do so without rebuilding the project, but rather by simply reconfiguring the application.

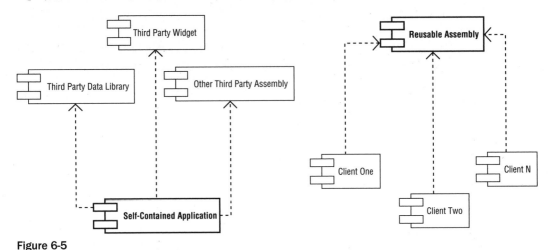

Figure 6-5

Check out the "Redirecting Assembly Versions" article in MSDN to see how applications can be reconfigured to make use of newer versions of assemblies. You can find the article here: `http://msdn.microsoft.com/en-us/library/7wd6ex19.aspx.`

If clients try to simply replace the old version with the new one — without rebuilding client applications after applying changes in the source code where needed — the upgrade will fail miserably.

It is worth noting that in .NET you can have multiple versions of assemblies registered side by side. When the client application that is making use of these assemblies is built, it is linked to a specific version. If you then install a new version, the original client application will continue to work with the original version of the assembly. In pre-.NET components based on COM technology, the newer version of the component replaced the old one. In cases where the compatibility between versions of the component was broken, a host of problems, also known as *DLL hell* ensued, resulting in broken applications.

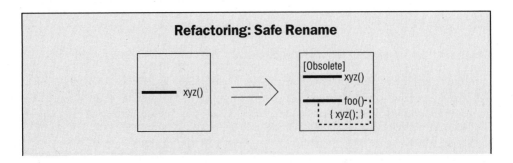

Motivation

The basic motivation for this refactoring is the same as that for the simple Rename refactoring: making code communicate its purpose and respecting the naming guidelines. However, in this case you are dealing with an element that belongs to the published interface, and you cannot reach all invocations of this element. You need to perform the renaming in a safe way.

Related Smells

Use this refactoring to eliminate the Unrevealing Names smell or to rename elements that do not comply with general naming guidelines.

Mechanics

This refactoring is generally performed on methods and properties. It is performed in a few consecutive steps:

1. Declare the method or property in your class with the same signature as the targeted method and give it a new, improved name.

2. Cut the code from the original method or property and paste it into a newly created method with an improved name.

3. Make the original method or property delegate the call to the newly created method.

4. Mark the original method with ObsoleteAttribute and the System.Component Model.EditorBrowsable(EditorBrowsableState.Never) attribute. ObsoleteAttribute marks the invocation code of the original method with a warning, while EditorBrowsable(EditorBrowsableState.Never) hides the original method from IntelliSense.

Before

```
public class FemalePatient:Patient{

    // ...

    //The name DailyCalRec uses abbreviations
    //and does not communicate very well
    public decimal DailyCalRec(){
        return 655 + (4.3 * WeightInPounds) +
        (4.7 * HeightInInches) - (4.7 * Age);
    }
}

[TestFixture]
public class TestFemalePatient{
    // ...
    [Test]
    public void TestDailyCaloriesRecommended(){
        FemalePatient femalePatient = new  FemalePatient();
        femalePatient.Height = 72;
```

Continued

```
                femalePatient.Weight = 110;
                femalePatient.Age = 30;
                decimal expectedResult = 1015.2;
                //The method DailyCalRec is invoked here
                decimal realResult = femalePatient.DailyCalRec();
                Assert.AreEqual(expectedResult, realResult);
            }
        }
```

After

```
    public class FemalePatient:Patient{

    // ...

        [ObsoleteAttribute("This method has been renamed." +
        "Use DailyCaloriesRecommended instead")]
        [EditorBrowsable(EditorBrowsableState.Never)]
        public decimal DailyCalRec(){
            return DailyCaloriesRecommended();
        }

        public decimal DailyCaloriesRecommended(){
            return 655 + (4.3 * WeightInPounds) +
            (4.7 * HeightInInches) - (4.7 * Age);
        }
    }

    [TestFixture]
    public class TestFemalePatient{
        // ...
        [Test]
        public void TestDailyCaloriesRecommended(){
            FemalePatient femalePatient = new  FemalePatient();
            femalePatient.Height = 72;
            femalePatient.Weight = 110;
            femalePatient.Age = 30;
            decimal expectedResult = 1015.2;
            //The method DailyCalRec is invoked here
           decimal realResult = femalePatient.DailyCaloriesRecommended();
            Assert.AreEqual(expectedResult, realResult);
        }
    }
```

Modifying the Published Interfaces

You can use certain tactics to minimize the ripple effect of changes in reusable assemblies. Refactoring enables you to change code freely, but in the case of published interfaces you have to conduct yourself in a more conservative manner. This means that published interfaces should be well thought out, built to last, and as extensible as possible.

Keeping Interfaces Stable and Lean

In this case it is necessary to do a little bit of planning and to try to anticipate how the module might look in the future. This is a tricky thing to do, but making reusable components is not easy. In addition, bear in mind the open-closed principle (mentioned later in the sidebar "Object-Oriented Design Principle: Open-Closed Principle"): Keep your assemblies open for extension and closed for change.

Publishing As Little and As Late As Possible

In a way, the open-closed principle is an extension of the encapsulation principle discussed in Chapter 5: Keep the scope and access level of different elements to a bare minimum. Because every development process is susceptible to changes in requirements and design, postponing the publishing date as long as possible increases your probability of publishing a more mature and stable version of your software.

In addition, avoid publishing inside the team that has access to the same code base, because it will slow down your development and make it less agile.

Implementing and Adhering to Versioning Policies

In .NET, you should use assembly version information to communicate version data. The important part of assembly version information is the assembly version number. This is the number used by the .NET runtime to bind assemblies together. Once the assembly is built referencing one specific version of another assembly, it uses this same version of the collaborating assembly at runtime. In .NET, multiple versions of an assembly can exist in parallel (something not possible with COM DLLs). If necessary, assemblies can be redirected to use other versions of collaborating assemblies by means of configuration files, machine configuration files, or publisher policy files.

The format of an assembly version number is as follows:

```
[major version].[minor version].[build number].[revision]
```

Your versioning policy should convey information about the amount of changes that each version brings. The client should always be able to conclude from version information whether the new version is compatible with the previous one. Here is a sample policy that you might follow.

- ❑ **Different build numbers**: Compatible; no changes to published interfaces allowed
- ❑ **Different minor versions**: Backwardly compatible; additive; nonbreaking changes to published interfaces and making elements obsolete allowed
- ❑ **Different major versions**: No compatibility guaranteed

Table 6-2 shows some examples of compatibility between versions. A "No" in the "Is Compatible" column means that the two versions are not guaranteed to be compatible, although they may be compatible by coincidence.

Using "Safe" Refactorings When Performing Changes

When you perform safe refactorings, the new version of the code is kept compatible with the previous version, but the modified element is declared obsolete. All the work is delegated to a new element. This means that all client code continues to operate as before, but users are warned that certain elements are to be discarded in the near future. For the mechanics of safe refactorings, take a look at the Safe Rename refactoring discussion earlier in the chapter.

Table 6-2: Compatibility between Different Versions of an Assembly

Original Version	New Version	Is Compatible
1.5.1254.0	1.5.2311.0	Yes
1.5.1254.0	1.5.0000.0	Yes
1.8.1114.0	1.9.1114.0	Yes
1.8.1114.0	1.7.1114.0	No
2.1.2325.0	3.0.1.2990.0	No
2.1.2325.0	1.5.8856.0	No

Announcing Your Changes

By using ObsoleteAttribute, you can communicate to your users the decision to eliminate certain elements in the near future. If you do this in timely manner, you give them the opportunity to prepare for modifications and avoid the surprise and confusion produced by abrupt changes to published interfaces. Never use exceptions for this purpose. Exceptions artificially maintain versions as compatible, but applications break unexpectedly at runtime. You can recognize this incorrect use of exceptions when you see a method that has only a single statement, one that is throwing an exception under any circumstances in which that method might be called.

Thinking About Extensibility

When you are making reusable components — because refactoring can't be performed as freely as usual — you should give more thought to design than you usually do. The following sections discuss three examples of typical choices you can make when designing your components, and how they affect extensibility.

Fields versus Properties

If you use public fields instead of properties, you cannot change the underlying representation of the data or add data-validation routines if it later becomes necessary. You have to change a field to a property, and that is a change that breaks binary compatibility between versions of published interfaces. This said, remember that the best option is to keep your field completely private when possible. Not all of an object's necessary data has to be visible from the outside.

Interface versus Abstract Class

The main difference between the interface and the abstract class in C# is that the abstract class can also hold implementation for a method that is not marked as abstract. This leads to an interesting afterthought: If you add a new method to an abstract class and provide it with the default implementation, then you keep the code compatible with the original version.

However, if you add a method to an interface, all classes implementing this interface have to be changed, because the newly added method has to be implemented somewhere along the hierarchy.

Hiding versus Overriding

Remember that in order to achieve polymorphic behavior, you must override elements in the base class. That means those elements have to be declared virtual in the first place. Consequently, if you are not sure whether you or someone else might need to override some method or property, you should declare it virtual just in case, unless you have compelling reasons not to do so.

If you are unsure about how hiding and overriding work in C#, take a look at the article "Versioning with the Override and New Keywords (C# Programming Guide)" on MSDN: http://msdn.microsoft.com/en-us/library/6fawty39.aspx.

Object-Oriented Design Principle: Open-Closed Principle

Change is a prevalent force in software development and there is no use fighting it. New and changing requirements are the order of the day for any typical software development shop. Changes present problems when they start producing an uncontrolled ripple effect inside your code, wreaking havoc and unexpectedly breaking code or introducing bugs in the least expected manner.

If you are able to write code in such a manner that new features can be written as additions that don't require you to compile the original assembly again, you can be sure that no change has been introduced into the assembly.

Definition

According to Bertrand Meyer, in *Object-Oriented Software Construction* (Prentice Hall, 1988), "software entities (classes, modules, functions, etc.) should be open for extension, but closed for modification."

Let's examine this definition.

First, you should understand what is meant by "closed for modification." When you create a piece of software, you need to go through the significant effort of analyzing the problem, gathering the requirements, designing the software, implementing the solution, and testing the result. Each time you introduce a change to your code, you have to repeat more or less the same cycle. If not, you risk shipping software that is fraught with bugs. Therefore, once you ship your assembly, you should try not to modify it unless you need to fix a bug. This is what is meant by "closed for modification."

However, you need to be able to respond to requests for new features. The solution is to be able to extend the behavior of your assembly. This is why entities should be "open for extension."

The way to achieve this in object-oriented software is through abstraction. The "client" class should always depend on the abstraction, not on the concrete implementation.

This way, you can modify the client and add new functionality by creating new implementations of the abstraction. In C#, you generally use interfaces and abstract classes to express these abstractions. An example will demonstrate how this works in more concrete terms.

Definition

Recall from Chapter 2 that at one point my `Patient` class had a host of *Man and *Woman methods. For example, if I wanted to calculate the recommended daily amount

Continued

of calories for a male patient, I'd call the `DailyCaloriesRecommendedMan` method. For a female patient, I'd call `DailyCaloriesRecommendedWoman`. I also created the `PatientHistoryXMLStorage` class to take care of the persistence functionality of the application. I generated XML to save patient data. Had I kept the *Man and *Woman methods, I would have had to program an XML generation routine like the following (fragment shown):

```
"<dailyCaloriesRecommended>" +
(patient.Gender == Gender.Male ?
patient.DailyCaloriesRecommendedMale.ToString() :
patient.DailyCaloriesRecommendedFemale.ToString()) +
"</dailyCaloriesRecommended>"
```

The problem with this code is that it is not open for extension. Suppose I wanted to later to add new functionality to my application so that it could calculate a recommended daily amount of calories for child patients. The only solution would be to modify `PatientHistoryXMLStorage`'s XML-generation routine by changing the ternary operator for a longer if-else statement:

```
decimal dailyCaloriesRecommended = 0;
if (patient.Gender == Gender.Male)
{
    dailyCaloriesRecommended =
        patient.DailyCaloriesRecommendedMale;
}
else if (patient.Gender == Gender.Female)
{
    dailyCaloriesRecommended =
        patient.DailyCaloriesRecommendedFemale;
}
else if (patient.Gender == Gender.Child)
{
    dailyCaloriesRecommended =
        patient.DailyCaloriesRecommendedChild;
}
//...
"<dailyCaloriesRecommended>" +
    dailyCaloriesRecommended +
    "</dailyCaloriesRecommended>"
//...
```

I have implemented new functionality, but it is more complicated than necessary and error prone. Moreover, I had to modify and rebuild the original assembly, exactly what we should try to avoid according to the open-closed principle.

Fortunately, I spent some time refactoring my application so that by the end of Chapter 2, the XML-generation routine looked like this:

```
//...
"<dailyCaloriesRecommended>" +
    patient.DailyCaloriesRecommended +
    "</dailyCaloriesRecommended>"
//...
```

The `patient` variable references the instance of either `MalePatient` or `FemalePatient`. In both cases, the code of the XML-generation routine is the same. This is possible because both the `MalePatient` and `FemalePatient` classes are extending the common parent class, `Patient`, and the routine was programmed to an abstraction, not to an implementation. Now suppose I need to calculate a recommended daily amount of calories for child patients. All I need to do is add another class to my project: `ChildPatient`. This class, just like `MalePatient` and `FemalePatient`, needs to extend the common abstraction, the `Patient` class:

```
public class ChildPatient:Patient
```

The variable `patient` in this case points to an instance of `ChildPatient`, and the XML-generation routine is left untouched. This means that the code is open for extension.

Rename and Safe Rename Refactoring in the Rent-a-Wheels Application

With just a very superficial visual analysis, you can see a number of obvious flaws in the naming practices for the Rent-a-Wheels application code. The mix of abbreviations and Hungarian notation used in the code means you have to perform extensive code modifications. Table 6-3 shows some of the Rename refactorings that need to be performed.

Table 6-3: Rename Refactoring and the Rent-a-Wheels Application

Original Name	New Name
FrmRt	VehicleRental
FrmCat	VehicleCategoriesMaintenance
oCn	connection
oCmd	command
oAdapter	adapter
txtName	BranchName
FrmBranch_Load	BranchMaintenance_Load

Most of this refactoring work goes smoothly, but keep the following in mind:

❑ When you rename a control or a form in Visual Studio, event-handling routines are not updated. You must rename event-handling routines manually. For example, you must manually change the name `btnCancel_Click` to `cancel_Click` after the form `btnCancel` is renamed `cancel`.

❑   Sometimes local variable names can clash with field names. In that case you can resolve the naming conflict either by qualifying the field with `this`, as in `this.branches = branches.Tables[0]`, or by choosing different names for fields and local variables, as in `this.branches = data.Tables[0]`.

Because Rent-a-Wheels is a self-contained executable, there is no need to use Safe Rename refactoring.

Summary

You have seen in this chapter how there is more to names than you might think at first. They help you establish the link between the problem domain and the source. In order for this link to be effective, it is important to formalize the language you are using in the project through a common vocabulary; and because you will rarely get things just right the first time around, you can use Rename refactoring to correct and improve the word choices you have made in your code.

You obtain further benefits in code comprehensibility and maintainability by consistent naming practices. To this end, always follow C# and .NET naming conventions and guidelines. A much more complex issue is the right words to employ when writing code. Try to base your word choice on problem and solution domains, stick with a single meaning for each word, and use each word to represent a single concept in your code. In addition, try to create names that are easy to memorize and pronounce.

When dealing with reusable assemblies, you do not have the same freedom with your code that you do when working on self-contained projects. While you are still free to change the underlying implementation, any change to the interface used by others can result in numerous problems for clients. You cannot assume that clients should rebuild and modify their applications with each release you perform. Instead, you need to clearly identify published interfaces, those that are freely exposed to users of your reusable assemblies. You must deal with such interfaces with utmost care, always announcing incoming changes before implementing them, respecting versioning policies, performing refactorings safely, and designing the code in such a way that it can withstand the changes and is open for extensibility.

In the next chapter you'll dive right into the world of object orientation, including its basic principles and some very common refactorings that will enable you to efficiently combat complex and unstructured code on the method level.

7

The Method Extraction Remedy for Duplicated Code

In this chapter you will go back to the basics of object-oriented (OO) principles:

❑ **Encapsulation:** You have certainly heard of encapsulation, but the benefits of encapsulation, like those of information and implementation hiding, are not automatically obtained. Nor can you guarantee them by using OO-capable language.

❑ **Method extraction:** You will also investigate the simplest form of encapsulation: a function. The same principles that can be used to improve function organization can be used with methods. You will see why long methods are problematic and how they can be improved by method extraction.

❑ **Duplicated code:** Next, you will face the dark side of programming in its worst form: duplicated code. You will see how duplicated code is potentially disastrous and why you should try to avoid it. You will also see how even simple refactoring, such as the Extract Method, can go a long way toward avoiding code duplication.

❑ **Magic literals:** Finally, you will take a look at one of the oldest ailments from which your code can suffer: magic literals. Fortunately, you are going to learn about the remedy and how magic literals can be replaced with constants and enumerations.

Encapsulating Code and Hiding the Details

You may have heard that encapsulation is the first pillar of object orientation, but encapsulation in software did not start with object orientation. It was actually invented a long time before that.

In the very early days of programming, people noticed that certain patterns of instructions repeated themselves many times in the code. In those days, computer memory was a limited resource, so putting these instructions in only one place could result in significant memory savings. Soon programmers were putting those instructions together instead of writing them each time they were needed, and calling them by a single name, the *subroutine*.

Very soon, an interesting side effect was noticed: Subroutines made the code easier for programmers to grasp. Since the human brain is also limited in memory and in the number of ideas it can process, hiding certain details from a direct view had the very positive result of simplifying the code for the programmer. A program could be composed of smaller units, thus making it easier to tackle complex problems, which could also be decomposed. This was much more convenient than using control flow and numerous GOTO statements for the same purpose, which can produce very complex, tangled code, called *spaghetti code*, that is difficult to understand and follow.

> **Definition:** *Spaghetti code* has a complex and tangled control structure resulting from extensive use of GOTOs and other unstructured constructs. Such code is very difficult to read, understand, debug, modify, test, and maintain.

Code like this inspired what is probably one of the most famous essays in software literature, "Go To Statement Considered Harmful," by Edsger Dijkstra.

A few other benefits also resulted from use of the subroutine:

- ❏ Improved reuse resulted in better productivity, because the same solution for a certain problem could be used repeatedly. Improved reuse meant less code and less duplication.

- ❏ Readability of the code was improved, because chunks of code could be given human-readable names. This enabled programmers to establish a link between the code and the problem domain. (Chapter 6 covers the benefits of establishing a link between the code and the problem domain.)

- ❏ Because you can reference a piece of code by its name, encapsulation means there's no need to know any details of its implementation, which is generally referred to as *information and implementation hiding*.

Information and Implementation Hiding

If a chunk of code can receive parameters and return values, then it can be observed from the outside as a unit that receives input, does some processing, and produces the desired output. When viewing the code from the outside, you are not concerned about implementation details; all you need to know about the function is its interface or the public part. You don't need to know any implementation details, such as which operations or local variables the method is using. Simply put, to use the function you need to know the declaration, but you don't need to know anything about the body of the function. For example, consider a function that returns a sorted array of Account objects:

```
public static Account[] sort(Account[] account)
```

You don't need to know which sort of algorithm was used by the programmer who implemented the method. That programmer may have used bubblesort, quicksort, heapsort, or any other algorithm.

Thankfully, in order for you to get your sorted array of the Account object, you don't need to know any of these algorithms or even whether any of them has been used. Without having to write this code, or even understand it, you can still use it and profit from it. (Of course, as an accomplished programmer, you should be familiar with these sorting algorithms.)

Moreover, if the encapsulated code needs to be changed later, you do not have to change any other parts of your code; the change is successfully localized. (This is only true as long as you do not change any parts of the interface.) This effectively minimizes the possible ripple effect of changes in your code.

Encapsulation and information and implementation hiding have more sophisticated meanings in object-oriented programming. You will learn more about these topics in Chapter 11, but you should first take a look at how it all works on a procedural level.

In order to organize your code in the form of well-structured, well-encapsulated methods that are easy to use, reuse, and understand, you should apply certain heuristics, as described next.

Refactoring: Extract Method

Motivation

Small, well-named, granular methods will benefit your code in a number of ways:

- **Better code comprehension:** You can easily understand the purpose of the few instructions in the code without getting bogged down with implementation details.

- **Increased reuse:** There is a greater probability for more granular methods to be reused.

- **Minimized code duplication:** With more effective reuse, code duplication is minimized.

- **Encapsulation of code:** You don't necessarily need to understand how a method is programmed in order to use it.

- **Changes can be performed in isolation:** As long as the public part of a method is not changed, the body of the method can be changed without a ripple effect on the rest of the code.

- **Methods can be unit-tested:** If you test large methods, the benefits of unit testing are reduced. You may be able to detect the error, but you will still have to determine where exactly the error was produced.

- **Describe code better than comments:** Comments can easily become obsolete. Because the comments do not have any effect during execution, it is very easy

Continued

---

to change the code but forget to change the comments. Such old comments are misleading and counterproductive.

This is one of the most basic and most common refactorings, and it is performed often. It is essential for simplifying your code and making it easier to maintain and comprehend.

Related Smells

Use this refactoring to eliminate Long Method, Duplicated Code, and Comments smells.

Mechanics

There are no strict definitions for a long method, but as soon as a method is doing more than one thing or the comments are used to explain what a section of the method is doing there is a pretty good chance the method is longer than it should be. If you can see that certain sections of code repeat themselves in more than one place, it is time to decompose the method by means of method extraction. Depending on local variables, this process can be more or less complicated. In its complete form, the process is made up of the following five steps:

1. Identify the section of the original method you will extract to a new method and think of a name that explains the intent well.

2. Declare a new method and then copy the section of code you are extracting to the new method.

3. Search for local variables used only inside the new method and then declare them inside the new method.

4. Search for local variables from the original method that are only read in the new method. These variables should be declared as method parameters.

5. Search for a local variable that has been modified in the extracted section. This value should be returned by the method. If more than one variable is modified in the extracted section, then you need to further simplify the code before performing the extraction. Refer to the Replace Temp with Query and Split Temporary Variable refactorings in Chapter 8 to see how this can be performed.

Local variables can make method extraction much more difficult. Passing too many parameters and returning too many values will result in an unnecessarily complicated method wherein the benefits of extraction are lost. In those cases, you should try to simplify the code before performing an extraction. For example, you can eliminate some local variables by performing Replace Temp with Query and Split Temporary Variable refactoring (see Chapter 8).

Before

```
public string RenderFundsTotalCell()
{
    decimal total;
    foreach (Account account in this.accounts)
    {
```

```
            total += account.Balance;
        }
        string formattedTotal;
        formattedTotal = "<P>Total:<B>" + total.ToString("C") + "</B></P>";
        return "<TD>" + formattedTotal + "</TD>";
    }
```

After

```
    public string RenderFundsTotalCell()
    {
        return "<TD>" + FormatTotal() + "</TD>";
    }

    private decimal CalculateFundsTotal()
    {
        decimal total = 0;
        foreach (Account account in this.accounts)
        {
            total += account.Balance;
        }
        return total;
    }

    private string FormatTotal()
    {
        return "<P>Total:<B>" +
            this.CalculateFundsTotal().ToString("C") +
            "</B></P>";
    }
```

Decomposing Methods

Almost every long method can be decomposed into a number of smaller, more granular methods that are easier to manipulate and that make your code more readable. This process of decomposition of larger methods into smaller ones is called *method extraction*. In order for you to perform this process effectively, extracted methods should contain code that fits well together, performs a meaningful single operation with clearly defined input and output, and is named in such a way that it easily establishes the link with the problem domain.

Circumference Calculation — Long Method Example

There is no clear-cut formula for performing method decomposition, so it is probably best to begin with an example: calculating the circumference of circle given the center coordinates and the coordinates of an arbitrary point on the circumference. You can visualize this by taking a look at Figure 7-1.

When you look at the drawing, the solution to the problem becomes pretty obvious. It comes down to two geometrical formulae. This becomes clear if you decompose the problem into two calculations:

❑   Because you have the coordinates of point C — the circle's center and point P, which is a point on the circumference — you can see that the distance between these two points represents a circle radius. If you calculate the radius, then you can use the following formula to calculate circumference length: circumference $= 2r\pi$.

❑   You can see also see on the diagram that the a, b, and r lines form a right triangle, where r is the hypotenuse. This means that r can be calculated as $r^2 = a^2 + b^2$, according to the Pythagorean theorem.

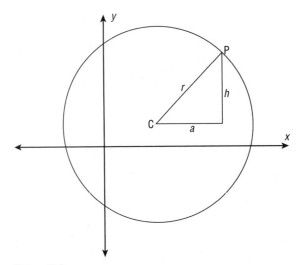

Figure 7-1

Because methods are really quite similar to functions — the difference being that a method is associated with an object and a function is not (more on that in some of the following chapters) — I have programmed the first version of the solution using the static Main function in a procedural style (as shown in Listing 7-1). You will see how you can decompose functions as you start to extract code from static void Main. In Chapter 9, you will see the solution programmed in an object-oriented way.

Listing 7-1: Calculating Circumference Length — Unstructured Example

```
using System;

namespace RefactoringInCSharpAndASP.Chapter7
{
    struct Point
    {
        public double X;
        public double Y;
    }

    class CircleCircumferenceLength
    {
        static void Main(string[] args)
        {

            Point center;
```

```
        Point pointOnCircumference;
        //read center coordinates
        Console.WriteLine("Enter X coordinate " +
            "of circle center");
        center.X = Double.Parse(Console.In.ReadLine());
        Console.WriteLine("Enter Y coordinate " +
            "of circle center");
        center.Y = Double.Parse(Console.In.ReadLine());
        //read some point on circumference coordinates
        Console.WriteLine("Enter X coordinate " +
            "of some point on circumference");
        pointOnCircumference.X =
            Double.Parse(Console.In.ReadLine());
        Console.WriteLine("Enter Y coordinate " +
            "of some point on circumference");
        pointOnCircumference.Y =
            Double.Parse(Console.In.ReadLine());
        //calculate and display the length of circumference
        Console.WriteLine("The length of circle "
            + "circumference is:");
        //calculate the length of circumference
        double radius;
        radius = Math.Sqrt(Math.Pow(pointOnCircumference.X - center.X,
                        2) +
                    Math.Pow(pointOnCircumference.Y - center.Y,
                        2)
                );
        double lengthOfCircumference;
        lengthOfCircumference = 2 * 3.1415 * radius;
        Console.WriteLine(lengthOfCircumference);
        Console.Read();
    }
  }
}
```

If you test this code manually, you will see that it performs the calculation correctly. However, this code is poorly structured and a single method contains all the code used to solve the problem. You can also see that some comments are marking different sections in the code. If you analyze the code further, you can see that some of the code is concerned with communicating with the user for the purposes of obtaining the data for the calculation and displaying the result, while other code is performing the actual calculation. This is an important conclusion that serves as the basis for the function extraction you are going to perform in the next section.

Smell: Long Method

Detecting the Smell

Long methods are easy to detect upon visual inspection. Sheer quantity of lines can be a good starting point. There is no strict rule governing when a method is too long, but if it is doing more than one thing it should be split into several methods. Another certain

Continued

sign that a method is just too long are comments explaining the purpose of certain sections of the method.

Related Refactoring

Use Extract Method refactoring to eliminate this smell.

Rationale

Long methods are difficult to understand, debug, reuse, maintain, and unit test. These problems can be remedied by the extraction of sections of code from the original method into a new, more granular method.

Extracting Circumference Length Calculation Code

You will begin your refactoring of the sample application by moving the code related to mathematical calculation into a separate function. Because this code calculates circumference length, you will declare a new function CalculateCircumferenceLength and copy the code that performs the calculation into the new function. Note that the comment on that section reflects the name I have chosen for the new function. The new function's code is shown in Listing 7-2.

Listing 7-2: Calculating Circumference Length Function Extraction — Steps 1 to 3

```
private static void CalculateCircumferenceLength() {
    double radius;
    radius = Math.Sqrt(Math.Pow(pointOnCircumference.X - center.X,
                        2) +
                        Math.Pow(pointOnCircumference.Y - center.Y,
                        2)
                    );
    double lengthOfCircumference;
    lengthOfCircumference = 2 * 3.1415 * radius;
}
```

Smell: Comments

Detecting the Smell

Code comments are easily detected by visual examination. When you see that the comments are carrying information that should be communicated by code element names, or that this information is superfluous or obsolete, you have detected comments that should be refactored out of your code.

Related Refactoring

Use Extract Method or Rename refactoring to eliminate this smell.

Rationale

The use of comments is traditionally considered a good programming practice for the same reasons that you like to refactor your code — comments help you understand what the code is doing. Sometimes they can even group sections of code together or help you establish a connection between the code and the problem domain. However, comments have one big disadvantage: They are not executed, so they are very prone to becoming obsolete.

You can easily change a piece of code and test the results without remembering to change the comments, and no one will notice. No one, that is, until a trusting mainte- nance programmer tries to understand the code by relying on now obsolete comments. There is probably nothing as frustrating as being led down the wrong path by obsolete comments.

Comments are sometimes used to help explain sections of poorly written code. In those cases, the valid solution lies not in the comments but in refactoring the problematic code.

Instead of relying on comments to explain the purpose your code, use information provided by the names of elements in your code to communicate your intention. This information is always available and is less prone to becoming obsolete.

This does not mean that all forms of comments are bad. For example, XML comments are used to generate documentation, and provide information displayed by IntelliSense and the Object Browser.

As soon as you paste the code, two variables, `pointOnCircumference` and `center`, are marked by the IDE as undeclared. This is because these variables are at the beginning of the `Main()` function. These variables are read inside the `CalculateCircumferenceLength` function, so you need to pass them to the `CalculateCircumferenceLength` function. You can do that by declaring these variables as parameters of the function. Now the declaration of `CalculateCircumferenceLength` looks like this:

```
private static void CalculateCircumferenceLength(
    Point center, Point pointOnCircumference)
```

Using this, the IDE does not report errors anymore.

Now the code compiles correctly, but `CalculateCircumferenceLength` is not really of much use. It calculates the circumference length and stores the value in the `lengthOfCircumference` variable, but then does nothing with it. You can see that in the original function, `Main`, the value of this variable is displayed to the user, and its calculation is actually the whole purpose of the application.

What you need to do is pass this value as a return value of the `CalculateCircumferenceLength` function, so that it is again available to the code in the `Main` function. This also means you need to declare the return type of the `CalculateCircumferenceLength` function and return the value. The `CalculateCircumferenceLength` function that returns the value of the calculation is displayed in Listing 7-3.

Listing 7-3: Calculating Circumference Length Function Extraction — Steps 4 and 5

```
private static double CalculateCircumferenceLength(
    Point center, Point pointOnCircumference)
```

Continued

Listing 7-3: Calculating Circumference Length Function Extraction — Steps 4 and 5 *(continued)*

```
{
    double radius;
    radius = Math.Sqrt(Math.Pow(pointOnCircumference.X - center.X,
                          2) +
                       Math.Pow(pointOnCircumference.Y - center.Y,
                          2)
                      );
    double lengthOfCircumference;
    lengthOfCircumference = 2 * 3.1415 * radius;
    return lengthOfCircumference;
}
```

Now that you have successfully extracted the `CalculateCircumferenceLength` function, all that is left to do is eliminate the extracted code section from the `Main` function and make use of the `CalculateCircumferenceLength` function instead.

Before doing that, you should write a unit test for the extracted function, but that task is omitted here for brevity. Once you have transformed the `Main` code so it is calling the `CalculateCircumferenceLength` function, you can eliminate the comment "calculate and display the length of circumference" both because it is now superfluous and because the name of the new function is eloquent. The code is shown in Listing 7-4.

Listing 7-4: Complete Code after Calculate Circumference Length Function Extraction

```
using System;

namespace RefactoringInCSharpAndASP.Chapter7
{
    struct Point
    {
        public double X;
        public double Y;
    }

    class CircleCircumferenceLength
    {
        static void Main(string[] args)
        {

            Point center;
            Point pointOnCircumference;
            //read center coordinates
            Console.WriteLine("Enter X coordinate " +
                "of circle center");
            center.X = Double.Parse(Console.In.ReadLine());
            Console.WriteLine("Enter Y coordinate " +
                "of circle center");
            center.Y = Double.Parse(Console.In.ReadLine());
            //read some point on circumference coordinates
            Console.WriteLine("Enter X coordinate " +
                "of some point on circumference");
            pointOnCircumference.X =
```

```
            Double.Parse(Console.In.ReadLine());
        Console.WriteLine("Enter Y coordinate " +
            "of some point on circumference");
        pointOnCircumference.Y =
            Double.Parse(Console.In.ReadLine());
        //calculate and display the length of circumference
        Console.WriteLine("The length of circle "
            + "circumference is:");
        double lengthOfCircumference = CalculateCircumferenceLength(
            center, pointOnCircumference);
        Console.WriteLine(lengthOfCircumference);
        Console.Read();
    }

    private static double CalculateCircumferenceLength(
        Point center, Point pointOnCircumference)
    {
        double radius;
        radius = Math.Sqrt(Math.Pow(pointOnCircumference.X - center.X,
                        2) +
                        Math.Pow(pointOnCircumference.Y - center.Y,
                        2)
                    );
        double lengthOfCircumference;
        lengthOfCircumference = 2 * 3.1415 * radius;
        return lengthOfCircumference;
    }
  }
}
```

Extracting the Radius Calculation Code

You have successfully performed your first method extraction. However, you should not stop just yet. The new function can also be simplified, by the separation of the calculation into the two steps I mentioned when we analyzed the problem initially. The first two lines of the function are concerned with the radius calculation and therefore can be placed in a separate function. After these functions have been extracted, you can also take the opportunity to eliminate the temporary (local) variables radius and lengthOfCircumference, because they do not improve code clarity. You can see how the code looks after CalculateRadius function extraction in Listing 7-5.

Listing 7-5: Calculate Radius Function Extraction

```
    private static double CalculateCircumferenceLength(
        Point center, Point pointOnCircumference)
    {
        return 2 * 3.1415 * CalculateRadius(center, pointOnCircumference);
    }

    private static double CalculateRadius(Point center, Point pointOnCircumference)
    {
        return Math.Sqrt(Math.Pow(pointOnCircumference.X - center.X,
                        2) +
```

Continued

165

Listing 7-5: Calculate Radius Function Extraction *(continued)*

```
                            Math.Pow(pointOnCircumference.Y - center.Y,
                                2)
                    );
    }
```

Extracting the "Wait for User to Close" Code

If you take a look at the end of Main, you will see a somewhat curious line of code:

```
Console.Read();
```

Normally such code is used to read user input, but this code ignores the value the user entered.

You have probably guessed by now, but this line serves only to keep the console window open until the user decides to close it. If you comment this line, the application still functions correctly but the console window closes so rapidly that the user has no chance to read the result. Someone reading it might be puzzled by this line of code whose purpose is not obvious. To make its purpose clear, you can extract this single line of code into a separate method. In the following example, the method is named WaitForUserToClose:

```
            private static void WaitForUserToClose()
            {
                Console.Read();
            }
```

Even a single line whose purpose is not immediately obvious might be worthy of method extraction — if by doing so you make the code more readable.

Extracting the Read Coordinates Code

Now you should go back to the Main code. This function is still too long. An interesting observation can be made with regard to the coordinates' input code: The segment for reading the center coordinates is quite similar to the code for reading the coordinates for the point on the circumference. The only difference is in the literals containing the message for the user. You can do something about this.

Begin by declaring a new function for reading coordinates and copying the code for reading the center coordinate into the body of the new function. You should end up with the code shown in Listing 7-6.

Listing 7-6: Input Point Coordinates Extraction — Steps 1 and 2

```
    private static void InputPoint() {
        Console.WriteLine("Enter X coordinate " +
            "of circle center");
        center.X = Double.Parse(Console.In.ReadLine());
        Console.WriteLine("Enter Y coordinate " +
            "of circle center");
        center.Y = Double.Parse(Console.In.ReadLine());
    }
```

Because the code for reading both points is quite similar, you can try to make this method work for the input of coordinates of both points. That is why I have named the function InputPoint without using a specific point name.

The IDE now marks the variable center as not declared. You can declare it at the beginning of the function and rename it to point at the same time. This way, you can keep your method point-neutral, so it can be used for the input of any point's coordinates. Next, you should make the function return the point so that the original function can make use of this function. The code for this version of InputPoint function is shown in Listing 7-7.

Listing 7-7: Input Point Coordinates Extraction — Steps 3 and 4

```
private static Point InputPoint() {
    Point point = new Point();
    Console.WriteLine("Enter X coordinate " +
        "of circle center");
    point.X = Double.Parse(Console.In.ReadLine());
    Console.WriteLine("Enter Y coordinate " +
        "of circle center");
    point.Y = Double.Parse(Console.In.ReadLine());
    return point;
}
```

As shown here, the only thing that keeps this code related to the specific circle's center point is the two words circle and center, part of the literals displayed to a user. You can parameterize this code by adding the new parameter pointName to the InputPoint function. Then you can construct the message to the user by concatenating a string literal and the pointName parameter. The new version of the InputPoint function is shown in Listing 7-8.

Listing 7-8: Input Point Coordinates Extraction — Steps 3 and 4, Part 2

```
private static Point InputPoint(String pointName) {
    Point point = new Point();
    Console.WriteLine("Enter X coordinate " +
        "of " + pointName);
    point.X = Double.Parse(Console.In.ReadLine());
    Console.WriteLine("Enter Y coordinate " +
        "of " + pointName);
    point.Y = Double.Parse(Console.In.ReadLine());
    return point;
}
```

The only thing left to do is to make use of this function in Main. You will eliminate the original coordinate reading code and replace it with a call to the InputPoint function. You will also eliminate an unnecessary temporary variable in the process. (You'll learn about Inline Temp refactoring in the next chapter.) The final version of the code is shown in Listing 7-9.

Listing 7-9: Final Method Extraction Version of the Calculate Circumference Length Function

```
using System;

namespace RefactoringInCSharpAndASP.Chapter7
{
    struct Point
    {
        public double X;
        public double Y;
    }
```

Continued

Listing 7-9: Final Method Extraction Version of the Calculate Circumference Length Function *(continued)*

```
class CircleCircumferenceLength
{
    static void Main(string[] args)
    {

        Point center = InputPoint("circle center");
        Point pointOnCircumference = InputPoint("point on circumference");
        //calculate and display the length of circumference
        Console.WriteLine("The length of circle "
            + "circumference is:");
        double lengthOfCircumference = CalculateCircumferenceLength(
            center, pointOnCircumference);
        Console.WriteLine(lengthOfCircumference);
        WaitForUserToClose();
    }

    private static Point InputPoint(String pointName) {
        Point point = new Point();
        Console.WriteLine("Enter X coordinate " +
            "of " + pointName);
        point.X = Double.Parse(Console.In.ReadLine());
        Console.WriteLine("Enter Y coordinate " +
            "of " + pointName);
        point.Y = Double.Parse(Console.In.ReadLine());
        return point;
    }

    private static double CalculateCircumferenceLength(
        Point center, Point pointOnCircumference)
    {
        return 2 * 3.1415 * CalculateRadius(
            center, pointOnCircumference);
    }

    private static double CalculateRadius(
        Point center, Point pointOnCircumference)
    {
        return Math.Sqrt(Math.Pow(pointOnCircumference.X - center.X,
                            2) +
                        Math.Pow(pointOnCircumference.Y - center.Y,
                            2)
                );
    }

    private static void WaitForUserToClose()
    {
        Console.Read();
    }

    }
}
```

This final version of the sample application looks a lot better. You now have code that is a lot easier to read and debug. For example, if you have a calculation error, you can easily test two functions in charge of mathematical computation and soon find where you made your mistake. You have also made a method shorter by extracting two very similar sections of code in a single method. This way, you eliminate duplicated code from the application. Duplicated code is a probably the worst smell that your code can suffer from, and in fact is so important that an entire section is dedicated to it later in this chapter.

Before ending this section on method extraction, I want to define another important smell very typical of GUI code, and the cause of many poorly written routines. While misuse of event-handling routines can be interpreted as just another form of the Long Method smell, programmers who use GUI-generation tools, such as Windows Forms Designer, to generate event hooks fall into this trap so easily that I decided to define it here as a smell on its own.

Smell: Event-Handling Blindness

Detecting the Smell

Large portions of code in the application are placed inside event-handling routines.

Related Refactoring

Use Extract Method refactoring to eliminate this smell.

Rationale

While this is only a special case of the Long Method smell, it is so common with GUI designer generated code that it deserves special mention. The typical scenario is as follows: You begin your project by placing components on the form and filling in the event-handling routines whose declaration is generated by the IDE when you click the components on the form. As the project progresses, more and more code is simply added to existing event handlers. The rapid application development (RAD) paradigm offers an important productivity boon, but if it is not coupled with good design and programming practices, all the benefits are lost over the long term.

To complete this discussion of method extraction, I want to share something that will make performing it immensely easier: refactoring with Visual Studio.

Extract Method Refactoring in Visual Studio

This is my favorite of Visual Studio's refactoring possibilities, and the one, together with Rename refactoring, that I use the most. When you are dealing with complex methods, keeping track of all local variables can be complicated and time-consuming. When extracting a method, Visual Studio will track which variables are passed to a new method, which are returned by the method's return value as output parameters. This can be a real time-saver. You can see Visual Studio's Extract Method preview window in Figure 7-2.

Visual Studio will correctly pass all variables read in the extracted method as parameters, and all variables assigned in the extracted segment as output parameters, using `ref` or `out` keyword.

Figure 7-2

Definition: You use the *ref* keyword to pass an argument by reference that has to be initialized before passing it to the method. You use the *out* keyword to pass an argument by reference that doesn't necessarily have to be initialized before passing it to the method.

If only one variable in the segment has been assigned, then Visual Studio will use this variable as the return value of the method. If no variables are being assigned in the new method, then Visual Studio will give this method void for a return type.

When you are writing methods, strive to write them in such a way that they return only one value. Use of output parameters is discouraged because it is probably a sign that the method is doing more than it should.

In case you select a block of code that cannot be extracted to a separate method and click Extract Method, Visual Studio will offer you the opportunity to expand the selection to a valid expression. This message box is visible in Figure 7-3.

However, using the extract method in Visual Studio does have a few quirks. If you select an arbitrary block of code that spans more than one method, Extract Method in Visual Studio will still be enabled.

Once you click Extract Method, you get the message "The selected text is not inside a method." You can see this message in Figure 7-4.

In addition, if you click Extract Method without making any selection in your code, you will get a similar message: "The selection is empty. Please select some code to be able to extract a method." In the last two cases, I would prefer if Visual Studio would disable the Extract Method menu item. What is the point of invoking the operation in Visual Studio just to get a message that it cannot be performed?

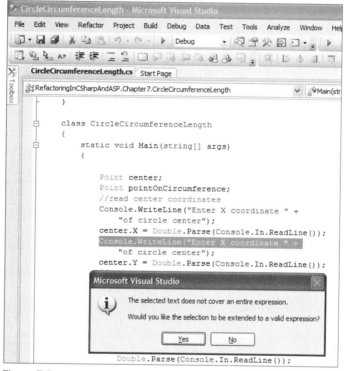

Figure 7-3

Finally, check out a tip for extracting the right side of an assignment statement. This type of method extraction is more common than you might expect.

In order to extract the right side of an assignment statement to separate a method, be sure not to make the ending semicolon or the assignment operator part of your selection. Correct selection for extracting the right side of an assignment statement is shown in Figure 7-5.

Inlining Methods

As you progress with the book, you will notice that most of the refactorings I cover are concerned with lack of structure in your code. Their aim is to help you introduce and organize structure in your code. Lack of structure is more common and probably the first type of smell you will encounter. Such lack of structure is well depicted with smells such as Long Method or Large Class.

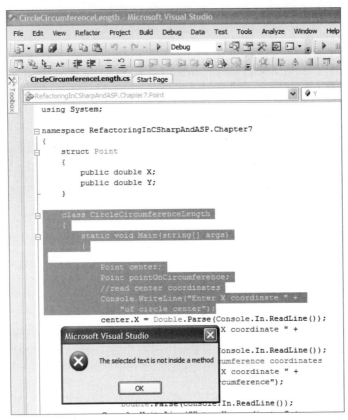

Figure 7-4

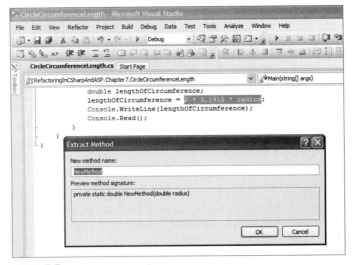

Figure 7-5

Smell: Lazy Method

Detecting the Smell

A method is extremely short, has no substance, and the name of the method does not aid in understanding the code.

Related Refactoring

Use Inline Method refactoring to eliminate this smell.

Rationale

Unnecessary indirection makes your code less efficient and more difficult to understand and maintain. Such methods can appear after some intense refactoring on your code base has been performed or as a result of modification. If you end up with Lazy Method, the best thing to do with it is to eliminate it altogether.

Some smells, however, deal with *excess* of structure. For example, it could be that a class is doing nothing but delegating execution to some other class and for no real purpose; or a method has a single line of code and a name that doesn't help you in understanding the code, such as in the Lazy Method smell example. Such smells are the result of excessive code structuring. Sometimes they can be a result of some overly ambitious pattern or some other profound refactoring or modifications to your code. When properly done, eliminating unnecessary elements can be as beneficial as providing structure.

You have undoubtedly heard that "all problems in computer science can be solved by another level of indirection." However, this doesn't mean you should aim for indirection *per se;* fortunately, most refactorings have the directly inverse refactoring whose effects are similar to an "undo". For example, Extract Method refactoring can be undone with Inline Method. This means that there are refactorings that will help you eliminate smells originating from excessive structuring.

One such type of refactoring is the Inline Method. It will help you eliminate the method whose body is as explicative as its name.

Refactoring: Inline Method

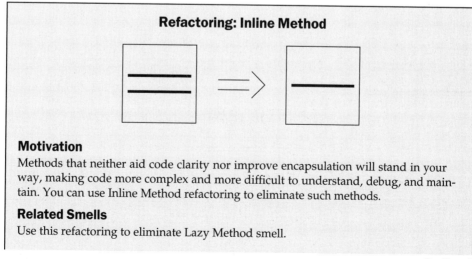

Motivation

Methods that neither aid code clarity nor improve encapsulation will stand in your way, making code more complex and more difficult to understand, debug, and maintain. You can use Inline Method refactoring to eliminate such methods.

Related Smells

Use this refactoring to eliminate Lazy Method smell.

Continued

Mechanics

While some tools can automate this refactoring, it can also be performed relatively easy manually. Here are the steps to follow:

1. Comment the method you plan to inline and recompile the code in order for Visual Studio to mark all occurrences in the code where a call to this method is made.

2. Replace the call to the method with the method body.

3. Eliminate the method.

In case the method belongs to a published interface, start by marking the method with Obsolete attribute and then perform the inlining in a future version of your product.

Before

```
static void Main(string[] args)
{

    Point center = InputPoint("circle center");
    Point pointOnCircumference = InputPoint("point on circumference");
    //calculate and display the length of circumference
    Console.WriteLine("The length of circle "
        + "circumference is:");
    double lengthOfCircumference = CalculateCircumferenceLength(
        center, pointOnCircumference);
    Console.WriteLine(lengthOfCircumference);
    WaitForUser();
}

private static void WaitForUser()
{
    WaitForUserToClose();
}

private static void WaitForUserToClose()
{
    Console.Read();
}
```

After

```
static void Main(string[] args)
{

    Point center = InputPoint("circle center");
    Point pointOnCircumference = InputPoint("point on circumference");
    //calculate and display the length of circumference
    Console.WriteLine("The length of circle "
        + "circumference is:");
    double lengthOfCircumference = CalculateCircumferenceLength(
```

```
                center, pointOnCircumference);
        Console.WriteLine(lengthOfCircumference);
        WaitForUserToClose();
    }

    private static void WaitForUserToClose()
    {
        Console.Read();
    }
}
```

The Duplicated Code Smell

At the last step in refactoring the original circumference calculation application, I identified two similar sections of code, extracted and parameterized a function, and replaced the two sections with a call to the newly extracted function. While the two sections were not completely identical, I managed to recognize the similarity, parameterize the difference, and effectively eliminate duplication from the code.

However, I still haven't discussed the problems that can occur with duplicated code. The following list shows the problems duplicated code can create and discusses why it should be eliminated from your code base:

❑ **Duplicated code adversely affects the maintainability of your code:** If you need to modify a piece of code that has been duplicated, you need to search for all occurrences of the code and modify it more than once. This will obviously make you work much more than necessary, and with a greater probability of error.

❑ **Duplicated code is a frequent source of bugs:** Imagine you need to modify your code. Because keeping track of code duplication is not very plausible, you are very likely to end up with a number of occurrences of the same code that you missed and where you failed to implement the change. Now you have a number of segments that do not behave as expected. This means that you have introduced a bug into your code.

❑ **Duplicated code makes it difficult to establish a link between your code and the problem domain:** Because the same code is present in more than one place, it is difficult to understand how your code relates to concepts from the problem domain. This means that the semantic value of your code is lost and the general design quality of your code is poor.

❑ **Duplicated code promotes longer methods:** If you are simply copying the code, you are not preoccupied with structuring your code. This can often lead to the proliferation of long, nongranular methods. (See the sidebar on the Long Method smell earlier in the chapter to understand the adverse effect longer methods can have on your code.)

❑ **Duplicated code means a bigger code base:** Keeping the number of lines needed in your application at a minimum simply means that there's less you need to deal with. In this sense, less code generally means less work. You will benefit from a smaller code base when optimizing, unit testing, maintaining, comprehending, and generally dealing with your code.

Now that you understand why you should avoid code duplication at all costs, you can take look at the most common sources of code duplication. This way, you will be able to recognize duplication-producing behavior when you program, and prevent code duplication right from the outset.

Smell: Duplicated Code

Detecting the Smell

Sometimes detecting duplicated code can be easy, because you can visually spot almost identical sections of code in more than one place. This duplication can be the result of a simple copy-paste operation. At other times, duplication is not at all obvious, and some level of pattern recognition is required. Once the similarity between sections of code has been identified, further analysis is necessary to isolate duplication from the differentiating code. For example, a method can be parameterized so it can be used to replace similar sections of code.

Some tools can perform static analysis of code in search of duplication, but generally this does not go beyond a simple textual comparison of code segments. Nonetheless, this is still useful for detecting the copy-paste form of duplication.

Related Refactoring

A number of refactorings can be employed to eliminate this smell: Extract Method, Extract Class, Extract Superclass, Pull Up Method, Pull Up Property, and so on.

Rationale

Duplicated code results in a code base that is more difficult to maintain, because each modification has to be performed in more than one place. Such code is also more difficult to comprehend, because it is hard to understand the purpose of the code sections. Code duplication is a sign of poorly designed code.

Sources of Duplicated Code

Several sources of duplicated code exist:

- ❏ The most common source of duplicated code is copy-paste programming. This style of programming is so important it deserves its own section, which follows shortly.

- ❏ Another source of duplicated code can be simple unawareness that the code already exists in the project you are working on. Maybe the project is too large, or maybe it is written in such a way that it is not easy to understand what the code is doing, so you are not able to find the class that is performing the action you need to implement.

- ❏ Sometimes the code can be so badly implemented that you prefer to write new code yourself.

- ❏ Today, open source has become ubiquitous, and a solution for numerous problems can be found online. It is ever so easy to simply copy the code you need into your own project.

- ❏ Finally, literal values can become a source of duplication, as you will see later in this chapter.

Whatever the reason, you should try to avoid the duplication. When you are not able to find your way around in the project you are working on, it is a good signal that the project code should be refactored. If you implemented some functionality on your own and consciously avoided using some unruly code, you should eliminate that unruly code from the code base altogether and use your improved version instead. When using open-source code, try to use a compiled binary, which will enable you to have an easier time upgrading new versions of the component.

Copy-Paste Programming

This style of programming is common with novice or inexperienced programmers. It is often the first mechanism of reuse that a programmer learns, and it can lead to a significant productivity boost in the initial phase of learning the craft. Sometimes it is even used by more experienced programmers when they are faced with tight deadlines. It is so simple to just copy and paste sections of code that you need.

Code Snippets in Visual Studio

The Code Snippets feature in Visual Studio enables you to paste predefined or custom code snippets inside your code. The code snippets that come with Visual Studio can help you write some very common lines of code by enabling you to paste skeleton code directly into the file you are working on. This feature can improve productivity, especially for some novice programmers. However, if abused, this feature can become a real hotbed of duplicated code. Beware of the trap of copy-paste programming with this feature.

Even if you did duplicate code on purpose, the drawbacks are the same. This style of programming is discouraged in favor of better, object-oriented methods of reuse such as delegation and inheritance. Refactoring techniques are very efficient in promoting reuse and eliminating duplicated code, and many refactorings have as a specific purpose the elimination of duplicated code. These techniques should be adopted as part of an overall style that promotes better design and reuse.

The next sidebar and section take a look at another dubious programming practice that often results in duplicated code, *magic literals* — one of the oldest programming ailments.

Smell: Magic Literals

Detecting the Smell

Probably the best way to start out is to analyze code visually or by performing a text search. Once you have spotted a literal, you can use the IDE's text search to look for other occurrences of the same value. Often you will come upon a magic literal value while modifying the code: You should use that opportunity to replace the value with a constant.

Related Refactoring

Use Replace Magic Literal with Constant refactoring to eliminate this smell.

Rationale

Literal values disseminated liberally in your code can easily lead to duplication. The purpose of such values is not immediately obvious. That can lead to code that is difficult to maintain, and it increases the likelihood of bugs.

Magic Literals

Magic literals are hard-coded values of numbers and strings that are disseminated liberally inside the code. These values have a special meaning with regard to program logic, but when they are placed as literals just anywhere in the code, the purpose of these values becomes less than obvious. In order to make the purpose of these variables explicit, you should give them names.

In C# you can declare constant values by means of the const keyword. These values are guaranteed not to change during program runtime. Sometimes constant values can be logically grouped together; in these cases, enumerations (using the enum keyword) can be used instead of constants.

To resolve the problem with magic literals, you should replace them with constants or enumerations. This way, your code will become easier to understand and modify, because the values can be changed in a single location, instead of requiring that you search the entire code for occurrences of the same literal values.

As with any other refactoring, you should use good judgment when you apply Replace Magic Literal with Constant refactoring. In some cases it just doesn't make sense. Consider the code example in the "Refactoring: Replace Magic Literal with Constant" sidebar. In that example I have extracted pi, but have left the number 2 inside the code. Both methods are implementations of mathematical formulae, but here the number 2 is just that, a number inside a formula, and replacing it with a constant wouldn't make sense.

Refactoring: Replace Magic Literal with Constant

Motivation

Magic literals make your code more difficult to understand. The purpose of literal values has to be understood from the context. Because the use of magic literals leads to duplication, it makes the code more prone to bugs and more difficult to maintain. Instead of replacing a value in a single place, the programmer has to hunt for and replace each occurrence of the magic literal in the code. Declaring literals as constants can reduce typographical errors, because the compiler can check a constant or an enumeration, but cannot check a literal value. Finally, declaring literals as constants can increase productivity and make your code less prone to bugs, because autocomplete can be used to search for the value, rather than you having to memorize it.

Related Smells

Use this refactoring to eliminate Magic Literals smell.

Mechanics

After you have identified the magic literal, declare a constant of the same type, give it a meaningful name, and initialize it with the same value of the magic literal. Now replace the literal with the constant. Search in your code for other occurrences of the same magic literal; and if they are used for the same purpose, replace them with the newly created constant also.

If you come upon magic literal values that are logically related and can be grouped, an enumeration is a better choice for replacement than a constant. Use the enum keyword

---

to declare the enumeration and to enumerate these values. Now you can replace magic literals with values from the enumeration.

Before

```
public class Circle
{
    private double radiusValue;
    public double Radius
    {
        get { return radiusValue; }
        set { radiusValue = value; }
    }
    public double CircumferenceLength()
    {
        return 2 * 3.1415 * Radius;
    }
    public double Area()
    {
        return 3.1415 * Math.Pow(Radius, 2);
    }
}
```

After

```
public class Circle
{
    private const double PI = 3.1415;
    private double radiusValue;
    public double Radius
    {
        get { return radiusValue; }
        set { radiusValue = value; }
    }
    public double CircumferenceLength()
    {
        return 2 * PI * Radius;
    }
    public double Area()
    {
        return PI * Math.Pow(Radius, 2);
    }
}
```

Extract Method and Replace Magic Literal Refactoring in the Rent-a-Wheels Application

After this chapter you will certainly look at the existing Rent-a-Wheels code with different eyes. Even upon superficial examination, you can see that the Rent-a-Wheels code suffers from the Event-Handling Blindness smell. In short, 100 percent of the code is placed in event-handling routines in different form classes.

Now examine the code further, in search of more unpleasant aromas. Here are the problems I am able to identify so far:

- ❏ **Event-handling blindness:** As I have already mentioned, this special case of Long Method smell, very popular with RAD programmers, is the most obvious smell in the Rent-a-Wheels code.

- ❏ **Magic literals:** A number of magic literals are present in the code — most notably, the database connection string is duplicated inside every routine that needs to make use of the persistence services.

- ❏ **Duplicated code:** Many methods contain very similar, sometimes even identical, code. Literal values are also duplicated in the code.

- ❏ **Copy-paste programming:** There is no doubt that the majority of the code in the Rent-a-Wheels application was written using copy-paste style, resulting in numerous duplications and general code proliferation. For those with detective instincts, it will suffice to make a comparison between the comments in some methods. Many were left in their original forms after being pasted, without being updated to a new context. This is a clear testimony to the copy-paste process.

- ❏ **Comments:** Because you performed a Rename refactoring in the previous chapter, the majority of comments have already become somewhat obsolete. However, they are still used to explain the purpose of certain blocks of code inside the method, which is a strong signal that the methods are too long and that method extraction should be performed.

Although these smells say a lot about the numerous deficiencies of the existing code, I will ask you to be patient for the moment and not perform any refactorings right now. In the next chapter you are going to learn a number of refactorings that can greatly simplify the work on method extraction. Therefore, leave Rent-a-Wheels as is for one more chapter; you'll come back to it once you have a complete arsenal of refactorings for method extraction at your disposal.

Summary

The chapter you have just read describes refactorings that can result in important and extensive "small scale" changes to your code. Fortunately, these are the kind of changes that bring a fast return. The code will immediately become easier to understand and maintain.

You have also seen some underlying object-oriented principles that can motivate these refactorings. It touched upon encapsulation, and you have seen the ways it can help you deal with complexity in your code. We started with the simplest kind of encapsulation: a function. Functions are very similar to methods, and all refactorings that can be applied to a function work with methods as well. You have seen how Extract Method refactoring can greatly simplify methods by extracting blocks of code into new, separate methods, and you now know how method extraction can be employed to make methods more granular and reusable, to eliminate duplication, to replace comments, and to make code easier to read.

This chapter also dealt with duplication, the most destructive force in the development process. Duplicated code will lead you on the road to unmanageable, bloated code that can be a real nightmare for any programmer who has to maintain it. Unfortunately, duplication is sometimes used deliberately, as a mechanism of reuse, a double-edged sword if ever there was one. Generally, programmers who use copy-paste style are unaware of the perils that duplication brings even in the short term, or they are simply trading code correctness for some very immediate gains in a project's schedule.

Magic literals are the last issue covered in this chapter. While magic literals are not very complex, the negative impact that they can have on code is very important.

In the next chapter you are going to see a few method-level refactorings that can greatly simplify method decomposition and which are generally used to prepare the ground for method extraction. With that, you will be ready to deal with even the most complex methods, and you will be able to take the first and most important step in bringing your code out of chaos and into the structured world.

8

Method Consolidation and Extraction Techniques

In the previous chapter, you saw the benefits that can be gained from keeping your code granular and well encapsulated on the most basic level: the method level. You also saw the importance of organizing the code in the form of small methods with well-chosen names.

When you come across long or poorly structured methods, the most common solution is to perform method extraction. You have also seen the mechanics behind method extraction, different illustrations of this refactoring, and how the whole process can be automated with the refactoring tool.

However, in the real world, method extraction is seldom straightforward. If a method merits extraction, then it was not well written in the first place, so you cannot expect that it will lend itself to extraction easily. Very often, you will have to perform a number of preparatory steps to make method extraction meaningful. These steps may involve the following:

❑   Dealing with temporary variables that stand in the way of method extraction

❑   Regrouping statements so that blocks of code can be extracted in one step

❑   Dealing with temporary variable declaration and initialization statements

This chapter describes a number of refactorings that can be used as preliminary steps to method extraction. If you are able to apply these refactorings efficiently, you will be able to perform method extraction on even the most complicated and tangled methods.

Dealing with Temporary Variables

Temporary variables are among the biggest impediments to efficient method extraction. Because the only place you can reach the local variable is within the method that hosts it, the more temporary variables you have in the method, the longer the method has to be.

> **Definition:** A temporary or local variable is a variable declared inside a method or property and which is visible only inside the containing method or property.

While you can perform method extraction by passing local variables as parameters, creating numerous methods with long parameter lists will not do much to improve code clarity. Such code goes against the idea of encapsulation, and you need a more efficient means at your disposal when performing method extraction.

In this section you are going to see how you can deal with temporary variables:

- ❏ The simplest case is that in which the variable reach is only inside the block you are going to extract. In that case, the variable becomes local to the newly created method and does not stand in the way of method extraction.

- ❏ In other cases you have to think about ways to avoid passing the variable as a parameter to a method.

- ❏ Sometimes you can inline the variable.

- ❏ In some cases you can replace it with a query and make the result available to more than one method.

- ❏ Sometimes even temporary variables can be abused. This is the case when the temporary variable holds two or more unrelated values during its lifetime. Such a variable makes the code much more difficult to read, because its role depends on context. It also works against method extraction, because it has a longer reach than necessary. The solution is to split this variable into two or more variables.

The following sections examine these valuable temporary-variable-management techniques in detail.

Move Declaration Near Reference Refactoring

Some programmers are used to placing temporary variable declarations at the top of the method. This should improve the readability of the method and make it tidier, but I am not so sure about this old piece of wisdom. Let me explain why.

First of all, decision and control structures in C# are scoped. This means that by placing all variables you use in a method at the beginning of the method, you are declaring them with greater visibility than necessary, and because I have already discussed the benefits of well-encapsulated code you know that such visibility works against encapsulation. However, such placement has another consequence as well. If the variable is initialized inside the decision or control block and declared outside, you will not be able to move initialization to declaration. (I talk about moving initialization to variable declaration in the next section.)

Second of all, placing variables at the beginning of the method instead of placing them in the part of the method where they are used makes Extract Method refactoring much more difficult to perform. As you saw in the previous chapter, when you extract methods, either manually or using a refactoring tool, you select a contiguous block of code and move it to the extracted method. If you are not able to reach the variable, you have to declare it as a parameter of the newly extracted method. Had you declared the variable where it was used, you would be able to select the variable declaration as well, thus removing the necessity for parameter passing.

I generally declare variables as I need them. I find such code easier to read this way. Because I do not need to search for code that assigns to a variable, I can understand immediately what value the variable holds. Whenever I see that a method has grown a bit out of proportion, I try to consolidate it by refactoring. Finally, once you have finely-grained methods, you will probably end up declaring variables at the beginning of the method anyway. Finely-grained methods are generally so short they don't leave you with any other option.

Refactoring: Move Declaration Near Reference

Motivation

By placing the variable declaration far away from the line where it is first referenced, you are making code more difficult to read, because it is not immediately clear how the variable was initialized.

In addition, declaring variables well ahead of time makes the method more difficult to refactor. If you try to extract a part of the method in which the variable was referenced, you have to pass the variable as a parameter to a newly extracted method, even though the declaration could possibly have been placed inside the extracted block.

Related Smells

Use this refactoring to prepare methods for method extraction and to eliminate the Long Method and Overexposure smells.

Mechanics

Find all variables in the method that are declared but not initialized at the same line. After that, look for the line where the variable is first referenced. Possibly the method is long, and the variable can be enclosed in a more restricted scope, or the line where the variable is referenced for the first time belongs to a block that does something different from the rest of the method and can be extracted. Cut the line with the variable declaration and paste it one line above the one in which the variable was referenced for the first time.

Before

```
static void Main(string[] args)
{
    Point center;
    Point pointOnCircumference;
    double radius;
    double lengthOfCircumference;
    //read center coordinates
    Console.WriteLine("Enter X coordinate " +
        "of circle center");
    center.X = Double.Parse(Console.In.ReadLine());
    Console.WriteLine("Enter Y coordinate " +
        "of circle center");
    center.Y = Double.Parse(Console.In.ReadLine());
    //read some point on circumference coordinates
    Console.WriteLine("Enter X coordinate " +
        "of some point on circumference");
    pointOnCircumference.X =
```

Continued

```
        Double.Parse(Console.In.ReadLine());
    Console.WriteLine("Enter Y coordinate " +
        "of some point on circumference");
    pointOnCircumference.Y =
        Double.Parse(Console.In.ReadLine());
    //calculate and display the length of circumference
    Console.WriteLine("The length of circle "
        + "circumference is:");
    //calculate the length of circumference
    radius = Math.Sqrt(Math.Pow(pointOnCircumference.X - center.X,
                            2) +
                        Math.Pow(pointOnCircumference.Y - center.Y,
                            2)
                    );
    lengthOfCircumference = 2 * 3.1415 * radius;
    Console.WriteLine(lengthOfCircumference);
    Console.Read();
}
```

After

```
static void Main(string[] args)
{
    //read center coordinates
    Console.WriteLine("Enter X coordinate " +
        "of circle center");
    Point center;
    center.X = Double.Parse(Console.In.ReadLine());
    Console.WriteLine("Enter Y coordinate " +
        "of circle center");
    center.Y = Double.Parse(Console.In.ReadLine());
    //read some point on circumference coordinates
    Console.WriteLine("Enter X coordinate " +
        "of some point on circumference");
    Point pointOnCircumference;
    pointOnCircumference.X =
        Double.Parse(Console.In.ReadLine());
    Console.WriteLine("Enter Y coordinate " +
        "of some point on circumference");
    pointOnCircumference.Y =
        Double.Parse(Console.In.ReadLine());
    //calculate and display the length of circumference
    Console.WriteLine("The length of circle "
        + "circumference is:");
    //calculate the length of circumference
    double radius;
    radius = Math.Sqrt(Math.Pow(pointOnCircumference.X - center.X,
                            2) +
                        Math.Pow(pointOnCircumference.Y - center.Y,
                            2)
                    );
    double lengthOfCircumference;
    lengthOfCircumference = 2 * 3.1415 * radius;
```

```
        Console.WriteLine(lengthOfCircumference);
        Console.Read();
}
```

Move Initialization to Declaration Refactoring

In C# you can initialize the variable on the same line on which you have declared it. By placing initialization code as a continuation of the variable declaration, you are making the code more compact and easier to read. You do not have to scan the code in the search of the line that initialized the variable.

More important, this refactoring will help you prepare the variable for Replace Temp with Query refactoring. Sometimes variable initialization might depend on certain conditions. In that case, the variable cannot be initialized on the same line on which it is declared. For example, take a look at the variable connection in the following code extract:

```
IDbConnection connection;
if (this.DatabaseProviderImplementation == ProviderImplementation.MSSql)
{
    connection = new SqlConnection();
}
else if (this.DatabaseProviderImplementation == ProviderImplementation.Oracle)
{
    connection = new OracleConnection();

}
//...
```

In this case, it is not possible to initialize the variable connection on the same line on which it was declared. However, if the code for some reason is changed in such a way that conditional initialization is not necessary anymore and the conditions have been eliminated, you can use Move Initialization to Declaration refactoring to consolidate your code. For example, if the code you just saw is changed to look as follows, you can apply Move Initialization to Declaration:

```
IDbConnection connection;
connection = CreateConnection();
```

Now you can easily Move Initialization to Declaration. The code is converted to the following form:

```
IDbConnection connection = CreateConnection();
```

The next section covers overburdened or multipurpose temporary variables.

Refactoring: Move Initialization to Declaration

Motivation

By initializing the variable on the same line on which the variable is declared, you will improve code readability.

Continued

187

Related Smells

Use this refactoring to prepare methods for method extraction and to eliminate the Long Method and Overexposure smells.

Mechanics

Find all variables in the method that are declared but not initialized at the same line. If necessary, perform Move Declaration Near Reference refactoring before consolidating initialization.

Before

```
IDbConnection connection;
connection = CreateConnection();
```

After

```
IDbConnection connection = CreateConnection();
```

Split Temporary Variable Refactoring

The longer the temporary variable reach in a method, the more intertwined the method is and the more complex any method extraction becomes. If the same variable is used inside the method for more than one purpose, it will have a longer reach than necessary. Furthermore, if you use a temporary variable to hold more than one unrelated value, the code becomes less comprehensible for the reader.

Smell: Overburdened Temporary Variable

Detecting the Smell

A variable that holds more than one unrelated value is generally considered overburdened. It is a variable that has been assigned more than once, and it is neither a looping nor a collecting variable. Sometimes these variables are given generic names like `result` or `temp`.

The mere existence of overburdened variables can be a good indicator that the method could benefit from method extraction.

Related Refactoring

Use Split Temporary Variable refactoring to eliminate this smell.

Rationale

Overburdened variables are serving more than one role in a method. In a sense they have a longer "reach," making method extraction more difficult and the method more intertwined. Because the role of the variable is not clear, it is not possible to establish the link between the name and the purpose of the variable, making the code more complex and difficult to understand.

I've already mentioned some very good reasons why a temporary variable in a method should be used for a single purpose, but why are temporary variables used for more than one purpose to begin with? Programmers sometimes use a single variable for more than one purpose, such as to save memory or to type less. Neither reason really holds water because any gains are outweighed by negative effects. Sometimes convoluted temporary usage is not really intentional. Whatever the origin of the multipurpose temporary variable, the variable should be split; and for each usage a new temporary variable should be declared. You can see this technique in the following example:

```
public void PrintReport()
{
    double result = 0;
    foreach (Vehicle vehicle in this.Vehicles)
    {
        if (vehicle.Rented)
        {
            result += 1;
        }
    }
    PrintJob.PrintLine("Total vehicles rented:" + result);
    result = 0;
    foreach (Rental rental in this.Rentals)
    {
        result += rental.AmountDue;
    }
    PrintJob.PrintLine("Total amount due:" + result);
}
```

In this example, the variable `result` first holds a value that represents the number of currently rented vehicles; later, the same variable holds the total amount of pending payments.

Sometimes a good sign of an overburdened variable is the name chosen for it. If it is some generic term like `result`, `temp`, or `var`, this may be because the variable is used for more than one purpose, so a more specific name would not fit well. After the variable has been split, newly created and original variables can be created, with names that are more in accordance with the single role each variable now performs.

Retaining Looping and Collecting Variables

The fact that a variable has been assigned more than once does not automatically signal that the variable should be split. Sometimes the variable has to be assigned more than once, and that is fine. Typical cases of such variables are looping variables — for example, an index when iterating an array or a collection. This variable has to be changed with each pass through the cycle. In C#, the `foreach` construct minimizes the necessity for declaring looping variables.

Another case when assigning a variable more than once occurs is when you need to collect certain values, such as when you are concatenating strings or calculating some totals. Take a look at the following code:

```
private decimal CalculateFundsTotal()
{
    decimal total = default(decimal);
    foreach (Account account in this.accounts)
```

```
    {
        total += account.Balance;
    }
    return total;
}
```

In this case, the variable `total` is a collecting variable, and incrementing it by each cycle helps you calculate the total balance for all accounts in the collection. In this example, splitting the variable does not make sense.

Refactoring: Split Temporary Variable

Motivation

Each temporary variable in a method should have a single role. Otherwise, its role can be understood only from the context, making the code less explicit and more difficult to read.

Such variables have a longer reach, and they make a method extraction much more difficult to perform. By splitting the variable so that the variable is really assigned only once (unless it is a collecting or looping variable), you make the purpose of the variables much more explicit and greatly simplify method extraction.

Related Smells

Use this refactoring to eliminate the Overburdened Temporary Variable smell.

Mechanics

Find all variables that are assigned more than once. Make sure these are neither collecting nor looping variables.

1. Rename the variable at the declaration (until the second assignment), with a name that clearly explains its first usage. Rely on the compiler to discover all occurrences of the variable:

```
public void PrintReport()
{
    double vehiclesRented = 0;
    foreach (Vehicle vehicle in this.Vehicles)
    {
        if (vehicle.Rented)
        {
            vehiclesRented += 1;
        }
    }
    PrintJob.PrintLine("Total vehicles rented:" +
    vehiclesRented);
    result = 0;
    foreach (Rental rental in this.Rentals)
    {
        result += rental.AmountDue;
    }
    PrintJob.PrintLine("Total amount due:" + result);
}
```

---

2. Change the second assignment to a declaration. Confirm that the code compiles correctly:

```
public void PrintReport()
{
    double vehiclesRented = 0;
    foreach (Vehicle vehicle in this.Vehicles)
    {
        if (vehicle.Rented)
        {
            vehiclesRented += 1;
        }
    }
    PrintJob.PrintLine("Total vehicles rented:" +
    vehiclesRented);
    double result = 0;
    foreach (Rental rental in this.Rentals)
    {
        result += rental.AmountDue;
    }
    PrintJob.PrintLine("Total amount due:" + result);
}
```

3. Perform Rename refactoring on the newly declared variable so that the name of the second occurrence of the original variable corresponds to its purpose.

4. Because the variable can be assigned more than twice, repeat this process until each usage of the variable is split into its own separately declared variable.

Before

```
public void PrintReport()
{
    double result = 0;
    foreach (Vehicle vehicle in this.Vehicles)
    {
        if (vehicle.Rented)
        {
            result += 1;
        }
    }
    PrintJob.PrintLine("Total vehicles rented:" + result);
    result = 0;
    foreach (Rental rental in this.Rentals)
    {
        result += rental.AmountDue;
    }
    PrintJob.PrintLine("Total amount due:" + result);
}
```

Continued

191

After

```
public void PrintReport()
{
    double vehiclesRented = 0;
    foreach (Vehicle vehicle in this.Vehicles)
    {
        if (vehicle.Rented)
        {
            vehiclesRented += 1;
        }
    }
    PrintJob.PrintLine("Total vehicles rented:" + vehiclesRented);
    double amountDueTotal = 0;
    foreach (Rental rental in this.Rentals)
    {
        amountDueTotal += rental.AmountDue;
    }
    PrintJob.PrintLine("Total amount due:" + amountDueTotal);
}
```

Next you are going to take a look at the most simple way to eliminate a temporary variable.

You will learn about the new C# 3.0 initializer syntax in Chapter 13, where C# 3.0 features are introduced.

Inline Temp Refactoring

One way to deal with temporary variables is to eliminate them altogether. If the variable has been assigned only once with a simple expression, you can eliminate the temporary variable and use the expression instead.

Smell: Superfluous Temporary Variable

Detecting the Smell

A superfluous temporary variable is generally detected only on close inspection of the method. It is the variable that is assigned a value once by an expression and is used once, without any operation on the received value. If you can instead directly use the expression that gives value to the variable, and the variable is contributing nothing to code clarity, then you have identified a superfluous variable.

Related Refactoring

Use Inline Temp refactoring to eliminate this smell.

Rationale

When a temporary variable adds nothing to code clarity, it is best to eliminate it. The way a variable can add to code clarity is through its name. If the expression that provides values to a variable is equally descriptive and the variable is not used for any additional operation, then it has no use. Each superfluous symbol in the code means more unnecessary complexity. Not only that, but a superfluous temporary variable will often stand in the way of Extract Method refactoring, so your best option is to eliminate the variable altogether.

As you might guess, the first motivation for this refactoring can be found in the context of Extract Method refactoring. It can help you eliminate annoying temporary variables and facilitate method extraction. Another time to inline temporary variables is when they are plainly unnecessary, and the expression can be read as easily as the variable, as in the following example:

```
public int VacantVehiclesCount()
{
    int numberOfVehicles = 0;
    numberOfVehicles = this.VehiclesCount;
    return numberOfVehicles - this.RentedVehiclesCount;
}
```

In this case, the temporary variable `numberOfVehicles` is not adding any clarity to the code because the property name `this.VehiclesCount` reads just as well. You can also encounter a similar situation when a temporary variable is used to represent a return value of the method, but the method name is sufficient to identify its purpose. Such a method might benefit from temp inlining for the sake of simplicity.

Refactoring: Inline Temp

Motivation

You can reduce the number of temporary variables in a method by performing Inline Temp refactoring. This is especially useful if the local variable is standing in the way of method extraction. Another good time to inline variables is when they add nothing to improving code readability.

Related Smells

Use this refactoring to prepare methods for method extraction and to eliminate the Superfluous Temporary Variable smell (a temporary variable that adds nothing to code clarity) and as a step that precedes and facilitates method extraction. (Take a look at Extract Method refactoring in Chapter 7 to see the smells that it can remedy.)

Mechanics

If the variable has been assigned more than once, perform Split Temporary Variable refactoring before embarking on Inline Temp refactoring.

Continued

```
Before

    public double VacancyPercentage()
    {
        double vacancyPercentage = 0;
        vacancyPercentage = 100 *
            (this.VehiclesCount - this.RentedVehiclesCount)
            / this.VehiclesCount;
        return vacancyPercentage;
    }

After

    public double VacancyPercentage()
    {
        return 100 *
            (this.VehiclesCount - this.RentedVehiclesCount)
            / this.VehiclesCount;
    }
```

Sometimes a temporary variable is assigned more than once, and the initialization expression lends itself to inlining. In this case, perform Split Temporary Variable before Inline Temp.

Finally, if the variable has been initialized by the result of multiple statements, you can perform Extract Method refactoring on these statements so that the variable is initialized by a simple expression and Inline Temp refactoring is then made available.

Next on the list of refactorings you can use to eliminate temporary variables is Replace Temp with Query Refactoring.

Replace Temp with Query Refactoring

Sometimes the expression that initializes the temporary variable is not very simple, nor its meaning very obvious, so inlining the variable will make the code *less* legible in the end. However, the temporary variable stands in the way of method extraction, so you need to find a way to deal with it. One thing that instance methods or properties can access easily is another instance method or property, and this is a good hint about the solution to the problem: You can replace a temporary variable with a read-only property or a method.

The case for this refactoring is even stronger if the same temporary variable initialization code is present in more than one method. If you replace the temporary variable with a read-only property or a method in more than one encompassing method, you not only make methods much more prone to extraction, but also reduce duplication in your code. This is a typical technique for a situation in which you would like to have a temporary variable available to more than one property or a method.

Is It a Method or a Property?

If a method returns a single value and has no output parameters, it can easily be changed to a read-only property and vice-versa. While the difference is mostly syntactical, it is nevertheless important to choose the right form for the extracted block. So, when replacing the temporary variable with a query, should you choose a property or a method?

In most cases, the solution can be reached intuitively. Properties are used to represent data — for example, to encapsulate access to fields of an object — whereas methods are used for sending messages between objects. For more borderline cases, see Table 8-1 for guidance.

Table 8-1: Deciding Between Method and Property for Extracted Query Code

Use a property when . . .	Use a method when . . .
The value it returns is coherent data value.	The value is the result of conversion — for example, `ToInt(...)`.
There are no observable side-effects to calling the property.	There might be observable side-effects.
Successive calls will always return the same result.	Successive calls do not necessarily return the same result.
The order of execution does not influence the result.	The order of execution may influence the result.
The call is not computationally costly.	The call is costly.

In some cases, although a variable might be assigned more than once, you would still like to replace it with a query. Use Split Temporary Variable refactoring before Replace Temp with Query refactoring to eliminate any secondary assignment, and perform Replace Temp with Query refactoring afterward.

If temporary variable initialization code comprises multiple statements, you can use Extract Method refactoring to consolidate the initialization code and perform initialization in a single statement.

Refactoring: Replace Temp with Query

Motivation

Sometimes you can see essentially the same value calculated and assigned to a temporary variable in more than one method. In order to reduce the duplication, you can extract the code into a separate query method or a property. You can follow the same steps before performing method extraction to avoid creating unnecessary parameters.

Continued

Related Smells

Use this refactoring to eliminate the Duplicated Code smell and to prepare a method for extraction.

Mechanics

If the variable has been assigned more than once, split it before replacing it with a query.

1. Perform Extract Method on the expression that assigns to the variable. For the newly created method, make the return type the same as that of the variable and make the method return the value of the expression.

2. Eliminate the variable by replacing it with a method call.

Before

```
public void PrintReport()
{
    //...
    int vacantVehicles = 0;
    vacantVehicles = this.VehiclesCount - this.RentedVehiclesCount;
    PrintJob.PrintLine("Total vehicles vacant:" +
        vacantVehicles.ToString());
    //...
}
public double GetVacancyPercentage()
{
    return 100 * (this.VehiclesCount - this.RentedVehiclesCount)
        / this.VehiclesCount;
}
```

After

```
public void PrintReport()
{
    //...
    PrintJob.PrintLine("Total vehicles vacant:" +
        VacantVehiclesCount.ToString());
    //...
}
public double GetVacancyPercentage()
{
    return 100 * (this.VacantVehiclesCount)
        / this.VehiclesCount;
}
private int VacantVehiclesCount
{
    get
    {
        return this.VehiclesCount - this.RentedVehiclesCount;
    }
}
```

Method Reorganization Heuristics

By this point in the chapter you have seen a number of refactorings that can help you consolidate your methods and make them prone to extraction. Method extraction is the most common remedy for long and amorphous methods. It is also the most common reason to apply the refactorings in this chapter. While the refactorings featured in this chapter have merits of their own, they are especially useful in the context of method extraction. As you become more experienced, you will be able to apply these refactorings more naturally, and you will learn to recognize patterns that lead to extraction. However, at this point you might ask yourself how and where to start the whole process. Here are some hints that might help you confront some more complex methods as you start out:

❑ **Search for duplication:** If you can get rid of duplication by extracting duplicated code as a method, do it right away. You will rarely have to go back if you use this step to reduce duplicate code. Doing this will make an original method a bit shorter.

❑ **Analyze comments:** Very often, comments are a good hint that certain sections of code belong together. However, sometimes the original author may have fallen a step short of placing the blocks of code in separate methods. You can go one step further and use methods to mark the blocks instead of comments. Again, this step will make the original method a bit shorter.

❑ **Search for sections of the method that stick well together and have a greater chance of reuse:** When you are confronted with long methods, you will often find sections that can be extracted as separate methods. Make the original method thinner by extracting these sections into separate methods.

As you go through these steps, you will often have to shuffle the code in a method in order to deal with temporary variables. You may have to move initialization near the reference, split temporary variables, inline them, or replace them with queries as the need arises. With practice, you will soon become more confident and better able to apply the techniques you have seen in this chapter. In time, you will see how your code becomes more expressive and leaner, and contains less duplication. When you finish with one cycle, go back for another iteration (and another), until you are finally satisfied.

These are more or less the heuristics I tried to apply to the Rent-a-Wheels application; but before discussing how these refactorings apply to Rent-a-Wheels, let's take a look at a refactoring that does the opposite of eliminating temporary variables; it introduces them.

Introducing Explaining Temporary Variables

Most of the refactorings you have seen in this chapter so far deal with eliminating temporary variables. On certain occasions, however, you might profit from introducing new temporary variables. The most common motive for creating new temporary variables is to improve code readability. You might have a complicated expression or a conditional that could profit from being separated into a few steps with the help of temporary variables. Or maybe you are dealing with a third-party or legacy API that publishes some dubious naming methodology. Sometimes you will create temporary variables while trying to understand a complex method, as a tool that will help you understand the underlying logic, only to eliminate them once you are done or after you successfully simplify or decompose the method.

Because a temporary variable spans only a single method, you will be better off using some other way to improve code readability, such as extracting an expression segment into the separate method or a property, if this is possible. You will be able to use such a method from other methods as well, thus reducing duplication in your code. This is not possible with temporary variables.

Refactoring: Introduce Explaining Temporary Variable

Motivation

A complex expression might be improved in the readability department by introducing a new temporary variable.

Related Smells

Use this refactoring to improve code that is difficult to read and understand.

Mechanics

Start by declaring the temporary variable. Set the value of the variable to the result of expression you wish to replace with the newly declared variable. Replace all the occurrences of the expression that the variable was assigned to with the variable itself.

Before

```
double lengthOfCircumference = 2 * 3.1415 *
    Math.Sqrt(Math.Pow(pointOnCircumference.X - center.X,
                    2) +
                Math.Pow(pointOnCircumference.Y - center.Y,
                    2)
            );
```

After

```
double radius = Math.Sqrt(Math.Pow(pointOnCircumference.X - center.X,
                    2) +
                Math.Pow(pointOnCircumference.Y - center.Y,
                    2)
            );
double lengthOfCircumference = 2 * 3.1415 * radius;
```

Dealing with Long and Nested Conditionals

A very common way to make a method unmanageable is to write long conditional statements. The typical scenario goes like this: Before executing the method, you have to check that certain conditions have been fulfilled. To make things more complicated, there may be more than one condition, and one piece of the method may be conditioned in a different way than the rest of the method. You end up with a number of long and nested if statements. The following code listing illustrates this situation rather well:

```
private void toMaintenance_Click(object sender, EventArgs e)
{
    string selectedLicensePlate = null;
    if (MessageBox.Show("Are you sure?", "Confirm",
    MessageBoxButtons.OKCancel) == DialogResult.OK)
```

```
{
    //Check that user has made a selection
    if (feetViewGrid.SelectedRows.Count > 0)
    {
        //Read value from first cell as Vehicle Id
        selectedLicensePlate =
        feetViewGrid.SelectedRows[0].
        Cells[0].Value.ToString();
        SqlConnection connection = new SqlConnection(
        "Data Source=TESLATEAM;" +
        "Initial Catalog=RENTAWHEELS;" +
        "User ID=RENTAWHEELS_LOGIN;" +
        "Password=RENTAWHEELS_PASSWORD_123");
        SqlCommand command;
        string sql = "Update Vehicle " +
                "Set Operational = 1 " +
                "WHERE LicensePlate = @SelectedLP";
        command = new SqlCommand();
        try
        {//open connection
            connection.Open();
            //Set connection to command
            command.Connection = connection;
            //set Sql string to command object
            command.CommandText = sql;
            //Add parameter to command
            command.Parameters.AddWithValue(
                "@SelectedLP", selectedLicensePlate);
            //execute command
            command.ExecuteNonQuery();
            //close connection
            connection.Close();
        }
        catch
        {
            MessageBox.Show("A problem occurred" +
            "and the application cannot recover! " +
            "Please contact the technical support.");
        }
    }
    else
    {
        //Warn user if no selection made in table and exit
        MessageBox.Show("Please select vehicle first!");
    }
}
}
```

Reading this method is not an easy task: It is difficult to say where each of the conditions ends up. Reading it will probably involve selecting brackets in the IDE in order to see where they are closing, and it might also involve a lot of scrolling. Nor will these conditions help method extraction.

The solution to this problem is to convert conditionals to guard clauses. This way, all conditions are written at the beginning of the method. If guard clause is not fulfilled, then the method simply exits. Take a look at the previous method refactored in this manner and after method extraction has been performed:

```
private void toMaintenance_Click(object sender, EventArgs e)
{
    if (!SelectionMade())
    {
        AskUserToMakeSelection();
        return;
    }
    if (!UserConfirms())
    {
        return;
    }
    VehicleToMaintenance();
    display_Click(null, null);
}
```

One argument against using guard clauses is that methods with guard clauses do not follow the "single exit point" structured programming rule. The reasoning behind single exit point is that it can help understand the method, especially because it simplifies resource deallocation, which means there is a single place to dispose of the resource. In C#, you won't worry about resource deallocation, as you can count on the garbage collector to do it for you. (The garbage collector might use a helping hand with unmanaged resources, and for that purpose C# has been endowed with the using and finally keywords.)

In addition, methods written with guard clauses look a lot easier to understand. If guard clauses are not making a method easier to read, then the method is probably too long anyway.

Refactoring: Replace Nested Conditional with Guard Clause

Motivation

Nested, long conditional statements can make a method more difficult to read and understand. If one branch of the conditional is used only to exit the method early or to raise the exception, then it can be replaced with the guard condition at the beginning of the method. Placing the guard condition at the beginning of the method makes it easier to follow the method's execution flow, and eliminates long, nested conditionals.

Related Smells

Use this refactoring to eliminate long and nested conditional blocks from your code.

Mechanics

Search for branches of if-else statements that consist of exiting the method or raising the exception only. Such branches are not part of the main (or normal) execution flow. The main purpose of the execution flow is to check for some condition that has to be satisfied before executing the main flow of the method; these are also known as *guard clauses*.

Move guard clauses to the beginning of the method so the method is exited early if the conditions are fulfilled. Sometimes, in order to move a guard clause to the beginning of the method, you will have to reverse the conditional first.

Before

```
private void toMaintenance_Click(object sender, EventArgs e)
{
    if (SelectionMade())
    {
        if(UserConfirms()){
            VehicleToMaintenance();
            display_Click(null, null);
        }
        return;
    }else{
        AskUserToMakeSelection();
    }
}
```

After

```
private void toMaintenance_Click(object sender, EventArgs e)
{
    if (!SelectionMade())
    {
        AskUserToMakeSelection();
        return;
    }
    if (!UserConfirms())
    {
        return;
    }
    VehicleToMaintenance();
    display_Click(null, null);
}
```

Method Reorganization and Rent-a-Wheels

I ended Chapter 7 with an analysis of the problems present in the Rent-a-Wheels application, which can be identified based on the smells described so far. If you remember, the smells identified and explained in the Rent-a-Wheels code were as follows:

- ❑ Event-handling blindness
- ❑ Magic literals
- ❑ Duplicated code
- ❑ Copy-paste programming
- ❑ Comments

This section illustrates these smells with code examples. A single method from the Rent-a-Wheels application neatly sums up all the smells identified thus far. In Listing 8-1, commented code that is highlighted with a gray background marks these smells.

Listing 8-1: Button save Click Event-Handling Code in Branch Maintenance Form

```
//Event-handling blindness - event handler as a sole function
private void save_Click(object sender, EventArgs e)
{
    string sql;
    //Connection String as Magic Literal
    SqlConnection connection = new SqlConnection(
        "Data Source=TESLATEAM;" +
        "Initial Catalog=RENTAWHEELS;" +
        "User ID=RENTAWHEELS_LOGIN;Password=RENTAWHEELS_PASSWORD_123");
    SqlCommand command = new SqlCommand();
    if (id.Text.Equals(""))
    {
        //Create Sql String with parameter @SelectedLP
        sql = "Insert Into Branch (Name) " +
        "Values(@Name)";
        //add parameter name
        command.Parameters.AddWithValue("@Name", name.Text);
    }
    else
    {
        //Create Sql String with parameter @SelectedLP
        sql = "Update Branch  Set Name = @Name " +
        "Where BranchId = @Id";
        //add parameter name
        command.Parameters.AddWithValue("@Name", name.Text);
        //Duplicated code - parameter adding statements are repeated

        //add parameter Id
        command.Parameters.AddWithValue("@Id", Convert.ToInt16(id.Text));
    }
    try
    {
        //Redundant comments
        //open connection
        connection.Open();
        //Set connection to command
        command.Connection = connection;
        //set Sql string to command object
        command.CommandText = sql;
        //exexute command
        command.ExecuteNonQuery();
        //close connection
        connection.Close();
    }
    catch
    {
        MessageBox.Show("A problem occurred and the application cannot recover! " +
```

```
            "Please contact the technical support.");
    }
    BranchMaintenance_Load(null, null);
}
```

There is one more detail that I decided to include in this chapter. It is related to the `SqlCommand` class. The class that implements a certain interface has to implement all the members declared in that interface, but it is free to declare additional members. In this case, the `AddWithValue` method is a member of `System.Data.SqlClient.SqlCommand`, but it is not a member of `System.Data.IDbCommand`. It seems that Microsoft provided a convenient way to add command parameters, but it is exposed only if you work directly with the `SqlCommand` type.

If we want to make our code provider-neutral, we have to use the `AddParameter` method, which belongs to the `IDbCommand` interface. This way, if we decide to use another database engine, all we need to do is change the single line of code where the command is created. The underlying principle can be summed with the dictum "Program to an abstraction and not to an implementation," which I discuss in depth in Chapter 10.

The method selected in Listing 8-1 illustrates a general pattern followed in the Rent-a-Wheels implementation, and you'll find that the rest of the code suffers from more or less similar problems. The first smell I attacked was duplicated code.

Removing Duplication in Rent-a-Wheels

After my first visual inspection, I was able to identify a number of event-handling routines containing completely identical blocks of code. The first of such blocks was control-populating code found in all the navigational buttons and in the `BranchMaintenance_Load` routine. Just in case you don't remember what the Branch Maintenance form looks like, take a look at Figure 8-1.

Figure 8-1

In this case, the navigational buttons are the small buttons at the bottom of the form that help you move between different branch records in the database. Event handlers for all of these buttons, including the `BranchMaintenance_Load` routine, have a few lines of identical code. Listing 8-2 shows two such routines for illustration purposes.

Chapter 8: Method Consolidation and Extraction Techniques

Listing 8-2: Navigational Button Event Handlers

```csharp
private void right_Click(object sender, EventArgs e)
{
    if (branches.Rows.Count > currentRowIndex + 1)
    {
        currentRowIndex++;
        DataRow row = branches.Rows[currentRowIndex];
        id.Text = row["BranchId"].ToString();
        name.Text = row["Name"].ToString();
    }
}

private void left_Click(object sender, EventArgs e)
{
    if (currentRowIndex - 1 >= 0 & branches.Rows.Count > 0)
    {
        currentRowIndex--;
        DataRow row = branches.Rows[currentRowIndex];
        id.Text = row["BranchId"].ToString();
        name.Text = row["Name"].ToString();
    }
}
```

The identical code in both routines is highlighted in gray. I decided to extract repeated code in a separate method and call it `DisplayCurrentRow`, as shown in Listing 8-3.

Listing 8-3: The DisplayCurrentRow Extracted Method

```csharp
private void DisplayCurrentRow()
{
    DataRow row = branches.Rows[currentRowIndex];
    id.Text = row["BranchId"].ToString();
    name.Text = row["Name"].ToString();
}
```

There is a portion of code in Listing 8-1 that is related to adding a parameter to a database command object. Once I reverted the code to use `IDbCommand`'s `AddParameter` method, more duplication was introduced. The parameter definition code now looks like this:

```csharp
IDbDataParameter idParameter = command.CreateParameter();
parameter.ParameterName = "@Id";
parameter.DbType = DbType.Int32;
parameter.Value = id.Text;
command.Parameters.Add(idParameter);

IDbDataParameter nameParameter = command.CreateParameter();
parameter.ParameterName = "@Name";
parameter.DbType = DbType.String;
parameter.Value = name.Text;
command.Parameters.Add(nameParameter);
```

In this case, extraction is not so straightforward. While the code is very similar, there are differences in each section. In order to solve this problem, I needed to parameterize the extracted method. At the same time, I will revert to the AddParameter method of IDbCommand and call the newly extracted method AddParameter, which receives four parameters. You can see this in Listing 8-4.

Listing 8-4: The AddParameter Extracted Method

```
private void AddParameter(IDbCommand command, string parameterName,
    DbType parameterType, object parameterValue)
{
    IDbDataParameter parameter = command.CreateParameter();
    parameter.ParameterName = parameterName;
    parameter.DbType = parameterType;
    parameter.Value = parameterValue;
    command.Parameters.Add(parameter);
}
```

This way, calling the AddParameter method is relatively simple. You need to add two more parameters compared to using SqlCommand's AddWithValue method. Because you are improving the code's database neutrality, this is not too high a price to pay.

Large portions of the code deal with ADO.NET objects. I extracted the part that creates the connection, sets the connection string to the connection, opens the connection, sets SQL code to the command, and adds a connection to the command to separate the PrepareDataObjects method. Now take a look at Listing 8-5.

Listing 8-5: The PrepareDataObjects Extracted Method

```
private IDbConnection PrepareDataObjects(IDbCommand command, string sql)
{
    IDbConnection connection = new SqlConnection(ConnectionString);
    connection.Open();
    command.Connection = connection;
    command.CommandText = sql;
    return connection;
}
```

Another interesting method I used for extraction is ExecuteNonQuery. Shown in Listing 8-6, its purpose is to execute a command.

Listing 8-6: The ExecuteNonQuery Extracted Method

```
private void ExecuteNonQuery(IDbCommand command, string sql)
{
    IDbConnection connection = PrepareDataObjects(command, sql);
    command.ExecuteNonQuery();
    connection.Close();
}
```

Using an adapter to fill the dataset, code that was originally found inside the Form-Load event handler can also be extracted into a separate method. The FillDataset method is shown in Listing 8-7.

Listing 8-7: The FillDataset Extracted Method

```
private DataSet FillDataset(IDbCommand command, string sql)
{
    IDbConnection connection = PrepareDataObjects(command, sql);
    IDbDataAdapter adapter = new SqlDataAdapter();
    DataSet branches = new DataSet();
    adapter.SelectCommand = command;
    adapter.Fill(branches);
    connection.Close();
    return branches;
}
```

One last obvious source of duplication is exception-handling code. The code in each catch block is completely identical (it is limited to showing users a message):

```
catch
{
    MessageBox.Show("A problem occurred and the application cannot recover! " +
    "Please contact the technical support.");
}
```

All unhandled exceptions in .NET are routed through the AppDomain class UnhandledException event. If I can hook up my code and write a handler for the UnhandledException event, I can place my exception-handling code inside the handler, thereby eliminating it from the rest of the application. In order to do that, I need to modify the Program class found in the Program.cs file. You can see the Program class code in Listing 8-8.

Listing 8-8: Program Class with Global Exception-Handling Code

```
using System;
using System.Windows.Forms;

namespace RentAWheel
{
    static class Program
    {
        /// <summary>
        /// The main entry point for the application.
        /// </summary>
        [STAThread]
        static void Main()
        {
            Application.EnableVisualStyles();
            Application.SetCompatibleTextRenderingDefault(false);
            Application.Run(new FleetView());

            AppDomain.CurrentDomain.UnhandledException +=
            new UnhandledExceptionEventHandler(HandleUnhandledException);
        }
```

```
static void HandleUnhandledException(object sender,
    UnhandledExceptionEventArgs e)
{
    MessageBox.Show("A problem occurred " +
        "and the application cannot recover! " +
        "Please contact the technical support.");
    }
  }
}
```

Now I will show you some other smells that I noticed in the Rent-a-Wheels application, and how you can deal with them.

Magic Literals, Comments, and Event-Handling Blindness in Rent-a-Wheels

One of the easiest things I've had to deal with is comments in the code. After method extraction, most of those comments proved to be redundant, and they could simply be deleted.

Literal values were replaced with constants. For example, a literal string containing branch-deletion SQL code was replaced with a constant, deleteBranchSql (see Listing 8-9).

Listing 8-9: Literal Value SQL String Replaced with a Constant

```
private const string deleteBranchSql = "Delete Branch Where BranchId = @Id";
//...
private void DeleteBranch() {
    IDbCommand command = new SqlCommand();
    AddParameter(command, idParameterName,
        DbType.Int32, Convert.ToInt32(this.id.Text));
    ExecuteNonQuery(command, deleteBranchSql);
}
```

I also decided to separate code dealing with the GUI from code dealing with the database, as shown in Listing 8-10. As a result, event-handling blindness was eliminated.

Listing 8-10: Separation of GUI Automation Code from Database Code

```
private void delete_Click(object sender, EventArgs e)
{
    DeleteBranch();
    BranchMaintenance_Load(null, null);
}

private void DeleteBranch() {
    IDbCommand command = new SqlCommand();
    AddParameter(command, idParameterName,
        DbType.Int32, Convert.ToInt32(this.id.Text));
    ExecuteNonQuery(command, deleteBranchSql);
}
```

Chapter 8: Method Consolidation and Extraction Techniques

As I performed these latest refactorings, I could see that the code was visually much more pleasing. The longest method is now no more than ten lines long. It can easily be read and debugged. There is no duplication, and there are no unnecessary comments or scattered literals. You can judge the result for yourself. Listing 8-11 shows the code for the complete `BranchMaintenance` form. This listing should also help you understand how all the pieces just discussed fit together.

Listing 8-11: Branch Maintenance Form Code

```csharp
using System;
using System.Data;
using System.Data.SqlClient;
using System.Windows.Forms;

namespace RentAWheel
{
    public partial class BranchMaintenance : Form
    {
        private const String connectionString = "Data Source=TESLATEAM;" +
            "Initial Catalog=RENTAWHEELS;" +
            "User ID=RENTAWHEELS_LOGIN;Password=RENTAWHEELS_PASSWORD_123";

        private const string branchTableIdColumnName = "BranchId";
        private const string branchTableNameColumnName = "Name";

        private const string selectAllFromBranchSql =
            "Select * from Branch";
        private const string deleteBranchSql =
            "Delete Branch Where BranchId = @Id";
        private const string insertBranchSql =
            "Insert Into Branch (Name) Values(@Name)";
        private const string updateBranchSql =
            "Update Branch  Set Name = @Name Where BranchId = @Id";

        private const string idParameterName = "@Id";
        private const string nameParameterName = "@Name";

        private const int singleTableInDatasetIndex = 0;

        private DataTable branches;
        private int currentRowIndex;

        public BranchMaintenance()
        {
            InitializeComponent();
        }

        private void new_Click(object sender, EventArgs e)
        {
            id.Text = String.Empty;
            name.Text = String.Empty;
        }

        private void BranchMaintenance_Load(object sender, EventArgs e)
        {
```

```
        LoadBranches();
        if ((this.branches.Rows.Count > 0))
        {
            currentRowIndex = 0;
            DisplayCurrentRow();
        }
}

private void LoadBranches()
{
    IDbCommand command = new SqlCommand();
    DataSet branches = FillDataset(command, selectAllFromBranchSql);
    this.branches = branches.Tables[singleTableInDatasetIndex];
}

private void right_Click(object sender, EventArgs e)
{
    if (branches.Rows.Count > currentRowIndex + 1)
    {
        currentRowIndex++;
        DisplayCurrentRow();
    }
}

private void left_Click(object sender, EventArgs e)
{
    if (currentRowIndex - 1 >= 0 & branches.Rows.Count > 0)
    {
        currentRowIndex--;
        DisplayCurrentRow();
    }
}

private void first_Click(object sender, EventArgs e)
{
    if (branches.Rows.Count > 0)
    {
        currentRowIndex = 0;
        DisplayCurrentRow();
    }
}

private void last_Click(object sender, EventArgs e)
{
    if (branches.Rows.Count > 0)
    {
        currentRowIndex = branches.Rows.Count - 1;
        DisplayCurrentRow();
    }
}

private void DisplayCurrentRow()
{
    DataRow row = branches.Rows[currentRowIndex];
```

Continued

Listing 8-11: Branch Maintenance Form Code *(continued)*

```
        id.Text = row["BranchId"].ToString();
        name.Text = row["Name"].ToString();
}

private void save_Click(object sender, EventArgs e)
{
    SaveBranch();
    BranchMaintenance_Load(null, null);
}

private void SaveBranch()
{
    IDbCommand command = new SqlCommand();
    if (String.IsNullOrEmpty(id.Text))
    {
        AddParameter(command, nameParameterName,
            DbType.String, name.Text.ToString());
        ExecuteNonQuery(command, insertBranchSql);
    }
    else
    {
        AddParameter(command, nameParameterName,
            DbType.String, name.Text.ToString());
        AddParameter(command, idParameterName,
            DbType.Int32, Convert.ToInt32(this.id.Text));
        ExecuteNonQuery(command, updateBranchSql);
    }
}

private void delete_Click(object sender, EventArgs e)
{
    DeleteBranch();
    BranchMaintenance_Load(null, null);
}

private void DeleteBranch() {
    IDbCommand command = new SqlCommand();
    AddParameter(command, idParameterName,
        DbType.Int32, Convert.ToInt32(this.id.Text));
    ExecuteNonQuery(command, deleteBranchSql);
}

private void reload_Click(object sender, EventArgs e)
{
    BranchMaintenance_Load(null, null);
}


private void AddParameter(IDbCommand command, string parameterName,
    DbType parameterType, object parameterValue)
{
    IDbDataParameter parameter = command.CreateParameter();
```

```
            parameter.ParameterName = parameterName;
            parameter.DbType = parameterType;
            parameter.Value = parameterValue;
            command.Parameters.Add(parameter);
        }

        private IDbConnection PrepareDataObjects(IDbCommand command, string sql)
        {
            IDbConnection connection = new SqlConnection(connectionString);
            connection.Open();
            command.Connection = connection;
            command.CommandText = sql;
            return connection;
        }

        private void ExecuteNonQuery(IDbCommand command, string sql)
        {
            IDbConnection connection = PrepareDataObjects(command, sql);
            command.ExecuteNonQuery();
            connection.Close();
        }

        private DataSet FillDataset(IDbCommand command, string sql)
        {
            IDbConnection connection = PrepareDataObjects(command, sql);
            IDbDataAdapter adapter = new SqlDataAdapter();
            DataSet branches = new DataSet();
            adapter.SelectCommand = command;
            adapter.Fill(branches);
            connection.Close();
            return branches;
        }
    }
}
```

If you take a look at the rest of the Rent-a-Wheels classes, you will find that a similar pattern was followed, resulting in much cleaner and more compact code. However, if you carefully inspect the complete code, you will probably notice that while there is no more duplication inside a single class, many methods are still duplicated between classes. Like any other duplicated code, this is outright smell; but don't worry — our work on Rent-a-Wheels does not end here. In the following chapters you will see ways to deal with this and other problems that can still be found in the code.

Summary

Method extraction is arguably the most common refactoring you will perform. It is the step that carries the brunt of transforming your code from a primordial mess to organized code structures. However, when you are dealing with long, complicated, and poorly structured methods, method extraction is seldom straightforward. To reap the benefits of extraction, you often have to perform a number of preparatory steps.

This chapter explained some simple yet important refactorings that help prepare the code for method extraction. These refactorings are mostly concerned with solving the problem of temporary variables, the biggest impediment to effective method extraction.

You have also learned how to internally reorganize methods by bringing the declaration near the variable initialization. Because in C# you can initialize the variable in the declaration statement, you have seen how to do this and how it can benefit code legibility.

Sometimes temporary variables have more than one role, which makes the code more complex and difficult to understand, and works directly against method extraction, because a long-reaching temporary variable has to be passed in and out of the method as a parameter. The solution for these overburdened variables is Split Temporary Variable refactoring.

In some cases it is beneficial to eliminate a temporary variable altogether. If the temporary variable has been assigned only once — and with a simple expression — you can replace the variable with the expression itself by *inlining* the temporary variable.

Another way to eliminate a temporary variable is to replace it with a query method or a property. Because a method or property can be reached from other methods or properties, a newly created, extracted method can use the query instead of parameter-passing. Better yet, if the query code was present in more than one method, you can additionally reduce duplication by replacing all occurrences of the repeated expression with the query.

You are now ready to take your refactoring to the next level. When refactoring, it is not enough to analyze a single class in isolation. In the next chapter, you will see how refactoring works on the class level.

9

Discovering Objects

In theory, you could write programs in C# without ever using a class or creating an object. Thanks to C#'s static methods, you could write your programs in a procedural style without knowing the first thing about object orientation. In practice, such a style is rare, and to be honest I never come across it, except in some ad hoc and demo applications. Actually, misuse and poor design of objects are much more common. At the root of such code is a poor understanding of object orientation.

When designing an object-oriented system, you need to think of it as a system of communicating and collaborating objects. However, the step of converting analysis artifacts to object-oriented code is neither trivial nor straightforward, yet it is often crucial for the project. While you have seen in this book so far that avoiding any change to code is impossible and that no design decision is irrevocable, in this chapter you'll see how identifying the classes for the first time establishes the foundations of your design, and probably leads the design in certain directions later.

In this chapter, you'll learn the following:

- ❑ First you will get a brief overview of object-oriented programming (OOP). This will help you understand the design techniques and refactorings covered later in this chapter in a deeper context. You will also see that there is more to encapsulation when you're dealing with objects than when you're dealing with functions.

- ❑ Also discussed are some topics already touched on in Chapter 6 and Chapter 7. You will see how analysis artifacts such as user stories or use cases serve as the basis for the design of the system. However, the gap between the code and the diagrams and text written in natural language is not easy to bridge. You'll learn some techniques you can employ in this endeavor.

- ❑ You'll also see what to do if you stray along the wrong path in designing your code. All is not lost; you can use diverse refactoring techniques to consolidate your design.

- ❑ This chapter also describes how to convert procedural or database-driven design to object-oriented design.

By the end of this chapter, you will have a better understanding of object-oriented design as a dynamic, adaptable process that can be modified to maximize code quality and respond to changing requirements.

A Brief Object-Oriented Programming Overview

As indicated in the chapter opener, this first section offers a short overview of some key, object-oriented programming concepts. This is not meant to be in any way comprehensive, and no doubt many of you will be familiar with much of the material. Rather, this section is meant as a quick refresher on some key concepts/features of object-oriented programming that the refactorings in this chapter involve or take advantage of. I have found that such overviews can be useful even for those familiar with the subject in question for identifying possible gaps or blind spots in understanding. Once you have identified them, you can fill in those gaps in order to complete your knowledge of object-oriented programming.

If you want to head straight to the refactorings discussed in this chapter, you can skip down to the "Designing Classes" section of the chapter and start reading there. However, if you keep reading, you will refamiliarize yourself with some of the unique characteristics of object-oriented programming that refactoring really uses to full advantage.

Objects in OOP

In procedural programming, you write programs by invoking functions and asking them to perform some operation on the data you generally supply as arguments. Sometimes those functions return some data as a result of an operation. Conversely, in object-oriented programming, you construct systems by sending messages to objects and asking them to perform some operations.

Objects work as small, independent, and encapsulated machines, each of which has its own piece of responsibility. I have already talked about encapsulation in Chapter 7, but without talking explicitly about object-oriented programming. I want to start this chapter by taking a look at how encapsulation works with objects.

Encapsulation and Objects

With objects, encapsulation works on another level. Here information and operations go together. Objects are constructed from information representing state, and operations that permit access to the information. Thanks to encapsulation, you never access the information directly. The data is hidden, and accessible only through properties and methods that provide another internal level of control. These public properties and methods that can be used by other objects to communicate with the object are called an *interface*.

In that sense, from the outside objects look like black boxes that expose some functionality through a well-defined interface. However, you have no idea what is inside the box or how this functionality is implemented internally. It also means that the data, implemented as object attributes, can be stored in one form internally and in another form visible to the public.

The following `Account` class code illustrates techniques for hiding both information and implementation:

```
public class Account
{
    //Balance is internally kept as decimal
    private decimal balance;

    //This attribute is not publicly visible
    private bool preferredCustomer;

    //Balance is publicly visible as String
    public string Balance
    {
        get { return balance.ToString(); }
    }
    //...
}
```

In the class `Account`, the field `preferredCustomer` is not visible from the outside, meaning this piece of information is hidden from the public but is used by the object internally. The property `Balance` is visible to the public as a string, but it is kept internally as a decimal. Figure 9-1 illustrates an object in the form of a machine, in this case a control panel, accessed through an interface. Just as an operator communicates with a machine through the control panel, unaware of what happens inside the machine, so the programmer using only the class has no knowledge of the inner workings of an object that programming is instantiating and using.

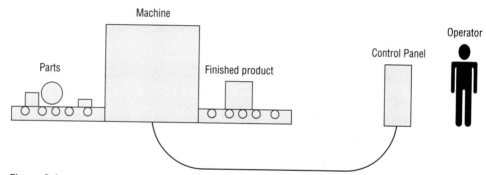

Figure 9-1

In Chapter 7 I talked about the welcome consequences of encapsulation known as information and implementation hiding. They bring more flexibility to the system because some internal design and implementation decisions can be changed without affecting anyone on the outside, thus localizing the change and preventing its ripple effect. For example, in the `Account` example class, you could change the internal implementation of the `Balance` property without affecting existing clients. For instance, you could make use of the `Format` method of the `String` class to format the `Balance` property as currency, with the currency prefix taking regional settings into account when making `Balance` available to the public:

```
//Balance is publicly visible as String
public string Balance
{
```

```
    get {
        return String.Format("{0:c}", balance);
    }
}
```

Hiding makes the system much easier to maintain, but the benefits do not end there. Representation and information content are separated, so the client is not coupled to a format used internally to represent the information.

Finally, encapsulation is the basis of modularity, which can help you construct complex systems by combining smaller components. This is crucial for taming complexity, something that object-oriented programming can be very good at.

Before continuing, I want take a look at how Visual Studio can automate the process of encapsulating fields by generating property setter and getter definitions. After that, we will return to the overview of key object-oriented concepts.

Encapsulate Field Refactoring in Visual Studio

You can invoke this refactoring by placing the cursor over the field name in the field declaration statement. Visual Studio adds the "get" and "set" part of the property declaration. Get returns the value of the field, while set assigns a value to the field. The name that Visual Studio chooses for a newly created property will be the same as that of the field, in uppercase, while the field name will not be changed. The property is declared as public, while the visibility of the field is changed to private, if the field was not private to start with.

Figure 9-2 shows the Encapsulate Field refactoring dialog window in Visual Studio.

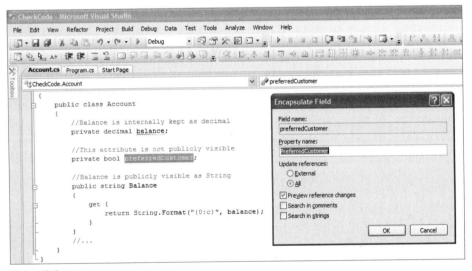

Figure 9-2

Refactoring: Encapsulate Field

Motivation

The reasons for encapsulating a field can be numerous, but the basic one is information hiding. A property can hide the internal data representation from the public view. Moreover, a property can control the data access, validate the data, and inform the object that the data is being accessed or modified. A property is also the easiest means of implementing read-only data in an object.

Even when a property's set and get blocks do nothing other than read and write the field value, you should encapsulate such a field if the class it belongs to is part of the published interface. Changing a field to a property later will break binary compatibility between the two versions of the class, so you should avoid such situations early, by using a property instead of a field. While C# syntax for referencing fields and properties is the same, CIL syntax for the two differs, resulting in binary incompatibility between versions of the classes such that one exposes a field and the other a property with the same name.

Related Smells

Use this refactoring to eliminate the Overexposure smell and to prepare a class for Move Field refactoring.

Mechanics

1. Create a property with the same name as the original name of the field but starting with an uppercase letter that assigns to and reads from the field.

2. Change the field visibility to private and then compile.

Before

```
public class Account
{
    public decimal balance;
    //...
}
```

After

```
public class Account
{
    private decimal balance;

    public decimal Balance
    {
        get { return balance; }
        set { balance = value; }
    }
    //...
}
```

Object State Retention

One very important characteristic of objects is that they retain their state during their lifetime. For example, one client might call upon an object providing some information. Another client could call upon the same object later, asking for the same information. The result it receives would be the same information that the first client provided if the object was internally implemented to provide the same information, because the clients generally don't know what happens inside the object, as you learned in the previous section. Thus, the object is capable of preserving its state indefinitely — or at least for as long as it is alive.

This is not the case in procedural programming. When the function is invoked, all data (except for global data) lives as long as the function invocation itself. Once the function is executed, the data is discarded, and there is no trace of the execution left when the function is invoked again. Take a look at the following code snippet:

```
ShoppingBasket basket = new ShoppingBasket();
basket.AddItem(new Product(12));
basket.AddItem(new Product(32));
Console.WriteLine(basket.ItemCount);
```

When this code is executed, the console will print "2" as a result. This is due to the capability of the object basket to retain state between the calls.

Classes

When you program in C#, you design and code classes. Classes have methods, properties, and events. During runtime, object instances are created based on classes in a process similar to using a mold to create and give shape to some artifact. Once you create an instance from a certain class, you can be certain that this particular object will have the same properties, methods, and events as any other object ever created from that same class.

There is another type of member that is not passed over to instances. Classes can have their own class-level members. These members are known as *static*. If one instance (of any class) updates the shared property, all instances will see the updated value, and they will retain this value as long as the program is running.

To create an instance of a class, you use C#'s new operator. Once the statement containing the new keyword is executed, a special method is executed next. This procedure in C# is known as a constructor. The constructor method in C# is declared as a method with no return value and with the name same as the class name. Because the constructor method is executed at the moment of instance creation, this makes it convenient for executing some operations related to object creation, such as field initialization. The constructor declared with no parameters is called the *default constructor*. It does not have to be written explicitly; if you do not declare it, the compiler will create it for you. If you declare a parameterized constructor, the default constructor will not be created automatically. This way, you force the programmer who is creating instance of your class to pass a parameter to the constructor at the moment of instantiation.

Based on what I just said about constructors and static members, you could easily write code that keeps a count of the instances of a class that are created by means of these two elements. Take a look at the following MyClass code:

```
class MyClass
{
    private static int numberOfInstances = 0;

    public static int NumberOfInstances {
        get { return numberOfInstances;  }
    }

    public MyClass() {
        numberOfInstances++;
    }
}
```

In this example, you can see how the value of a static property is incremented by one each time a new instance of MyClass is created, making this information available to all active objects in the program.

I mentioned earlier that all instances of the same class have the same members, including properties. Usually, the values that these properties hold are different from instance to instance. Sometimes, however, it happens that you have two instances that hold identical values for all the properties, making it difficult for you to tell these objects apart. Nonetheless, C#'s runtime has no such problems. This is thanks to another important characteristic of objects: *object identity*.

Object Identity

Every object, even if it is created from the same class as others and even if the values of all its properties are the same as those of another object, is unique in the system and can be distinguished by its runtime. This is because every object is assigned its own memory space; you can be sure that the handle to an object will point to the same unique object as long as you do not explicitly assign another object to it. You use variables to keep the handle to an object. In case you need two variables to point to the same object, you can use the Equals method. Consider the following code:

```
static void Main(string[] args)
{
    object object1 = new object();
    object object2 = new object();
    Console.WriteLine(object1.Equals(object2));

    //Make object1 and object2 variable point to the same object
    object2 = object1;
    Console.WriteLine(object1.Equals(object2));

    Console.ReadLine();
}
```

If you execute the preceding code, the output will be as follows:

```
False
True
```

The default implementation of the Equals method, inherited from the Object class, uses reference semantics, meaning it will return True if the variables point to the same address in memory.

Generally, the Equals method should be overridden so that it takes into account the value of significant properties in the object. This is called *value semantics*. For example, if you have a class that represents a date and you have created two instances of that class that represent the same calendar date — say, January 1, 2008 — it is logical that their comparison should yield the result True even if they occupy different memory spaces, such as in the following code using the .NET framework's System.DateTime type:

```
static void Main(string[] args)
{
    DateTime date1 = new DateTime(2009, 6, 6);
    DateTime date2 = new DateTime(2009, 6, 6);
    DateTime date3 = new DateTime(2010, 6, 6);

    Console.WriteLine(date1.Equals(date2));
    Console.WriteLine(date1.Equals(date3));

    Console.ReadLine();
}
```

The output after executing the preceding code is as follows:

```
True
False
```

For a detailed explanation of the rules you should follow when overriding the method Equals, *see the article "Guidelines for Overriding Equals() and Operator ==," at MSDN* (http://msdn.microsoft.com/en-us/library/ms173147.aspx).

Objects As Basic Building Blocks

Some older languages make a strict distinction between primitive types such as int or char and objects such as Collection, ComboBox, and so on. Primitive types were created to hold some data values and were often used as basic building blocks when you were writing your own custom classes.

In .NET, even simple types such as Integer can be treated as fully capable objects. Thanks to the .NET boxing and unboxing feature, the distinction between simple types, value types, and reference types is almost completely blurred. Therefore, in .NET it is completely legal to write code like the following:

```
static void Main(string[] args)
{
    string stringFromNumberLiteral = 623.ToString();
    Console.WriteLine(stringFromNumberLiteral);

    Console.ReadLine();
}
```

The output, as you might expect, will be 623. In VB 6, for example, calling a method on a literal representing a primitive was not possible. In .NET, this *is* possible because value types can be automatically boxed inside an instance of the object reference type.

Be aware, however, that there is a performance penalty for treating values as reference types.

Root Object

In .NET, each time you write a class, it implicitly inherits the .NET root object: `System.Object`. You can even inherit this object explicitly without any consequence. Therefore, whether you declare your class as `class MyClass` or `class MyClass:Object`, the result is the same: Any object you create will already have a few methods implemented. The public methods are as follows:

- Equals
- GetHashCode
- GetType
- ToString
- Finalize
- MemberwiseClone

This is also true for value types, because the base class for value type `System.ValueType` also inherits `System.Object`. If you declare a variable as `SomeType`, the variable will be able to point to an instance of that or any other subtype of `SomeType`, because of the polymorphic behavior inherent in C# code. As a result, if you declare a variable as `Object`, because all types in .NET inherit `Object`, the variable will be able to point to any instance you can throw at it.

Because `System` is the default namespace, you are free to omit it and write just `Object`, which is more common than `System.Object`.

Object Lifetime and Garbage Collection

When I talked about object state, I said that objects retain state as long as they are alive. Objects can be alive as long as the program lives, but this would not be very practical, so most are discarded during program execution once they are not needed anymore. Objects come to life when you call the `new` operator. As you have already seen, the constructor method is called right after object creation. This is straightforward.

The next logical question is: When do objects die? The answer this time is not as simple. An object's lifetime is determined by its scope. This means that when the object goes out of scope, the runtime is free to reclaim the memory that the object has been occupying. However, this does not happen immediately. To understand what happens when an object goes out of scope, you need to understand a few facts about garbage collection.

Garbage collection is a mechanism for automated memory management. To run efficiently, the runtime needs to allocate memory for new objects and reclaim that memory once it has been left unused. Once an object has gone out of scope and become unreachable, the garbage collector is free to reclaim the memory space and use it for some other object. Failing to reclaim memory results in memory leakage; this is a perilous bug well known to COM programmers.

Reference Counting Garbage Collector

Pre-.NET Visual Basic programmers could also count on the runtime to liberate memory once the object was freed. In COM, garbage collection was based upon reference counting. Each time a new reference to an object was created in COM, the reference count was incremented by one. When the reference was removed, the count was decremented. When the count reached zero, the object was removed and the memory reclaimed.

C++ programmers dealing with COM had to invoke the `AddRef` and `Release` methods defined by the `IUnknown` interface explicitly in their code in order to interact with the reference counting mechanism.

Most of the time this worked well, but in some situations, such as when circular references are produced, for example, the count would fail to reach zero, and the memory would never be reclaimed. This is partly why VB 6 programmers were accustomed to helping the garbage collector by setting the variable value to nothing once they had no need for the object, basically manually decrementing the reference counter. However, this does not work in .NET anymore because in .NET the garbage collector is radically different.

Tracing Garbage Collector

In .NET, Microsoft has implemented a *tracing garbage collector*. That means that the collector starts at root objects (local variables and reference object parameters, global and static object pointers, and so on) and then creates a graph of objects that are reachable from the roots. Objects that are not in the graph are considered unreachable, and the collector is free to reclaim the memory.

To make garbage collection more efficient, you can use different collection optimization techniques, such as dividing objects into generations. This is an optimization technique used by the .NET garbage collector. The garbage collector's performance is one of the most critical performance aspects of the .NET runtime. However, a complete discussion of this subject is beyond the scope of this book. The important fact about the .NET garbage collector is that it is nondeterministic, meaning the programmer has no control over when garbage collection occurs. Although it is possible to invoke garbage collection explicitly, this is not recommended, as it means meddling with complex garbage-collection algorithms, and any performance gains are unlikely unless you know what you are doing.

In conclusion, objects are removed from memory when the garbage collector decides it is the best moment to do so. This has one very practical consequence. If you are using some limited resources, such as database connections, files, or the like, it may not be practical to wait for the garbage collector to kick in. In those cases, you can use C#'s `using` statement to mark the block after which the object should be disposed of. The `using` block can be written like this:

```
using (IDbConnection connection = new SqlConnection()) {
    //..
    }
```

This way, you are guaranteed that the connection object will be disposed of after the end of the `using` block has been reached. If you need to create your own class, which should release resources early by means of a `using` statement, your class should implement the `System.IDisposable` interface.

Garbage collection is a great feature of the .NET Framework. It relieves the programmer of one of the most tedious and bug-spawning tasks: manual memory management.

Messages

As mentioned earlier, the dynamics of the object-oriented system arise from message interchange between objects. When you write the code, you send the message to an object, asking it to perform some operation. This is radically different from calling functions while supplying them with data. As you will see in the next chapter, when you write the code, you may not know until runtime the exact function that will be executed as a consequence.

The previous sections have described some of the most important characteristics of object-oriented programming. It is very important to be aware of these characteristics in order to successfully design and write object-oriented code. Obviously, the story of object-oriented programming does not end here. The next chapter discusses inheritance and polymorphism, two other crucial mechanisms that any object-oriented environment should support.

Designing Classes

Now that you have reviewed the basic building blocks of object-oriented programs, you are ready to embark on the fundamental step in software designing: discovering classes and partitioning your code in the form of types. New classes can be created either starting from a "clean slate," based on your analysis artifacts, or some existing code can be restructured so new classes are introduced in order to better organize that code. One such restructuring is known as Extract Class refactoring. We begin by looking at the crucial step in the design process by which new classes are formed based on analysis artifacts.

Using Analysis Artifacts

In Chapter 6 I talked about the process of writing software, and about techniques you can use to understand the problem domain and gather the requirements. You have seen how in that phase of development, several diverse artifacts can be produced to help structure and organize knowledge about the requirements and problem domain, artifacts such as an agreed-upon vocabulary, use cases, and user stories. All these artifacts use some sort of natural language, diagrams, drawings, prototypes, user interface captures, and so forth to capture whatever functionality the system in question should perform.

However, that chapter ended before the next crucial step: using all this gathered information and transforming it into the code. Based on these artifacts, you can design the classes that are going to be the basic building blocks of your software.

This section describes some of the most popular approaches for the discovery of objects. These approaches should help you bridge a very difficult gap that lies between the natural language (and other artifacts made for human comprehension) and the program code, which is written for computer execution. Keep in mind the complexity of the task; these approaches are hardly foolproof. To apply them efficiently, you need a significant amount of experience and practice.

First and foremost, you need to identify objects belonging to the problem domain. Implementation details will be refined as you go along. When you are designing classes, the most important decisions are concerned with identifying the classes, along with their operations and attributes, and with the relationships that classes can have. Another aspect of the system you are designing that you must not overlook is its dynamics — that is, how objects collaborate and exchange messages.

After a quick look at the first refactoring of this chapter, you will start bridging the gap from concept to code with one popular approach, linguistic analysis.

Refactoring: Extract Class

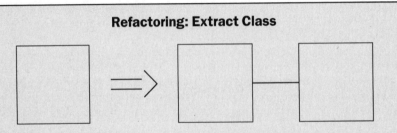

Motivation

Large classes are difficult to understand and maintain. They also make reuse much more difficult and can make you distribute unnecessary pieces of code. Large classes are also a breeding ground for uncontrolled dependencies. Extract Class provides the most direct manner for dealing with large classes.

You should start by looking at the features that are grouped and that go naturally together inside the class. Sometimes these features have a common prefix indicating that they belong together. For example, in the class Client you have properties prefixed by the word Telephone: TelephoneNumber, TelephoneAreaCode, TelephoneType. Such features can be extracted into a separate class.

Related Smells

Use this refactoring to eliminate the Large Class smell and to make a class comply with the Single Responsibility Principle (SRP). (Both the Large Class smell and the SRP are both defined later in this chapter.)

Mechanics

1. Create a class for features you would like to split into a separate class.

2. Make a link between an original class and a new class. The new class can become a field of the originating class.

3. Use Move Field refactoring on the originating class and bring a field into the new class.

4. Continue moving fields and methods (and rename them if needed after moving them) until you are done.

Before

```
public class ShoppingCart
{
    private IList products;
    private int customerNumber;
    private string customerName;
    private CustomerTypes customerType;
    public decimal CustomerDiscount()
    {
        if (this.CustomerType == CustomerTypes.Premium)
        {
            return 3;
        }
```

```
            else
            {
                return 0;
            }
        }
        public CustomerTypes CustomerType
        {
            get { return customerType; }
            set { customerType = value; }
        }
        public decimal CalculateTotal()
        {
            decimal total = default(decimal);
            foreach (Product product in this.Products)
            {
                total += product.Price;
            }
            total = total - (total / 100) * this.CustomerDiscount();
            return total;
        }
        public IList Products
        {
            get { return products; }
            set { products = value; }
        }
        //...
    }
```

After

```
    public class ShoppingCart
    {
        private IList products;
        private Customer customer = new Customer();
        public decimal CalculateTotal()
        {
            decimal total = default(decimal);
            foreach (Product product in this.Products)
            {
                total += product.Price;
            }
            total = total - (total / 100) * this.customer.Discount();
            return total;
        }
        public Customer Customer
        {
            get { return customer; }
            set { customer = value; }
        }
        public IList Products
        {
            get { return products; }
```

Continued

```
                set { products = value; }
        }
        //...
}

public class Customer
{
    private string name;
    private int number;
    private CustomerTypes type;
    public string Name
    {
        get { return name; }
        set { name = value; }
    }
    public int Number
    {
        get { return number; }
        set { number = value; }
    }
    public CustomerTypes Type
    {
        get { return type; }
        set { type = value; }
    }
    public decimal Discount()
    {
        if (this.Type == CustomerTypes.Premium)
        {
            return 3;
        }
        else
        {
            return 0;
        }
    }
}
```

Classes Are Nouns, Operations Are Verbs

Probably the most popular approach in object-oriented circles for developing code from the artifacts you have gathered is textual or linguistic analysis. During analysis, you have surely produced some text that describes the desired system behavior and some sample user-system interactions. Often, this text takes the form of use cases. You can analyze such text and find classes "buried in the text," along with their members, according to the following rules:

❏   Nouns become classes.

❏   Verbs become operations.

❏   Some nouns (or adjectives) become attributes of classes.

❏   An "is a" phrase indicates inheritance and a "has a" phrase indicates a strong association such as composition or aggregation.

You can see how this works on a sample use case from the Rent-a-Wheels application. You have already seen this use case in Chapter 4, and many more use cases are available in that chapter if you want to give this a try for yourself. This process generally goes through a few steps, and I will demonstrate them in the order in which they are performed.

Step 1: Mark All the Nouns

Start with a very simple operation, marking all nouns in the use case with bold. Here is the Rent a Vehicle use case with all the nouns identified:

1. **Receptionist** selects the **vehicle** from the **list** of available **vehicles**.
2. **Receptionist** inputs the **customer** data: **ID type** and **number**.
3. **Receptionist** marks the **vehicle** as "hand over."

Step 2: Eliminate the Actor

Generally, you do not need to model the actor as a part of your system. The actor is an external entity that interacts with the system. Actor elimination results in fewer selected nouns:

1. Receptionist selects the **vehicle** from the **list** of available **vehicles**.
2. Receptionist inputs the **customer** data: **ID type** and **number**.
3. Receptionist marks the **vehicle** as "hand over."

Step 3: Eliminate Duplicated Nouns

In a use case, the same noun can appear more than once. The same noun is usually transformed in the same class, at least when use cases are well written, so you end up with the following list of nouns:

1. Vehicle
2. List of vehicles
3. Customer
4. ID type
5. ID number

Step 4: Separate System Classes from Domain Classes

The system classes are those supporting classes that do not belong to the problem domain. Very often, you can count on the .NET Framework or third-party libraries to provide you with these classes. If you have some specific requirements that existing classes do not support, you might need to program these classes as well, or extend existing ones. In that case, you should consider them also. Often, however, the decision whether to use existing classes or to program custom classes is made later in the process, when more details about implementation are known, and you start by using existing ones.

In this example, you can see from the use-case content that "List of vehicles" is an object used for pre-sentational purposes, to render a list of vehicles to a user and enable that user to select a single vehicle from the list. It is probable that some existing widget can be used to instantiate an object that fulfills this purpose, so I'll put aside for the moment the "List of vehicles" noun in this design.

Step 5: Separate Attributes from Classes

If you read the use case carefully, you will find some compound nouns such as ID type and ID number. If you interpret the second statement in the use case, you will see that ID, in fact, refers to a form of identification, and that ID type and ID number refer to attributes of this class. Some attributes can be successfully represented with system classes. For example, an identification document number can be represented with a string (some documents, such as passports, can have characters in the identification number). You could also represent the identification document type with a simple string, but a more elaborate design would limit the choice of document types, so a better choice for the identification document type is an enumeration.

The rule about using adjectives to identify attributes will not work out well most of the time. Because of the style of writing that is common in use cases, you seldom find phrases like "The car is red." More often than not you will find a statement like "The color of the car is red." This means that an adjective (color, in this instance) is used in these cases to identify an attribute of a class.

Going back to the example, after this step you have the following classes and enumerations identified:

1. Vehicle
2. Customer
3. ID with attributes number and type:

    ❑ Attribute number is of String type

    ❑ Attribute type is of ID type enumeration

4. ID type (enumeration)

Smell: Data Class

Detecting the Smell

A class that has only properties and no methods is a data class. These classes and structures are generally easily discovered because they appear as long lists of fields and property blocks uninterrupted by method definitions.

Related Refactoring

Use Convert Procedural Design to Objects and Move Method refactorings to eliminate the smell.

Rationale

Object-oriented programming brings data and behavior together. A class consisting of fields and properties only is lacking methods that give life to data. This behavior is then implemented in some other place, maybe as a part of some other class or in the form of shared methods. Wherever the methods actually are, by not being in the right place they will stand in the way of encapsulation and make inheritance, polymorphism, and similar object-oriented techniques impossible to implement.

Step 6: Interpret "is a" and "has a" Phrases

Again, you need to do some interpretation of the use case text. You have already seen how ID type and ID number were hiding another class not directly mentioned, an ID document. This object is used to identify the customer.

In fact, you can now say that "the customer has an ID document." This means that there is some sort of stronger association between the customer and the ID document. I have chosen to represent this association as an aggregation, as the customer can probably exist in the system even without an ID document. (The type of association will have no consequence on the code of these classes. It might, however, influence how you program the system later.) This means that the customer will have a property of the type ID document. In a class diagram, this is represented with a line going from the IdDocument class to the Customer class with a diamond ending it (see Figure 9-3).

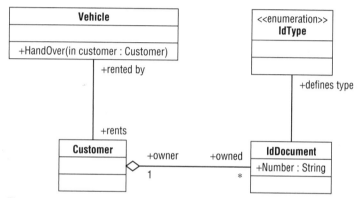

Figure 9-3

Step 7: Identify the Operations

The last sentence in the use case talks about an operation that is performed in the system. You have already identified the classes in the system; and as you have seen in the introductory part of this chapter, in object-oriented programs you ask an object to perform an operation by sending it a message. Sentence number three in the use case talks about handing over the vehicle, so you can add a handOver operation to the Vehicle class. You need to supply the Vehicle with a piece of information in order for it to be able to perform this operation — that is, you need to supply the Customer. In the end, the operation will look something like this once it is written down:

```
public class Vehicle
{
    public void HandOver(Customer customer)
    {
        //... to be implemented
    }
    //...
}
```

With this, the process of textual analysis is more or less complete. In real life, you iterate the process for other use cases. During iteration, you will discover new classes and more members and relations between existing classes. As you continue, more pieces of the picture are discovered, and you move one step closer to the first version of your application.

Now take a look at the classes you have identified so far, as shown in the diagram in Figure 9-3.

In the example you analyzed, you found no occurrences of an "is a" relation. Such a relation would indicate inheritance between classes and might be written as follows: "If a vehicle is a truck, then the hand-over operation is performed as follows." In that case, you would use another class, `Truck`, that inherits from `Vehicle`, to represent this new entity. The `Truck` class would override the `handOver` operation to realize a different set of steps that are performed when a truck is handed over to a customer.

As you can see, the class diagram contains all the classes, their operations and attributes, and the relationships between classes identified in the sample use case by means of textual analysis. If you go back to the Rent-a-Wheels code, you will find no mention of the classes you just identified. From that you can conclude that some other modeling technique was used to design the code. If you remember, the Rent-a-Wheels application layer design was preceded by database design; I call this technique database-driven design, and will talk about it in the context of anti-patterns. An anti-pattern is similar to a smell, only it generally works on a larger scale.

> **Definition: An anti-pattern is a repeated solution to a problem that presents a number of difficulties and design flaws. A better solution is possible but is not applied because of lack of knowledge or simple malpractice. An anti-pattern can generally be refactored into a more optimal solution.**

The next section explores another technique you have at your disposal when you are trying to identify classes to comprise the system you are building: thinking about objects in terms of classes, their responsibilities, and their collaborators.

Smell: Database-Driven Design

Detecting the Smell

A way to detect this smell is often indirect. Most of the design document is concerned with database design. The team talks about *database structure, data integrity,* and *normalization,* but is not very concerned with identifying classes, designing objects, or considering the interactions at work.

Such an approach often leads to a simplistic design wherein C# code fulfills the purpose of a simple data-flow conductor. Because there is no elaborate design, many more advanced object-oriented techniques such as inheritance and polymorphism are not present. The design does not reflect the problem domain.

Related Refactoring

Use Replace Row with Data Class, Convert Procedural Design to Objects, and Extract Class refactorings to eliminate the smell.

Rationale

Code whose only purpose is to store and retrieve data from the database does not comply with basic object-oriented principles and does not represent the problem domain or embody the business rules. Such C# code delegates all important logic to the SQL code layer. This means that a lot of duplicated and redundant code is present, making the application difficult to maintain and modify.

Classes, Responsibilities, and Collaborators

One way to think about the design of your system is to think about classes, their responsibilities, and the way they interact or collaborate. *Class-responsibility-collaborator cards* (CRC) are a brainstorming and design tool that can help you identify and design the classes for your system. The cards should help you think about classes in terms of their responsibilities and collaborators. This is a great tool for understanding the dynamics of the system and behavior of objects. The cards render naturally into an object-oriented design.

In a CRC-card design session, you start with a stack of blank 4″×6″ index cards. Each card should represent a single class. The cards have three compartments: top, left, and right. Each compartment should be filled in by the developer.

- ❏ **Top**: Place the class name in this compartment. Optionally, add a section for listing superclasses and subclasses.

- ❏ **Left**: List all the responsibilities that belong to the class in this section.

- ❏ **Right**: List all the collaborators that the class communicates with to perform its responsibilities.

Refactoring: Move Method

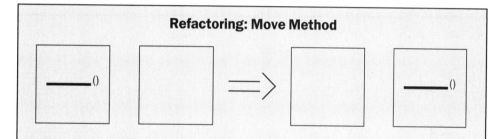

Motivation

Sometimes a method just seems more interested in other class's members than in members of its own class. In that case, the method makes more sense in the other class.

Related Smells

Use this refactoring to eliminate the Large Class, Data Class, and Procedural Design smells and to simplify classes that do not obey the SRP.

Mechanics

1. Start by copying the method into the new class. Rename it if you have a name that fits better and makes it work with data available in the new class.

2. If the method needs originating class members and there is no other way to get the necessary functionality, then pass the originating object as a parameter to a method.

3. If possible, make the clients use the new method and then delete the original method. If not, keep the delegation code in the original method.

Continued

Before

```
public class Point
{
    public double X;
    public double Y;
    public double CalculateCircumferenceLength(Point center,
        Point pointOnCircumference)
    {
        return 2 * 3.1415 * CalculateRadius(center,
            pointOnCircumference);
    }
    public double CalculateRadius(Point center,
        Point pointOnCircumference)
    {
        return Math.Sqrt(
                Math.Pow((pointOnCircumference.X - center.X), 2)
                + Math.Pow((pointOnCircumference.Y - center.Y), 2)
            );
    }
}

public class Circle
{
    private Point center;
    private Point pointOnCircumference;
    public Point Center
    {
        get { return center; }
        set { center = value; }
    }
    public Point PointOnCircumference
    {
        get { return pointOnCircumference; }
        set { pointOnCircumference = value; }
    }
}
```

After

```
public class Point
{
        public double X;
        public double Y;
    }
public class Circle
{
    private Point center;
    private Point pointOnCircumference;
    public Point Center
    {
        get { return center; }
        set { center = value; }
```

```
    }
    public Point PointOnCircumference
    {
        get { return pointOnCircumference; }
        set { pointOnCircumference = value; }
    }
    public double CalculateCircumferenceLength()
    {
        return 2 * 3.1415 * CalculateRadius();
    }
    public double CalculateRadius()
    {
        return Math.Sqrt(
                Math.Pow((this.PointOnCircumference.X
                    - this.Center.X), 2)
                + Math.Pow((this.PointOnCircumference.Y
                    - this.Center.Y), 2)
            );
    }
}
```

Moving features between classes is very common in the refactoring process. The following Move Field refactoring is similar to Move Method refactoring (shown in the preceding sidebar) and can be employed in its own right or as a part of other more complex refactorings such as Extract Method.

Refactoring: Move Field

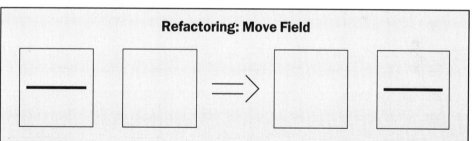

Motivation
Sometimes the methods of another class seem to be much more interested in the field in the class than are the methods in the class containing the field. This results in *high coupling* between classes and weakened encapsulation and modularity. While this refactoring can be used on its own, it is an essential part of Extract Class refactoring.

Related Smells
Use this refactoring to eliminate the Large Class, Data Class, and Procedural Design smells.

Mechanics

1. Start with Encapsulate Field refactoring, providing property access to a field, if the field is public and accessed directly. In the originating class, replace all field access with property access.

Continued

2. Copy the field and the property that encapsulates it to a targeted class.

3. Make the target class accessible to the originating class. Sometimes you can obtain a target instance from existing fields or methods. If not, you might need to add a field with a target instance.

4. Make the property in the originating class use the property on the target class instead of on the field.

5. Eliminate the field in the originating class.

Alternatively, if the originating class contains only a small number of references to a field, you can reference a property on the target class directly, eliminating the property in the originating class altogether.

Before

```
public class Rental
{
    //...
    private int numberOfDays;
    private Vehicle vehicle;
    public decimal DailyPrice;
    public int NumberOfDays
    {
        get { return numberOfDays; }
        set { numberOfDays = value; }
    }
    public Vehicle Vehicle
    {
        get { return vehicle; }
        set { vehicle = value; }
    }
    public decimal Total()
    {
        return this.NumberOfDays * this.DailyPrice
            + Vehicle.Tank.Price();
    }
}

public class VehicleType
{
    //...
    private string name;
    public string Name
    {
        get { return name; }
        set { name = value; }
    }
}
```

After

```
public class Rental
{
    //...
    private Vehicle vehicle;
    private decimal dailyPrice;
    public decimal DailyPrice
    {
        get { return this.Vehicle.Type.DailyPrice; }
        set { this.Vehicle.Type.DailyPrice = value; }
    }
    public int NumberOfDays
    {
        get { return numberOfDaysValue; }
        set { numberOfDaysValue = value; }
    }
    public Vehicle Vehicle
    {
        get { return vehicle; }
        set { vehicle = value; }
    }
    public decimal Total()
    {
        return this.NumberOfDays * this.DailyPrice +
            Vehicle.Tank.Price();
    }
}

public class VehicleType
{
    //...
    private string name;
    private decimal dailyPrice;
    public string Name
    {
        get { return name; }
        set { name = value; }
    }
    public decimal DailyPrice
    {
        get { return dailyPrice; }
        set { dailyPrice = value; }
    }
}
```

Employing Cards in Brainstorming Sessions

When starting a CRC-card design session, you should select a seemingly related set of use cases or user stories. You first identify the classes in a process similar to textual or linguistic analysis by transforming nouns into classes. Then you assign responsibilities to the classes. Again, you can use textual analysis to identify verbs, indicating the problem the class should solve. Finally, you should look for other classes that the class needs to successfully fulfill its responsibilities, and then list these classes in the Collaborators compartment on the card.

You generally work with cards in a team environment. As the session progresses, cards are refined, some are put aside, and new ones are created. The cards can be arranged on the table to reflect different scenarios. During this role-playing, each card can represent an instance of a class. As different scenarios and use cases are played out, the design is further refined and reinforced.

If a card becomes too crammed with features, that's a good indication that a new card should be introduced and some responsibilities passed to that new card. Because new cards are easily created and old ones are easily put aside or thrown back into play, cards are a great interactive and dynamic aid. Figure 9-4 shows two sample cards that were created based on the already familiar Rent-a-Vehicle use case, used for a textual analysis example in the previous section.

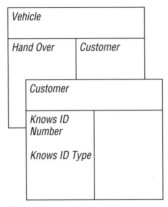

Figure 9-4

CRC cards are great tools for discovering classes that will comprise the design of your system. Their focus on responsibilities and object collaboration fits naturally into an object-oriented approach to software design and can be a great technique for bridging this ever-present gap between the analysis artifacts and the code.

Object-Oriented Design Principle: Single Responsibility

The Single Responsibility Principle (SRP) is a fundamental design principle that can help you produce a granular and reusable design that is resilient to change. SRP dictates that all members of a class should be similar and used to solve a single problem. This way, the motives for change will be much more homogenous and the impact of change will be localized.

Definition

In *Agile Software Development: Principles, Patterns, and Practices* (Prentice Hall, 2002), Robert C. Martin writes, "A class should have only one reason to change." Again, change is at the heart of this principle. While we cannot fight change in software, it is crucial that the process motivated by change is controlled and localized. The more

---

heterogeneous the members of the class, the more possible motives for change can be found. This can have huge consequences for application development. Once the responsibilities of a class become coupled, the effects of change become far-reaching and difficult to control, resulting in an application that breaks unexpectedly in different places as a result of change.

Imagine you have a Windows Forms class that can calculate the length of a circle's diameter. The class has both presentation and geometrical calculation code. Now imagine that the client needs to put this functionality on the web. For this, the presentation class you use will be some Active Server Page (ASP) class. Because the initial Windows Forms class has both presentation and calculation code, you'll have to either completely rewrite your Windows Forms class or distribute unnecessary Windows Forms code with an ASP application. Now, if your original application changes, you will also have to test the ASP application, distribute the Windows Forms class to the ASP application that will never make any use of this presentation code, version the class, and so on.

Example

I'll stick with the familiar subject for this example. Imagine you have programmed a Vehicle class as follows:

```
public class Vehicle
{
    public void HandOver(Customer customer)
    {
        if (!this.InMaintenance)
        {
            this.HandedOver = true;
        }
        else
        {
            throw new InvalidVehicleOperationException(
                "Cannot hand over vehicle. Vehicle in maintenance.");
        }
    }
    public void Update()
    {
        IDbConnection connection = new SqlConnection(connectionString);
        connection.Open();
        IDbCommand command = new SqlCommand();
        command.Connection = connection;
        command.CommandText = sql;
        command.ExecuteNonQuery();
        //etc..
    }
    //...
}
```

If you analyze this code, you can clearly see that the Vehicle class has more than one responsibility. It contains both rental business–elated code (the HandOver method) and persistence-related code (the Update method). This has a number of possible consequences:

Continued

❑ If you change the persistence mechanism, the class has to change.

❑ If you change some business logic, the class has to change.

❑ If one of the responsibilities of the class changes, you have no guarantee that the other one still works correctly until you test that functionality also.

❑ If you would like to reuse the business-related code, you have to distribute persistence code in the same package, and vice versa.

It is often an initial reflex to put persistence logic inside the domain class. After all, the data and the operations with the object go together and should not be separated. However, if you think about it carefully, the Update method is not really concerned with Vehicle data. It needs this data to be able to persist a vehicle instance, but it is really more concerned with the behavior of the database provider object.

Clearly, this class should be split into two classes. One should contain only business-related logic, and the other only persistence code. As a result, I'll keep the Vehicle class and leave the HandOver method inside it. I will create a new VehicleDataStore class and move the Update method to this new class. The code that follows now obeys the SRP:

```
public class Vehicle
{
    public void HandOver(Customer customer)
    {
        if (!this.InMaintenance)
        {
            this.HandedOver = true;
        }
        else
        {
            throw new InvalidVehicleOperation(
                "Cannot hand over vehicle. Vehicle in maintenance.");
        }
    }
    //...
}

public class VehicleDataStore
{
    public void Update(Vehicle vehicle)
    {
        IDbConnection connection = new SqlConnection(connectionString);
        connection.Open();
        IDbCommand command = new SqlCommand();
        command.Connection = connection;
        command.CommandText = sql;
        command.ExecuteNonQuery();
        //etc..
    }
    //...
}
```

The next section describes another approach to modeling your system, one more fit for modeling the data than for modeling your classes, but still practiced by many teams when they are designing C# applications.

Entities and Relationships

The entity-relationship model is a standard method for designing database structures. This model presents a logical view of the data whereby you think about the system in terms of entities, their attributes, and the relationship between the two. Such a view is easily translated to a relational database design in which entities correspond to tables, attributes to columns, and relationships to relational constraints or relation tables.

Database design is generally motivated by a desire for data retrieval and storage efficiency, data consistency, elimination of redundant data, and so on. Often the design is further refined through a normalization process. Such a process is guided by some mathematical rules that optimize data structuring, and it resembles the refactoring of object-oriented systems.

> The ADO.NET Entity Framework abstracts the entity-relationship model such that the conceptual entity-relationship schema is mapped to a database schema, removing the direct coupling of the data persistence layer and the application layer.

However, object-oriented design is a design guided by software design principles. You can often find redundant data in object-oriented systems, while this is undesirable from the database design viewpoint. You navigate through objects by following the relations; in databases, you join tables. You can group objects inside the collection, while in databases, you store rows inside the table. There are a number of different principles that work in one technology but are not applicable in the other.

This modeling technique can help you visualize some static relations, but the dynamics of the system and object communication patterns will not be covered. In addition, some complex relationships between objects, such as inheritance, will not be identified.

If a project's general application design is driven by database design, you encounter the Database-Driven Design smell. In such cases, the design of classes and Visual Basic code is often neglected and simply functions as database storage and retrieval. While this can be considered malpractice, it is often the design approach taken by traditional C# development teams.

Object-Relational Impedance Mismatch

This term refers to the problem of programs written in some object-oriented language using relational databases. The problem arises because the two technologies are not completely analogous. While at first glance there is a correspondence between classes and tables, databases are not capable of expressing more complex relations between classes, such as inheritance, that are present in object-oriented systems. As a result, a lot of boilerplate code has to be produced in order for a database to be used for object storage. A number of products, ranging from object-oriented databases to object-relation mapping tools, have been developed that can deal with this problem to a greater or lesser extent.

At this point, you have seen what to do during the analysis phase. You also know the techniques you have at your disposal to transform the analysis artifacts into the design of your classes. Very often, however, you will already have at your disposal operational code with all the classes identified and structured. In the next section, you'll see how to deal with such code.

Discovering Hidden Classes

In the first section of this chapter, you reviewed some basic characteristics of object-oriented code. These characteristics should be taken into account when you design your system and write code for your classes. Following that material, you learned how you can make a transition from analysis artifacts toward the design of your application.

At this point, you might be wondering what to do with already operational code that is not well structured and that you sense has other classes that are not identified. In this section, you'll deal with this very common situation — that is, poorly structured code that has classes buried and hidden within it. A typical characteristic of such code is that it does not comply with the SRP.

You will also learn how to identify over-encumbered classes and discover what techniques you have at your disposal to refactor such code and distribute the responsibilities between classes in a more balanced way. You can start with a very common situation: code that communicates directly with a database without embodying the rules of the problem domain.

Smell: Large Class

Detecting the Smell
A long list of properties and methods is the first sign of the Large Class smell, and the easiest to detect. Another good indicator of a large class is a long and heterogeneous import section. A large class is often accompanied by long methods.

Related Refactoring
Use Extract Method, Extract Class, and Extract Superclass refactorings to eliminate this smell.

Rationale
A large class is often a manifestation of some other, more specialized smell such as Event-Handling Blindness, Database-Driven Design, or a similar problem caused by mixing presentation and domain classes. Whatever the reason for its existence, it suffers from too many responsibilities. That means the class can suffer change from many different motives and is a source of spiraling dependencies and cascading changes.

A large class is difficult to read and understand. Sometimes only part of its attributes has meaning relatable to class name, and some methods are used under specific circumstances, or its execution is conditioned.

Sometimes a large class appears and grows with time. As new functionalities are requested, the easiest way to implement them is to add more code to existing classes. This is a sign of decaying design, in which not enough care is taken to refactor the application in time.

Dealing with Database-Driven Design

A very common approach in database-driven development is to concentrate your design on the database. The data vocabulary is created, tables are designed with data integrity and normalization in mind, and indexes are created for optimal access.

After that, the rest of the application code is developed as the sole function of the database. Often, in such cases, applications are built in the form of a two-tiered architecture wherein the presentation layer is used to communicate directly with the database, as a sort of data conductor, using the database provider API directly in the presentation classes.

Refactoring: Replace Row with Data Class

Motivation

An application can be built in the form of a two-tiered architecture, wherein the presentation layer communicates directly with the database. Database access and some other APIs often use a row paradigm in the communication layer for retrieval of sets of data, such as the `System.Data.DataRow` class in the .NET Framework.

If such row objects are used, directly evading the use of a business (or domain) layer, the code will probably suffer from duplication and be difficult to understand and maintain. As a step toward more complete object-oriented design, you can replace rows with a simple data class that has only properties. Each property should correspond to an item in a row. Such a class contains only data, a signal that the design is not complete and that you should complete it by moving related methods inside the class. You should consider this as only a first step in the right direction: toward defining the domain layer for your application.

Related Smells

Use this refactoring to eliminate Duplicated Code, Large Class, and Database-Driven Design smells and to make classes comply with the SRP.

Mechanics

A need for defining the domain layer appears often in two-tiered applications that have no domain layer. In such applications, presentation and other client layers communicate directly with the database by means of a row paradigm.

1. Create a class that will represent a row structure. One instance of a class corresponds to one row.

2. For each item in the row, create a property in your class.

3. Instead of using the rows directly, make the code create instances of the data class and return them to the client.

Before

```
//...
public class AccountView
{
    //...
```

Continued

```
            private void viewAccountDetails_Click(
                object sender, System.EventArgs e)
        {
            IDbConnection connection = new SqlConnection(connectionString);
            IDbDataAdapter adapter = new SqlDataAdapter();
            DataSet accountDataSet = new DataSet();
            IDbCommand command = new SqlCommand();
            string sql = "Select * from Accounts "
                + "where Number = " + this.Number.Text;
            connection.Open();
            command.Connection = connection;
            command.CommandText = sql;
            adapter.SelectCommand = command;
            adapter.Fill(accountDataSet);
            connection.Close();
            accountTable = accountDataSet.Tables[0];
            DataRow accountRow = accountTable.Rows[0];
            //Fill controls on the form
            this.Name.Text = accountRow["Name"].ToString();
            this.Type.Text = accountRow["Type"].ToString();
            if (!Convert.ToBoolean(accountRow["Blocked"]))
            {
                this.Balance.Text = accountRow["Balance"].ToString();
            }
            else
            {
                this.Balance.Text = "Blocked";
            }
        }
    }
```

After

```
//...
public class AccountView
{
    //...
    private void viewAccountDetails_Click(object sender,
        System.EventArgs e)
    {
        Account account = GetAccount(this.Number.Text);
        this.Name.Text = account.Name;
        this.Type.Text = account.Type;
        if (!account.Blocked)
        {
            this.Balance.Text = account.Balance.ToString();
        }
        else
        {
            this.Balance.Text = "Blocked";
        }
    }
```

```
    private Account GetAccount(string number)
    {
        IDbConnection connection = new SqlConnection(connectionString);
        IDbDataAdapter adapter = new SqlDataAdapter();
        DataSet accountDataSet = new DataSet();
        IDbCommand command = new SqlCommand();
        string sql = "Select * from Accounts " +
            "where Number = " + number;
        connection.Open();
        command.Connection = connection;
        command.CommandText = sql;
        adapter.SelectCommand = command;
        adapter.Fill(accountDataSet);
        connection.Close();
        accountTable = accountDataSet.Tables[0];
        DataRow accountRow = accountTable.Rows(selectedRow);
        Account account = new Account();
        account.Number = accountRow["Number"].ToString();
        account.Name = accountRow["Name"].ToString();
        account.Type = accountRow["Type"].ToString();
        account.Balance = Convert.ToDecimal(accountRow["Balance"]);
        account.Blocked = Convert.ToBoolean(accountRow["Blocked"]);
        return account;
    }
    //...
}

//New class defined to replace DataRow
public class Account
{
    private string number;
    private string name;
    private AccountType type;
    private decimal balance;
    private bool blocked;

    public string Number
    {
        get { return number; }
        set { number = value; }
    }
    public string Name
    {
        get { return name; }
        set { name = value; }
    }
    public AccountType Type
    {
        get { return type; }
        set { type = value; }
    }
    public decimal Balance
    {
```

Continued

```
            get { return balance; }
            set { balance = value; }
        }
        public bool Blocked
        {
            get { return blocked; }
            set { blocked = value; }
        }
    }
```

Another place to look for hidden objects is in code written in a procedural style. As you probably know, it has taken software science a few decades to move from procedural to object-oriented programming, but in the next section you will do it in whirlwind fashion.

Moving from Procedural to Object-Oriented Design

As I have already mentioned, it is possible to write C# programs without ever coding a class or instantiating an object. Static members are remnants of C#'s procedural origins. You can invoke static methods without creating an instance of a class to which they belong. Still another sign of procedural design is data without behavior. In C#, such data can be found inside a class or structure that has only fields and simple properties declared that do nothing other than return the values of private fields.

As mentioned previously, data can feel lonely without behavior, as can behavior without data. It is only natural to try to bring them together. Chapter 7 includes an excellent example of procedural style, the CircleCircumferenceLength example. In this chapter, you can start just where you left off, at Listing 7-9 in that chapter.

Smell: Procedural Design

Detecting the Smell
This smell is easily detected because of the excessive presence of C# static methods and fields (or properties).

Another sign of procedural design is classes or structures comprising properties and no methods (Data Class smell): a type having data but no behavior. Because behavior is not part of the type, it is most probably implemented in the form of static functions.

Related Refactoring
Use Convert Procedural Design to Objects refactoring to eliminate this smell.

Rationale
Procedural design is often a remnant of old styles and practices. When using procedural design, you cannot benefit from inheritance, polymorphism, higher-level encapsulation, or a host of other benefits object-oriented design can bring to your code.

The first thing that you can observe is that two methods, CalculateRadius and CalculateCircumferenceLength, have the same parameter list: center and pointOnCircumference points. In this example, these two points are used to define the circle. Because they define a single circle, they should be used as properties of that object, so you can add to your solution a class Circle with two properties of type Point: Center and PointOnCircumference. Listing 9-1 shows the code.

Listing 9-1: Circle Class Creation

```csharp
public class Circle
{
    private Point center;
    private Point pointOnCircumference;

    public Point Center
    {
        get { return center; }
        set { center = value; }
    }
    public Point PointOnCircumference
    {
        get { return pointOnCircumference; }
        set { pointOnCircumference = value; }
    }
}
```

This is still a simple data class, but don't worry — this is just the beginning. Now you should make the code use this class instead of passing circle points as unrelated objects. Take a look at the Main method of the CircleCircumferenceLength class using the Circle class in Listing 9-2.

Listing 9-2: CircleCircumferenceLength Class After the Circle Class Is Introduced

```csharp
using System;

namespace RefactoringInCSharpAndASP.Chapter9
{
    public struct Point
    {
        public double X;
        public double Y;
    }

    class CircleCircumferenceLength
    {
        static void Main(string[] args)
        {
            Circle circle = new Circle();
            circle.Center = InputPoint("circle center");
            circle.PointOnCircumference = InputPoint("point on circumference");
            //calculate and display the length of circumference
```

Continued

Listing 9-2: CircleCircumferenceLength Class After the Circle Class Is Introduced
(continued)

```
            Console.WriteLine("The length of circle "
                + "circumference is:");
            double lengthOfCircumference = CalculateCircumferenceLength(circle);
            Console.WriteLine(lengthOfCircumference);
            WaitForUserToClose();
        }

        private static Point InputPoint(String pointName)
        {
            Point point = new Point();
            Console.WriteLine("Enter X coordinate " +
                "of " + pointName);
            point.X = Double.Parse(Console.In.ReadLine());
            Console.WriteLine("Enter Y coordinate " +
                "of " + pointName);
            point.Y = Double.Parse(Console.In.ReadLine());
            return point;
        }

        private static double CalculateCircumferenceLength(Circle circle)
        {
            return 2 * 3.1415 * CalculateRadius(circle);
        }

        private static double CalculateRadius(Circle circle)
        {
            return Math.Sqrt(Math.Pow(circle.PointOnCircumference.X
                                    - circle.Center.X,
                            2) +

                            Math.Pow(circle.PointOnCircumference.Y
                                    - circle.Center.Y,
                            2)
                        );
        }

        private static void WaitForUserToClose()
        {
            Console.Read();
        }
    }
}
```

All you have to do now is look for behavior that you can move inside the `Circle` class. There are two methods in a `CircleCircumferenceLength` class that receive all the data they use as a circle parameter. If these methods could access the data in the form of instance data, instead of parameters, it would mean less writing. Moving these methods inside the `Circle` class enables just that.

To accomplish this, just copy the methods into the `Circle` class. Then delete the parameter declaration and replace the `circle` parameter name with the `this` keyword if some of the values from the circle are referenced. If the parameter is only referenced directly, then simply delete it. Once you have moved the methods to the `Circle` class, you have to change the visibility to public, as they will be invoked from another class. Because these are now instance methods, the keyword `static` has to be erased from the method declaration. The resulting code is shown in Listing 9-3.

Listing 9-3: Circle Class After Move Method Refactoring

```csharp
namespace RefactoringInCSharpAndASP.Chapter9
{
    public class Circle
    {
        private Point center;
        private Point pointOnCircumference;

        public Point Center
        {
            get { return center; }
            set { center = value; }
        }
        public Point PointOnCircumference
        {
            get { return pointOnCircumference; }
            set { pointOnCircumference = value; }
        }

        public double CalculateCircumferenceLength()
        {
            return 2 * 3.1415 * CalculateRadius();
        }

        public double CalculateRadius()
        {
            return Math.Sqrt(Math.Pow(this.PointOnCircumference.X
                                    - this.Center.X,
                                2) +
                            Math.Pow(this.PointOnCircumference.Y
                                    - this.Center.Y,
                                2)
                            );
        }
    }
}
```

All that is left is to make the `CircleCircumferenceLength` class use `Circle` methods instead of its own. This is easily accomplished. All `CircleCircumferenceLength` class has to do is call the method on the `Circle` instance. Listing 9-4 shows the final version of the code.

Listing 9-4: CircleCircumferenceLength Calculation Code Converted to Object Design

```csharp
using System;

namespace RefactoringInCSharpAndASP.Chapter9
{
    public struct Point
    {
        public double X;
        public double Y;
    }

    class CircleCircumferenceLength
    {
        static void Main(string[] args)
        {
            Circle circle = new Circle();
            circle.Center = InputPoint("circle center");
            circle.PointOnCircumference = InputPoint("point on circumference");
            //calculate and display the length of circumference
            Console.WriteLine("The length of circle "
                + "circumference is:");
            double lengthOfCircumference = circle.CalculateCircumferenceLength();
            Console.WriteLine(lengthOfCircumference);
            WaitForUserToClose();
        }

        private static Point InputPoint(String pointName)
        {
            Point point = new Point();
            Console.WriteLine("Enter X coordinate " +
                "of " + pointName);
            point.X = Double.Parse(Console.In.ReadLine());
            Console.WriteLine("Enter Y coordinate " +
                "of " + pointName);
            point.Y = Double.Parse(Console.In.ReadLine());
            return point;
        }

        private static void WaitForUserToClose()
        {
            Console.Read();
        }
    }
```

```
public class Circle
{
    private Point center;
    private Point pointOnCircumference;

    public Point Center
    {
        get { return center; }
        set { center = value; }
    }
    public Point PointOnCircumference
    {
        get { return pointOnCircumference; }
        set { pointOnCircumference = value; }
    }

    public double CalculateCircumferenceLength()
    {
        return 2 * 3.1415 * CalculateRadius();
    }

    private double CalculateRadius()
    {
        return Math.Sqrt(Math.Pow(this.PointOnCircumference.X
                                    - this.Center.X,
                        2) +
                        Math.Pow(this.PointOnCircumference.Y
                                    - this.Center.Y,
                        2)
                );
    }
}
}
```

Note two other interesting items in this refactoring:

❑   Because there is no need to access the `CalculateRadius` method from the outside, you can hide the method by reducing its visibility to private. This demonstrates how encapsulation works on another level with objects.

❑   Looking at the `Circle` class, note that it contains no data input code. In the example module, you used the `Console` interface to enable users to communicate with the application. If you now decide you would prefer to implement a Windows Forms interface, you can easily reuse the `Circle` class. This is possible because the domain is separated from presentation, which is the subject of the next section.

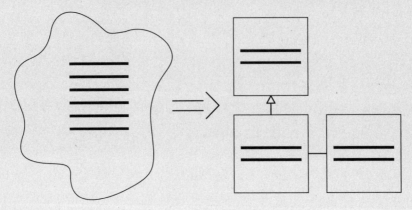

Refactoring: Convert Procedural Design to Objects

Motivation

This refactoring is motivated by the advantages provided by the object-oriented paradigm when compared to procedural programming. Object-oriented programming is a superior, more robust, and more productive paradigm that builds upon, but supersedes, procedural programming.

Related Smells

Use this refactoring to eliminate Procedural Design and Data Class smells.

Mechanics

1. If you don't have data structures in your code (you are using a `DataRow`, for example), start by creating data classes from rows by means of Replace Row with Data Class refactoring. If you have data clumps (data that generally goes together but is not structured, such as repeatable parameter lists), start by grouping them in the form of data classes.

2. Move all your procedural code (static methods) into the single class. This will be handy when you move methods to a class.

3. Perform Extract Method on all the long methods in a module to make them more granular and easier to use.

4. For each method, look for a data class on which methods operate. This probably means that the instance of the data class is passed to a static method as a parameter. Move the method to a data class and make it use the data class property directly as an instance member, instead of passing it as a parameter. Continue until you move all the methods into classes.

5. Delete the class that previously contained static methods from the solution if you managed to empty it.

Before

```
struct ShoppingCart
{
    public IList Products;
}

struct Product
{
    public decimal Price;
}

class OnlineShop
{
    public static decimal CalculateTotal(ShoppingCart cart)
    {
        decimal total = 0;
        foreach (Product product in cart.Products)
        {
            total += product.Price;
        }
        return total;
    }
    //...
}
```

After

```
class ShoppingCart
{
    public IList Products;

    public decimal CalculateTotal()
    {
        decimal total = 0;
        foreach (Product product in this.Products)
        {
            total += product.Price;
        }
        return total;
    }
}

class Product
{
    public decimal Price;
}
```

Separating Domain, Presentation, and Persistence

You have certainly experienced how C#'s rapid application development (RAD) features can entice you to confront the problems head-on, coding your way out right from the outset. It is great that you can fire up the C# IDE and just fill in the event handlers, but that can be a misleading, double-edged advantage that leads you toward coupled, nonreusable code.

This situation is well known to veteran programmers on the Microsoft platform. In the COM (Component Object Model) era, the prevailing architectural pattern was two-tiered, a pattern also known as *client/server*. Relational databases provided robust back ends, and Visual Basic was a tool that permitted a very fast application development, whereas C++ was used for more low-level plumbing. Then came the Web, and enterprises wished to put their businesses on the Internet. Unfortunately, domain logic coupled with presentation inside event-handling routines proved very difficult to reuse, spawning a new architectural style known as *three-tiered architecture*. Figure 9-5 illustrates three-tier application separation.

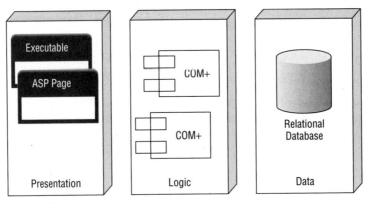

Figure 9-5

This separation is often logical and physical, meaning different tiers reside on different machines. However, as long as the logical separation is correctly performed and the classes are well-structured and organized, the physical distribution is a less complicated issue.

The tier separation does not end there. Inside the logic tier, you can have further layering and separation between purely domain logic and between persistence code and presentation code.

When you have to deal with code for which tier separation is not correctly performed, the best way to start is by separating the domain code from the presentation code.

Separating Domain from Presentation Code

This large-scale refactoring is performed in a few steps. Let's continue the refactoring example using the `AccountView` and `Account` classes from the "Refactoring: Replace Row with Data Class" sidebar earlier in the chapter.

Defining a Data Class for the Domain

The first step in separating the domain from the presentation is often Replace Row with Data Class refactoring. By creating data classes based on table rows, you can often identify the core of the classes that will comprise your domain layer. This step was already performed in the example shown in the "Refactoring: Replace Row with Data Class" sidebar.

Moving Domain Logic Inside the Data Class

If you analyze the original `AccountView` code, you will be able to identify one business rule coded inside an event handler:

```
if (!account.Blocked)
{
    this.Balance.Text = account.Balance.ToString();
}
else
{
    this.Balance.Text = "Blocked";
}
```

You can interpret this rule as follows: If the account is blocked, then hide the account balance. You will move this rule to the `Account` class. For that, you need to modify the `Balance` property as follows:

```
public decimal Balance
    {
        get {
            if (blocked)
            {
                return 0;
            }else{
                return balance;
            }
        }
        set { balance = value; }
    }
```

This way, if the account is blocked, the balance will stay hidden from anyone using the `Account` class.

Moving Persistence Logic Inside the Data Class

You need to keep the presentation layer free of all nonpresentation code. For that purpose, you will move all persistence code to the domain class.

In this example from the "Replace Row with Data Class" refactoring sidebar, the `GetAccount` method is used to read the account data from the database. This method can be moved into the `Account` class and converted into a parameterized constructor. The code for the constructor looks like this:

```
public Account(string number) {
    IDbConnection connection = new SqlConnection(connectionString);
    IDbDataAdapter adapter = new SqlDataAdapter();
    DataSet accountDataSet = new DataSet();
    IDbCommand command = new SqlCommand();
    string sql = "Select * from Accounts " +
        "where Number = " + number;
    connection.Open();
```

```
        command.Connection = connection;
        command.CommandText = sql;
        adapter.SelectCommand = command;
        adapter.Fill(accountDataSet);
        connection.Close();
        accountTable = accountDataSet.Tables[0];
        DataRow accountRow = accountTable.Rows(selectedRow);
        Account account = new Account();
        this.Number = accountRow["Number"].ToString();
        this.Name = accountRow["Name"].ToString();
        this.Type = accountRow["Type"].ToString();
        this.Balance = Convert.ToDecimal(accountRow["Balance"]);
        this.Blocked = Convert.ToBoolean(accountRow["Blocked"]);
    }
```

Now all the code you have left inside the `AccountView` class is purely presentation-related. The original event handler now looks like this:

```
private void viewAccountDetails_Click(object sender, System.EventArgs e)
{
    Account account = new Account(this.number.Text);
    this.Name.Text = account.Name;
    this.Type.Text = account.Type;
    if (!account.Blocked)
    {
        this.Balance.Text = account.Balance.ToString();
    }
    else
    {
        this.Balance.Text = "Blocked";
    }
}
```

You have successfully separated persistence code from domain code. However, your work is not over yet. Some persistence-related code exists inside your domain class, and such code does not comply with the SRP. You need to move the persistence-related code to a separate class.

Separating Domain Code from Persistence Code

You often find designs in which persistence classes contain database access code. In these cases, if you need to change the database or the persistence method, the changes will affect your domain classes as well. To avoid this situation, the solution is to extract the database code to separate classes. You should begin by defining one data access class for each persisted domain object. Then you extract methods and move database access code to newly defined data access classes.

In the following example, you will define a new `AccountData` class, and move the persistence code from the constructor to the newly created class. This method can be called `GetAccount`. Moving this method finishes the transformation of this example. Take a look at the final version in Listing 9-5.

Listing 9-5: AccountView Example After Separation of Domain and Persistence Code

```
public class Account
{
    private string number;
    private string name;
    private AccountType type;
    private decimal balance;
    private bool blocked;

    public Account(string number, string name, AccountType type,
        decimal balance, bool blocked) {
            this.number = number;
            this.name = name;
            this.type = type;
            this.balance = balance;
            this.blocked = blocked;
    }

    public decimal Balance
    {
        get {
            if (Blocked)
            {
                return 0;
            }else{
                return balance;
            }
        }
        set { balance = value; }
    }

    public string Number
    {
        get { return number; }
        set { number = value; }
    }

    public string Name
    {
        get { return name; }
        set { name = value; }
    }

    public bool Blocked
    {
        get { return blocked; }
        set { blocked = value; }
    }

    public AccountType Type
    {
```

Continued

Listing 9-5: AccountView Example After Separation of Domain and Persistence Code
(continued)

```
        get { return type; }
        set { type = value; }
    }

}

class AccountData
{
    public Account GetAccount(string number) {
        IDbConnection connection = new SqlConnection(connectionString);
        IDbDataAdapter adapter = new SqlDataAdapter();
        DataSet accountDataSet = new DataSet();
        IDbCommand command = new SqlCommand();
        string sql = "Select * from Accounts " +
            "where Number = " + number;
        connection.Open();
        command.Connection = connection;
        command.CommandText = sql;
        adapter.SelectCommand = command;
        adapter.Fill(accountDataSet);
        connection.Close();
        accountTable = accountDataSet.Tables[0];
        DataRow accountRow = accountTable.Rows[0];
        return new Account(
            Convert.ToInt32(accountRow["Number"]),
            accountRow["Name"].ToString(),
            new AccountType(accountRow["Type"]),
            Convert.ToDecimal(accountRow["Balance"]),
            Convert.ToBoolean(accountRow["Blocked"]));
    }
}

public class AccountView
{
    //...
    private void viewAccountDetails_Click(object sender, System.EventArgs e)
    {
        AccountData data = new AccountData();
        Account account = data.GetAccount(this.number.Text);
        this.Name.Text = account.Name;
        this.Type.Text = account.Type;
        if (!account.Blocked)
        {
            this.Balance.Text = account.Balance.ToString();
        }
        else
        {
            this.Balance.Text = "Blocked";
        }
    }
}
```

Sometimes the code you deal with is so simple that you can extract the domain and persistence layer in parallel. However, your approach depends on your needs:

❏ If you need to free the domain layer from the presentation, then begin by moving domain and persistence code out of the presentation.

❏ If you need to liberate the persistence layer, then begin by forming this layer first.

❏ If your code is simple enough, you can try to do refactorings in parallel.

You've covered many significant refactorings in this chapter so far. Now it's time to turn back to the Rent-a-Wheels application and apply that new knowledge to it.

Discovering Objects and the Rent-a-Wheels Application

This content of this chapter promises to introduce some fundamental changes to the Rent-a-Wheels application. On close inspection, you can see that Rent-a-Wheels suffers from nearly all the maladies you have encountered in this chapter: large classes; mixed presentation, domain, and persistence code; encumbered classes that are not compliant with SRP; and so on. You need to take following transformations one step at a time. Fortunately, you already know your first step.

Applying Replace Row with Data Class

Begin with the refactoring that is a good starting point in cases like this: Replace Row with Data Class. By looking at the `BranchMaintenance` form, you can see that you need to declare the `Branch` class. Listing 9-6 shows the `Branch` class code.

Listing 9-6: Newly Defined Branch Data Class

```
using System;

namespace RentAWheel
{
    class Branch
    {
        private int id;
        private string name;

        public Branch(int id, string name) {
            this.id = id;
            this.name = name;
        }

        public int Id
        {
            get { return id; }
            set { id = value; }
        }

        public string Name
        {
            get { return name; }
```

Continued

Listing 9-6: Newly Defined Branch Data Class *(continued)*

```
                set { name = value; }
        }
    }
}
```

The `Branch` class has two properties: a database-generated Id and a Name. In addition, a convenient parameterized constructor is defined so that the class can be instantiated and initialized with data on the same line.

Now, instead of operating directly with `DataRow` objects in the `BranchMaintenance` form, you use the row to initialize the instance of the `Branch` class. You then display the `branch` object data in the form. Listing 9-7 shows an example of using the `branch` object in the `DisplayCurrent` method in Listing 9-7.

Listing 9-7: Displaying the branch Object on the Form

```
//Replaces DisplayCurrentRow method
private void DisplayCurrent()
{
    Branch branch = branches[current];
    id.Text = branch.Id.ToString();
    name.Text = branch.Name;
}
```

You need to take a similar approach with the rest of the methods that communicate with the database. That is, you will make the rest of the methods use the `Branch` data class. After that, you need to take care of domain and persistence, and you can start by moving the domain logic into the data class.

Separating Domain from Presentation

In Chapter 4, which introduced the Rent-a-Wheels application, you saw a number of details regarding vehicle operation and vehicle state — for example, how the vehicle is periodically sent to maintenance and how, during that period, the vehicle is removed from circulation, as you would expect.

In the existing Rent-a-Wheels application, you implement rules regarding vehicle state by manipulating controls on the `FleetView` form. If the vehicle is in maintenance, then the Hand Over button is disabled. This rule belongs to the domain layer, so you need to move this logic inside the `Vehicle` class. Listing 9-8 shows how this is accomplished.

Listing 9-8: Vehicle Data Class Becomes Domain Class

```
public void HandOver()
{
    if (this.Operational.Equals(Operational.InMaintenence))
    {
        throw new InvalidVehicleStateException(
            "Vehicle in maintenance. Cannot be handed over.");
    }
    if (!this.RentalState.Equals(RentalState.Rented))
    {
```

```
        throw new InvalidVehicleStateException(
            "Vehicle not rented. Cannot be handed over");
    }
    this.RentalState = RentalState.HandedOver;

}
```

Implementation of the maintenance-related rule is simple: If someone tries to hand over a non-operational vehicle, then an exception is thrown.

Separating Persistence Code from Presentation

To extract the persistence code from the presentation classes, you define a data access class for each data class you have defined. Therefore, for the Branch class, you define a new BranchData class. This class holds all the persistence-related code.

You should start by moving the simplest method — in this case, the Delete method — to BranchData. As you move this method, you have to move the rest of the members this method is referencing. For now, just copy the necessary methods into the BranchData class. As you progress, more and more persistence-related code will find its way into the BranchData. Once everything is finished, you can delete all the unused persistence-related methods in the BranchMaintenance class. Listing 9-9 shows the final result for the branch-related code.

Listing 9-9: Branch-Related Classes: BranchMaintenance, Branch, and BranchData

```
//separate file

using System;

namespace RentAWheel
{
    public class Branch
    {
        private int id;
        private string name;

        public Branch(int id, string name) {
            this.id = id;
            this.name = name;
        }

        public int Id
        {
            get { return id; }
            set { id = value; }
        }

        public string Name
        {
            get { return name; }
            set { name = value; }
        }
```

Continued

Listing 9-9: Branch-Related Classes: BranchMaintenance, Branch, and BranchData
(continued)

```csharp
        }
    }


using System;
using System.Collections.Generic;
using System.Data;
using System.Data.SqlClient;

namespace RentAWheel
{
    class BranchData
    {
        private const String connectionString = "Data Source=TESLATEAM;" +
        "Initial Catalog=RENTAWHEELS;" +
        "User ID=RENTAWHEELS_LOGIN;Password=RENTAWHEELS_PASSWORD_123";

        private const string branchTableIdColumnName = "BranchId";
        private const string branchTableNameColumnName = "BranchName";

        private const string selectAllFromBranchSql =
            "Select BranchId as BranchId, Branch.Name as BranchName from Branch";
        private const string deleteBranchSql =
            "Delete Branch Where BranchId = @Id";
        private const string insertBranchSql =
            "Insert Into Branch (BranchName) Values(@Name)";
        private const string updateBranchSql =
            "Update Branch  Set BranchName = @Name Where BranchId = @Id";

        private const string idParameterName = "@Id";
        private const string nameParameterName = "@Name";

        private const int singleTableInDatasetIndex = 0;

        public IList<Branch> GetAll()
        {
            IList<Branch> branches = new List<Branch>();
            IDbCommand command = new SqlCommand();
            DataSet branchesSet =
                FillDataset(command, selectAllFromBranchSql);
            DataTable branchesTable =
                branchesSet.Tables[singleTableInDatasetIndex];
            foreach(DataRow row in branchesTable.Rows){
                branches.Add(BranchFromRow(row));
            }
            return branches;
        }

        public static Branch BranchFromRow(DataRow row)
        {
```

```
            return new Branch(Convert.ToInt32(row[branchTableIdColumnName]),
                        Convert.ToString(row[branchTableNameColumnName]));
}

public void Delete(Branch branch)
{
    IDbCommand command = new SqlCommand();
    AddParameter(command, idParameterName,
        DbType.Int32, branch.Id);
    ExecuteNonQuery(command, deleteBranchSql);
}

public void Update(Branch branch)
{
    IDbCommand command = new SqlCommand();
    AddParameter(command, nameParameterName,
        DbType.String, branch.Name);
    AddParameter(command, idParameterName,
        DbType.Int32, branch.Id);
    ExecuteNonQuery(command, updateBranchSql);
}

public void Insert(Branch branch)
{
    IDbCommand command = new SqlCommand();
    AddParameter(command, nameParameterName,
        DbType.String, branch.Name);
    ExecuteNonQuery(command, insertBranchSql);
}

private void AddParameter(IDbCommand command, string parameterName,
    DbType parameterType, object paramaterValue)
{
    IDbDataParameter parameter = command.CreateParameter();
    parameter.ParameterName = parameterName;
    parameter.DbType = parameterType;
    parameter.Value = paramaterValue;
    command.Parameters.Add(parameter);
}

private IDbConnection PrepareDataObjects(IDbCommand command, string sql)
{
    IDbConnection connection = new SqlConnection(connectionString);
    connection.Open();
    command.Connection = connection;
    command.CommandText = sql;
    return connection;
}

private void ExecuteNonQuery(IDbCommand command, string sql)
{
    IDbConnection connection = PrepareDataObjects(command, sql);
    command.ExecuteNonQuery();
```

Continued

261

Listing 9-9: Branch-Related Classes: BranchMaintenance, Branch, and BranchData
(continued)

```
                connection.Close();
        }

        private DataSet FillDataset(IDbCommand command, string sql)
        {
            IDbConnection connection = PrepareDataObjects(command, sql);
            IDbDataAdapter adapter = new SqlDataAdapter();
            DataSet branches = new DataSet();
            adapter.SelectCommand = command;
            adapter.Fill(branches);
            connection.Close();
            return branches;
        }
    }
}


using System;
using System.Collections.Generic;
using System.Windows.Forms;

namespace RentAWheel
{
    public partial class BranchMaintenance : Form
    {
        private BranchData data = new BranchData();
        private IList<Branch> branches;
        private int current;

        public BranchMaintenance()
        {
            InitializeComponent();
        }

        private void new_Click(object sender, EventArgs e)
        {
            id.Text = String.Empty;
            name.Text = String.Empty;
        }

        private void BranchMaintenance_Load(object sender, EventArgs e)
        {
            LoadBranches();
            if ((this.branches.Count > 0))
            {
                current = 0;
                DisplayCurrent();
            }
        }
```

```
private void LoadBranches() {
    this.branches = data.GetAll();
}


private void right_Click(object sender, EventArgs e)
{
    if (branches.Count > current + 1)
    {
        current++;
        DisplayCurrent();
    }
}

private void left_Click(object sender, EventArgs e)
{
    if (current - 1 >= 0 && branches.Count > 0)
    {
        current--;
        DisplayCurrent();
    }
}

private void first_Click(object sender, EventArgs e)
{
    if (branches.Count > 0)
    {
        current = 0;
        DisplayCurrent();
    }
}

private void last_Click(object sender, EventArgs e)
{
    if (branches.Count > 0)
    {
        current = branches.Count - 1;
        DisplayCurrent();
    }
}

private void DisplayCurrent()
{
    Branch branch = branches[current];
    id.Text = branch.Id.ToString();
    name.Text = branch.Name;
}

private void save_Click(object sender, EventArgs e)
{
    SaveBranch();
```

Continued

Listing 9-9: Branch-Related Classes: BranchMaintenance, Branch, and BranchData *(continued)*

```
                BranchMaintenance_Load(null, null);
        }

        private void SaveBranch()
        {
            if (String.IsNullOrEmpty(id.Text))
            {
                data.Insert(new Branch(0, name.Text));
            }
            else
            {
                Branch branch = branches[current];
                branch.Name = name.Text;
                data.Update(branches[current]);
            }
        }

        private void delete_Click(object sender, EventArgs e)
        {
            data.Delete(branches[current]);
            BranchMaintenance_Load(null, null);
        }

        private void reload_Click(object sender, EventArgs e)
        {
            BranchMaintenance_Load(null, null);
        }
    }
}
```

This code looks much better. The classes are not encumbered with more responsibilities than necessary, so they do not violate the SRP; presentation, domain, and persistence code are clearly separated; and the size of the classes is getting closer to the normal limits.

When you try to run the sample code for this chapter, be sure to execute the database modification script included in the downloaded code. I have renamed a few table columns in order to make the SQL code more compact. (All the code for this book is available at the book's web site at www.wrox.com.)

I have made some small functional changes to the code. For example, in Vehicle Maintenance Form, now you can enter vehicle mileage and tank level. This way, any error during vehicle reception can be mended.

Note another detail on the implementation level: I have eliminated the tables used to map ID with entity name for the Category, Branch, and Model combo boxes. I have used combo box's DataSource property instead, such as in the following routine:

```
private void LoadModelCombo()
{
    this.models = modelData.GetAll();
    model.DataSource = models;
```

```
        model.DisplayMember = "Name";
        model.ValueMember = "Id";
}
```

I am sure that if you inspect the code in detail you will find more small-scale changes similar to this one. What is more important, however, is the bigger picture.

A very similar general pattern is applied to the rest of the Rent-a-Wheels classes. If you take a look at those classes, you will see that many methods between the classes look exactly the same. You have already done a lot of work to eliminate duplication from the code, but it seems that there is still some work to be done. The next chapter deals with that. There, you will see how code duplicated between classes can be extracted and the duplication eliminated.

Summary

You covered a lot of ground in this chapter. If someone asked me to select the most important chapter in the book, I might well name this one. You began by looking at an overview of object-oriented programming concepts such as encapsulation, object state and identity, object lifetime, garbage collection, and messages.

After looking at objects from a theoretical point of view, you saw analysis techniques you can apply in order to identify the classes that can serve as the pillars of your application design.

When you program, you don't always start out with a clean slate. Indeed, you often need to manipulate already existing code. In C# code, presentation, domain, and persistence code can be mixed sometimes. You have seen how you can extract the relevant classes and separate the code. You can often start out by replacing rows with data classes.

Finally, you have once again applied your knowledge to the Rent-a-Wheels application, making profound changes to its code. Many new classes have been identified, and the code is more evenly spread out, so that each class takes some responsibility.

In the next chapter, you will encounter some other important characteristics of object-oriented programming. You will see how techniques such as inheritance, polymorphism, and genericity can be further used to construct robust and reusable code.

10

Advanced Object-Oriented Concepts and Related Refactorings

In the previous chapter you explored some of the basic concepts in object-oriented programming theory. In this chapter, you will work with some more advanced, but also fundamental, capabilities of object-oriented programming environments.

This chapter progresses as follows:

- ❑ You will first learn how you can employ inheritance, polymorphism, and genericity to further improve the design of your code, remove unnecessary duplication, and enhance encapsulation. These capabilities of C# are fundamental for implementing advanced reusability mechanisms and for the creation of frameworks and toolkit libraries.

- ❑ As shown many times in this book already, you won't often reach optimal design during the first iteration of code. Therefore, the second part of this chapter describes how you can refactor your code by extracting classes and interfaces, moving methods up and down in the hierarchy, employing generic types, and so on. This way, you make use of these advanced object-oriented capabilities and thus take the design of your code to the next level.

- ❑ The end of the chapter takes you back to the Rent-a-Wheels application. You will see that although the number of classes in the application has increased substantially, the overall complexity of the application and even the simple line count has been reduced.

We begin this chapter by going back to some of the key concepts of object-oriented theory.

Inheritance, Polymorphism, and Genericity

C# was conceived as a modern, fully capable object-oriented language. It has drawn on the best features of languages like Java and Delphi and can be considered a next stage in the evolution of C++, with which it shares a lot of common syntax, but whose many features have been superseded in C#.

For best results, C# requires an object-oriented savvy programmer. This means having full command of mechanisms such as interface and implementation inheritance, polymorphism, genericity, and others. By correctly applying these mechanisms, you will be able to make your code much more compact and robust, and avoid unnecessary duplication.

The evolution of C# is continuous. In version 2.0, generics were the most important feature added to the language. Other important features include partial and static classes, nullable types, anonymous delegates, and more.

This evolution continues with C# 3.0, which adds to the language important features such as LINQ, lambda expressions, type inference, extension methods, automatic properties, and others. The next section covers some fundamental object-oriented features present in C# from its inception (with the exception of genericity).

Inheritance

You have already seen examples of refactorings that can be used to reduce code duplication. You have seen the devastating consequences that duplicated code can have on the maintainability of your code base. Until now, though, you haven't seen any technique that can solve duplication spread among different classes. How can you solve a situation in which the same members exist in more than one class?

Imagine you have programmed the class named Customer for a local opera house. This class has typical properties and methods such as Name, Address, Telephone, PurchaseHistory, and so on. It also has a DiscountPercent method that takes into account the total number of purchases made:

```
public class Customer
    {
        //...
        private PurchaseHistory purchaseHistory;

        public PurchaseHistory PurchaseHistory
        {
            get { return purchaseHistory; }
            set { purchaseHistory = value; }
        }
        public decimal DiscountPercent()
        {
            if (this.PurchaseHistory.TotalPurchases > 10)
            {
                return 3;
            }
            else if (this.PurchaseHistory.TotalPurchases > 100)
            {
                return 5;
            }
```

```
        else
        {
            return 0;
        }
    }
}
```

As usual, very soon you have to add some new functionality. Opera management has decided that all senior citizens get a 50 percent discount for all of their purchases. At this point, you remember the open-closed principle discussed in Chapter 6, and you decide to modify the existing Customer class.

Instead, you can define a new SeniorCitizen class. Obviously, you do not want to copy all the content of the Customer class into SeniorCitizen; you want to change only the single method.

One option is to declare the Customer class as a property of SeniorCitizen. Then you make SeniorCitizen hand over the execution to Customer. The only method that contains some new logic is DiscountPercent. Such code would look like this:

```
public class SeniorCitizen
{
    private Customer customer;
    public Customer Customer {
        get { return customer; }
        set { customer = value; }
    }
    public string FirstName {
        get { return this.Customer.FirstName; }
        set { this.Customer.FirstName = value; }
    }
    //... and so on for every member that Customer declares
    public decimal DiscountPercent()
    {
        //only method that does not delegate to Customer
        return 50;
    }
}
```

As you can see, this is quite cumbersome and requires a lot of coding. Actually, this is what your code would look like if you decided to use the "favor composition over inheritance principle" discussed later in this chapter to the extreme. (Don't do it — inheritance has its purposes and is a valid option in some situations.)

Here is where inheritance comes into play. The better solution is simply to inherit the Customer class and override the DiscountPercent method:

```
public class SeniorCitizen : Customer {

    public override decimal DiscountPercent() {
        return 50;
    }
}
```

```
public class Customer
{
    //...
    private PurchaseHistory purchaseHistory;

    public PurchaseHistory PurchaseHistory
    {
        get { return purchaseHistory; }
        set { purchaseHistory = value; }
    }

    public virtual decimal DiscountPercent()
    {
        if (this.PurchaseHistory.TotalPurchases > 10)
        {
            return 3;
        }
        else if (this.PurchaseHistory.TotalPurchases > 100)
        {
            return 5;
        }
        else
        {
            return 0;
        }
    }
}
```

In order to accomplish overriding the DiscountPercent method in the SeniorCitizen class, you had to change the source code of class Customer as well. This is because C# is "closed for override" by default (and consequently "closed for extension" by default to some extent). The same is true for the VB.NET programming language. This was a deliberate decision on the part of Microsoft's language design team, whereby they decided to favor security and preserve original design intent over extensibility. Some other languages, such as Java, are "open for override" by default. Bear this in mind when designing classes; it often makes sense to leave a door open for override. Seldom can you foresee all possible uses your classes might have in the future. In C# 3.0 and later, there is a way to add members to an interface and provide default behavior via extension methods. Check out Chapter 13 for more discussion on the subject.

However, the story does not end here. You are again faced with some new requirements. The opera house has also decided to provide walker aids for interested seniors. You can easily describe this requirement by defining an additional property, RequiresAssistance, in the SeniorCitizen class:

```
public class SeniorCitizen : Customer {

    private bool requiresAssistance;

    public override decimal DiscountPercent() {
        return 50;
    }

    public bool RequiresAssistance {
        get { return requiresAssistance; }
```

```
            set { requiresAssistance = value; }
    }
}
```

In this case, the new property is accessible only if the variable is declared and created as `SeniorCitizen`, as in `SeniorCitizen customer = new SeniorCitizen()`. If it is declared as `Customer`, as in `Customer customer = new SeniorCitizen()`, the newly added `RequiresAssistance` property will not be accessible. This way, the `SeniorCitizen` class can expose behavior that characterizes only itself and not the parent class.

When the class is inherited, the following things are accomplished automatically:

❑   All the members that belong to the superclass, except private ones, are immediately available to subclasses as if they were the subclasses' own.

❑   A subclass automatically implements the interface of the superclass, making the child subclass a valid substitute in polymorphic behavior.

❑   A subclass can, by means of overriding, provide different implementation for certain members marked as overrideable in the superclass.

❑   A subclass can provide additional new behavior by defining new members.

> *As mentioned in Chapter 6, if you have any questions about how hiding and overriding work in C#, see the article "Versioning with the Override and New Keywords (C# Programming Guide)" on MSDN:* `http://msdn.microsoft.com/en-us/library/6fawty39.aspx`.

Inheritance is not limited to classes. Interfaces can also be inherited by other interfaces or implemented in a class. This is referred to as *interface inheritance*.

> **If you inherit the class and then declare a method or property with the same signature in the subclass, the method will be hidden by default, and the compiler will warn you.**
>
> **Sometimes hiding is the desired behavior. In order to override the member, you have to use the `override` keyword. For further explanation on this subtle but crucial distinction, consult the MSDN.**

Class versus Interface Inheritance

The purpose of the interface construct in C# is to explicitly define a class interface. You have already seen how interfaces help encapsulate objects by making objects accessible through a single access point only, and by hiding object internals. Every class has an interface that consists of all public members of that class. The interface construct helps you define a group of members that will be visible under the name of the interface, thus reducing the visible footprint of a class if the class is accessed through an interface.

Sometimes you don't know what the implementation of an interface is going to look like. In these cases, an interface can serve as a contract that communicating objects have to obey. The object that exposes the interface guarantees that it is capable of receiving a certain message, and a client object has to send the message in the exact form defined through its signature in the interface.

An interface cannot be instantiated and has only abstract members. Abstract members have only a signature and no implementation. A class implements an interface by means of the colon symbol (:). In contrast to a class inheritance, a class can implement multiple interfaces. This is a form of *multiple inheritance*, a powerful object-oriented concept. When you are inheriting classes, however, only a single inheritance is permitted.

Now you can continue working on the opera example. Define an ICustomer interface and make the class Customer implement the newly created interface. This way, the Customer class will be visible through a newly created interface whenever a variable pointing to an instance of Customer has been declared as ICustomer. The same is true for SeniorCitizen. Because inheritance is transitive, all children implement or inherit all types that their parents implement or inherit. The code with the ICustomer interface will, therefore, look like this:

```
public interface ICustomer {

    PurchaseHistory PurchaseHistory {
        get;
        set;
    }

    decimal DiscountPercent();
}
```

```
public class Customer: ICustomer
{
    //...
    private PurchaseHistory purchaseHistory;

    public PurchaseHistory PurchaseHistory
    {
        get { return purchaseHistory; }
        set { purchaseHistory = value; }
    }
    public virtual decimal DiscountPercent()
    {
        if (this.PurchaseHistory.TotalPurchases > 10)
        {
            return 3;
        }
        else if (this.PurchaseHistory.TotalPurchases > 100)
        {
            return 5;
        }
        else
        {
            return 0;
        }
    }
}
```

Interfaces are closely related to polymorphic behavior. In order to be able to perform type substitution, an object has to implement an interface or inherit the class.

Polymorphism

In the example used so far in this chapter, you have seen how a class can inherit other classes and override some members, and implement an interface; but so far you have not seen what happens from the client's point of view. For that purpose, you can add an additional class to the example, a PurchaseForm class that has a Customer property. You will also add another DisplayForm with two buttons, InstantiateAsCustomer and InstantiateAsSeniorCitizen, whose sole purpose is to pass an instance of Customer and then an instance of SeniorCitizen to PurchaseForm:

```csharp
public partial class PurchaseForm : Form
{
    private ICustomer customer;

    public PurchaseForm()
    {
        InitializeComponent();
    }

    public ICustomer Customer {
        get { return customer; }
        set { customer = value; }
    }

    private void PurchaseForm_Activated(object sender, EventArgs e)
    {
        this.discount.Text = customer.DiscountPercent().ToString() ;
    }
}

public partial class DisplayForm : Form
{
    public DisplayForm()
    {
        InitializeComponent();
    }

    private void instantiateAsCustomer_Click(object sender, EventArgs e)
    {
        PurchaseForm purchaseForm = new PurchaseForm();
        purchaseForm.Customer = new Customer();
        purchaseForm.Activate();
        purchaseForm.Show();
    }

    private void instantiateAsSeniorCitizen_Click(object sender, EventArgs e)
    {
        PurchaseForm purchaseForm = new PurchaseForm();
        purchaseForm.Customer = new SeniorCitizen();
        purchaseForm.Activate();
        purchaseForm.Show();
    }
}
```

The code displayed here is programmer-generated code of the `PurchaseForm` *class. Any Windows Forms class is a partial class, and IDE-generated code is placed in another file. I have omitted the IDE-generated code for this example because of space considerations. The complete code for this example is available for download from* `www.wrox.com`.

Run this example with the following two actions:

❑ Press the `InstantiateAsCustomer` button. The `PurchaseForm` will show 0 as the discount percent. (Assume that purchase history is empty by default.)

❑ Press the `InstantiateAsSeniorCitizen` button. The `PurchaseForm` will show 50 as the discount percent.

In the first case, the `DiscountPercent` method implemented in `Customer` was executed; in the second, the `DiscountPercent` method implemented in `SeniorCitizen` was executed.

This is an example of *polymorphic* behavior, wherein the same variable can point to different instances of different classes. The same operation was defined and implemented differently in different classes. An important thing to notice is that the exact type of the instance to which the variable is pointing is not known until runtime.

In this example, that means you can use the same form and the same code to perform purchases for both `Customer` and `SeniorCitizen`. The `PurchaseForm` is oblivious to the implementing type of the `ICustomer` interface. This helps improve the encapsulation of the system and makes reuse even more efficient.

Object-Oriented Design Principle: Program to an Abstraction

In order to keep your code flexible and open for extension, you should always try to depend on the highest abstraction in the inheritance hierarchy. You can generally consider parent classes or interfaces to be more abstract, and child classes more concrete or specialized. If you adhere to this principle, the client code will happily accept different implementations without needing modification or any type of intervention.

Definition

A definition of this principle from *Design Patterns: Elements of Reusable Object-Oriented Software* (Addison-Wesley, 1995) is expressed as follows: "Program to an abstraction, not an implementation."

Remember that greater abstraction is always found higher up in the inheritance hierarchy and is often represented through interfaces or abstract class constructs.

Example

Imagine you have a `PurchaseHistory` class that holds a list of all the purchases a customer has made. A possible implementation would look as follows:

```
public class PurchaseHistory
{
    //...
    private ArrayList purchases;
}
```

In this case, `PurchaseHistory` is dependant on one specific implementation of a list, `System.Collections.ArrayList`, and will not accept any other. However, it is better to make `PurchaseHistory` dependant on list abstraction, defined by the `System.Collections.IList` interface:

```
public class PurchaseHistory
{
    //...
    private IList purchases;
}
```

This way, not only can `ArrayList` be used as a purchase list implementation, but any other class that implements the `IList` interface. Such a class could be, for example, `System.Collections.Generic.List(Of T)`.

Interface versus Abstract Class

Somewhere between classes and interfaces are abstract classes. These classes in C# are defined by means of the `abstract` keyword. Neither abstract classes nor interfaces can be instantiated. Abstract classes can contain both abstract and concrete methods. This means that abstract classes might be a good choice in situations where you know how to implement some methods but not others.

Important things to remember when choosing an abstract class over an interface include the following:

❑   You can inherit only a single abstract class, and you can implement as many interfaces as you want. Interfaces are a more flexible option in this respect.

❑   Abstract classes can contain implemented members, so they are a good choice if you want to provide or enforce some common behavior for all subclasses.

❑   Abstract classes can declare nonpublic members; interfaces can't.

❑   If you declare a type as an interface and then add a member, you force all the implementers to implement the new method and be recompiled. If you choose an abstract class instead and add a new method, you can ship a default implementation with the class itself. This way, you avoid recompiling classes that inherit your abstract class. This effect can be especially relevant when you are programming frameworks.

❑   Abstract classes, like any other class, can also implement interfaces. This is actually a common pattern that makes it possible to provide a partial default implementation for a certain interface, if you can make use of such an implementation. If the implementation provided by an abstract class does not serve the purpose, you are free to implement an interface and write the class from scratch. When an abstract class implements an interface, you are free to implement only the members of the interface you choose. Because the class is abstract, you are free to leave interface members of your choice unimplemented.

While abstract classes can contain both abstract and concrete members, there is no reason why you couldn't write an abstract class containing purely abstract members. Such an approach is beneficial for framework programmers because it frees them to add new members to the abstract class in the next version of the class, as long as they provide a default implementation for such members. This way, binary compatibility between classes will not be broken. In the case of interfaces, any new member in a new version of an interface means that all implementors have to be recompiled in order to implement newly defined members. As an alternative, you can add members to interfaces and provide default behavior with extension methods, a feature present in C# since version 3.0. I talk about extension methods in more detail in Chapter 13.

Genericity

This is another feature, available in C# since the C# 2.0 and Visual Studio 2005 incarnation of the language, that enables you to avoid writing a lot of boilerplate code and can also provide additional type safety. *Generic types*, also known as *parameterized types*, enable you to define other types that a class uses at the point of usage, and that are not in the class itself. This way, the same class can work with many types that can be used to parameterize the class.

The Typed Container Problem

Generics are easiest to understand in the context of container types. Standard containers from the System.Collections namespace provide convenient placeholders for groups of objects and their manipulation, such as position or key-based retrieval. Because these containers are general-purpose, they let you add to and retrieve from the container any type of object. After the object is retrieved, it has to be cast back into the expected type. (In practice, you will rarely need to hold objects of different types in the same container.) There are at least two problems with the general-purpose container scheme:

❑ **There is no guarantee that all the objects in the container will be of the type you expect:** There is nothing to prevent the addition of any object of any type to the container; and if you come across an invalid type, a runtime System.InvalidCastException is thrown when that object is retrieved and cast into the expected type. There should be some way for the compiler to ensure that only expected types are added to the container.

❑ **After retrieving the type, you have to write the code that casts the object into the expected type:** Such code is redundant, and therefore should not be necessary.

There is a solution, even with standard containers, to the problems just listed. It consists of writing your own typed container wrappers. Your container wrapper delegates all the work to a standard container it hides from the public. The sample code for this solution is shown in Listing 10-1.

Listing 10-1: Custom-Typed Container Implementation Using Standard Containers

```
public class CustomerList
{
    private IList list;
    //... Other list-like members
    public int Add(Customer customer)
    {
        //delegate to internal list
        this.list.Add(customer);
    }
    public Customer Item
    {
        get {
```

```
                    return (Customer)list.Item(index);
                }
        set {
                this.list.Item(index) = value;
                }
        }
    }
}
```

The custom-container approach has two major drawbacks:

❑   It is repetitious and requires a lot of work and discipline. In practice, it is easier not to go to all the trouble of writing a custom container, and instead use a general-purpose container.

❑   Because custom container wrappers do not implement standard non-type-safe container interfaces (for instance, System.Collections.IList), they are not easily interchangeable through polymorphism with other container implementations that do implement those interfaces. For example, it is not easy to replace your CustomerList with a standard ArrayList.

The Generic Container Solution

Generics are an elegant solution to the problem of typed containers. They enable you to specify the type of contained objects at the point of usage and in a single place. After such a container is instantiated, it will receive and return only objects of the specified type, resolving the problem of type safety and casting code. You can easily define a type-safe container by using < and > brackets, enclosing a generic type parameter.

```
    private IList<Customer> list;
```

No more do you need to cast an object to Customer after retrieval or worry about an object of some other type cropping up from the container. It is worth mentioning that all container implementations from the System.Container.Generic namespace also implement interfaces from the standard container namespace, making them valid replacements for nongeneric implementations. For example, System.Container.Generic.List implements the System.Container.IList interface, making it a valid replacement for System.Container.ArrayList as long as the ArrayList is accessed through a System.Container.IList interface (see the sidebar "Object-Oriented Design Principle: Program to an Abstraction" earlier in the chapter).

Generics are not container-only. They can be used for many other purposes as well. In C#, you are free to write your own generic classes when you need them, and these can be used for various purposes.

Like any other powerful tool, these advanced object-oriented language capabilities just described are useful only if employed well and in the right circumstances. In the hands of an inexperienced user, these advanced object-oriented features can be completely counterproductive, leading to poorly designed software. Therefore, the next step is to take a look at the most common errors that programmers make when applying these features, and how refactoring can help remedy those errors.

Inheritance Abuse and Refactoring Solutions

You should be aware of a few things when applying inheritance. When you inherit a class, the link between the parent class and the child class (often referred to as superclass and subclass) is established at compilation time. This link is strong in nature, because all nonprivate members in the parent are also visible in the child class. This has the following consequences:

❑ The behavior that the child class has inherited from the parent cannot be changed at runtime.

❑ Reusing a child class means also reusing the parent. If there is a need to change some behavior in the parent class, this will most probably provoke a change in a child class, because of the tight coupling between the two.

You have just seen the arguments that inspired the writers of *Design Patterns: Elements of Reusable Object-Oriented Software* (Addison-Wesley, 1994) to coin the "favor object composition over class inheritance" design principle. This is sometimes simplistically interpreted as meaning that class inheritance is not necessary at all. Depending on the circumstances, either composition or inheritance can be beneficial for the design. Nonetheless, inheritance is often abused as a reuse technique because it is so easy to implement.

Object-Oriented Design Principle: Favor Object Composition over Class Inheritance

Class inheritance is a powerful and easily accessible reuse technique. A child class has immediate access to functionality provided by a parent class, and can override some of the parent's functionality or provide new functionality. Inheritance should be used in cases where the child specializes or extends behavior provided by the parent. It reflects an "is a kind of" relationship between the two.

This link between the child and the parent is established at compile time and cannot be changed at runtime. The link is strong in nature, exposing the child to the inner workings of the parent. The consequences are as follows:

❑ Inherited behavior cannot be changed at runtime.

❑ Changes in the parent class will most probably provoke a change in all child classes.

This makes class composition and reuse based on delegation a more flexible and better choice when the reused behavior should be changed at runtime. It can be a better choice for more granular and more encapsulated design. Finally, it is better suited for expressing a "has a" relationship instead of an "is a kind of" relationship between types.

Definition
In *Design Patterns: Elements of Reusable Object-Oriented Software*, the principle is formulated as follows: "Favor object composition over class inheritance."

Example
In a system that controls a reactor in an atomic plant, you need to read reactor temperature and operate on control rods. Imagine a design in which the `AtomicReactor` class inherits the `Thermometer` implementation:

```
public class BimetalThermometer
{
    public decimal GetCurrentTemperature()
```

```
        {
            //...
        }
    }
    public class AtomicReactor : BimetalThermometer
    {
        public void ControlTemperature()
        {
            if (GetCurrentTemperature() <
                TemperatureLevels.DangerousLow)
            {
                RaiseAlarm();
                EmergencyReactionIncrease();
                return;
            }
            else if (GetCurrentTemperature() >
                TemperatureLevels.DangerousHigh)
            {
                RaiseAlarm();
                EmergencyReactionDecrease();
                return;
            }
            else if (GetCurrentTemperature() <
                TemperatureLevels.Low)
            {
                IncreaseReaction();
            }
            else if (GetCurrentTemperature() >
                TemperatureLevels.High)
            {
                DecreaseReaction();
            }
        }
    }
    //...
```

In such a design, thermometer functionality is deceptively easy to use. However, the problems such a design imposes are various:

❑   The reactor is not "a kind of thermometer," so from a problem domain point of view, inheritance is not employed correctly.

❑   The reactor is coupled with a specific implementation of the thermometer. If at some point another type of thermometer were used, the application would have to be recompiled.

The relationship between the reactor and thermometer is much better expressed by a composition relationship between the two:

```
public interface IThermometer
{
```

Continued

```
        decimal GetCurrentTemperature();
}

public class BimetalThermometer : IThermometer
{
    public decimal GetCurrentTemperature()
    {
        //...
    }
}

public class InfraredThermometer : IThermometer
{
    public decimal GetCurrentTemperature()
    {
        //...
    }
}

public class AtomicReactor
{
    private IThermometer thermometer;

    public IThermometer Thermometer
    {
        get { return thermometer; }
        set { thermometer = value; }
    }

    public void ControlTemperature()
    {
        if (thermometer.GetCurrentTemperature()
            < TemperatureLevels.DangerousLow)
        {
            RaiseAlarm();
            EmergencyReactionIncrease();
            return;
        }
        else if (thermometer.GetCurrentTemperature()
            > TemperatureLevels.DangerousHigh)
        {
            RaiseAlarm();
            EmergencyReactionDecrease();
            return;
        }
        else if (thermometer.GetCurrentTemperature()
            < TemperatureLevels.Low)
        {
            IncreaseReaction();
        }
```

```
            else if (thermometer.GetCurrentTemperature()
                > TemperatureLevels.High)
        {
            DecreaseReaction();
        }
    }
}
```

Now the reactor uses the `Thermometer` object to obtain temperature readings. The reactor does not depend on a specific implementation of `Thermometer`, and this implementation can be changed at runtime. Both `BimetalThermometer` and `InfraredThermometer` implement the `IThermometer` interface, and either can be used by the reactor to perform readings.

Finally, this example demonstrates how inheritance and composition are used together to make a more flexible and robust design.

You will now see some typical examples of inheritance misuse, beginning with composition that is mistaken for inheritance.

Definition: A *fragile base class problem* refers to the inability of the base class designer to predict the effect of changes introduced to the base class and released in a new version just by looking at the base class code, but not at the code of all the classes that inherit from the base class. Whereas in self-contained applications the designer might have access to child classes, when creating reusable modules framework and similar, looking at the code of the child classes is not an option. One fallback remedy to this problem built into the .NET Framework is the versioning mechanism. An assembly containing the child classes will not be forced to use a new version of the assembly containing the new version of the base class once the new base class assembly is installed, as the new and old version of the base class assembly can exist in parallel, as explained in Chapter 6.

Composition Mistaken for Inheritance and Other Misuses

You are used to classifying things in your life. You know that a car is a kind of vehicle, that a human is a primate, and that a triangle is a kind of geometric shape. However, such relationships between different entities are not simple to establish and have been the subject of scientific and philosophical investigation from ancient times. When classifying, you try to establish a relationship between things. You look into common characteristics and then group things according to commonality. You rightfully expect any member of a group to share all common characteristics of that group.

Smell: Refused Bequest

Detecting the Smell

A child class that refuses to implement certain parent members is a sign of a refused bequest. The compiler will oblige a programmer to make a child class seemingly compliant with the parent, but a programmer is able to find a way around this obligation imposed by the compiler. The refusal can take a form of an empty overriding method implementation, an overriding function that returns a null object — nothing — or a member that does nothing but raise an exception.

Related Refactoring

Use Replace Inheritance with Delegation refactoring to eliminate this smell.

Rationale

A child class should support the parent's interface in its totality. A child that is refusing some of the parent's members results in clients having to know the child, which will ultimately break encapsulation and polymorphic code. Here is an example of seemingly correct inheritance in which the child is refusing some of the parent's behavior:

```
public abstract class Bird
{
    //...
    public abstract void Fly();
}

public class Ostrich:Bird
{
    //...
    public void Fly() {
        throw new InvalidOperationException(
            "Ostrich cannot fly, silly!");
    }
}
```

A more benign case of the smell is when the child is not making use of all members that the parent provides, but when the child refuses the parent's interface, refactoring has to take place.

Inheritance should be used to express a relationship between more general and more specific cases, often expressed as an "is a" or an "is a kind of" relationship. However, these relationships can often work out differently in science, in laypeople's understanding of the world, and, finally, in programming.

In programming, when designing inheritance, you base your thinking on generalization and an "is a" principle. However, everyday classifications do not always translate well into the programming world. When writing code, you have to be strict in the application of principles that govern software design. For example, if you randomly ask any person to name the most typical bird characteristic, he or she will most probably reply, "flying." If you ask this same person what an ostrich is, he or she will probably serenely reply, "A bird." Although the classifications we normally use are far from perfect, they generally do not interfere with our everyday life. However, similar imperfections in software can have much farther-reaching consequences.

Refactoring: Replace Inheritance with Delegation

Motivation

Using delegation instead of inheritance can often result in much more flexible, more encapsulated, and more robust design. This is expressed in the "favor object composition over class inheritance" design principle. In this case, delegation refers to having another object to do the work, another object to which the work is being delegated. Often the relationship between the two objects is one of composition.

In some cases, the inheritance relationship between two classes is unfounded, because the child class refuses some of the parent's interface, which makes it nonconformant in type. Such a situation should be remedied by refactoring, and often the best solution is to replace inheritance with delegation.

When you program, it is often convenient to start by extending an already existing class that provides ready behavior that you can reuse. In some cases, you may find that you do not want all the behavior exposed through inheritance to be visible. If you need to hide some of the parent's members, it is best to replace inheritance with delegation.

Related Smells

Use this refactoring to eliminate the Refused Bequest smell and to make the design more flexible by using delegation instead of inheritance as a reuse mechanism.

Mechanics

The refactoring is performed in a few sequential steps. You can start by analyzing the sample code used in this refactoring. The `PerishableContainer` class discards items that have passed in storage more times than permitted. The class inherits the standard `ArrayList` and extends its functionality with methods for adding and retrieving perishable items. The problem with the class is that it also exposes all the public members of `ArrayList`, making it easy for the client to circumvent time-restricted methods. The solution is to replace inheritance with delegation.

Continued

Before

```
public class PerishableContainer : ArrayList
{
    private int perishIntervalInSeconds;

    public int PerishIntervalInSeconds
    {
        get { return perishIntervalInSeconds; }
        set { perishIntervalInSeconds = value; }
    }

    public void LeaveInStorage(PerishableItem item)
    {
        base.Add(item);
    }

    private PerishableItem TakeOldestFromStorage()
    {
        if (base.Count > 0)
        {
            PerishableItem item = (PerishableItem)base[0];
            base.Remove(item);
            if (!HasPerished(item))
            {
                return item;
            }
        }
        return null;
    }

    public PerishableItem TakeFromStorage()
    {
        PerishableItem item = null;
        while (base.Count > 0)
        {
            item = TakeOldestFromStorage();
            if (item != null)
            {
                break;
            }
        }
        return item;
    }

    private bool HasPerished(PerishableItem item)
    {
        if (item.CreationTime.AddSeconds(
            perishIntervalInSeconds) > System.DateTime.Now)
        {
            return false;
```

```
            }
        return true;
    }
}

public interface PerishableItem
{
    System.DateTime CreationTime
    {
        get;
        set;
    }
}
```

1. Create a parent type field in the child and initialize it with the object itself (this):

```
public class PerishableContainer : ArrayList
{
    private ArrayList list;

    public PerishableContainer() {
        this.list = this;
    }
    //...
}
```

2. Make the code in the child use the newly defined field "list" instead of base:

```
//...
private PerishableItem TakeOldestFromStorage()
{
    if (list.Count > 0)
    {
        PerishableItem item = (PerishableItem)list[0];
        list.Remove(item);
        if (!HasPerished(item))
        {
            return item;
        }
    }
    return null;
}
```

3. Remove the inheritance clause from the class declaration and initialize the field created in Step 1 with a new instance of the would-be parent:

```
public class PerishableContainer
{
    /...
```

Continued

```
          private ArrayList list;

          public PerishableContainer()
          {
              this.list = new ArrayList();
          }

          /...


      }
```

4.   Expose all members from the parent used by the clients with simple delegation code:

```
// ...
public int Count
{
    get { return list.Count; }
}
```

After

```
public class PerishableContainer
{
    private int perishIntervalInSeconds;

    private ArrayList list;

    public PerishableContainer()
    {
        this.list = new ArrayList();
    }

    public int PerishIntervalInSeconds
    {
        get { return perishIntervalInSeconds; }
        set { perishIntervalInSeconds = value; }
    }

    public void LeaveInStorage(PerishableItem item)
    {
        list.Add(item);
    }

    private PerishableItem TakeOldestFromStorage()
    {
        if (list.Count > 0)
        {
            PerishableItem item = (PerishableItem)list[0];
            list.Remove(item);
```

```
                if (!HasPerished(item))
                {
                    return item;
                }
            }
        return null;
    }

    public PerishableItem TakeFromStorage()
    {
        PerishableItem item = null;
        while (list.Count > 0)
        {
            item = TakeOldestFromStorage();
            if (item != null)
            {
                break;
            }
        }
        return item;
    }

    private bool HasPerished(PerishableItem item)
    {
        if (item.CreationTime.AddSeconds(
            perishIntervalInSeconds) > System.DateTime.Now)
        {
            return false;
        }
        return true;
    }

    public int Count
    {
        get { return list.Count; }
    }
}

public interface PerishableItem
{
    System.DateTime CreationTime
    {
        get;
        set;
    }
}
```

It is best to start inheritance misuse analysis with an example that demonstrates possible pitfalls with inheritance application. You will then see how the pitfall can be resolved by means of different refactorings. The next section starts by looking at a peculiar print-system design.

Refactoring for Inheritance — Print-System Example

In this particular print-system design, shown in Listing 10-2, the central class in the design is an abstract PrintService class. This class declares an abstract PrintJob method that is implemented by different classes that inherit PrintSystem. Child classes, such as LexmarkX500 and HPLaserJet, implement physical device-specific code that has to take care of communicating with the device and rendering the data in the form that the device understands.

In a system designed like this, each time you need to add another physical device to the group of supported devices, you need to add another sibling to the class hierarchy. It is up to the child class to implement all device-specific code.

Listing 10-2: Print System Using Inheritance to Incorporate Different Printing Devices

```csharp
public enum ServiceState
{
    Idle,
    Processing,
    Stopped
}

public abstract class PrintService
{
    private IList<PrintJob> jobsInQueue;
    private ServiceState serviceState;
    public IList<PrintJob> JobsInQueue
    {
        get { return jobsInQueue; }
        set { jobsInQueue = value; }
    }
    public ServiceState ServiceState
    {
        get { return serviceState; }
        set { serviceState = value; }
    }
    public PrintJob CreatePrintJob()
    {
        return new PrintJob();
    }
    private void print()
    {
        while (JobsInQueue.Count > 0)
        {
            PrintJob(JobsInQueue[0]);
        }
    }
    protected abstract void PrintJob(PrintJob job);
}
public class HPLaserJet : PrintService
{
    private bool initialized;
```

```csharp
    private bool Initialized
    {
        get { return initialized; }
        set { initialized = value; }
    }
    protected override void PrintJob(PrintJob job)
    {
        if (!this.Initialized)
        {
            this.Initialize();
        }
        StartDocument();
        Stream renderedDocument = RenderDocument(job);
        WriteDocumentToDevice(renderedDocument);
        EndDocument();
    }
    private Stream RenderDocument(PrintJob job)
    {
        //device specific code
        return null;
    }
    private void WriteDocumentToDevice(Stream data)
    {
        //device specific code
    }
    private void Initialize()
    {
        //device specific code
    }
    private void StartDocument()
    {
        //device specific code
    }
    private void EndDocument()
    {
        //device specific code
    }
}

public class LexmarkX500 : PrintService
{
    private bool initialized;
    private bool Initialized
    {
        get { return initialized; }
        set { initialized = value; }
    }

    protected override void PrintJob(PrintJob job)
    {
        if (!this.Initialized)
        {
            this.Initialize();
        }
        StartDocument();
```

Continued

Listing 10-2: Print System Using Inheritance to Incorporate Different Printing Devices *(continued)*

```
            Stream renderedDocument = RenderDocument(job);
            WriteDocumentToDevice(renderedDocument);
            EndDocument();
        }
        private Stream RenderDocument(PrintJob job)
        {
            //device specific code
            return null;
        }
        private void WriteDocumentToDevice(Stream data)
        {
            //device specific code
        }
        private void Initialize()
        {
            //device specific code
        }
        private void StartDocument()
        {
            //device specific code
        }
        private void EndDocument()
        {
            //device specific code
        }
    }
    public class PrintJob
    {
        //...
    }
```

There are several problems with this design. Take a look at some of the immediately obvious ones:

❏ Each time a different physical device is connected, the client application has to instantiate a different child class. It can still use different device-specific print services in a polymorphic way, thanks to the inheritance relationship between the abstract parent PrintService class and the device-specific child classes.

❏ Each time a new physical device has to be supported, a new class has to be added to the hierarchy. The client has to be aware of the class name, and the client code has to be recompiled in order to use the new class (unless a more complex solution is implemented on the client side).

❏ In this design, one physical device corresponds to one printing system. In the future, this might prove not to be flexible enough. What if you have more than one physical device? You then have to instantiate a different print service for each device. The inheritance relationship between device-specific and general print functionality makes it complex for the service to support more than one physical device.

❑ Thinking in problem domain terms, you can see that the functionality between PrintService and the child classes is not particularly related. Child classes do not override any of the PrintService methods, except the device-specific PrintJob. However, they add a number of device-specific methods. This can make you wonder whether the relationship between PrintService and the children is really of an "is a" type.

❑ If you would like one day to reuse device-specific code contained in the LexmarkX500 and HPLaserJet classes, you would be obliged to bring along PrintService code. This is not very flexible.

From this analysis, it seems that the inheritance relationship between PrintService and the device-specific LexmarkX500 and HPLaserJet classes is not entirely justified. LexmarkX500 and HPLaserJet fit into the picture better as classes that PrintService can delegate to in order to communicate with a physical device.

Extracting the Device Interface

You can start by noting that PrintService has a single abstract method. The abstract PrintJob method is implemented by both the LexmarkX500 and HPLaserJet classes. This means that PrintService has no knowledge of concrete child types such as LexmarkX500 and HPLaserJet. This is actually a good thing, so when moving from inheritance to delegation in the design of this print system, you can try to use LexmarkX500 and HPLaserJet in a polymorphic way. In order to do so, you need to extract an IPrintDevice interface that has a single PrintJob method.

First, you have to make the method PrintJob public. Then, you can use Visual Studio's Extract Interface refactoring to perform the extraction. Alternatively, you can perform the extraction manually. Next, you need to disassociate the LexmarkX500 and HPLaserJet classes from PrintService by removing the inheritance clause from the class declaration. The result of interface extraction is shown in Listing 10-3.

Listing 10-3: Extracted IPrintDevice Interface

```
interface IPrintDevice
{
    void PrintJob(PrintJob job);
}

public class HPLaserJet : IPrintDevice
{
    //...
    void IPrintDevice.PrintJob(PrintJob job)
    {
        //device-specific code
    }

}
```

This refactoring makes it possible to use all IPrintDevice implementors in a polymorphic way, which simplifies things greatly when you are going from an inheritance to a composition relationship between the PrintService and the LexmarkX500 and HPLaserJet classes.

Refactoring: Extract Interface

Motivation

Sometimes you want to expose only a part of the functionality offered by a class. This is especially true if some clients use only a subset of the functionality provided by the class.

Another need for this refactoring results when some classes have a part of their interface in common, but implementation of these members is different. In order for these classes to be used in a polymorphic way, they should share a common interface.

Related Smells

Use this refactoring to eliminate the Duplicated Code smell and to provide polymorphic access to classes.

Mechanics

1. Declare the interface with all the members that you wish to expose through the interface.

2. Make the classes implement the interface by adding the colon symbol and interface name to the class declaration.

3. Make the clients use the interface and not the concrete classes.

Before

```
public class Customer
{
    private string firstName;

    private PurchaseHistory purchaseHistory;

    public string FirstName
    {
        get { return firstName; }
        set { firstName = value; }
    }

    public PurchaseHistory PurchaseHistory
    {
        get { return purchaseHistory; }
        set { purchaseHistory = value; }
    }

    public decimal DiscountPercent()
    {
        if (this.PurchaseHistory.TotalPurchases > 10)
        {
            return 3;
        }
```

```
        else if (this.PurchaseHistory.TotalPurchases > 100)
        {
            return 5;
        }
        else
        {
            return 0;
        }
    }
}
```

After

```
interface ICustomer
{
    decimal DiscountPercent();
    string FirstName { get; set; }
    PurchaseHistory PurchaseHistory { get; set; }
}

public class Customer : ICustomer
{
    private string firstName;

    private PurchaseHistory purchaseHistory;

    public string FirstName
    {
        get { return firstName; }
        set { firstName = value; }
    }

    public PurchaseHistory PurchaseHistory
    {
        get { return purchaseHistory; }
        set { purchaseHistory = value; }
    }
    public decimal DiscountPercent()
    {
        if (this.PurchaseHistory.TotalPurchases > 10)
        {
            return 3;
        }
        else if (this.PurchaseHistory.TotalPurchases > 100)
        {
            return 5;
        }
        else
        {
            return 0;
        }
    }
}
```

Extract Interface Refactoring in Visual Studio

In order to activate Extract Interface refactoring in Visual Studio, you should select the class name in the class declaration statement in the source code editor. After selecting the Extract Interface menu item, you will be presented with the Extract Interface dialog, where you can add the name of the new interface and select any class members that you want to include in forming it. You are offered only the class's public methods in the list of members available for extraction, and you are prompted to name the interface based on the class name, prefixed by the letter "I," as shown in Figure 10-1.

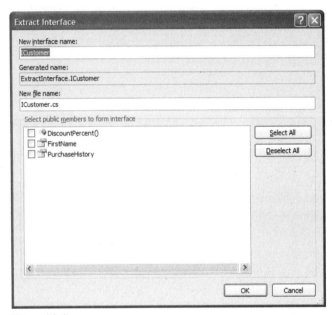

Figure 10-1

Delegation Instead of Inheritance Inside the Print System

Now you are ready to modify `PrintService` so it delegates to `IPrintDevice` instead on relying on a subclass to implement device-specific behavior. `PrintService` is no longer abstract, so the `abstract` keyword can be removed from the declaration. The abstract `PrintJob` method now delegates to a device, and it should be declared private. Listing 10-4 shows the code for `PrintService` after it has been refactored to use delegation instead of inheritance.

Listing 10-4: Delegation Instead of Inheritance for PrintService

```
public class PrintService : PrintSystem.IPrintDevice
{
    private IPrintDevice device;
    private IList<PrintJob> jobsInQueue;
```

```
    private ServiceState serviceState;

    public IList<PrintJob> JobsInQueue
    {
        get { return jobsInQueue; }
        set { jobsInQueue = value; }
    }

    public ServiceState ServiceState
    {
        get { return serviceState; }
        set { serviceState = value; }
    }

    public PrintJob CreatePrintJob()
    {
        return new PrintJob();
    }

    private void print()
    {
        while (JobsInQueue.Count > 0)
        {
            PrintJob(JobsInQueue[0]);
        }
    }

    public void PrintJob(PrintJob job) {
        this.device.PrintJob(job);
    }
}
```

Eliminating Duplication by Means of Inheritance

If you go back to Listing 10-2 for a moment and compare the implementation of the PrintJob method in LexmarkX500 and HPLaserJet, you can see that these methods are identical. The same goes for the property Initialized. One way that classes can share implementation is by means of inheritance. The solution in this case is to extract the superclass from which both LexmarkX500 and HPLaserJet inherit. You can name this class PrintDevice. Because the PrintJob method is calling other device-specific methods, you need to declare those methods in PrintDevice as well. However, because implementations of these methods differ from device to device, they have to be declared abstract, meaning the extracted superclass has to be abstract as well. PrintDevice has to implement the IPrintDevice interface. You can see the result of superclass extraction in Listing 10-5.

Listing 10-5: Extracted PrintDevice Abstract Superclass

```
public abstract class PrintDevice : IPrintDevice
{
    public void PrintJob(PrintJob job)
    {
        if (!this.Initialized)
```

Continued

295

Listing 10-5: Extracted PrintDevice Abstract Superclass *(continued)*

```
            {
                this.Initialize();
            }
            StartDocument();
            Stream renderedDocument = RenderDocument(job);
            WriteDocumentToDevice(renderedDocument);
            EndDocument();
        }
        protected abstract Stream RenderDocument(PrintJob job);
        protected abstract void WriteDocumentToDevice(Stream data);
        protected abstract void Initialize();
        protected abstract void StartDocument();
        protected abstract void EndDocument();
        public abstract bool Initialized
        {
            get;
            set;
        }
    }

    public class HPLaserJet : PrintDevice
    {
        private bool initialized;

        public override bool Initialized
        {
            get { return initialized; }
            set { initialized = value; }
        }

        protected override Stream RenderDocument(PrintJob job)
        {
            //device specific code
            return null;
        }

        protected override void WriteDocumentToDevice(Stream data)
        {
            //device specific code
        }

        protected override void Initialize()
        {
            //device specific code
        }
```

```
        protected override void StartDocument()
        {
            //device specific code
        }

        protected override void EndDocument()
        {
            //device specific code
        }
}

public class LexmarkX500 : PrintDevice
{
    private bool initialized;

    public override bool Initialized
    {
        get { return initialized; }
        set { initialized = value; }
    }

    protected override Stream RenderDocument(PrintJob job)
    {
        //device specific code
        return null;
    }

    protected override void WriteDocumentToDevice(Stream data)
    {
        //device specific code
    }

    protected override void Initialize()
    {
        //device specific code
    }

    protected override void StartDocument()
    {
        //device specific code
    }

    protected override void EndDocument()
    {
        //device specific code
    }
}
```

Refactoring: Extract Superclass

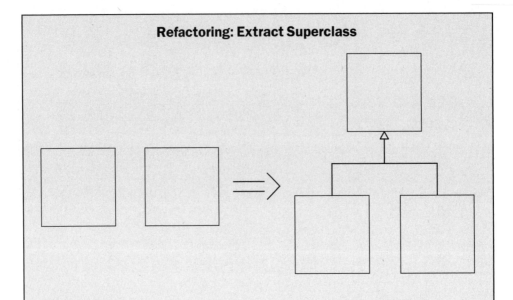

Motivation

One way that different classes can share implementation is through inheritance. Unfortunately, you cannot always identify duplicated implementations before you actually code the classes. Sometimes this duplication can be the result of newly added features or some other refactoring. Whatever the origin of duplication, you can eliminate it by extracting a superclass.

Sometimes the classes share implementation for some members and only declaration for others. In those cases, the extracted class should be abstract, because that permits both abstract and concrete methods. If classes share only an interface, then you should use Extract Interface refactoring instead.

This refactoring is an alternative to Extract Class refactoring, which promotes reuse by means of delegation. If you later decide that delegation was a better choice, you can apply Replace Inheritance with Delegation refactoring in order to reverse the situation.

Related Smells

Use this refactoring to eliminate the Duplicated Code and Large Class smells.

Mechanics

1.   Create an empty abstract superclass and make the targeted class inherit the superclass.

2.   Start moving class members up to the superclass one by one. If only the declaration is common between future subclasses, pull only the declaration to the superclass and make the member abstract. If member implementation is common as well, pull up the complete member.

3.   Execute tests after each pull.

4. If a subclass ends up having no members of its own because all have been pulled up to the superclass, you can eliminate it altogether.

5. Inspect the clients. If all members they now use are superclass members, change the declared type to superclass.

6. If the superclass contains only non-abstract members, remove the `abstract` keyword from the class declaration.

Before

```
public class OrdinaryCustomer
{
    private string firstName;
    private ShoppingBasket basket;
    public string FirstName
    {
        get { return firstName; }
        set { firstName = value; }
    }
    public ShoppingBasket Basket
    {
        get { return basket; }
        set { basket = value; }
    }
    public decimal CalculateDiscount()
    {
        if (Basket.Total > 3000)
        {
            return 2;
        }
        return 0;
    }
}

public class RegisteredCustomer
{
    private string firstName;
    private ShoppingHistory history;
    private ShoppingBasket basket;
    public string FirstName
    {
        get { return firstName; }
        set { firstName = value; }
    }
    public ShoppingBasket Basket
    {
        get { return basket; }
        set { basket = value; }
    }
    public decimal CalculateDiscount()
    {
```

Continued

```
            if (History.Total > 3000)
            {
                return 3;
            }
            else if (History.Total > 10000)
            {
                return 5;
            }
            return 0.5m;
        }
        public ShoppingHistory History
        {
            get { return history; }
            set { history = value; }
        }
    }
```

After

```
    public abstract class Customer
    {
        private string firstName;

        private ShoppingBasket basket;

        public string FirstName
        {
            get { return firstName; }
            set { firstName = value; }
        }

        public ShoppingBasket Basket
        {
            get { return basket; }
            set { basket = value; }
        }

        public abstract decimal CalculateDiscount();
    }

    public class OrdinaryCustomer:Customer
    {
        public override decimal CalculateDiscount()
        {
            if (Basket.Total > 3000)
            {
                return 2;
            }
            return 0;
        }
    }
```

```
public class RegisteredCustomer:Customer
{

    private ShoppingHistory history;

    public override decimal CalculateDiscount()
    {
        if (History.Total > 3000)
        {
            return 3;
        }
        else if (History.Total > 10000)
        {
            return 5;
        }
        return 0.5m;
    }
    public ShoppingHistory History
    {
        get { return history; }
        set { history = value; }
    }
}
```

You have now eliminated some code duplication that occurred between LexmarkX500 and HPLaserJet. As it happens, though, not all the code duplicated between the two classes has been identified. You need to refactor these classes further to remove the leftover duplication, as described in the following section.

Eliminating Duplication by Pulling Up Members

Very often, code duplicated between sibling classes can surface as a result of other refactorings, such as method extraction and method parameterization. Another source of duplication is indiscriminate feature expansion, which occurs when a member is added to one class and later added to another sibling without first checking the code in the other siblings.

The solution for cases in which code is duplicated between all the siblings is to pull the member up to a parent class. This way, the duplication is eliminated and common features are maintained in the parent class. If you compare the LexmarkX500 and HPLaserJet classes from the print-system example, you will see that the property Initialized is identical in both classes. The solution is to pull up the Initialized property to the PrintDevice class. The resulting code is shown in Listing 10-6.

Listing 10-6: Pulling Up the Initialized Property of LexmarkX500 and HPLaserJet

```
public abstract class PrintDevice : IPrintDevice
{
    private bool initialized;

    public bool Initialized
    {
```

Continued

Listing 10-6: Print System Using Inheritance to Incorporate Different Printing Devices
(continued)

```
        get { return initialized; }
        set { initialized = value; }
    }

    public void PrintJob(PrintJob job)
    {
        if (!this.Initialized)
        {
            this.Initialize();
        }
        StartDocument();
        Stream renderedDocument = RenderDocument(job);
        WriteDocumentToDevice(renderedDocument);
        EndDocument();
    }
    protected abstract Stream RenderDocument(PrintJob job);
    protected abstract void WriteDocumentToDevice(Stream data);
    protected abstract void Initialize();
    protected abstract void StartDocument();
    protected abstract void EndDocument();

}

public class HPLaserJet : PrintDevice
{

    protected override Stream RenderDocument(PrintJob job)
    {
        //device specific code
        return null;
    }

    protected override void WriteDocumentToDevice(Stream data)
    {
        //device specific code
    }

    protected override void Initialize()
    {
        //device specific code
    }

    protected override void StartDocument()
```

```
        {
            //device specific code
        }

        protected override void EndDocument()
        {
            //device specific code
        }
    }

public class LexmarkX500 : PrintDevice
{
        protected override Stream RenderDocument(PrintJob job)
        {
            //device specific code
            return null;
        }

        protected override void WriteDocumentToDevice(Stream data)
        {
            //device specific code
        }

        protected override void Initialize()
        {
            //device specific code
        }

        protected override void StartDocument()
        {
            //device specific code
        }

        protected override void EndDocument()
        {
            //device specific code
        }
    }
```

This concludes the redesign of the print system. In the first stage, inheritance was replaced with delegation, only to be introduced again later. First, interface inheritance was introduced to provide polymorphic access to print devices, and then class inheritance was used to reduce duplication between different devices.

Such gradual changes to code are not uncommon, because some smells become visible only after more immediate ones are eliminated. The optimal design is hardly a tangible set of classes and their relations; it is a continuously changing set of decisions that corresponds best to current circumstances.

Refactoring: Pull Up Method

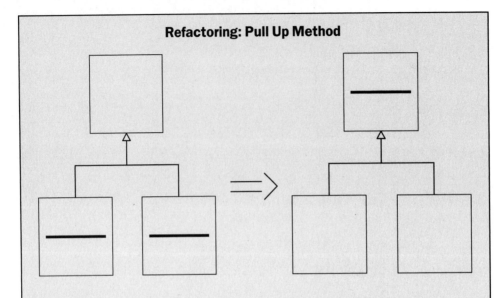

Motivation

A way to share implementation between classes is to have a common ancestor. All members common to all the siblings should be contained in the parent class, in order to avoid unnecessary duplication.

When a member is completely identical in all of the child classes, in order to avoid duplication, the member should be moved from the child classes to a parent class or interface.

Related Smells

Use this refactoring to eliminate the Duplicated Code and Large Class smells.

Mechanics

The simplest case in which to use this refactoring is when the methods in child classes are completely identical. Sometimes, however, this refactoring should be preceded by other refactorings, such as method extraction and method parameterization, until the methods are made equal.

The mechanics are similar but simpler when you are pulling up abstract method declarations to a parent abstract class or interface.

1. Cut and paste the method from the child class to the base class.

2. If the recently moved method is using some other methods in the child classes, declare the method as abstract in the parent and make the child classes override it. If the method is using a property available only in child classes, then consider moving the property up as well.

3. Delete the method from the rest of the siblings.

4. Compile and test.

Before

```
public abstract class Customer
{
    //...
    private string firstName;

    private ShoppingBasket basket;

    public string FirstName
    {
        get { return firstName; }
        set { firstName = value; }
    }

    public ShoppingBasket Basket
    {
        get { return basket; }
        set { basket = value; }
    }

    public abstract decimal CalculateDiscount();
}

public class OrdinaryCustomer:Customer
{
    //...
    private IList wishList;

    private SpecialOffersService specialOfferService;

    public override decimal CalculateDiscount()
    {
        if (Basket.Total > 3000)
        {
            return 2;
        }
        return 0;
    }

    public IList PersonalizeOffer() {
        IList personalizedOffer = new ArrayList();
        IList itemsOnOffer = specialOfferService.ItemsWithSpecialOffer();
        foreach (Product productFromWishList in wishList) {
            if (itemsOnOffer.Contains(productFromWishList)) {
                personalizedOffer.Add(productFromWishList);
            }
        }
        return personalizedOffer;
    }
}
```

Continued

```
public class RegisteredCustomer:Customer
{
    //...
    private IList wishList;

    private SpecialOffersService specialOfferService;

    private ShoppingHistory history;

    public override decimal CalculateDiscount()
    {
        if (History.Total > 3000)
        {
            return 3;
        }
        else if (History.Total > 10000)
        {
            return 5;
        }
        return 0.5m;
    }

    public ShoppingHistory History
    {
        get { return history; }
        set { history = value; }
    }

    public IList PersonalizeOffer()
    {
        IList personalizedOffer = new ArrayList();
        IList itemsOnOffer = specialOfferService.ItemsWithSpecialOffer();
        foreach (Product productFromWishList in wishList)
        {
            if (itemsOnOffer.Contains(productFromWishList))
            {
                personalizedOffer.Add(productFromWishList);
            }
        }
        return personalizedOffer;
    }
}
```

After

```
public abstract class Customer
{
    //...
```

```csharp
        private IList wishList;

        private SpecialOffersService specialOfferService;

        private string firstName;

        private ShoppingBasket basket;

        public string FirstName
        {
            get { return firstName; }
            set { firstName = value; }
        }

        public ShoppingBasket Basket
        {
            get { return basket; }
            set { basket = value; }
        }

        public IList PersonalizeOffer()
        {
            IList personalizedOffer = new ArrayList();
            IList itemsOnOffer = specialOfferService.ItemsWithSpecialOffer();
            foreach (Product productFromWishList in wishList)
            {
                if (itemsOnOffer.Contains(productFromWishList))
                {
                    personalizedOffer.Add(productFromWishList);
                }
            }
            return personalizedOffer;
        }

        public abstract decimal CalculateDiscount();
}

public class OrdinaryCustomer:Customer
{
    //...
    public override decimal CalculateDiscount()
    {
        if (Basket.Total > 3000)
        {
            return 2;
        }
        return 0;
    }
}
```

Continued

```
public class RegisteredCustomer:Customer
{
    //...
    private ShoppingHistory history;

    public override decimal CalculateDiscount()
    {
        if (History.Total > 3000)
        {
            return 3;
        }
        else if (History.Total > 10000)
        {
            return 5;
        }
        return 0.5m;
    }

    public ShoppingHistory History
    {
        get { return history; }
        set { history = value; }
    }
}
```

Making Use of Generics

Generics add additional type safety to your code and liberate you from writing tedious typecasting code. Existing classes can often be further enhanced by the means of generics, which permit parameter type to be declared at the point of usage.

Very often, a good signal that generics can be employed is when the Object type is used in declarations. An additional signal of the possibility for upgrade to generic types is the use of container types from the System.Collections namespace. Generic containers are placed inside the System.Collections.Generic namespace and have close correspondence with containers from the System.Collections namespace.

In practice, you rarely operate in the same way on objects that are different in type. You can operate on objects of different types, but through polymorphic mechanisms, meaning those objects belong to the same supertype. Even in those cases, a class can be made generic, and a parameter type can be a common supertype.

When introducing generics, you should make sure that all uses of Object correspond to the same type. Generic types can be parameterized with more than one parameter type, so for each implicit type, a new parameter type should be used.

Refactoring: Replace General-Purpose Reference with Parameter Type

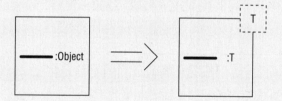

Motivation

Before generics were introduced in C#, the only way you could write code that dealt with objects of any type was to declare a reference as an `Object`. Sometimes it is useful to limit the type of manipulated objects at the point of usage for the following reasons:

- ❑ Additional type safety is provided.
- ❑ Duplicate typecasting code can be eliminated.

Related Smells

Use this refactoring to eliminate the duplicated code and to turn dynamically typed code into strongly statically typed explicit code.

Mechanics

General-purpose references can often be found when the type `Object` is employed as the declaring type.

1. Identify how many different underlying types are declared as `Object`. For example, the `IList` interface references only one type, one that is added and retrieved from the list, whereas `IDictionary` references two: one is used as key, and the other is stored in the dictionary.

2. For each different underlying type discovered in Step 1, add one type parameter in the class declaration.

3. Replace `Object` with the parameter type declared in Step 2.

4. Compile and test.

Before

```
public class PerishableContainer
{
    private ArrayList list = new ArrayList();

    private int perishIntervalInSeconds;

    private IDictionary timeInStorage = new Hashtable();
```

Continued

```
public int PerishIntervalInSeconds
{
    get { return perishIntervalInSeconds; }
    set { perishIntervalInSeconds = value; }
}

public void LeaveInStorage(object item)
{
    list.Add(item);
    timeInStorage.Add(item, DateTime.Now);
}

private object TakeOldestFromStorage()
{
    if (list.Count > 0)
    {
        object item = (object)list[0];
        list.Remove(item);
        if (!HasPerished(item))
        {
            return item;
        }
    }
    return null;
}

public object TakeFromStorage()
{
    object item = null;
    while (list.Count > 0)
    {
        item = TakeOldestFromStorage();
        if (item != null)
        {
            break;
        }
    }
    return item;
}

private bool HasPerished(object item)
{
    if (((DateTime)timeInStorage[item]).
        AddSeconds(perishIntervalInSeconds)
        > System.DateTime.Now)
    {
        return false;
    }
    return true;
}

public int Count
```

```
    {
        get { return list.Count; }
    }

    //...
}
```

After

```
public class PerishableContainer<Perishable>
{
    private ArrayList list = new ArrayList();

    private int perishIntervalInSeconds;

    private IDictionary timeInStorage = new Hashtable();

    public int PerishIntervalInSeconds
    {
        get { return perishIntervalInSeconds; }
        set { perishIntervalInSeconds = value; }
    }

    public void LeaveInStorage(Perishable item)
    {
        list.Add(item);
        timeInStorage.Add(item, DateTime.Now);
    }

    private Perishable TakeOldestFromStorage()
    {
        Perishable item = default(Perishable);
        if (list.Count > 0)
        {
            item = (Perishable)list[0];
            list.Remove(item);
            if (!HasPerished(item))
            {
                return item;
            }
        }
        return item;
    }

    public Perishable TakeFromStorage()
    {
        Perishable item = default(Perishable);
        while (list.Count > 0)
        {
            item = TakeOldestFromStorage();
            if (item != null)
            {
```

Continued

```
                    break;
              }
        }
        return item;
    }

    private bool HasPerished(Perishable item)
    {
        if (((DateTime)timeInStorage[item]).
            AddSeconds(perishIntervalInSeconds)
            > System.DateTime.Now)
        {
            return false;
        }
        return true;
    }

    public int Count
    {
        get { return list.Count; }
    }

    //...
}
```

Inheritance and Generic Types in the Rent-a-Wheels Application

You have probably noticed by now in the Rent-a-Wheels application that various Data classes (BranchData, ModelData, and so on) have a number of identically declared and implemented methods. In addition, these classes are used in a similar way, except for the domain objects they work upon. The presence of identical methods means that code duplication exists between the classes. From this, a few conclusions can be reached:

❑   Data classes share some of their implementation, mainly private methods such as AddParameter or ExecuteNonQuery.

❑   Interfaces are almost identical, except for the single object on which the classes operate. For example, the method Delete is in BranchData declared as public void Delete(Branch branch), whereas in ModelData, the method is declared as public void Delete(Model model).

❑   Duplication can be avoided by superclass extraction.

Extracting Super

Because some of the methods between different Data classes differ in implementation, the superclass has to be abstract. You can call it AbstractData, and move all identical methods to it. Because the majority of these methods are private, visibility has to be changed to protected so that subclasses can make use of these methods. These methods are AddParameter, ExecuteNonQuery, FillDataset, and so on.

After this extraction is performed, it becomes obvious that some of the methods, such as PrepareDataObjects, are used only by methods that found their way to the superclass, meaning that these methods can remain private.

Employing Generics

The declaration of public methods differs only in the type of domain object that the Data class manipulates. You can make AbstractData a parameterized class and enable the domain object to be defined at the point of usage. Therefore, AbstractData is declared as a generic class:

```
public abstract class AbstractData<Persisted>
{

    //...

    public abstract void Delete(Persisted persisted);

}
```

The public methods now receive the Persisted instance and can be overridden and implemented in each of the child data classes.

It is actually the child Data (BranchData, ModelData, and so on) that parameterizes the abstract superclass AbstractData and defines the parameter type as Branch, Model, and so on. Therefore, BranchData is declared as follows:

```
class BranchData : AbstractData<Branch>
{

    //...
    public override void Delete(Branch branch)
    {
        IDbCommand command = new SqlCommand();
        AddParameter(command, idParameterName,
            DbType.Int32, branch.Id);
        ExecuteNonQuery(command, deleteBranchSql);
    }
}
```

This way, AbstractData can expose a common interface in the form of public methods such as Delete and Update that use a parameterized type. Only the parameterized GetAll method provokes change in form classes, because it uses a parameterized list to return a list of all domain objects. The declaration of the GetAll method in BranchData looks like this:

```
public override IList<Branch> GetAll()
```

It seems that the Data class can be a very useful and reusable class that can serve as a base for future concrete Data class implementations. With this, you have managed to organize the Data classes into a hierarchy that both reduces duplication and makes it possible for Data classes to be used in a polymorphic manner.

You may still be concerned with one thing, however. `AbstractData` depends on a concrete ADO.NET provider, meaning it would not be easy to change the system so that it uses a different database motor.

Extracting the DataObjectsProvider Class

To make `AbstractData` database-neutral, you can extract the data provider object-creation code to separate the `AbstractDataObjectsProvider` class:

```
public abstract class AbstractDataObjectsProvider
{
    public abstract System.Data.IDbDataAdapter InstantiateAdapter();

    public abstract System.Data.IDbConnection InstantiateConnection();

    public abstract System.Data.IDbCommand InstantiateCommand();
}
```

`AbstractData` can hold a field of `AbstractDataObjectsProvider` and delegate data-object creation to this class. You can also make the child classes supply the concrete `DataObjectsProvider` through a constructor method, together with a connection string.

The `BranchData` constructor now looks like this:

```
public BranchData():base(BranchData.MSSQLConnectionString,
    new MSSQLDataObjectsProvider()) {
}
```

The `MsSqlDataObjectsProvider` code contains simple creation code:

```
public class MSSQLDataObjectsProvider : AbstractDataObjectsProvider
{
    public override System.Data.IDbDataAdapter InstantiateAdapter()
    {
        return new SqlDataAdapter();
    }

    public override System.Data.IDbConnection InstantiateConnection()
    {
        return new SqlConnection();
    }

    public override System.Data.IDbCommand InstantiateCommand()
    {
        return new SqlCommand();
    }
}
```

With this you have moved the dependency on a certain data provider down in the hierarchy. More important, provider creation code is concentrated on a single line, so all it takes to change the provider is changing a single line in the concrete data classes and implementing another `DataObjectProvider`. You can see the resulting design in Figure 10-2.

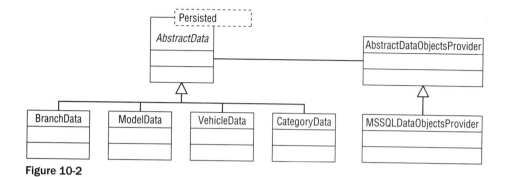

Figure 10-2

Listing 10-7 shows the most important new code for Rent-a-Wheels that resulted from the refactorings described in this chapter.

Listing 10-7: Selected Rent-a-Wheels Classes After Advanced Refactorings

```
public abstract class AbstractData<Persisted>
{
    private String connectionString;

    private AbstractDataObjectsProvider provider;

    public AbstractData(String connectionString,
        AbstractDataObjectsProvider provider) {
        this.connectionString = connectionString;
        this.provider = provider;
    }

    private String ConnectionString
    {
        get { return connectionString; }
        set { connectionString = value; }
    }

    private AbstractDataObjectsProvider Provider
    {
        get { return provider; }
        set { provider = value; }
    }

    private IDbConnection CreateConnection()
    {
        IDbConnection connection = Provider.InstantiateConnection();
        connection.ConnectionString = this.ConnectionString;
        return connection;
    }

    private IDbConnection PrepareDataObjects(IDbCommand command, string sql)
    {
```

Continued

315

Listing 10-7: Selected Rent-a-Wheels Classes After Advanced Refactorings *(continued)*

```
        IDbConnection connection = CreateConnection();
        connection.Open();
        command.Connection = connection;
        command.CommandText = sql;
        return connection;
    }

    protected void AddParameter(IDbCommand command, string parameterName,
    DbType parameterType, object paramaterValue)
    {
        IDbDataParameter parameter = command.CreateParameter();
        parameter.ParameterName = parameterName;
        parameter.DbType = parameterType;
        parameter.Value = paramaterValue;
        command.Parameters.Add(parameter);
    }

    protected DataSet FillDataset(IDbCommand command, string sql)
    {
        IDbConnection connection = PrepareDataObjects(command, sql);
        IDbDataAdapter adapter = provider.InstantiateAdapter();
        DataSet branches = new DataSet();
        adapter.SelectCommand = command;
        adapter.Fill(branches);
        connection.Close();
        return branches;
    }

    protected void ExecuteNonQuery(IDbCommand command, string sql)
    {
        IDbConnection connection = PrepareDataObjects(command, sql);
        command.ExecuteNonQuery();
        connection.Close();
    }

    protected IDataReader ExecuteReader(out IDbConnection connection, string sql)
    {
        IDbCommand command = provider.InstantiateCommand();
        connection = PrepareDataObjects(command, sql);
        return command.ExecuteReader();
    }

    public abstract IList<Persisted> GetAll();

    public abstract void Delete(Persisted persisted);

    public abstract void Update(Persisted persisted);

    public abstract void Insert(Persisted persisted);

}
```

```
class BranchData : AbstractData<Branch>
{
    private const String MSSQLConnectionString = "Data Source=TESLATEAM;" +
    "Initial Catalog=RENTAWHEELS;" +
    "User ID=RENTAWHEELS_LOGIN;Password=RENTAWHEELS_PASSWORD_123";

    private const string branchTableIdColumnName = "BranchId";
    private const string branchTableNameColumnName = "BranchName";

    private const string selectAllFromBranchSql =
        "Select BranchId as BranchId, Branch.Name as BranchName from Branch";
    private const string deleteBranchSql =
        "Delete Branch Where BranchId = @Id";
    private const string insertBranchSql =
        "Insert Into Branch (Name) Values(@Name)";
    private const string updateBranchSql =
        "Update Branch  Set Name = @Name Where BranchId = @Id";

    private const string idParameterName = "@Id";
    private const string nameParameterName = "@Name";

    private const int singleTableInDatasetIndex = 0;

    public BranchData():base(BranchData.MSSQLConnectionString,
        new MSSQLDataObjectsProvider()) {
    }

    public override IList<Branch> GetAll()
    {
        IList<Branch> branches = new List<Branch>();
        IDbCommand command = new SqlCommand();
        DataSet branchesSet =
            FillDataset(command, selectAllFromBranchSql);
        DataTable branchesTable =
            branchesSet.Tables[singleTableInDatasetIndex];
        foreach(DataRow row in branchesTable.Rows){
            branches.Add(BranchFromRow(row));
        }
        return branches;
    }

    public static Branch BranchFromRow(DataRow row)
    {
        return new Branch(Convert.ToInt32(row[branchTableIdColumnName]),
                        Convert.ToString(row[branchTableNameColumnName]));
    }

    public override void Delete(Branch branch)
    {
        IDbCommand command = new SqlCommand();
        AddParameter(command, idParameterName,
            DbType.Int32, branch.Id);
        ExecuteNonQuery(command, deleteBranchSql);
```

Continued

317

```
    }

    public override void Update(Branch branch)
    {
        IDbCommand command = new SqlCommand();
        AddParameter(command, nameParameterName,
            DbType.String, branch.Name);
        AddParameter(command, idParameterName,
            DbType.Int32, branch.Id);
        ExecuteNonQuery(command, updateBranchSql);
    }

    public override void Insert(Branch branch)
    {
        IDbCommand command = new SqlCommand();
        AddParameter(command, nameParameterName,
            DbType.String, branch.Name);
        ExecuteNonQuery(command, insertBranchSql);
    }
}
```

As is the case with other chapters, the complete code is available for download at the book's website at www.wrox.com, and I recommend you analyze it in more depth. The refactorings performed on Rent-a-Wheels in this chapter were quite complex and have significantly changed the application's internals.

Summary

This chapter dealt with some advanced and powerful object-oriented concepts. You have witnessed the power and dangers of inheritance. With great power comes great responsibility, so you have to be careful not to misuse inheritance, or your losses will soon outweigh the benefits.

Even when inheritance has been poorly applied, there is still a solution. You can refactor your code so it uses delegation instead of inheritance; and in cases where inheritance is well applied, it still might need a bit of tweaking. You can do this by moving members up and down the hierarchy.

In cases where you can see that you could benefit from inheritance, you can perform Extract Interface and Extract Superclass refactoring. By extracting an interface, you open the door for polymorphic mechanisms in your code; and by extracting a superclass, you reduce code duplication between the siblings.

In the Rent-a-Wheels example, you have seen these advanced refactorings in practice and how, when combined, they can provide a solution to a number of problems, increasing the flexibility and reuse value of your code.

The next chapter wraps up the story on inheritance. It also covers large-scale code organization and provides some insight into the concepts of namespace, assembly, and related refactorings.

11

Code Organization on a Large Scale

Until now, I have hardly mentioned C#'s large-scale organizational mechanisms, such as namespaces and assemblies. The organization of your project and the partitioning of types to namespaces and assemblies can have a profound effect on the maintainability of your project and the development process in general.

Many of these issues are not apparent with small projects. They become much more relevant as projects grow and the number of types reaches hundreds or even thousands. Dependencies, an important aspect of large scale organization, conversely, are notorious for multiplying with the age of the project. This does not mean that these issues should be taken lightly with smaller projects. Projects have a tendency to grow, and decisions that you make early on can have important consequences much later.

This chapter covers the following:

❑   Criteria that can be applied when using namespaces and assemblies to organize your project

❑   Dependencies, including why it is important to keep dependencies between different organizational units at bay

❑   File-level organization of code and partial types, and how this affects forms inheritance in C#

Namespaces

Many real-life projects can amass hundreds, if not thousands, of types. Without namespaces, it would be difficult for programmers to find their way around projects that large. Namespaces enable you to group related types and avoid name collisions. Each class (or any other type like interface, structure, or enumeration, and so on) has a full name that consists of the type name itself plus the name of the namespace to which it belongs.

For example, the `ArrayList` class belongs to the `System.Collections` namespace. The namespace is actually more than simply a label for a class, and it is important to choose its name wisely.

Naming Guidelines and Namespace Organization

One of the most important things to remember when creating namespaces is to choose appropriate, logical names. The guidelines for choosing namespace names do not differ that much from the guidelines for naming classes. Names should be descriptive and clearly indicate the purpose of the namespace. For example, the system namespace `System.IO` clearly indicates that types in that namespace are used for reading and writing to files and data streams.

Therefore, placement of a type inside a certain namespace is by no means arbitrary. All types in a namespace should have a related purpose. This helps produce consistent library design and facilitates the use of types. Such organization is easily navigated with the help of IntelliSense in Visual Studio, as you can appreciate in Figure 11-1.

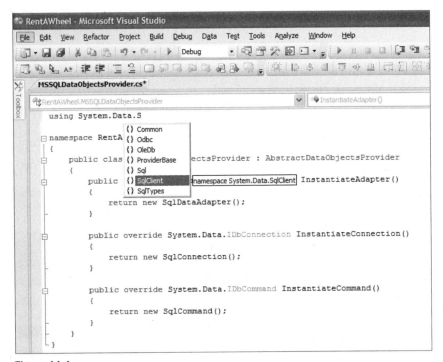

Figure 11-1

Nested Namespaces

Because namespaces can be nested, they can form logical hierarchies whereby more general types are placed further up in the hierarchy and more specific types are placed further down the hierarchy chain. For example, the `System.Data` namespace contains general data interface types such as `IDbConnection`, while `System.Data.SqlClient` contains implementation classes specific to the Microsoft SQL Server data provider such as `System.Data.SqlClient.SqlConnection`.

Changing the Default Namespace Name

When you create a new project in Visual Studio, it is automatically assigned a default namespace, based on the project name. This name chosen by the IDE can be changed and need not have any relation with the project or assembly name. The default namespace can be changed from the Project Properties page.

Microsoft recommends using `CompanyName.TechnologyName` as a root namespace, so you can set this plus the project-related name to be a default namespace for your project. This will save you from typing a namespace declaration every time you add a new code item to your project.

If you add a new class to the project using the Visual Studio Add➤Class option, the generated class file will contain the default namespace declaration, and the newly added class will be placed inside it. This is the only role the default namespace plays in a C# project, and you can always change the namespace to which a class belongs by changing the namespace declaration in the source code.

If you add a folder to your project and then add a new class to your project while the folder selected, the namespace declaration for the newly added class will be generated as the default namespace name plus the folder name. This way, the Visual Studio–generated namespace structure follows a physical folder structure. This is the most logical way to organize your namespaces.

Smell: Implicit Imports

Detecting the Smell

This smell is generally easily detected by simple visual inspection. Long Pascal-cased statements such as `System.Collections.Generic.IList` should stand out from the rest of the code in the body of the class.

Related Refactoring

Use Explicit Imports refactoring to eliminate this smell.

Rationale

Using long type names in the body of your type means more clutter and more duplication in your code. It also renders a "Using" section uninformative, because there is no guarantee that it contains all the namespaces used by your class.

Employing Using Directives

When you program, you always use the full name of the class. The compiler will not find any class only by its short name unless the class belongs to the built-in `System` namespace, such as `String` or `Object`. To avoid typing long names, which would be rather tedious, you can use a `using` directive in a "using" section at the top of the file that enables you to specify the long name one time only or import the containing namespace.

Avoid using full type names in the body of your type because they make the code harder to read. Not only does this mean more clutter in the body of the type, it also means that the "using" section will fail to provide useful dependency information when you scan your code in browsing mode.

Because you import the whole namespace by means of a `using` directive, you should strive to maintain the number of classes in the namespace at a moderate level. Even so, a name collision can occur. Name collision happens when two or more imported namespaces contain a type with the same name. In those cases, you can use a `using` directive to declare an alias name in order to disambiguate collided names. The following snippet shows an example:

```
using System.Xml;
using ExtendedNode = ParsingCompany.ExtendedParser.XmlNode;
```

Because `System.Xml` contains the `XmlNode` class, it collides with `ParsingCompany.ExtendedParser.XmlNode`. By introducing the `ExtendedNode` alias for `ParsingCompany.ExtendedParser.XmlNode`, you can use short names for both types in the same class.

Refactoring: Explicit Imports

Motivation

Using long type names in your code adds more clutter to your code and makes it difficult to read. It also means that you cannot count on the Imports section to give you the full breakdown of your type's dependencies. Finally, it means more duplication, which can be avoided by means of `using` directives.

Related Smells

Use this refactoring to eliminate Implicit Imports smell.

Mechanics

1. Add the `using` directives for the type that was used implicitly.
2. Eliminate the full name part from the type that was used implicitly.
3. Perform a textual search on the imported namespace in order to discover other instances of implicit imports. If more instances are discovered, then proceed to eliminate the namespace part from the name of the type.

Before

```
public class PurchaseHistory
{
    private System.Collections.Generic.IList<Item> itemsValue;
    //...
}
```

After

```
using System.Collections.Generic;

public class PurchaseHistory
{
    private IList<Item> itemsValue;
    //...
}
```

Your C# project can contain a number of namespaces; each namespace can spawn several source files and even several projects, but the most common way to organize a namespace is to place it inside the single project. That way, when you compile your project, your namespace will be contained inside the assembly, and this will convert the assembly to the unit of release and deployment.

Assemblies

An assembly is the compiled product of your C# project. Assemblies can contain a number of namespaces that in turn can contain a number of types. Besides compiled code, each assembly contains a Win32 header; a CIL header; type metadata; an assembly manifest; and, optionally, resources as images and string tables if added to the assembly. Assemblies are large, physical building blocks. In .NET you construct your applications by combining different assemblies.

If you choose Windows Application as the application type of your assembly, the compiler generates an executable file, and you can run your process assembly as an application under Windows. Double-clicking the file initiates the execution by launching a startup object that can be a Windows form or a `static void Main` method.

If you choose Class Library as the assembly application type, then the compiler generates a dynamically linked library, and you can invoke and use this assembly from some other assembly. This way, you can reuse the compiled assembly without ever seeing the code that was used to produce it. This type of reuse is known as *binary reuse*, and it offers a number of benefits compared to reuse on the code level.

Binary Reuse

Imagine you have programmed a number of classes that resolve important functionality in your application. Then you start working on some other application, and you are faced with almost the same problem. Obviously, if you have already programmed the code that solves this problem, you don't want to write it again. One option is to add all the source files from the original project to the new project, thereby reusing the code. All types, including ones that were developed for the first project, are compiled into the new assembly. This type of reuse is known as *source-based reuse*.

Another option is to add a reference to the original project's compiled assembly and then reuse the functionality provided by the assembly. This type of reuse is known as *binary reuse*. Binary reuse is in many ways superior to source-based reuse. The following sections take a look at some of the benefits that binary reuse brings to your development process.

Encapsulation and Modularity

The great thing about programming is that you can count on many ready-made building blocks when you construct your application. Because you can compose your application out of different pieces, you can attack bigger problems by dividing them into smaller ones. Many times, you can find assemblies that solve several of the problems you need to resolve in order to construct your application. In this way, the assembly becomes the largest building block of your development process.

Because an assembly is a binary, most of the time you do not have access to the code that was used to create it. Generally, you get the documentation, you can see types and signatures in an object browser, and you can count on help from IntelliSense in order to make use of the assembly. However, code and internal implementation details are hidden from your view. At first, this can be seen as a limitation, and you might be tempted to look into the code of the assembly you are using.

In fact, this lack of access to an assembly's source code is just another level of encapsulation, and it removes an enormous amount of complexity from your shoulders. Just imagine a project containing the code for the System.IO and System.Data namespaces inside it. This would raise the line count and complexity of your project by several orders of magnitude. Even the simplest program might turn unmanageable once you start to suspect that there is a bug somewhere inside the System namespace and place a breakpoint inside the code in order to investigate it.

Versioning

When you use someone else's assembly, you expect it to be tried and tested, well documented, and with a well-designed API that is easy to use. Not only this, but you can rightfully expect the assembly's creator to maintain the assembly. If a bug is detected, then the creator should provide a new release that resolves the bug; and because the creator is in the business of making software, it is only logical to expect the assembly to evolve in time, and that the creator will provide more and better functionality in the next major release of the assembly. Therefore, you need to be able to use assemblies that change over time, but you also want to avoid the problems that can result from the evolution of those assemblies:

❑   Because the assembly interface can change over time, you do not want your application to break when a new version of the assembly you are using is released.

❑   You do not want to be forced to recompile and redistribute your assembly just so you can use a minor new bug-fixing version of some assembly that you use.

❑   Finally, you want to be able to manage your own schedule of assembly upgrades.

Because .NET assemblies are versioned, and assembly versioning mechanisms are built into the .NET runtime, you can avoid all of the aforementioned problems. You can declare that your assembly depends on a specific version of some other assembly, and you can choose whether you want your assembly to use a newer version. Just imagine the complexity of these versioning procedures if you had to perform them on the source-code level.

> See Chapter 6 for more information on assembly versioning schemas and .NET version management mechanisms.

Memory Resources

Because assemblies in .NET are dynamically linked and loaded, multiple application domains can reference a single assembly that can be distributed in its own file. This reduces disk memory consumption and can reduce the time to download and start the application over the Internet. Each assembly is loaded only once into the computer RAM, which means that multiple running applications using the same assembly at the same time does not require loading the assembly multiple times, resulting in more efficient use of system resources. In order for application domains to share the JIT-compiled code, an assembly must be marked as domain-neutral.

For more information on assembly loading options and domain-neutral assemblies, take a look at the article "Application Domains and Assemblies" on MSDN: http://msdn.microsoft.com/en-us/library/43wc4hhs.aspx.

Strong Security

Assemblies can be given strong names and can be digitally signed. This way, you can guarantee that your application is not using some other assembly that happened to have the same name as the one used by your application and that could have been maliciously substituted for the original assembly. You can also guarantee that the original assembly has not been tampered with in any way; and that when a new version is provided, it is indeed provided by the same trusted author. You can also define permissions and security policies for your assemblies. The comprehensive set of security features makes assemblies safe for use and distribution even in the most demanding environments, such as the Internet.

Intellectual Property Protection

As mentioned earlier, assemblies do not contain source code. When obfuscated, they can be extremely difficult to reverse engineer. This makes an assembly an excellent platform for commercial software distribution. It also adds an additional level of security to your project, because no one can analyze the original source in search of possible vulnerabilities. You can rest assured that generating the source code from the binary and then using and modifying the code in order to compile malicious surrogate versions of the assembly will be extremely difficult and complex.

Multilanguage Reuse

An assembly programmed in any .NET language can be referenced from any .NET assembly no matter what language it is programmed in. This makes it possible for an assembly programmed in C# to reuse code programmed in Visual Basic or managed C++, which provides additional flexibility to your development process and opens up the field for reuse in .NET.

Now that you have seen some of the benefits of binary reuse, you are probably thinking about assembly organization. How do you decide which namespaces the assembly should contain? What criteria should you apply when placing types inside the namespaces? The next section addresses those questions.

Namespace Organization Guidelines

As projects grow in size, using classes as the sole organizational unit soon becomes insufficient. The namespace is a higher-level organizational unit that can group classes. The design of namespaces evolves over time, as a result of changes in class organization that affect the way you build and maintain the system, and perform reuse. Sometimes these forces can work against each other, or over time the balance can change. Therefore, it's important to start by looking into how namespace organization affects the maintainability of your code.

Smell: Large Namespace

Detecting the Smell

Use class view to detect this smell. If you expand the namespace and it shows a large list of classes, you should investigate further such namespace organization.

Related Refactorings

Use Move Class to Namespace and Extract Namespace refactorings to eliminate this smell.

Rationale

Namespaces are higher-order organizational units. By using them improperly, you reduce the maintainability and reusability of your code. A large namespace, especially if coupled with a non-coherent namespace, is poised to become a magnet and hotbed for sprouting dependencies.

Maintainability

In Chapter 9 you saw how the Single Responsibility Principle works on classes. Recall that it states that a class should have only one reason to change. The same principle can be applied at the namespace level. If new requirements for changes appear, it is best if those changes can be limited to a minimum number of namespaces. If classes are conceptually closely related or, because of the way they are implemented, they belong inside the same namespace, then this principle applied to namespaces means that classes belonging to the same namespace should have the same motive for change.

Smell: Non-Coherent Namespace

Detecting the Smell
This smell can often be discovered indirectly. If you look at the package diagram, this namespace can have a large number of incoming and outgoing dependencies.

Related Refactorings
Use Move Class to Namespace and Extract Namespace refactorings to eliminate this smell.

Rationale
A non-coherent namespace can appear in many forms. For example, it can be a namespace that mixes the following:

❑   Classes intended for reuse with classes not intended for reuse

❑   Classes with different responsibilities

❑   Classes with different levels of abstractness and stability

---

Reuse

The first principle regarding reuse and class distribution is the Reuse-Release Equivalence principle. Reusable classes are not just programmed and compiled; such classes have to be supported by an integral development process. In order to be able to put versioning and release practices in place, you should separate classes intended for reuse from classes not intended to be reused.

Object-Oriented Design Principle: Reuse-Release Equivalence

In order to be able to successfully reuse classes, it is not enough for the class to be well written and well designed. Some development process considerations, besides pure software design arguments, have to be taken into account. When you reuse some classes, you have to be sure that you will get support when you need it and that any bugs you might encounter will be resolved; but first you need a mechanism that will make it possible to identify the exact version of the classes you are using. Reusable classes have to be released with versioning policies in place and in such a manner that the programmer using the classes can decide what version to use and when to perform an upgrade.

Definition

To quote Robert C. Martin, "The granule of reuse is the granule of release" (from *Agile Software Development: Principles, Patterns, and Practices*, Prentice Hall, 2002).

As a consequence, you should keep classes intended for reuse together, and apart from classes not intended for reuse.

Example

While programming an online store purchase form, you create a new zip code validator class and place it in the same namespace and assembly as the web GUI classes:

```
namespace BookStore.Web.Purchase
{
    public class PurchaseForm
    {
        //...
    }
    public class ZipValidator
    {
        //...
    }
}
```

The problem with such partitioning is that a reusable ZipValidator class is placed inside the same namespace and assembly as other classes not intended for reuse. If you reuse the ZipValidator, then you have to accept the versioning and release cycle that is influenced by other non-reusable classes, if such mechanisms are put in place for the GUI classes:

```
namespace BookStore.Web.Purchase
{
    public class PurchaseForm
    {
        //...
    }
    //...
}

namespace Web.Common.Validators
{
    public class ZipValidator
    {
        //...
    }
    //...
}
```

By placing the validator class together with other reusable classes, you are not susceptible to the effects that changes in GUI classes can produce. This way, the validator class is part of the namespace intended for reuse and the release cycle and versioning

Continued

policies intended and planned for reuse. Bear in mind that your assembly organization should be in sync with your namespace organization.

Needless to say, just placing the class inside the right namespace cannot fix your development process; correct development practices have to be followed.

Distinguishing classes intended for reuse from classes programmed without such a purpose in mind is only the first indicator of how to organize your classes through namespaces. Different groups of classes are reused for different purposes. For example, a ShoppingBasket class can be used while building an online store application, whereas an IDbConnection interface can be used for interacting with a database store in any application that needs to provide persistence features.

However, as it happens, some classes are reused together. It is highly probable that if you use a ShoppingBasket class, you will also use a BasketItem class. Similarly, if you use an IDbConnection interface, you will likely also use an IDbCommand interface. This leads to the following conclusion: Certain related classes are reused together. When you place classes inside namespaces, you should try to put classes that are reused together inside the same namespace.

As an additional illustration, take a look at the existing .NET Framework classes in the System.Collections.Generic namespace. If you use the Dictionary class, you will most probably also make use of the KeyValuePair and KeyNotFoundException classes.

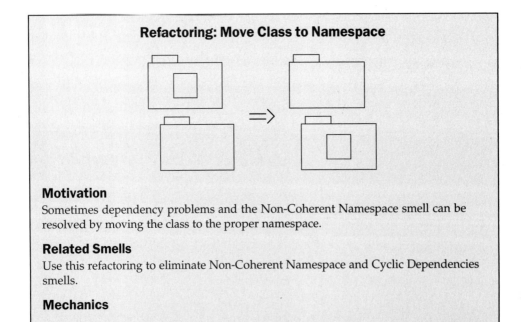

Refactoring: Move Class to Namespace

Motivation
Sometimes dependency problems and the Non-Coherent Namespace smell can be resolved by moving the class to the proper namespace.

Related Smells
Use this refactoring to eliminate Non-Coherent Namespace and Cyclic Dependencies smells.

Mechanics

1. If the originating and target namespaces are in different assemblies, start by moving the source file to the target assembly. (If there are multiple types in

the source file, you need to perform Move Type to File refactoring before this step.)

2. Change the namespace declaration in the class to the targeted namespace. Remember that assemblies often declare the root namespace.

3. Search for references to the type. Use the compiler to locate places where the type was used. It will display a "Type typename could not be found . . ." message. Modify the Imports section so it imports the namespace to which the type now belongs.

Before

```
namespace Web.ShoppingBasket
{
    public class PerishableContainer
    {
        //...
    }
    public class Basket
    {
        //...
    }

    }
    //...
}
```

After

```
namespace Web.ShoppingBasket
{
    public class Basket
    {
        //...
    }
    //...
}

namespace Common.Containers
{
    public class PerishableContainer
    {
        //...
    }
    //...
}
```

What is the benefit of placing classes reused together in the same package? The response to this question is related to the issue of dependencies. The next section takes a look at what dependencies are and why they are important for your development process and application architecture.

Dependency Considerations

When you reference a certain type in your code, you are establishing the dependency between the type you referenced and the type that is making the reference. The effect of dependency is as follows:

❑ If the type that your type depends upon changes, you most probably have to change and recompile the dependent type.

❑ Even when the change in the type that other class depends upon is implementation-only, meaning that no signatures in the type have changed, you still have to test the dependent type in order to ensure that the latest change didn't result in a new bug.

❑ If the dependency-related types belong to different namespaces, then there is a dependency relationship between the containing namespaces; and if the containing namespaces belong to different assemblies, then there is also a dependency relationship between the containing assemblies.

In other words, the effect of dependencies on the architecture of your application and development process in general is profound. This makes dependency management one of the most important aspects of the large-scale design of your application. Take a look now at how dependencies influence some crucial aspects of the development process.

Build Process, Testability, and Distribution

In order to compile a dependent class, a compiler needs to have a compiled version of the class on which the dependent class is dependent. If the dependency is circular, it turns into a kind of chicken or egg question for the compiler. Visual Studio will not even let you establish cyclic dependency between projects in the solution.

However, you can still establish cyclic dependencies by referencing the compiled assembly. The effect of cyclic dependencies is such that you are not able to normally control the versioning process in your solution.

Imagine that two projects, A and B, both depend on each other, and a group of programmers is working on these two projects in parallel. If you try to release new versions of these two projects, you will find that you cannot release them independently of each other. The solution is arduous integration work that in practice converts the two projects into a single project physically divided into two assemblies. These two assemblies are still a single monolithic software product from a development process point of view. The software has to be compiled, tested, and distributed together.

When there are no circular dependencies in your solution, then each project can follow its own release timeline. Each dependent project can choose when to make use of the new version of the project it depends upon.

Refactoring: Extract Namespace

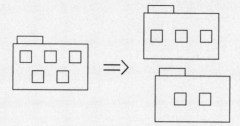

Motivation

Namespaces containing too many types increase code clutter and make it more difficult for programmers to find and use classes. Large namespaces will negatively impact reuse and maintenance characteristics in your code. Such namespaces can be reduced in size by namespace extraction.

Sometimes, namespace extraction can resolve the problem of cyclic dependencies. By extracting offending classes to a separate namespace, you can make both namespaces depend on the extracted namespace, instead of having them depend on each other.

The namespace is a higher order organizational unit. By placing related classes in separate namespaces, you improve the organization and coherence of your code.

Related Smells

Use this refactoring to eliminate Non-coherent Namespace and Cyclic Dependencies smells.

Mechanics

1. If the originating and target namespaces are in different assemblies, start by moving the source file to the target assembly. (If there are multiple types in the source file, you need to perform Move Type to File refactoring before this step.)

2. Change the namespace declaration in the class to the targeted namespace. Remember that assemblies often declare the root namespace.

3. Search for references to the type. Use the compiler to locate places where the type was used. It will display a "Type typename could not be found . . ." message. Modify the Imports section so it imports the namespace to which the type now belongs.

Before

```
namespace RentAWheels.Business
{
    public class Vehicle
    {
        //...
    }
```

Continued

```
            public class Branch
            {
                //...
            }

            public class VehicleCategory
            {
                //...
            }

            public class User
            {
                //...
            }

            public class Profile
            {
                //...
            }

            public class Permission
            {
                //...
            }
        }
```

After

```
        namespace RentAWheels.Business
        {
            public class Vehicle
            {
                //...
            }

            public class Branch
            {
                //...
            }

            public class VehicleCategory
            {
                //...
            }

        }

        namespace RentAWheels.Users
        {
```

```
        public class User
        {
            //...
        }

        public class Profile
        {
            //...
        }

        public class Permission
        {
            //...
        }
}
```

Breaking Dependency Cycles

Fortunately, there are methods to deal with dependencies in your projects. One such method can help you invert the dependency and in that way break the dependency cycle. Cycles often involve multiple projects. These complex relationships are best analyzed by viewing UML package diagrams that can show namespace structures and their relationships, and that are being generated by some tool from the same code that is being executed. In order to keep things simple, use only two namespaces belonging to two different assemblies for this illustration.

Smell: Cyclic Dependencies

Detecting the Smell

This smell is not easily detected on any but the smallest projects. Typically, it is not something you give too much thought as you program. Some code analysis tools are capable of identifying dependency cycles. One such tool is NDepend (www.ndepend.com). Another alternative is visually inspecting static structure UML diagrams.

If the cycle encompasses projects, Visual Studio refuses adding cyclical references between the projects in the solution. However, you are still able to reference the compiled assembly in a cyclical manner.

Related Refactoring

Use Move Class to Namespace and Extract Namespace refactorings and invert dependencies in order to eliminate cyclical dependencies from your project.

Rationale

Cyclic dependencies work against the modularity of your code. Items joined through cyclic dependencies have to be tested, released, and reused together.

Imagine you have a typical GUI namespace whose classes are interacting with a faxing service in another namespace. The mock-up code is shown in Listing 11-1.

Listing 11-1: Cyclic Dependency between GUI and Faxing Service Namespaces

```
namespace Faxing
{
    public class FaxService
    {
        private FaxingDevice faxingDevice;

        public void SendFax(FaxJob job)
        {
            try
            {
                faxingDevice.Dial(job.Number);
                faxingDevice.Transmit(job.Content);
                faxingDevice.EndTransmission();

            }
            catch (FaxingException e)
            {
                GUI.ErrorForm errorForm = new GUI.ErrorForm();
                errorForm.ShowErrorMessage(e.Message);
            }
        }
    }
}

namespace GUI
{
    public partial class FaxingForm
    {

        private void sendFax_Click(object sender, EventArgs e)
        {
            Faxing.FaxService faxService = new Faxing.FaxService();
            faxService.SendFax(this.Job);
        }
    }
}
```

If you were to present this in a diagram depicting dependencies between namespaces, it would look something like Figure 11-2.

Even from the simple look of the diagram, it is obvious that there is a problem with the design. The Faxing namespace groups classes related to faxing functionality. The GUI namespace groups forms that render the user interface, and contains this particular application's logic. Unfortunately, a circular dependency is present between the two. Where does this problem come from?

If you were to design the faxing service as a reusable component, then depending on the particular application and its GUI is not such a good idea. If you analyze the faxing service code carefully, you can see that it uses an ErrorForm to inform users that something went wrong with a faxing operation. This is the source of the circular dependency and the weakest link between the two. You can try to eliminate this dependency.

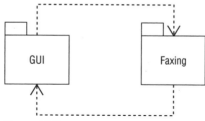

Figure 11-2

Inverting Dependencies

You need to eliminate the `FaxingService` dependency on `ErrorForm`, but at the same time you need to keep the functionality that enables you to inform the user of any problem with the faxing operation. The solution is to invert the dependency between `FaxingService` and `ErrorForm`.

Consider extracting the error-reporting code to a separate method and naming it `OnFaxingError`:

```
public void OnFaxingError(FaxingException e)
{
    ErrorForm errorForm = new ErrorForm();
    errorForm.ShowErrorMessage(e.Message);
}
```

This method is now called from a catch block. Now, you can perform Extract Interface refactoring with this method. Name it `ErrorReporter`, but instead of `FaxService` implementing this method, you can let clients interested in error messages from `FaxService` implement this method.

Instead of using `ErrorForm`, `FaxingService` can use a newly defined interface that has the same purpose and that resides in the same namespace as `FaxingService`. Objects interested in getting information about faxing problems can implement this interface and subscribe to listening for errors messages from `FaxingService`. The code for the solution is shown in Listing 11-2.

Listing 11-2: Cyclic Dependency between GUI and Faxing Service Namespaces Inverted

```
namespace Faxing
{
    public interface ErrorReporter {
        void ReportFaxingError(String message);
    }

    public class FaxService
    {
        //...
```

Continued

Listing 11-2: Cyclic Dependency between GUI and Faxing Service Namespaces Inverted *(continued)*

```csharp
        private ErrorReporter errorReporter;

        private FaxingDevice faxingDevice;

        public void SendFax(FaxJob job)
        {
            try
            {
                faxingDevice.Dial(job.Number);
                faxingDevice.Transmit(job.Content);
                faxingDevice.EndTransmission();

            }
            catch (FaxingException e)
            {
                OnFaxingError(e);
            }
        }

        public ErrorReporter ErrorReporter
        {
            get { return errorReporter; }
            set { errorReporter = value; }
        }

        public void OnFaxingError(FaxingException e)
        {
            ErrorReporter.ReportFaxingError(e.Message);
        }
    }
}

namespace GUI
{
    public partial class FaxingForm : Faxing.ErrorReporter
    {
        //...

        Faxing.FaxService faxService;

        public FaxingForm() {
            faxService = new Faxing.FaxService();
            faxService.ErrorReporter = this;
        }

        private void sendFax_Click(object sender, EventArgs e)
        {
            faxService.SendFax(this.Job);
        }
```

```
    public void ReportFaxingError(String message) {
        ErrorForm errorForm = new ErrorForm();
        errorForm.ShowErrorMessage(e.Message);
    }
  }
}
```

The cycle between the two namespaces is eliminated. The new state of affairs is depicted graphically in Figure 11-3.

An alternative to declaring an interface and subscribing to a callback method is for FaxingService *to declare an error event to which anyone interested in faxing operation success could subscribe.*

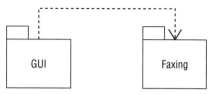

Figure 11-3

When you are looking to break cycles, the best methodology is to search for the weakest link. If you break the cycle at one point, it means you have done away with the cycle. Dependency inversion is a powerful tool for controlling spiraling dependencies. It can be applied to break circular dependencies and reduce dependencies in general. While dependencies have a negative impact on your design, making it more rigid and less modular, they cannot be avoided altogether.

Object-Oriented Design Principle: Acyclic Dependencies Principle

Cyclic dependencies work directly against the modularity of your software. If you let such dependencies grow, you soon lose the benefits of modular design. You have to start treating all the projects in your solution as a single project, meaning that you cannot test, release, and reuse each assembly in an independent manner. Your build process suffers, because all dependent namespaces and assemblies have to be released together.

Definition

Again quoting Robert C. Martin, "Allow no cycles in the package-dependency graph." (*Agile Software Development: Principles, Patterns, and Practices*, Prentice Hall, 2002)

In C#, you can interpret a package as a namespace.

Example

Cyclic dependencies are best observed on package diagrams. Figure 11-2 shows the simplest case of cyclic dependencies.

C# Project File Structure Organization

C# is very flexible in regard to organizing your project's file structure. You can place your source code files inside an arbitrary directory structure, and you can place an arbitrary number of types inside a single source code file. You can even distribute a single type over more than one source code file, as you will soon see in the section dedicated to partial classes later in the chapter.

With all this flexibility at hand, you really need to choose a uniform schema for project file organization. One such schema that can help you avoid clutter in Solution Explorer and find your way around source code files faster is the following:

❑ Mimic the namespace hierarchy with the directory hierarchy. For example, place the `PurchaseForm` class belonging to `BookStore.Web.Purchase` namespace inside the `[Project Root Directory]\BookStore\Web\Purchase` directory. You can ignore the root namespace for this purpose.

❑ Place a single type inside a single source code file. This enables you to specify a "using" section in such a way that it refers to a single type. Remember, there is only a single "using" section per source code file, so placing multiple types in a single file will make all the types in the file share the same "using" section. It also makes it easier to move the class to another namespace or assembly, because you can simply move the file in Solution Explorer.

❑ Use the class name for the source filename. For example, if the file contains `PurchaseForm`, name it `PurchaseForm.cs`.

In case you have followed a different schema and now you wish to place a single type inside a single file, you can apply Move Type to File refactoring to single types inside the single source code file.

Refactoring: Move Type to File

Motivation

Multiple types in a single source file can make your code more difficult to work with. Because a file is the smallest unit under source code control, by placing multiple types in single file you increase the probability that more than one developer works on the same file, thereby increasing the probability of conflicting changes.

Multiple types in a single file make some large-scale organizational refactorings such as Extract Namespace and Move Class to Namespace more difficult. While these refactorings do not have to be performed on the file level, it is recommended. Physical project structures in which directory and file hierarchy mimic namespace hierarchy make your project organization more logical and coherent.

Related Smells

Use this refactoring to place types in separate source files and to prepare your project for refactorings such as Move Class to Namespace and Extract Namespace.

Mechanics

1. Create a new source file for the type you wish to move to a separate file. Use the type name for the newly created filename.

2. Cut and paste the type code to the new file.

---

3. Remove unused, and sort remaining, `using` directives. Remove imports that are no longer used in the original file and be careful to copy to the new file only those imports that are used by the type you have just moved.

Before

```
Vehicle.cs file content:
    public class Vehicle
    {
        //...
    }

    public class Branch
    {
        //...
    }
```

After

```
Vehicle.cs file content:
    public class Vehicle
    {
        //...
    }

Branch.cs file content:
    public class Branch
    {
        //...
    }
```

Next, you will turn to another peculiar schema for source code organization. Partial classes enable you to spread a single type across multiple source code files.

Partial Classes

Partial classes are another interesting C# feature that appeared in the 2005 (C# 2.0) version of the language. This feature permits one class to span more than one source code file. It is primarily intended for code-generation tools such as Windows Forms Designer. All tool-generated code can be placed in a separate file, out of the programmer's sight, because it was never intended to be manipulated directly by the programmer anyway. In this sense, partial classes are similar to the Region directive of C#. (Region directives enable you to mark the section of source code so it can be collapsed and hidden in the C# editor.)

> One caveat about partial types: You should not use them as a replacement for traditional object-oriented techniques. Remember that a partial type spread across several source code files is in the end still a single type and will be treated by the compiler and client programmers as such. If you let such a type grow out of proportion, it will suffer all the problems that any other class suffering Large Class smell would: It will be difficult to maintain and reuse, prone to change, and would not abide by the Single Responsibility Principle (SRP) or the Open-Closed Principle (OCP).

Partial classes are related to another feature in C#, one related to Windows Forms inheritance.

Inherited Form

Inherited Form is a built-in Visual Studio template that helps you inherit the form class. If you already have a form class in your solution and you decide to invoke the Inherited Form template through the Add New Item dialog, as shown in Figure 11-4, Visual Studio displays the Inheritance Picker dialog and prompts you to select the parent form class. Figure 11-5 shows the Inheritance Picker dialog.

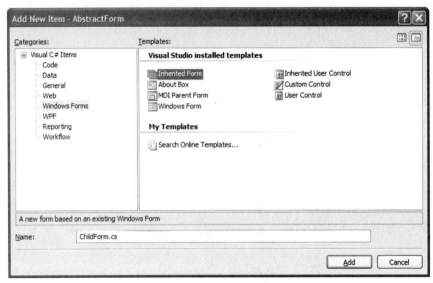

Figure 11-4

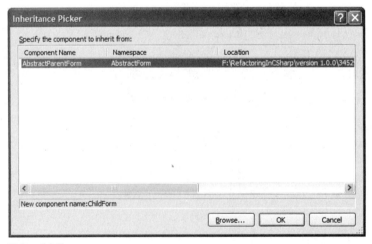

Figure 11-5

After you select the parent form, Visual Studio adds another form to your project that inherits the selected parent. In design view, you can see all the controls that were placed on the parent form, but they are marked with a special lock icon. You cannot modify these controls in the child form. If you modify the controls placed on the parent form, these changes are reflected in the child form only after you build the project containing the parent form.

For the C# compiler, the form class is the same as any other class. The same is true for an inherited form.

Abstract Form Inheritance

Because form classes can be considered normal C# classes, they should support all legal code manipulation that is permitted by the C# language. When using inheritance, you might well wish to make the form abstract. The following example tries to do just that:

1. Create a new Windows Forms Application project named `AbstractForm`.

2. Rename `Form1`, added to the project by default, to `AbstractParentForm`.

3. Change the `AbstractParentForm` Text property in the Properties window to "Abstract Parent Form."

4. Build the project. Otherwise, Visual Studio will complain that no form can be found in the project when you try to add the inherited form in the next step.

5. Add an inherited form named `ChildForm` to the project and using the Inheritance Picker, select `AbstractParentForm` as the "component to inherit from."

6. Make `ChildForm` the startup object for the project. In order to do this, you need to modify the `Program` class. Replace the `AbstractParentForm` with `ChildForm` in the `Application.Run` method invocation. The modified code for the `Program.cs` file is shown in Listing 11-3.

Listing 11-3: Setting ChildForm As the Project's Startup Object

```
static class Program
{
    /// <summary>
    /// The main entry point for the application.
    /// </summary>
    [STAThread]
    static void Main()
    {
        Application.EnableVisualStyles();
        Application.SetCompatibleTextRenderingDefault(false);
        Application.Run(new ChildForm());
    }
}
```

Looking at the `ChildForm` code, you can now see the following content:

```
public partial class ChildForm : AbstractParentForm
{
    public ChildForm()
    {
```

```
        InitializeComponent();
    }
}
```

Visual Studio generated code for `ChildForm` that makes `ChildForm` inherit the `AbstractParentForm`. So far, so good. If you run the project, you will see that it correctly displays `ChildForm`. In order to test how form inheritance works, you need to add a control to the parent form. Add a Button control to the `AbstractParentForm` and build and run the project. You will see the Button control displayed in `ChildForm`. This means inheritance is working for forms classes, as expected.

If you now open the `ChildForm` in Windows Forms Designer, you will see that the `button1` control has a special arrow in the left, upper corner indicating that the control is inherited. You cannot manipulate or move this control, but you can otherwise manipulate the form, add and remove other controls, and so on, just as you would when working with any other form.

It's time to test how forms inheritance works with abstract classes. Start by adding the keyword `abstract` to the `AbstractParentForm`. For illustration purposes only, you can add an abstract method to the form called `myAbstractMethod`. Then, you need to provide an implementation for this method in `ChildForm`. You can leave the implementation empty; all you need is to see how inheritance and abstract forms work in Visual Studio. The resulting code is shown in Listing 11-4.

Listing 11-4: Making AbstractParentForm Abstract

```
public abstract partial class AbstractParentForm : Form
{
    public AbstractParentForm()
    {
        InitializeComponent();
    }

    public abstract void myAbstractMethod();
}
public partial class ChildForm : AbstractParentForm
{
    public ChildForm()
    {
        InitializeComponent();
    }

    public override void myAbstractMethod() {
        //leave empty
    }
}
```

Build and run the project. Everything should be working as expected.

Now try to edit the `ChildForm` in the Windows Form Designer. However, instead of displaying the form, the error message is displayed:

```
The designer must create an instance of type 'AbstractForm.AbstractParentForm' but
it cannot because the type is declared as abstract.
```

If you have read this message carefully, you might think I made a mistake somewhere in the process of describing the previous steps. The Designer is saying it cannot create an instance of `AbstractParentForm` and you clicked the `ChildForm`?

In fact, no mistake was made. The Windows Forms Designer is implemented in such a way that it instantiates the parent form in the form hierarchy when displaying the Forms Designer window. Because in this example `ChildForm` inherits `AbstractParentForm`, the Designer tried to instantiate `AbstractParentForm`. Because the `AbstractParentForm` was marked as abstract, the Designer could not create an instance of it, and the error was produced.

This is an unfortunate limitation of the Window Forms Designer tool and Visual Studio. There is no reason why you shouldn't be able to program abstract parent Windows Forms and then design non-abstract children. Fortunately, there is a workaround for this problem.

Please note that this is not a limitation of the C# compiler or the .NET runtime. As I have demonstrated, a project using abstract parent forms will compile and run correctly; the problem is limited to the Windows Forms Designer tool.

Delegating Abstract Form Work to a Form Helper Class

Imagine you are programming reports in your application when you detect that all forms that are used to display reports have several identical members. You decide to extract the `AbstractReportForm` superclass and make all concrete report forms inherit the abstract report form. Each concrete report form has a different way of recollecting data for report generation, so you mark the `AddReportData` method as abstract using the `abstract` keyword and therefore make `AbstractReportForm` abstract.

Everything is working out fine, but the problem is designing concrete report forms. The Designer is reporting an error because `AbstractReportForm` is abstract. Is there a way that you could place common code inside the single parent class and still design forms in Windows Designer?

The solution comes in the form of Replace Inheritance with Delegation refactoring. The parent report form need not leave abstract methods that child forms have to implement. Instead, it can delegate all work to an `AbstractReportHelper` class. While Windows forms cannot be abstract, they can use other abstract classes without any problem. Therefore, a concrete report form can create an instance of a concrete helper class that overrides all abstract members declared in `AbstractReportHelper`. The code in Listing 11-5 illustrates this solution.

Listing 11-5: Delegating Work to AbstractHelper to Keep the Form Non-Abstract

```
public partial class GeneralReportForm : Form
{
    private AbstractReportHelper helper;

    public GeneralReportForm()
    {
        InitializeComponent();
    }

    protected AbstractReportHelper Helper
```

Continued

Listing 11-5: Delegating Work to AbstractHelper to Keep the Form Non-Abstract
(continued)

```csharp
        {
            get { return helper; }
            set { helper = value; }
        }
    }
    public abstract class AbstractReportHelper
    {
        private GeneralReportForm form;

        public AbstractReportHelper(GeneralReportForm form)
        {
            this.form = form;
        }
        internal void ViewReport()
        {
            //...
        }

        internal void SelectReportType()
        {
            //...
        }

        public GeneralReportForm Form
        {
            get { return form; }
            set { form = value; }
        }

        internal abstract void AddReportData();
    }
    public partial class AccountsReportForm : GeneralReportForm
    {
        public AccountsReportForm()
        {
            InitializeComponent();
            this.Helper = new AccountsHelper(this);
        }
    }
    public class AccountsHelper : AbstractReportHelper
    {
        public AccountsHelper(GeneralReportForm form)
            : base(form)
        {
        }

        internal override void AddReportData()
        {
            // Add accounts report data
        }
    }
```

With this finished, you are now ready to take another look at Rent-a-Wheels and see how the latest refactorings apply to the sample application.

Namespace Organization and Windows Forms Inheritance in Rent-a-Wheels

I start work on Rent-a-Wheels by sorting out one issue that was pending from the previous chapter. Even while making changes in the previous chapter, I noticed that all administration forms have a number of identical members. However, I didn't cover forms inheritance in the last chapter, so it was left for later. Now is the right moment to deal with duplicate code in the administration forms.

Extracting the Parent Administration Form Using the Abstract Form Helper Pattern

This chapter has discussed issues related to Windows Forms inheritance and the Window Forms Designer. You have seen how Designer generates separate files for Designer-generated code. You have also seen some of the Designer's limitations in regard to the use of abstract forms. Windows Forms Designer displays a similar limitation with parameterized types; in order to display the form in Windows Form Designer, the form cannot be parameterized (generic).

The first graphically obvious duplication between different administration forms in the Rent-a-Wheels application involves two groups of controls. The first group of controls is a navigation strip at the bottom of the form that enables you to navigate between different records in the table being maintained by the form. The second group comprises the New, Save, Delete, and Reload action buttons on the right side of the form.

Extract Parent Maintenance Form

Start by adding a new Windows form named `GeneralMaintenanceForm` to the project. Next, copy the controls from the random administration form and paste them on `GeneralMaintenanceForm`. Accommodate the controls on the form so that the position of the action and navigation button strips fit all of the existing administration forms. After all the specific label and text controls are added, they should be visible and not overlap with controls on the parent `GeneralMaintenanceForm` form class. Figure 11-6 shows the `GeneralMaintenanceForm` displayed by the Designer.

Copy all methods that have identical declaration and implementation in all forms to `GeneralMaintenanceForm`. Such a method is the button's `btnFirst` click event handler:

```
private void first_Click(object sender, EventArgs e)
{
    if (branches.Count > 0)
    {
        current = 0;
        DisplayCurrent();
    }
}
```

Figure 11-6

The only difference is in the variable branches, which in different forms has a different name, but the type of the variable is the same — a parameterized IList: System.Collections.Generic.IList<T>. Because the type of the variable is the same, you can treat all variables like branches, models, categories, and so on, in a uniform way, leaving out the parameterization to the concrete maintenance form. However, this means that the GeneralMaintenanceForm will have to be parameterized as well, which produces a problem when displaying the GeneralMaintenanceForm in Windows Form Designer, as you will soon see.

Some other methods, such as DisplayCurrent, have an identical declaration, but differ in their implementation in each form. Therefore, DisplayCurrent in BranchMaintenance is implemented as follows:

```
private void DisplayCurrent()
{
    Branch branch = branches[current];
    id.Text = branch.Id.ToString();
    name.Text = branch.Name;
}
```

The DisplayCurrent method in the ModelMaintenence form has a different implementation:

```
private void DisplayCurrent()
{
    Model model = models[current];
    id.Text = model.Id.ToString();
    name.Text = model.Name;
    category.Text = model.Category.Name;
}
```

You need to have the DisplayCurrent method in the GeneralMaintenanceForm so you can compile the project. For the moment, declare an empty DisplayCurrent and change its declaration to protected virtual. This way, child forms can override this method with code specific for the concrete administration form. The empty `DisplayCurrent` looks like the following:

```
protected virtual void DisplayCurrent() {

}
```

Do the same with the rest of the methods. In some cases you need to extract some event-handling code into a separate method. For example, you can extract the `new_Click` code to a new `CleanForm` method.

Finally, it is time to make all administration forms inherit `GeneralMaintenanceForm`. First, delete all the code already existing in `GeneralMaintenanceForm`, like all event-handling routines. Now, make each administration form inherit `GeneralMaintenanceForm`. In order to do this, you have to change the Designer-generated code. Because each form already has an inheritance declaration, all you need to do is change the inheritance declaration from the `System.Windows.Forms.Form` line to `GeneralMaintenanceForm`.

Run the application and make sure that everything works as it is supposed to. This is already a great step forward. I have reduced a huge amount of duplicated code and streamlined administration form construction. However, I am not happy to leave empty method declarations, such as the empty `DisplayCurrentObject` method, in the extracted super `GeneralMaintenanceForm`. Had it not been for problems with the Windows Forms Designer, I would have marked this method as abstract and the `GeneralMaintenanceForm` as abstract.

Resolving Windows Designer Problems via a Helper Class

In order to refactor the GUI layer of Rent-a-Wheels so it renders well in Windows Forms Designer, you need to introduce helper classes that contain the logic previously contained in the event-handler routines in the form classes. This way, you can extract a `FormHelper` class that contains all the code that is identical in the form classes and that contains some abstract method declarations. The `GeneralMaintenanceForm` ends up being an empty shell that delegates all the work to `MaintenanceFormAbstractHelper`. Take a look at `GeneralMaintenanceForm` in Listing 11-6.

Listing 11-6: GeneralMaintenanceForm Code

```
public partial class GeneralMaintenanceForm : Form
{

    public GeneralMaintenanceForm()
    {
        InitializeComponent();
    }

    private IMaintenanceFormHelper helper;

    public IMaintenanceFormHelper Helper
    {
        get { return helper; }
        set { helper = value; }
    }
```

Continued

Listing 11-6: GeneralMaintenanceForm Code *(continued)*

```
    private void btnNew_Click(object sender, EventArgs e)
    {
        Helper.btnNew_Click(sender, e);
    }

    private void btnSave_Click(object sender, EventArgs e)
    {
        Helper.btnSave_Click(sender, e);
    }

    private void btnDelete_Click(object sender, EventArgs e)
    {
        Helper.btnDelete_Click(sender, e);
    }

    private void btnReload_Click(object sender, EventArgs e)
    {
        Helper.btnReload_Click(sender, e);
    }

    private void btnFirst_Click(object sender, EventArgs e)
    {
        Helper.btnFirst_Click(sender, e);
    }

    private void btnLeft_Click(object sender, EventArgs e)
    {
        Helper.btnLeft_Click(sender, e);
    }

    private void btnRight_Click(object sender, EventArgs e)
    {
        Helper.btnRight_Click(sender, e);
    }

    private void btnLast_Click(object sender, EventArgs e)
    {
        Helper.btnLast_Click(sender, e);
    }

}
```

Note that the helper class is declared as `IMaintenanceFormHelper`. It is an interface that `MaintenanceFormAbstractHelper` implements. You might wonder why you need an interface. Why not use `MaintenanceFormAbstractHelper` directly? As it happens, Windows Forms Designer has a problem with designing generic form classes. Had I used `MaintenanceFormAbstractHelper` directly, I would need to declare `GeneralMaintenanceForm` as generic, like this:

```
public partial class GeneralMaintenanceForm<Maintained> : Form
{

    public GeneralMaintenanceForm()
```

```
    {
        InitializeComponent();
    }

    private MaintenanceFormAbstractHelper<Maintained> helper;
    //...

}
```

Because GeneralMaintenanceForm is in this case using MaintenanceFormAbstractHelper, it has to declare the type that parameterizes the MaintenanceFormAbstractHelper. GeneralMaintenanceForm does not know the type that is maintained, so it has to declare it as a parameterized type (generic). Unfortunately, Windows Forms Designer is not capable of displaying such a form, so that's where IMaintenanceFormHelper comes into play; it hides the generic side of MaintenanceFormAbstractHelper.

All the work has been moved to MaintenanceFormAbstractHelper. Because the helper class does not contain any GUI elements and therefore won't be manipulated in Windows Designer, it can be marked as abstract and can contain abstract members. The code for MaintenanceFormAbstractHelper and IMaintenanceFormHelper is shown in Listing 11-7.

Listing 11-7: Helper and Helper Interface Code

```
public interface IMaintenanceFormHelper
{
    void btnDelete_Click(object sender, EventArgs e);
    void btnFirst_Click(object sender, EventArgs e);
    void btnLast_Click(object sender, EventArgs e);
    void btnLeft_Click(object sender, EventArgs e);
    void btnNew_Click(object sender, EventArgs e);
    void btnReload_Click(object sender, EventArgs e);
    void btnRight_Click(object sender, EventArgs e);
    void btnSave_Click(object sender, EventArgs e);
    void GeneralMaintenanceForm_Load(object sender, EventArgs e);
}
public abstract class MaintenanceFormAbstractHelper<Maintained> :
IMaintenanceFormHelper
{
    private IList<Maintained> maintainedList;

    private int current;

    public MaintenanceFormAbstractHelper() {
        CreateData();
    }

    public IList<Maintained> MaintainedList
    {
        get { return maintainedList; }
        set { maintainedList = value; }
    }

    internal Maintained Current() {
```

Continued

Listing 11-7: Helper and Helper Interface Code *(continued)*

```
        return MaintainedList[current];
    }

    public void btnNew_Click(object sender, EventArgs e)
    {
        CleanForm();
    }

    public void btnDelete_Click(object sender, EventArgs e)
    {
        DeleteMaintained();
        GeneralMaintenanceForm_Load(sender, e);
    }

    public void btnSave_Click(object sender, EventArgs e)
    {
        SaveMaintained();
        GeneralMaintenanceForm_Load(sender, e);
    }

    public void btnReload_Click(object sender, EventArgs e)
    {
        GeneralMaintenanceForm_Load(sender, e);
    }

    public void btnFirst_Click(object sender, EventArgs e)
    {
        if (MaintainedList.Count > 0)
        {
            current = 0;
            DisplayCurrent();
        }
    }

    public void btnLeft_Click(object sender, EventArgs e)
    {
        if (current - 1 >= 0 & MaintainedList.Count > 0)
        {
            current--;
            DisplayCurrent();
        }
    }

    public void btnRight_Click(object sender, EventArgs e)
    {
        if (MaintainedList.Count > current + 1)
        {
            current++;
            DisplayCurrent();
        }
    }
```

```
    public void btnLast_Click(object sender, EventArgs e)
    {
        if (MaintainedList.Count > 0)
        {
            current = MaintainedList.Count - 1;
            DisplayCurrent();
        }
    }

    public void GeneralMaintenanceForm_Load(object sender, EventArgs e)
    {
        LoadMaintained();
        if ((this.MaintainedList.Count > 0))
        {
            current = 0;
            DisplayCurrent();
        }
    }

    protected abstract void CreateData();

    protected abstract void DisplayCurrent();

    protected abstract void CleanForm();

    protected abstract void LoadMaintained();

    protected abstract void DeleteMaintained();

    protected abstract void SaveMaintained();

}
```

Abstract methods are overridden in the concrete helper class. For example, you can see BranchMaintenanceHelper in Listing 11-8.

Listing 11-8: BranchMaintenanceHelper Implementing Abstract Methods

```
public class BranchMaintenanceHelper : MaintenanceFormAbstractHelper<Branch>
{
    private BranchData data;

    private BranchMaintenance form;

    public BranchMaintenance Form
    {
        get { return form; }
        set { form = value; }
    }

    protected override void DisplayCurrent() {
        Branch branch = Current();
```

Continued

Listing 11-8: BranchMaintenanceHelper Implementing Abstract Methods *(continued)*

```
        Form.id.Text = branch.Id.ToString();
        Form.name.Text = branch.Name;
    }

    protected override void CleanForm()
    {
        Form.id.Text = String.Empty;
        Form.name.Text = String.Empty;
    }

    protected override void LoadMaintained()
    {
        this.MaintainedList = data.GetAll();
    }

    protected override void CreateData()
    {
        this.data = new BranchData();
    }

    protected override void DeleteMaintained()
    {
        data.Delete(Current());
    }

    protected override void SaveMaintained()
    {
        if (String.IsNullOrEmpty(Form.id.Text))
        {
            data.Insert(new Branch(0, Form.name.Text));
        }
        else
        {
            Branch branch = Current();
            branch.Name = Form.name.Text;
            data.Update(Current());
        }

    }
}
```

All that is left for the concrete form is to instantiate the helper. Take a look at the BranchMaintenance form in Listing 11-9.

Listing 11-9: BranchMaintenance Form

```
public partial class BranchMaintenance : GeneralMaintenanceForm
{
    public BranchMaintenance():base() {
        BranchMaintenanceHelper helper = new BranchMaintenanceHelper();
```

```
        helper.Form = this;
        base.Helper = helper;
        InitializeComponent();

    }

    private void BranchMaintenance_Load(object sender, EventArgs e)
    {
        base.Helper.GeneralMaintenanceForm_Load(null, null);
    }
}
```

This way, you have overcome the limitation that Windows Forms Designer has with abstract classes. You are now able to display and design forms in Windows Forms Designer, and you are able to use abstract classes, an important feature of your code that will leave no loopholes and "apparently" implemented methods to implementors, as would be the case if you use parent Windows Forms that contain abstract logic. This completes the refactoring of GUI classes. Now it's time to do some large-scale reorganization of the project.

Namespace and Assembly Reorganization

At this point, you have a single project with a single namespace containing all the classes. If you analyze some of the rules discussed in this chapter, you will see that two primary forces can be applied to Rent-a-Wheels:

❏   Single Responsibility

❏   Reuse-Release Equivalence

The first principle dictates that you should keep GUI classes apart from business classes apart from data classes. The second principle dictates that you should keep abstract classes apart from concrete classes. Figure 11-7 presents this horizontal and vertical axis of separation schematically.

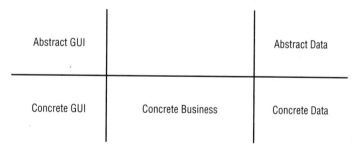

Abstract GUI		Abstract Data
Concrete GUI	Concrete Business	Concrete Data

Figure 11-7

The partitions depicted in Figure 11-7 look like a good way to partition Rent-a-Wheels into assemblies. All projects except for the concrete GUI will be class libraries. The concrete GUI assembly will be a Windows application. Each of the assemblies must be revised for imports, and in some cases will reference another Rent-a-Wheels assembly. Assembly dependencies are better depicted with the component diagram shown in Figure 11-8.

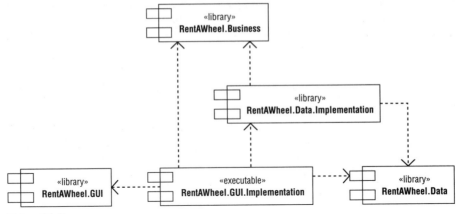

Figure 11-8

One important conclusion is immediately obvious from the diagram. The application has no circular dependencies. In addition, less abstract namespaces depend on more abstract ones; and there is a clear separation of concerns between the assemblies.

While organizing namespaces, we have also used an opportunity to organize class files into directories. This makes the project easier to browse in Solution Explorer. Figure 11-9 shows the Rent-a-Wheels Solution Explorer after reorganization.

Figure 11-9

This looks much more orderly and better organized, and I don't mean only the files; the whole solution is now much more coherent. You might even go so far as to say that there are no immediate problems in the application needing your attention. However, this does not mean that you cannot take the design even further, but that will have to wait for the next chapter.

Summary

This chapter dealt with some issues that often appear in large projects. You have seen how in C# you can use higher-level organizational structures to manage your projects. Organizing types inside namespaces and partitioning solutions into assemblies has to be done with an understanding of the principles governing large-scale organization.

These principles are applied in order to improve maintainability and reuse, and to minimize dependencies between different elements in a project. Unmanaged dependencies can have direct repercussions on your development process.

Luckily, you have the means to control and deal with dependencies. Minimizing dependencies between assemblies or namespaces can be as simple as moving a type to a proper namespace. In other cases, more elaborate solutions, such as dependency inversion, are necessary.

The smaller effects of large-scale code organization are not immediate. However, problems that can arise from improper organization can be crippling at later stages of a project. That is why you should think about a project's organization from its outset.

By finishing this chapter, you have covered most of the traditional refactoring techniques. You have seen how code can be reorganized from method level to namespace level. You have also seen a number of ailments that can plague your code, and how you can remedy them.

In the next chapter, which covers design patterns, you will go beyond the obvious. You will see how sometimes a design can appear to be problematic and "smelly" at first sight, but is actually an elegant solution to a specific problem when analyzed in depth.

12

Refactoring to Patterns

Until now, I have promoted a rather simple approach to refactoring. You inspect the code, find the smells, and then refactor it so the smells are eliminated or at least reduced. This approach focuses essentially on negative aspects of your code in an attempt to eradicate them. Many times, following such an approach, you can reach an overall improved and even sophisticated design for your code.

It is also possible to lead your design toward some thought-out design goal. Often, such a solution is neither immediately obvious nor the most simple. However, the benefits that such a premeditated design can bring often justify the added complexity.

In order to lead your code toward some predetermined design, you need to study and understand different design solutions. *Design patterns* were created for exactly that purpose: to share and disseminate knowledge about successful object-oriented designs that go beyond the ordinary and capture the brilliance of sophisticated object-oriented solutions.

Highlights of this chapter include the following:

- ❏ What design patterns are and how to make use of them
- ❏ Example of a design pattern
- ❏ The very influential Dependency Injection pattern
- ❏ Applying refactoring to pattern concepts and the Rent-a-Wheels application

Design patterns are a huge subject, and there is only so much that can be accomplished in the space of one chapter. Rather than provide specific knowledge about design patterns and refactoring combinations, the purpose of this chapter is to pique your interest in the subject and point you in the right direction. As you learn more about patterns, you will recognize situations where they can be applied and be able to devise refactorings that will help you incorporate them into real-life, operational code.

Design Patterns: What's All the Fuss About?

Design patterns came into prominence in the software industry with the publication of *Design Patterns: Elements of Reusable Software Design* by Erich Gamma, Richard Helm, Ralph Johnson, and John M. Vlissides (Addison-Wesley, 2004) some 15 years ago. Since then, they have been the subject of numerous books, articles, conference speeches, and lectures and have become a part of the mainstream object-oriented compendium.

Today, you will often hear developers discuss design not in terms of originality of the solution, but in terms of design patterns — what design patterns they used in their design and to which purpose. Patterns have become a part of not only the common corpus of knowledge, but also the programmer's common vocabulary.

To understand what a design pattern is, consider this analogy: Master chess players are capable of looking many moves ahead. To some extent, this is because of their experience and natural talent. In great part, however, this is thanks to the study of other players' moves. Once notable moves are played out in a tournament, they are analyzed and archived, and they become part of the global chess-playing body of knowledge. By studying previously played moves, learning openings and endgames, and studying common approaches to the middle game, a master player is capable of taking advantage of other people's inventiveness and hard work. Such study gives a player a much broader horizon, meaning that player is a lot less likely to be surprised or faced with a totally new situation. Study liberates a player from solving basic problems during each game and with each move. Instead of thinking two or three moves in advance, a sharp player can anticipate possible developments five or six moves ahead. Even an extremely talented self-taught player, when confronted with a learned player, will have little chance of success.

Design patterns provide you with similar insight in the area of software development. By learning design patterns, you can meet the best developers in the world and learn from them. Programming is often viewed as a craft; and in any craft, a master-apprentice relationship is very important for the learning process. Through design patterns, you can record and learn a good portion of an expert programmer's mastery. Unlike some crafts that are not easily described or translated into a written form, programming's final product is just that: source code in a written format. When you're not able to learn from a flesh-and-blood teacher, that teacher's wisdom recorded in writing is the next best thing.

> *Patterns record moments of a programmer's ingenuity, enabling the sharing of these moments. When you study patterns, you see that they always reflect a unique, nontrivial, and imaginative view of the problem.*

Defining Design Patterns

Patterns capture and share the experiences of others. They are a guide or template for a solution to a certain problem in software design. They describe collaborating objects and classes that have to be adapted to deal with certain problems, including their structure, roles, and responsibilities. Patterns abstract and identify key aspects of a design used to solve a single problem in a particular context.

Although patterns provide you with an immediate insight about how to deal with a certain problem, you still have to adapt the solution to your particular situation, choose the correct variation, and often compare and weigh different solutions for the same problem.

Although patterns often include sample code, they are not intended to be reused directly, at the code level — as, for example, components, frameworks, or reusable classes are. Instead of code reuse, they promote design reuse. By learning patterns, you learn to analyze, identify, and divide the problem; and you learn different techniques to structure and organize classes and objects. By comparing patterns and their trade-offs, you understand how they relate to one another.

While some patterns can be turned into reusable components, insisting on code reuse with patterns is contrary to pattern philosophy. Learning patterns means that you spend time analyzing, understanding, assimilating, and applying the pattern. This way, you improve your design and programming skills. By using ready-made pattern components, you can miss important aspects of object-oriented design. In this case, exposure to detail is desired, and encapsulation will not help you hone your design skills.

> **Definition:** *Design patterns* **represent a proven solution to a recurring problem in a given context.**

Classifying Patterns

Having in mind the construction of a design patterns catalog that could be easily searched and browsed, the authors of *Design Patterns: Elements of Reusable Software Design* proposed the following classification system, with all patterns categorized according to their purpose. These design patterns, called *Gang of Four (GoF)* design patterns because of the four authors, are general-purpose patterns that can be further classified into three groups:

- ❑ **Creational:** These patterns solve different problems related to object creation or instantiation.
- ❑ **Behavioral:** These patterns deal with the ways in which objects can communicate and share responsibilities in order to reach a certain goal.
- ❑ **Structural:** These patterns describe the assembly and composition of objects and classes used to solve certain problems.

Patterns can also describe designs related to a more specific field — for example, you can have real-time patterns, concurrency patterns, object-relational patterns, and so on. This chapter sticks to classic, mostly creational patterns.

Pattern Elements

In order for patterns to be efficiently consulted and used, they should be written in a concise and consistent form. The authors of *Design Patterns* used a template wherein each pattern definition consists of a number of sections. This is still a widely accepted form to describe a pattern. Whatever the form used to describe the pattern, it should explain the following four essential elements of each pattern:

- ❑ **Name:** A descriptive and original name is important for pattern recognition and memorization. As you study patterns, you will notice that the name is associated with the solution that the pattern provides.

❑ **Problem:** The problem section describes the scenario in which it makes sense to use the pattern. It describes context, conditions that need to be met in order to use the pattern, and the design problem that the pattern solves. It should also mention some examples of poor design that this pattern resolves.

❑ **Solution:** In this section, principal classes and objects representing the design are described, together with their responsibilities and collaboration. This section generally includes a UML diagram, most often the one depicting the static structure of the solution. It should also include some sample code that illustrates the design.

❑ **Consequences:** Here, different trade-offs that result from pattern usage are discussed. Often, this section mentions some real-world scenarios in which this pattern can be applied. Different patterns are compared and confronted, and cases when some patterns can be used jointly are described.

I try to follow this scheme later in the chapter when I describe individual patterns such as Abstract Factory and Dependency Injection.

Weighing the Benefits of Design Patterns

When you design software, you have to weigh the pros and cons of different solutions. You generally start the project by thinking about combining data and encapsulating it by writing classes. You have to consider granularity and work on eliminating duplication. As the project grows and progresses, your focus changes, and you start thinking more about flexibility, performance, and modularity. Over time, more importance is placed on aspects of growth, evolution, dependencies, and maintainability. Often, your focus is dedicated to only certain aspects of the design, those more prominent at certain stages of the project. You are not always able to envisage the future consequences because this is complex, and you lack the necessary experience.

You often hear it said that the decisions you make early in the project are those that have the greatest consequences and are hardest to change. This means you should take into consideration all of the afore-mentioned aspects of your design from the beginning. This does not mean that you need to start your project with a sophisticated design up front, but that you need to be aware of the trade-offs that different patterns bring into your design.

Design patterns help you understand these trade-offs and show you how to solve certain problems. They enable you to compare alternatives and understand different aspects right from the start, providing the necessary perspective that is impossible to have without the experience and shared, incremental knowledge.

Using Patterns

As mentioned earlier, when you learn patterns, you are not supposed to reproduce the solution you read in the exact form it is described. You have to choose what is best for your particular situation. Patterns can especially help you with the design of those classes that do not have direct correspondence in the real world, making your design more flexible and reusable. These classes are always present as your design becomes more sophisticated. As you assimilate patterns, you learn how to incorporate them in your design, how to choose between different alternatives, and how to combine and adapt the patterns until you reach a sophisticated design that has its own aesthetics and style.

Now that you have some grounding in what design patterns are, it's time to turn to an example.

Example Design Pattern: Abstract Factory

As this book demonstrates, I am a great proponent of evolutionary design. If you already have a lot of experience with a certain type of application, you may rely on your experience to start with a more sophisticated design up front. If not, it is best to refine your design continuously. As you work on the project, you can put your design to test in a real-life situation and adapt it to resolve unforeseen problems that might arise.

The following example of a design pattern illustrates this approach. Imagine you have to construct a very simple data maintenance application. Over time, new requirements are added, and the code is growing in quantity. In order to deal with increased complexity, the code has to be refactored and design patterns applied.

The merits of different refactorings including pattern incorporation are discussed as the example goes along. This way, you can see when the circumstances to introduce a pattern in your code are indicated and how that step is always motivated by a specific need in your design. You will have the opportunity to discuss and evaluate the pattern not in some abstract theoretical way but with a concrete problem at hand.

Using Abstract Factory

In this example, you will see how Abstract Factory is applied to resolve the problem of instantiation of related data provider objects such as connection, command, adapter, and others in a consistent polymorphic manner:

❑ The client code should not depend on specific types belonging to a provider such as Oracle or Microsoft SQL Server. In case a new database needs to be added to the list of supported databases, a new provider should be incorporated without requiring code modification in the client.

❑ The provider object should be instantiated in a consistent manner. If a client is using an object from one provider, then some mechanism should be in place so that only objects belonging to a specific provider are instantiated. For example, if a client is using `System.Data.SqlClient.SqlConnection`, then `System.Data.SqlClient.SqlCommand` should be created when the client asks for a command object, and not a command like `System.Data.OracleClient.OracleCommand` or similar.

Data Entry Sample Application

The initial version of the application is very simple. You have a few forms that enable you to display and modify data in a database, and they contain the typical Load, New, Save, and Delete buttons. The static class `Globals` holds the global `ConnectionString` variable. The database in question is the Microsoft SQL database, so the data provider from the `System.Data.SqlClient` namespace is used to query the database. The code behind the Delete button's click event is presented in Listing 12-1.

Listing 12-1: Simple Event-Handling Routine That Deletes a Database Record

```
private void delete_Click(object sender, EventArgs e)
{
    SqlConnection connection =
```

Continued

Listing 12-1: Simple Event-Handling Routine That Deletes a Database Record
(continued)

```
            new SqlConnection(Globals.ConnectionString);
        SqlCommand command =
            new SqlCommand("Delete [User] where [Id] = @Id", connection);
        command.CommandType = CommandType.Text;
        connection.Open();
        SqlParameter id = command.CreateParameter();
        id.ParameterName = "@Id";
        id.Value = this.id.Text;
        id.DbType = DbType.Int16;
        command.Parameters.Add(id);
        command.ExecuteNonQuery();
        connection.Close();
    }
```

This code represents a very simple approach that works for the time being. As a matter of fact, other routines are very similar to delete_Click, but because variables are initialized at the same line that declares them, the code looks more compact, and duplicated code does not look that worrisome at the moment.

Adding Multiple Database Engine Support via Polymorphism

A few finished forms later, you are informed by your client that some installations use the same database structure but a different database engine. This client would like to use the same application to access the data residing on Oracle, and in some cases even Microsoft Access, databases.

Your initial idea is to add a switch statement that will deal with this situation. You have added a global flag DatabaseProvider declared in the Globals module that can indicate the current provider. The same delete_Click routine programmed this way would then look something like the code in Listing 12-2.

Listing 12-2: Delete Routine with Different Case Block for a Different Database Provider

```
private void delete_Click(object sender, EventArgs e)
{
    switch (Globals.DatabaseProvider) {
        case DatabaseProvider.Microsoft:
            SqlConnection connection =
                new SqlConnection(Globals.ConnectionString);
            SqlCommand command =  new SqlCommand(
                "Delete [User] where [Id] = @Id", connection);
            command.CommandType = CommandType.Text;
            connection.Open();
            SqlParameter id = command.CreateParameter();
            id.ParameterName = "@Id";
            id.Value = this.id.Text;
            id.DbType = DbType.Int16;
            command.Parameters.Add(id);
```

```
            command.ExecuteNonQuery();
            connection.Close();
            break;
        case DatabaseProvider.Oracle:
            OracleConnection connectionOracle =
                new OracleConnection(Globals.ConnectionString);
            OracleCommand commandOracle = new OracleCommand(
                "Delete [User] where [Id] = @Id", connectionOracle);
            commandOracle.CommandType = CommandType.Text;
            connectionOracle.Open();
            OracleParameter idOracle = commandOracle.CreateParameter();
            idOracle.ParameterName = "@Id";
            idOracle.Value = this.id.Text;
            idOracle.DbType = DbType.Int16;
            commandOracle.Parameters.Add(idOracle);
            commandOracle.ExecuteNonQuery();
            connectionOracle.Close();
            break;
    }
}
```

It is immediately obvious that this approach will not get you very far. The code will multiply for each provider you might add, so is there another approach you might use?

If you analyze the code a bit you can see that the connection, command, and parameter declaration and the creation code are the only pieces of code that differ between the two case blocks. This is a good indication of the direction in which you should start looking for a better solution.

If you take a look at SqlConnection and OracleConnection in the Object Browser, you'll notice that they both implement a common IDbConnection interface. Because they have a common parent interface, if the variable type is declared correctly, they can be treated as the same type of object.

The example routines employ primarily those members of SqlConnection and OracleConnection that are defined in the IDbConnection interface. The situation is similar with SqlCommand and OracleCommand; they share a common IDbCommand interface. Finally, OracleParameter and SqlParameter share a common IDbParameter interface.

Now, if you treat your objects in polymorphic manner and declare the connection as IDbConnection, the command as IDbCommand, and the parameter as IDbParameter, the only difference between the two case blocks is the object creation code — namely, the new statement.

Upcasting an Object Declaration

Upcasting an object declaration means that you change the declaration so that the object is declared as some other type *higher* in the type hierarchy. You change the local variable declaration so that variables are declared as an interface from the System.Data namespace. The connection is declared as System.Data.IDbConnection, the command as System.Data.IDbCommand, and the parameter as System.Data.IDbDataParameter. In other routines, where some other objects such as reader or adapter are used, a similar procedure is followed. The code resulting from upcasting variables can be seen in Listing 12-3.

Listing 12-3: Variables Upcast to an Interface Common to All Data Providers

```
private void delete_Click(object sender, EventArgs e)
{
    IDbConnection connection =
        new SqlConnection(Globals.ConnectionString);
    IDbCommand command = new SqlCommand(
        "Delete [User] where [Id] = @Id");
    command.Connection = connection;
    command.CommandType = CommandType.Text;
    connection.Open();

    IDataParameter id = command.CreateParameter();
    id.ParameterName = "@Id";
    id.Value = this.id.Text;
    id.DbType = DbType.Int16;
    command.Parameters.Add(id);
    command.ExecuteNonQuery();
    connection.Close();
}
```

Split Initialization from Declaration Refactoring of Data Provider Objects

At this point, you need to isolate the lines that differ depending on which data provider is used. The only parts of code that differ in this example depending on the provider are the provider object instantiation statements: new SqlConnection, new SqlCommand, and so on. Because the data provider objects are currently initialized on the same line that is used to declare them, in order to isolate this code, it is best if you perform Split Initialization from Declaration refactoring on these variables. Listing 12-4 shows the resulting code.

Listing 12-4: Split Initialization from Declaration Refactoring for Data Provider Objects

```
private void delete_Click(object sender, EventArgs e)
{
    IDbConnection connection;
    connection = new SqlConnection(Globals.ConnectionString);
    IDbCommand command;
    command = new SqlCommand(
        "Delete [User] where [Id] = @Id");
    command.Connection = connection;
    command.CommandType = CommandType.Text;
    connection.Open();

    IDataParameter id = command.CreateParameter();
    id.ParameterName = "@Id";
    id.Value = this.id.Text;
    id.DbType = DbType.Int16;
    command.Parameters.Add(id);
    command.ExecuteNonQuery();
    connection.Close();
}
```

Extracting Data Provider Object Creation Code As Methods

If you were to introduce conditional code that creates different provider objects depending on specific providers, the `switch` block would be significantly smaller than the one shown in Listing 12-2. However, as provider creation code is common to a majority of routines in the form, the better solution is to extract these statements as separate methods.

You can extract connection and command object creation code to separate methods. Once that is done, all of the routines on the form can reference these extracted methods. The code resulting from data provider object creation methods extraction is shown in Listing 12-5.

Listing 12-5: CreateConnection and CreateCommand Methods Extracted

```csharp
public partial class UserMaintenance : Form
{
    //...
    private const String DeleteUserSql =
        "Delete [User] where [Id] = @Id";

    private void delete_Click(object sender, EventArgs e)
    {
        IDbConnection connection;
        connection = CreateConnection();
        IDbCommand command;
        command = CreateCommand();
        command.Connection = connection;
        command.CommandType = CommandType.Text;
        command.CommandText = DeleteUserSql;
        connection.Open();
        IDataParameter id = command.CreateParameter();
        id.ParameterName = "@Id";
        id.Value = this.id.Text;
        id.DbType = DbType.Int16;
        command.Parameters.Add(id);
        command.ExecuteNonQuery();
        connection.Close();
    }

    private static SqlCommand CreateCommand()
    {
        return new SqlCommand();
    }

    private static SqlConnection CreateConnection()
    {
        return new SqlConnection(Globals.ConnectionString);
    }
}
```

Introducing Provider Objects Creation Logic

Now that you have methods containing purely object creation code, you can finally introduce logic that instantiates a specific provider's objects depending on the currently configured data provider. The provider name is read from the application configuration file and then appropriate variables are set in the module Globals, declaring some global variables. The configuration section in the App.config file looks like the file shown in Listing 12-6.

Listing 12-6: ConnectionString Section in the App.config File

```
<?xml version="1.0" encoding="utf-8" ?>
<configuration>
    <!-- ... -->
    <connectionStrings>
        <add name="DataEntry"
        connectionString="Data Source=TESLATEAM;
        Initial Catalog=Users;
        Integrated Security=SSPI;"
        providerName="System.Data.SqlClient"/>
    </connectionStrings>
</configuration>
```

Note that the connectionStrings section contains a providerName attribute, and the value of the attribute is the namespace of a specific provider.

You can use the Application Startup event to read these settings and populate variables in the Globals module. The code for the Application Startup event is shown in Listing 12-7.

Listing 12-7: Reading Configuration Data on Application Startup in the Program Class

```
static class Program
{
    /// <summary>
    /// The main entry point for the application.
    /// </summary>
    [STAThread]
    static void Main()
    {
        Application.EnableVisualStyles();
        Application.SetCompatibleTextRenderingDefault(false);
        ReadConfiguration();
        Application.Run(new UserMaintenance());
    }

    private static void ReadConfiguration() {
        Configuration config =
        ConfigurationManager.OpenExeConfiguration(ConfigurationUserLevel.None);
        ConnectionStringsSection connectionStringsSection =
            config.ConnectionStrings;
        ConnectionStringSettings connectionStringSettings =
            connectionStringsSection.ConnectionStrings[
            Globals.DbConfigurationSectionName];
```

```
        Globals.ConnectionString = connectionStringSettings.ConnectionString;
        Globals.DatabaseProviderName = connectionStringSettings.ProviderName;
    }
}
```

The code for the static class `Globals`, used to hold the current data provider name and connection string, is shown in Listing 12-8.

Listing 12-8: Module Globals

```
public static class Globals
{
    public const String MsSqlProviderName = "System.Data.SqlClient";
    public const String OracleProviderName = "System.Data.OracleClient";

    public const String DbConfigurationSectionName = "DataEntry";

    private static String connectionString;

    private static String databaseProviderName;

    public static String ConnectionString
    {
        get { return Globals.connectionString; }
        set { Globals.connectionString = value; }
    }

    public static String DatabaseProviderName
    {
        get { return Globals.databaseProviderName; }
        set { Globals.databaseProviderName = value; }
    }
}
```

Now that you have seen how the data provider configuration is read from the configuration file and maintained in the module `Globals`, look at the code for two data provider object creation methods, shown in Listing 12-9.

Listing 12-9: CreateConnection and CreateCommand Methods with Conditional Logic

```
private static IDbCommand CreateCommand()
{
    IDbCommand command = null;
    switch (Globals.DatabaseProviderName)
    {
        case Globals.MsSqlProviderName:
            command = new SqlCommand();
            break;
        case Globals.OracleProviderName:
            command = new OracleCommand();
```

Continued

Listing 12-9: CreateConnection and CreateCommand Methods with Conditional Logic (continued)

```
            break;
        }
        return command;
    }

    private static IDbConnection CreateConnection()
    {
        IDbConnection connection = null;
        switch (Globals.DatabaseProviderName) {
            case Globals.MsSqlProviderName:
                connection = new SqlConnection(Globals.ConnectionString);
                break;
            case Globals.OracleProviderName:
                connection = new OracleConnection(Globals.ConnectionString);
                break;
        }
        return connection;
    }
}
```

Extracting Creation Methods to a Separate Class

As it soon becomes apparent, the same data provider object creation code is present in more than one form class. This means that the same code would be duplicated across numerous classes. In order to avoid duplication, you can extract the connection object and command object creation code into a separate class, as shown in Listing 12-10. Call this class DataProviderFactory.

Listing 12-10: A First Take at the Factory Class

```
class DataProviderFactory
{
    private IDbCommand CreateCommand()
    {
        IDbCommand command = null;
        switch (Globals.DatabaseProviderName)
        {
            case Globals.MsSqlProviderName:
                command = new SqlCommand();
                break;
            case Globals.OracleProviderName:
                command = new OracleCommand();
                break;
        }
        return command;
    }

    private IDbConnection CreateConnection()
    {
        IDbConnection connection = null;
        switch (Globals.DatabaseProviderName)
        {
            case Globals.MsSqlProviderName:
```

```
                connection = new SqlConnection(Globals.ConnectionString);
                break;
            case Globals.OracleProviderName:
                connection = new OracleConnection(Globals.ConnectionString);
                break;
        }
        return connection;
    }
}
```

Now that you have a class dedicated to data provider object creation, you can move global variables from the Globals class to this class. By moving variables to DataProviderFactory, the static class Globals is rendered empty, so it can be deleted from the project.

Global variables are one of the earliest recorded and most notorious code smells.

The code for DataProviderFactory after receiving variables from the Globals static class is shown in Listing 12-11.

Listing 12-11: DataProviderFactory with Provider-Related Variables

```
public class DataProviderFactory
{

    public const String MsSqlProviderName = "System.Data.SqlClient";

    public const String OracleProviderName = "System.Data.OracleClient";

    public const String DbConfigurationSectionName = "DataEntry";

    private static String connectionString;

    private static String databaseProviderName;

    public static String ConnectionString
    {
        get { return DataProviderFactory.connectionString; }
        set { DataProviderFactory.connectionString = value; }
    }

    public static String DatabaseProviderName
    {
        get { return DataProviderFactory.databaseProviderName; }
        set { DataProviderFactory.databaseProviderName = value; }
    }

    public IDbCommand CreateCommand()
    {
        IDbCommand command = null;
        switch (DataProviderFactory.DatabaseProviderName)
        {
            case DataProviderFactory.MsSqlProviderName:
```

Continued

Listing 12-11: DataProviderFactory with Provider-Related Variables *(continued)*

```
                command = new SqlCommand();
                break;
            case DataProviderFactory.OracleProviderName:
                command = new OracleCommand();
                break;
        }
        return command;
    }

    public IDbConnection CreateConnection()
    {
        IDbConnection connection = null;
        switch (DataProviderFactory.DatabaseProviderName)
        {
            case DataProviderFactory.MsSqlProviderName:
                connection = new SqlConnection(
                    DataProviderFactory.ConnectionString);
                break;
            case DataProviderFactory.OracleProviderName:
                connection = new OracleConnection(
                    DataProviderFactory.ConnectionString);
                break;
        }
        return connection;
    }
}
```

You now have a functional factory class. It provides methods that instantiate the correct connection object or command object for a certain provider. However, the class still has a few major problems:

❑ If you change the ProviderName property, you will be able to instantiate objects for different providers from the same factory. In addition, all instances of the factory share the ProviderName property, meaning that only one data provider can be current at a given time. You need to be able to create objects in a consistent form. If the factory has returned an instance of System.Data.SqlClient.SqlConnection when calling the CreateConnection method, then it is only logical that CreateCommand should return an instance of System.Data.SqlClient.SqlCommand and not some other command object.

❑ As you add new providers, you have to modify the factory class, adding another case block to the switch-case statement.

❑ The switch-case statement is duplicated between different methods. While this duplication is not yet very harmful, as you add more object creation methods and more providers, it will become more annoying.

❑ Finally, you have a single class referencing a number of providers. As providers are added, this will result in a growing using statement section and a class that centralizes dependencies on data providers. In order to compile the class, you must have at your disposal all the providers it references.

How should you go about addressing this? What is the next step you should take? Well, here is where the Abstract Factory pattern kicks in. It describes the solution that can be applied in a situation like this.

Solution

You have refactored the code in incremental steps up to this point. You have managed to improve the design, but a number of issues are still present in the code. However, the solution is not immediately visible.

Refactoring Creational Code to Abstract Data Provider Factory

The Abstract Factory pattern provides the solution to the problem at hand. It amounts to the following steps:

1. Create an abstract factory that defines interfaces for the creation of related objects.

2. Use concrete factories that inherit the Abstract Factory override and implement creational methods that instantiate related concrete types defined by Abstract Factory's abstract methods.

In this example, you will have a single factory for each data provider:

❏ For an Oracle data provider, you will create `OracleProviderFactory`.

❏ For a Microsoft data provider, you will create `MsSqlProviderFactory`.

❏ For an OLE DB provider, you will create `OleDbProviderFactory`.

You will add another concrete factory class for each provider you wish to support.

In this example, in order to refactor code to the Abstract Factory pattern, you perform Extract Subclass refactoring on the `DataProviderFactory` class from Listing 12-11. The extracted methods are `CreateConnection` and `CreateCommand`, and each subclass contains one case block. Finally, you make the `DataProviderFactory` class abstract, and mark `CreateConnection` and `CreateCommand` as abstract. These methods in `DataProviderFactory` contain no implementation. The resulting code is presented in Listing 12-12.

Listing 12-12: DataProviderFactory As Abstract Factory

```
public abstract class DataProviderFactory
{
    public const String MsSqlProviderName = "System.Data.SqlClient";

    public const String OracleProviderName = "System.Data.OracleClient";

    public const String OleDbProviderName = "System.Data.OleDb";

    public const String DbConfigurationSectionName = "DataEntry";

    private static String connectionString;

    private static String databaseProviderName;
```

Continued

Listing 12-12: DataProviderFactory As Abstract Factory *(continued)*

```
    public static String ConnectionString
    {
        get { return DataProviderFactory.connectionString; }
        set { DataProviderFactory.connectionString = value; }
    }

    public static String DatabaseProviderName
    {
        get { return DataProviderFactory.databaseProviderName; }
        set { DataProviderFactory.databaseProviderName = value; }
    }

    public static DataProviderFactory CreateDataProviderFactory(
        String providerName)
    {

        DataProviderFactory concreteFactory = null;
        switch (providerName) {
            case DataProviderFactory.MsSqlProviderName:
                concreteFactory = new MsSqlProviderFactory();
                break;
            case DataProviderFactory.OracleProviderName:
                concreteFactory = new OracleProviderFactory();
                break;
            case DataProviderFactory.OleDbProviderName:
                concreteFactory = new OleDbProviderFactory();
                break;
        }
        return concreteFactory;
    }

    public abstract IDbCommand CreateCommand();

    public abstract IDbConnection CreateConnection();
}
```

Note how both `CreateConnection` and `CreateCommand` return objects of interface type from the root data provider namespace `System.Data`. The class does not reference any concrete providers. The shared `CreateDataProviderFactory` method is used to return the concrete factory and contains a single switch-case statement. Listings 12-13 to 12-15 present the code of each concrete factory.

Listing 12-13: MsSqlProviderFactory Factory

```
using System.Data;
using System.Data.SqlClient;

namespace Users
{
    public class MsSqlProviderFactory: DataProviderFactory
    {
```

```
        public override IDbCommand CreateCommand() {
            return new SqlCommand();
        }

        public override IDbConnection CreateConnection() {
            return new SqlConnection();
        }
    }
}
```

Note how MsSqlProviderFactory imports only the System.Data.SqlClient namespace.

Listing 12-14: OleDbProviderFactory Factory

```
using System.Data;
using System.Data.OleDb;

namespace Users
{
    public class OleDbProviderFactory: DataProviderFactory
    {
        public override IDbCommand CreateCommand() {
            return new OleDbCommand();
        }

        public override IDbConnection CreateConnection() {
            return new OleDbConnection();
        }
    }
}
```

OleDbProviderFactory imports only the System.Data.OleDb namespace.

Listing 12-15: OracleProviderFactory Factory

```
using System.Data;
using System.Data.OracleClient;

namespace Users
{
    public class OracleProviderFactory:DataProviderFactory
    {

        public override IDbCommand CreateCommand() {
            return new OracleCommand();
        }

        public override IDbConnection CreateConnection() {
            return new OracleConnection();
        }
    }
}
```

Finally, OracleProviderFactory imports only the System.Data.OracleClient namespace. You can see this code represented graphically in Figure 12-1.

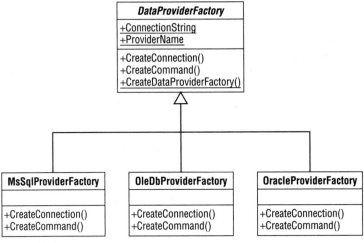

Figure 12-1

The future implementation and modification is easy to follow. For each new provider, a new concrete factory inheriting DataProviderFactory is added. For each new object — for example IDbDataAdapter — a new creation method (CreateDataAdapter) is added.

Consequences

Now that you have implemented the solution, you should understand the consequences of this pattern in detail. First, consider the benefits that this pattern brings to your design:

- ❑ **Clients can use the data provider in a polymorphic manner:** They never need to reference any concrete data provider class. All they need to know are interfaces from the System.Data namespace. This leads to less code and less duplication in your code, and all the other benefits that polymorphic behavior can bring.

- ❑ **Polymorphic use of providers makes exchanging different providers easy:** Clients are never aware of the concrete type of object that the factory creates. This makes it easy to add configuration capability to the application and to externalize to a configuration file a string that indicates the current provider. This way, there is no need to change the code or recompile the application in order to use different providers. This makes your code less dependent on a specific database and helps avoid vendor lock-in.

- ❑ **Only related objects are created:** This rule is enforced because once you create a factory, it returns provider objects of a specific provider only. MsSqlProviderFactory always creates objects from System.Data.SqlClient, SqlConnection, and SqlCommand — and none other. This makes creational code behave in a consistent and predictable manner.

- ❑ **From a testing perspective, the pattern makes client code easier to unit test:** All you need to do when executing tests is use MockDataProviderFactory, a factory that creates mocked data provider objects.

You should also understand some downsides to this pattern:

❑ **Creating another type that needs to be created by the factory is not easy:** For example, if you wish to add a creational method for Data Adapter, you need to add a new method to the abstract `DataProviderFactory` class. This, as a consequence, obliges you to implement this method in all concrete factory classes inheriting the `DataProviderFactory` class.

❑ **Adding a new family of objects (a new data provider in this example) is relatively costly:** That's because it requires you to implement a new concrete factory class for each family you add.

When you need to use the pattern, it does not mean that the design is cast in stone and that you have to follow the code from the pattern example line by line. You can modify and adapt the pattern so it suits your own needs. As explained earlier, that is the only correct way to use patterns. To illustrate this, the following section looks at some variations that can be applied to the Abstract Factory pattern.

Abstract Factory Variations

There are different ways to refine and implement this pattern. The following sections explore some of the variations you might use when implementing the pattern yourself.

Instantiating the Concrete Factory

Maybe the biggest problem with the solution is the concrete factory creation code from Listing 12-12. If you take a look at the shared `CreateDataProviderFactory` method, you can see that you need to modify the code of Abstract Factory by adding a new case block for each new concrete factory that needs to be incorporated. One solution is to use the concrete factory's name as a provider parameter (`ProviderName` property) and then instantiate the factory by means of reflection. This way, each time a new concrete factory is added, it is adequate to give the correct provider name parameter to instantiate the provider, and no modification to `DataProviderFactory` is required. If you wish, you can give it a try and implement `CreateDataProviderFactory` in this fashion.

Default Implementation

In some cases, it might be appropriate to have a default implementation for the factory. In that case, you could instantiate the `AbstractFactory` itself, which would provide some meaningful default implementation of the factory. Needless to say, this would convert the abstract factory into a concrete factory itself. It means you would have to delete the `abstract` keyword from the abstract factory's declaration and change the `abstract` keyword to `virtual` in the creation method's declaration, and provide default implementation for them. In this case, the OLE DB provider makes the most sense as a default implementation because of its versatility in connecting to different data sources (provided that necessary DLLs are available on the system hosting the factory).

Concrete Factories As Singletons

A singleton is another design pattern. It helps you enforce only a single instance of a certain type if your application is created during application lifetime. It makes sense to implement concrete factories as singletons, because only a single instance of each concrete factory will be needed anyway.

Factory Inheritance Hierarchies

In a similar way to how you create hierarchies of other objects, you can have hierarchies of factories. Imagine you have programmed an enhanced SQL Command object, capable of caching data parameters.

The `EnhancedSqlCommand` class works with the same `System.Data.SqlClient.SqlConnection` object as `System.Data.SqlClient.SqlCommand` does. You can program your `EnhancedMsSqlProviderFactory` to inherit `MsSqlProviderFactory` and override a single `CreateCommand` method that will return an instance of `EnhancedSqlCommand` instead of the standard `SqlCommand`.

Data Provider Factory in .NET Framework 2.0

If you are programming on .NET Framework 2.0 or later, you do not need to create your own data provider factories. Creators of the .NET Framework have realized the benefits of the Abstract Factory pattern and provided the classes that implement it. Take a look at the `System.Data.Common.DbProviderFactory` and `System.Data.Common.DbProviderFactories` classes and compare their design to the one used in this chapter.

The existence of these classes by no means renders our refactoring in the abstract factory exercise futile. The purpose of this example was not to solve a specific problem but to use a well-known problem to expose a possible solution to this and similar problems — that is, to demonstrate the effectiveness of the refactoring process in combination with design patterns. Now you have tasted the power of combining design patterns and refactoring. The next section continues this discussion with a few points about a related and very influential pattern.

Dependency Injection Pattern

While it is not one of the classic GOF patterns, the Dependency Injection (DI) pattern has become hugely influential of late. It has given rise to numerous lightweight containers and unobtrusive DI frameworks. It has changed the way many developers approach application design. However, be aware that any improvements this approach brings to your design, and especially to your development process, are not easily observable on a small scale. Nevertheless, it is important to learn more about this pattern and the benefits it offers.

Dependency Injection and Inversion of Control

DI is also often referred to by another name: *Inversion of Control (IoC)*. These terms are used more or less interchangeably throughout the chapter. However, Inversion of Control is a more general technique often used in programming whereby the programmer relinquishes some control to another entity. For example, when you code the Windows Form class, you implement different event handlers that react to user actions. In this case, you have no control over the flow of the program; it is the user who can choose to push any enabled button at any point in time. Conversely, had you programmed this process as a console application, asking the user to enter one bit of data at a time, you would interact with the user in a strictly defined order of execution that is under your complete control.

Problem Using Dependency Injection

When you write your typical industrial-strength application, you are faced with the great complexity characterized by typical real-life software projects. The common way to deal with the complexity in your project is modularity. Instead of making your application as a single monolithic construct, you assemble your application out of existing or newly created components and services. Each component and service has to solve a piece of the puzzle that your application represents.

Software Components and Services

Components are deployable binaries created to be reused as a part of some (often unknown) application. Component-based applications are created by composing, or assembling, different components. As a C# programmer, you are probably familiar with COM and COM+ components. (Software components are discussed in Chapter 6.)

Services are similar to components and they are also used by other applications. Services have the capacity to be accessed remotely, meaning they can be hosted by a remote machine, and generally execute in some other process. A typical example of a service is a web service that is accessed through the SOAP protocol.

Providing components with remote access is often technically straightforward, so the difference between the two can be blurred. It may depend only on how you deploy the component. In a .NET environment, you access and use services and components in the same way you would use and access any other object.

This modular approach is not without its own problems. These problems become more relevant with the scale and overall complexity of the application. Some of the problems you have to deal with include the following:

- ❏ How to create components and locate services
- ❏ How to deal with dependencies between your components and services
- ❏ How to avoid wedding yourself to a single implementation of the component or service
- ❏ How to test such an application easily
- ❏ How to configure the application in a uniform and consistent manner
- ❏ How to provide the application with additional services such as transaction support or object pooling without obliging components to implement specific interfaces or inherit specific classes

In any assembled application, you have two principal collaborators:

- ❏ Client
- ❏ Service

A client collaborator (often a service or component in its own right) asks a service collaborator to provide some service. Figure 12-2 represents this graphically.

Figure 12-2

In order to make this more illustrative, imagine that the client is an Online Purchase component and the service is a Credit Card Verification service.

The first problem the client has to resolve is getting a hold of the service. In a normal object-oriented scenario, the Online Purchase component would simply create a new instance of the Credit Card Verification service object. This is as simple as the following:

```
PremiumCreditCardVerificationService verificationService =
new PremiumCreditCardVerificationService();
```

The problems with this approach are numerous. Because you cannot easily switch to another a Credit Card Verification service implementation, the following problems are evident:

❏   You depend on a specific service implementation and service provider. What happens when another verification service charges less?

❏   Your application is not easy to test. Such services generally charge for use, so you wouldn't like to use a real service just to test your application.

❏   You are not isolated from changes to the verification service because you depend upon its implementation.

You can generally distinguish between a service implementation and a service interface, so you could reduce the dependency on the service by viewing the service through its interface, like this:

```
CreditCardVerificationService verificationService =
new PremiumCreditCardVerificationService();
```

However, while dependency is reduced to a single service-creation line, the Online Purchase component still depends on a specific Credit Card Verification Service implementation.

Earlier in this chapter, you saw how you can use factory classes to decouple the client from a specific class implementation. In the case of services, instead of factories, you rely on Service Locator classes to provide you with services you need. Online Purchase could use a Service Locator to obtain an instance of the Credit Card Verification service:

```
ServiceLocator locator = new ServiceLocator();
CreditCardVerificationService verificationService =
locator.find(premium);
```

Figure 12-3 presents this graphically in more general terms, using service- and client-generic names for collaborators.

Compared to previous solutions, this is obviously much better because you do not depend on a specific service implementation. There is one problem, however: The client still depends on the Service Locator. You have to ask the locator that you need to find a certain object (the service).

Depending on the Service Locator, this can be a limitation, but it isn't necessarily a deal breaker. Still, relying on the Service Locator requires writing a lot of boilerplate code. In addition, while pursuing more universal Service Locator solutions, you might end up writing less explicit code, such as this locator method declaration that returns an Object type:

```
public Object find(String serviceName)
```

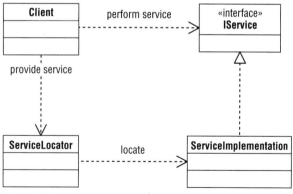

Figure 12-3

There is a way, however, to do without even the Service Locator. The solution is to have someone else inject a service inside the client. I will call such an entity an *assembler*. When creating clients, an assembler injects the client with a specific service implementation.

Solution

When you program your code following the Dependency Injection pattern, you pursue the following line of thinking, expressed here from the client's point of view: "Why should I create or locate components or services or even ask someone else to create or locate them for me? I'll just declare that I need components or services, and let someone else provide them for me."

This is where Inversion of Control comes from: The client is letting someone else create or locate components or services the client itself needs. Figure 12-4 shows what this would look like presented graphically.

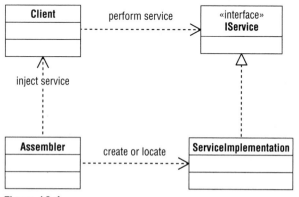

Figure 12-4

You can observe one very important effect. The client now depends only on the ISerivce interface. That means you have successfully resolved the service implementation location problem in such a way that your client does not depend even on a Service Locator anymore.

Note, however, that the assembler depends on both client and service implementation. You might think at first that all you have accomplished is moving dependencies from one place to another; but you will probably have numerous components, services, and clients in each application, so having a single place to reconfigure dependencies is already an important accomplishment. In addition, you are managing to create reusable components that do not depend on a specific context. If you consider that the client can also be a component, you have managed to reduce its dependencies on specific service implementations, factories, or service locators. Finally, assembler dependencies can often be removed by programmatic methods such as reflection. This is often the case with lightweight containers.

Constructor-Based Injection vs. Property-Based Injection

In order for DI to work, the client needs a mechanism for injecting dependencies. For this, we can count on standard object-oriented mechanisms — namely constructors and properties:

❏   If the client declares a service as a property, then all an assembler has to do is set the property to reference a service implementation instance. For example, an assembler can contain the following code:

```
OnlinePurchase purchase = new OnlinePurchase();
purchase.VerificationService = new PremiumCreditCardVerificationService();
```

❏   If the client declares a service as a constructor parameter, then all the assembler has to do is create the client invoking this parameterized constructor, passing a service implementation instance as a parameter:

```
OnlinePurchase purchase = new OnlinePurchase(
new PremiumCreditCardVerificationService());
```

Which way is better? There have been a lot of discussions on the subject. The advantage of constructor-based injection is that it instantiates objects in a legal state, with all dependencies provided in the constructor itself. The advantage of property-based injection is that it allows clients to have a default (nonparameterized) constructor, a requirement of some technologies. For example, if you wish to program COM components in C#, you must provide public default, nonparameterized constructors.

Finally, there are other forms of injection, such as interface-based. The best choice is more or less a question of specific context and maybe even personal preferences, so we won't dwell on the subject. Now that you can provide the client with the dependency, the question is, how does the assembler know what concrete service implementation it is supposed to inject?

What Service Implementation to Inject

Very often, you have at your disposal more than one implementation of a service or component. The following sections explore how the assembler knows which concrete implementation should be injected into the client.

Coded Assembler

In its most simple form, an assembler can contain literal code that creates and injects concrete dependencies into the client. Going back to the Online Purchase component and Credit Card Verification service example, Listing 12-16 shows an example of assembler-encoded injection.

Listing 12-16: Assembler-Encoded Injection

```
public class Assembler
{
    public void IntializeApplication()
    {
        OnlinePurchase purchase = new OnlinePurchase(
        new PremiumCreditCardVerificationService());
        //...set purchase client with instance of purchase
    }
    //...
}
```

When you construct applications, you generally end up with large object graphs. In this example, this means that the instance of Online Purchase, the client to the Credit Card Verification service, will probably be a component that is required by its own client, and so on.

Auto-wiring Assembler

Such an assembler is used in combination with other assembling approaches. The most basic way for a component to declare a certain dependency, and that it should be injected with a service, is on the code level. If a client has declared a writable property or a constructor parameter of a certain type, it means it depends on this type and needs to have an instance of that type injected. If only a single class is available at runtime that implements a certain service interface, then it is obvious that this class is exactly the implementation that client needs, as there is no other.

In such a case, many DI-based frameworks are capable of discovering and providing the client with the only available implementation because they are capable of inspecting components through introspection. This way, some dependencies can be resolved with no additional effort. This is an important characteristic of full-blown assemblers because it keeps applications simple. At the same time, it enables the principle of programming to an abstraction to be followed, without incurring additional configuration cost.

Metadata Assembler

This form of dependency resolution is the most common in full-blown DI frameworks. These assemblers enable you to externalize to a configuration file (often XML) the dependency information. Such an assembler is capable of resolving complex dependency graphs and enables you to mix standard configuration data with dependency information. Consider the following sample configuration file used by the Spring Framework for .NET:

```
<object id="onlinePurchase" type="OnlinePurchase, OnlinePurchaseAssembly ">
<property name=" verificationService" ref="premiumVerification"/>
</object>
<object id="premiumVerification" type="PremiumCreditCardVerificationService,
CreditCardVerificationAssembly"/>
```

You can see how each object is defined with a unique ID and type that consists of a full class name and assembly name. In this case, `onlinePurchase` is property-injected with the `premiumVerification` object, an instance of the `PremiumCreditCardVerificationService` class.

An alternative to configuration files is attributes. This technique is a bit more intrusive, as you have to recompile your code in order to change the way the application is assembled. Supported by Nano Container for .NET, an example follows:

```
[RegisterWithContainer]public class PremiumCreditCardVerificationService {
    //...
}
```

The `RegisterWithContainer` attribute registers `PremiumCreditCardVerificationService` with the assembler under a class name. The assembler is capable of discovering that `PremiumCreditCard VerificationService` is a type of `CreditCardVerificationService`.

Benefits of the DI Pattern

You can obtain numerous benefits by following the Dependency Injection pattern, as confirmed by the recent popularity of DI frameworks and lightweight containers:

- ❑ **Solution to component creation and service location code:** You are liberated from coding different factories or programming to different service locators, as this is not the concern of your component or service anymore. (Remember that a client of some service or component is most often a service or component itself).

- ❑ **Decoupling of the client from a specific implementation:** By not depending on a specific implementation, you are harvesting all the benefits of the polymorphic approach, and creating highly reusable, configurable components. Such components do not depend on a specific context to be reused.

- ❑ **Ease of configuration:** Your application is woven together from loosely coupled elements. You can exchange different implementations with ease, often just by changing the configuration file. The radically different approach to configuration, completely in the spirit of object-oriented programming, enables you to avoid programming configuration plumbing code. Through DI, configuration elements are just objects that you assign to other objects.

- ❑ **Ease of testing:** You can easily exchange a real implementation with stubs or a mocked implementation of services and components for testing purposes, facilitating different forms of testing without incurring any programming cost.

- ❑ **DI-based, lightweight containers make it easy to add support for other crosscutting services:** An example of this is transaction or pooling that can be added declaratively, without imposing any limitation on the component itself.

- ❑ **DI containers are unobtrusive:** This means you do not have to extend a class or implement a specific interface in order to use services they provide. Often, your class is not aware of the container's existence. This is not the case with heavyweight containers.

> **Definition: POCO is an acronym for Plain Old CLR Object. It refers to objects that are not forced to implement any specific interface or inherit any specific class in order to make use of the services that certain frameworks or containers provide.**

Note two negative aspects of the DI pattern:

❑ You create code that at first sight is not easy to follow (due to Inversion of Control).

❑ Some programmers are put off because they have to write additional configuration files, although often these files are larger than necessary because programmers do not use the auto-wiring capacities present in all major DI containers.

Lightweight vs. Heavyweight Containers

DI has led to the creation of numerous unobtrusive frameworks and lightweight containers. Probably the most popular lightweights on the .NET platform are Castle/Windsor, Spring .NET, Unity Application Block, and the Pico/Nano .NET container. These lightweight containers have certain advantages compared to traditional application server heavyweight containers such as Microsoft Transaction Serverx (MTS).

In this case, making a choice based on their names (lightweight versus heavyweight) would be a mistake, because the two container types differ in much more than simple size in bytes. The following list explores the differences between the two in greater detail.

What Is a Component Container?

In their simplest form, component containers are capable of hosting components and taking care of their life cycle. From a client point of view, when a component is hosted inside a container, the client does not need to take care of creating and initializing the component, because the container does this for the client. From a hosted component point of view, the component can count on the container to provide it with information about important events in the lifetime of the component, such as creation, that can be used by the component to perform necessary tasks, such as initialization or destruction and any necessary cleanup. In addition, containers can provide a host of additional services to components, such as assembly and dependency resolution, configuration, manageability, and so on.

❑ **DI support:** Both lightweight and heavyweight containers support DI, but MTS supports only the injection of services that are part of MTS and some simple configuration data through the "Object Construction" feature. Lightweight containers can host and inject any .NET object.

❑ **POCO programming model:** In order to host your component inside MTS, the implementing class must inherit the `System.EnterpriseServices.ServicedComponent` class. Because C# (like the majority of .NET languages) supports only single inheritance, this imposes an important limitation on the programming model you need to follow. Moreover, you won't be able to reuse other classes through inheritance when programming your component, nor will other classes be able to inherit your class, unless they are tied up with MTS libraries. Lightweight containers impose no such limitation. You can program your classes as simple POCOs, not tying them to a specific hosting environment. Crosscutting services such as transaction support are implemented in the form of interceptors and can be added declaratively.

❑   **Modular architecture:** Lightweight containers are generally programmed in a modular manner, so you can use only the services you need. This means you need to reference and distribute only the libraries you actually use. If necessary, you can program your own. MTS is a monolithic application and cannot be installed or distributed partially.

❑   **Embedding:** MTS is an application server that runs in a separate process from your own application. It is registered as a Windows service and has to be installed and administered separately from your application. This can be an advantage in certain circumstances — for example, in large enterprises that use components produced by different software companies — but this also dictates its size and complexity. Conversely, lightweight containers can be embedded and distributed as a part of your application. Core libraries are often so small that they can be embedded inside thick clients (as in a client/server model) and distributed over the Internet.

❑   **Ease of testing:** Thanks to DI, with lightweight containers, the implementation of different services can be easily replaced with stubs or mocks. This facilitates the testing process. With heavyweight containers, this is not possible.

❑   **Centralization:** Centralization is characteristic of heavyweight application servers. Because components are hosted in a centralized server, this can facilitate administration, monitoring, configuration, and assembly of applications in one central location. Lightweight containers are not installed separately and are bundled together with the application.

These differences between the two types of containers are summarized in Table 12-1.

Table 12-1: Lightweight Containers vs. Heavyweight Containers

Characteristics	Lightweight Containers	Heavyweight Containers
DI	Yes	Very Limited
POCO programming model	Yes	No
Modular architecture	Yes	No
Embedding	Yes	No
Ease of testing	Yes	No
Centralization	No	Yes

Noting the differences between the two types of containers, it seems that lightweight wins handily. Does this mean it's the end of the road for heavyweight containers? Well, not likely. They are still a proven technology and very useful for highly scalable, high-traffic, large enterprise-level applications that need to support redundancy and high availability.

Until recently, however, you could often find application servers used even for an application that benefited minimally from the services they provide and where using heavyweight containers is clearly overkill. The advent of lightweight containers should help developers program more productively and help place the heavyweight containers in their rightful niche.

Refactoring to DI

You have seen how code can be refactored to use DI, in the example used to discuss DI. You have also seen how the assembler is used to inject dependency into the client instead of having the client find the dependency.

To summarize: Instead of instantiating and using a factory to create a component, or instead of using a service locator to locate a service, you invert the control and let someone else inject the dependencies your component needs. The following section puts this into practice with the Rent-a-Wheels application.

Refactoring to Patterns and the Rent-a-Wheels Application

If you consider the refactorings performed in Chapter 10, you might recall a first attempt at Abstract Factory for data provider objects in the form of an AbstractDataObjectsProvider class with a concrete MSSQLDataObjectsProvider factory class.

Eliminating Code That Duplicates .NET Framework Functionality

Because the same functionality is provided by the DbProviderFactories and DbProviderFactory classes in the .NET Framework System.Data.Common namespace, you can eliminate AbstractData ObjectsProvider and MSSQLDataObjectsProvider and use classes provided by the .NET Framework instead. The former classes aren't adding any additional value, so the less code you have to maintain, the better. Because the DbProviderFactory class provides a comprehensive list of methods for data provider object creation, you can decouple the rest of the code from the Data classes (BranchData, ModelData, and so on) from the concrete data providers.

For example the ExecuteReader method in the AbstractData class used to look like this:

```
protected IDataReader ExecuteReader(out IDbConnection connection, string sql)
{
    IDbCommand command = provider.InstantiateCommand();
    connection = PrepareDataObjects(command, sql);
    return command.ExecuteReader();
}
```

After using the DbProviderFactory class from the System.Data.Common namespace, the code for the same method looks like this:

```
protected IDataReader ExecuteReader(out IDbConnection connection, string sql)
{
    IDbCommand command =
        DatabaseProviderFactory.CreateCommand();
    connection = PrepareDataObjects(command, sql);
    return command.ExecuteReader();
}
```

Injecting Data Classes to GUI Classes via Dependency Injection

In order to provide less coupling between the GUI and Data layers and make the `RentAWheel.Data` assembly nondependent on Rent-a-Wheels configuration specifics, you can do the following:

❑ Inject GUI classes with `Data` implementations, instead of having GUI classes creating instances of `Data`.

❑ Inject `Data` classes with a connection string and a concrete `DbProviderFactory`. This will decouple Data classes from the specific Rent-a-Wheels implementation and make `AbstractData` highly reusable.

Instead of incorporating third-party assemblers, you implement your own coded assembler. Application startup is a convenient moment for DI, so you can code your assembler as part of the `Program` class. The code for the `Program` class is shown in Listing 12-17.

Listing 12-17: Program Class As DI Assembler

```
static class Program
{
    private static ConnectionStringSettings connectionStringSettings;

    private const String DbStringConfigurationSectionName = "RentAWheels";

    private static VehicleData vehicleData;

    private static ModelData modelData;

    private static CategoryData categoryData;

    private static BranchData branchData;

    private static FleetView fleetView;

    static BranchMaintenance branchMaintenance;
    static VehicleCategoriesMaintenance categoryMaintenance;
    static ModelMaintenance modelMaintenance;
    static FleetMaintenance fleetMaintenance;
    static VehicleRental vehicleRental;
    static VehicleReception vehicleReception;
    static VehicleChangeBranch changeBranch;

    /// <summary>
    /// The main entry point for the application.
    /// </summary>
    [STAThread]
    static void Main()
    {
        Application.EnableVisualStyles();
        Application.SetCompatibleTextRenderingDefault(false);
```

```
        ReadConnectionSettings();
        CreateDataServices();
        CreateForms();
        SetupModelMaintenanceForm();
        SetupFleetMaintenanceForm();
        SetUpBranchMaintenanceForm();
        SetUpVehicleCategoriesMaintenanceForm();
        SetUpVehicleRentalForm();
        SetUpRentVehicleReceptionForm();
        SetUpRentVehicleChangeBranchForm();
        SetUpFleetViewForm();
        Application.Run(fleetView);

        AppDomain.CurrentDomain.UnhandledException +=
        new UnhandledExceptionEventHandler(HandleUnhandledException);
    }

    static void HandleUnhandledException(object sender,
        UnhandledExceptionEventArgs e)
    {
        MessageBox.Show("A problem occurred " +
            "and the application cannot recover! " +
        "Please contact the technical support.");
    }

    static void CreateDataServices() {
        vehicleData = new VehicleData();
        vehicleData.ConnectionStringSettings = connectionStringSettings;
        modelData = new ModelData();
        modelData.ConnectionStringSettings = connectionStringSettings;
        categoryData = new CategoryData();
        categoryData.ConnectionStringSettings = connectionStringSettings;
        branchData = new BranchData();
        branchData.ConnectionStringSettings = connectionStringSettings;
    }

    private static void ReadConnectionSettings()
    {
        Configuration config = ConfigurationManager.
            OpenExeConfiguration(ConfigurationUserLevel.None);
        ConnectionStringsSection connectionStringsSection =
            config.ConnectionStrings;
        connectionStringSettings = connectionStringsSection.
            ConnectionStrings[DbStringConfigurationSectionName];
    }

    private static void CreateForms()
    {
        fleetView = new FleetView();
        branchMaintenance = new BranchMaintenance();
        categoryMaintenance = new VehicleCategoriesMaintenance();
        modelMaintenance = new ModelMaintenance();
```

Continued

387

Listing 12-17: Program Class As DI Assembler *(continued)*

```
        fleetMaintenance = new FleetMaintenance();
        vehicleRental = new VehicleRental();
        vehicleReception = new VehicleReception();
        changeBranch = new VehicleChangeBranch();
    }

    private static void SetupModelMaintenanceForm()
    {
        ((ModelMaintenanceHelper)modelMaintenance.Helper).ModelData
            = modelData;
        ((ModelMaintenanceHelper)modelMaintenance.Helper).CategoryData
            = categoryData;
    }
    private static void SetUpFleetViewForm()
    {
        fleetView.BranchData = branchData;
        fleetView.CategoryData = categoryData;
        fleetView.VehicleData = vehicleData;
        fleetView.ModelMaintenance = modelMaintenance;
        fleetView.BranchMaintenance = branchMaintenance;
        fleetView.CategoryMaintenance = categoryMaintenance;
        fleetView.FleetMaintenance = fleetMaintenance;
        fleetView.VehicleReception = vehicleReception;
        fleetView.VehicleRental = vehicleRental;
        fleetView.ChangeBranchForm = changeBranch;
    }
    private static void SetupFleetMaintenanceForm()
    {
        ((FleetMaintenanceHelper)fleetMaintenance.Helper).BranchData
            = branchData;
        ((FleetMaintenanceHelper)fleetMaintenance.Helper).ModelData
            = modelData;
        ((FleetMaintenanceHelper)fleetMaintenance.Helper).VehicleData
            = vehicleData;
    }
    private static void SetUpChangeBranchForm()
    {
        changeBranch.BranchData = branchData;
        changeBranch.VehicleData = vehicleData;
    }
    private static void SetUpBranchMaintenanceForm()
    {
        ((BranchMaintenanceHelper)branchMaintenance.Helper).BranchData
            = branchData;
    }
    private static void SetUpVehicleReceptionForm()
    {
        vehicleReception.VehicleData = vehicleData;
    }
    private static void SetUpVehicleCategoriesMaintenanceForm()
```

```
    {
        ((VehicleCategoriesMaintenanceHelper)categoryMaintenance.Helper).
            CategoryData = categoryData;
    }
    private static void SetUpVehicleRentalForm()
    {
        vehicleRental.VehicleData = vehicleData;
    }
    private static void SetUpRentVehicleReceptionForm()
    {
        vehicleReception.VehicleData = vehicleData;
    }
    private static void SetUpRentVehicleChangeBranchForm()
    {
        changeBranch.VehicleData = vehicleData;
    }
}
```

This is not yet all I have to say about design patterns and Rent-a-Wheels. It seems that I have incorporated certain design patterns a lot before this chapter.

CRUD Persistence Pattern

If you take a look at different Data classes, you will see that they all inherit `AbstractData` and implement certain abstract methods that `AbstractData` declares:

```
public abstract IList<Persisted> GetAll();

public abstract void Delete(Persisted persisted);

public abstract void Update(Persisted persisted);

public abstract void Insert(Persisted persisted);
```

You can see that for each domain object, the data implements a few persistence methods. This pattern is actually not so new. It is often referred to by the acronym *CRUD*, which stands for create, retrieve, update, and delete. This pattern is popular today and often appears in similar forms and under different names, such as DAO for Data Access Object and others. Mind you, this implementation here is very basic. It doesn't have methods for parameterized querying, not to mention more advanced problems such as concurrency, stale data, transactions, lazy loading, and so on. Object persistence is a very complex field and is discussed in Chapter 13.

Summary

Software design patterns provide a wealth of programming wisdom and ingenuity. Learning patterns will greatly hone your designer skills but it is not enough for real-life pattern application. Because the only practical way to approach design is evolutionary, you will have to learn techniques for refactoring your code so that it incorporates solutions described by design patterns.

This chapter gave you a first taste of the design patterns and refactoring to patterns process. When refactoring to patterns, you are not guided only by the immediate goal of eliminating undesired qualities from your code or smells; you are led forward by a clear vision of the design you wish to implement.

You have seen how the problem of creating related objects can be resolved by an Abstract Factory pattern, decoupling the client from the knowledge of the concrete family it will use. You have also seen how typical creational code can be refactored along the lines of the Abstract Factory pattern.

This chapter also discussed the Dependency Injection pattern, an increasingly influential design pattern that is changing the way typical applications are programmed and assembled. DI can be applied in a very simple form or it can be implemented with the help of DI-based containers. You have seen the benefit of the pattern and how containers based on DI compare to traditional heavyweight containers and application servers.

I hope that after reading this chapter you can appreciate the importance of design patterns and the benefits they can bring to your development process; and that you will be inspired to learn more about patterns and to devise ways you can refactor your code along the lines of solutions proposed by certain patterns.

The next chapter takes a look at what the latest version of C# and Visual Studio offers you. LINQ and other new features that ship with Visual Studio 2008 are discussed.

13

LINQ and Other C# 3.0 Enhancements

Visual Studio 2008 brings probably the most important version of C# since the first one in .NET. This is not because of the novelties in the integrated development environment (IDE) itself; more important are the new features that ship with version 3.5 of the .NET Framework and, especially interesting for those involved in refactoring, C# version 3.0.

This chapter discusses the following features:

❑   LINQ technology brings additional power to working with data in C#. Different data sources can now be queried in a uniform and language-native manner. LINQ paves the way for the implementation of different technologies such as object-relational mapping frameworks and others.

❑   In the 2008 version, C# is additionally equipped with features such as automatic properties, new object initializer syntax, extension methods, local variable type inference, and many others.

Type Inference for Local Variables

You know that in a statically typed language the type of a variable is declared explicitly by the programmer as a part of variable declaration. By declaring it as a certain type, you give a variable a certain meaning and purpose, and you specify how the variable can be manipulated. This is the basis of the type system. With that information, the compiler provides you with *type safety*; it will confirm that only those members that are declared in the variable's type can be invoked, while the IDE will provide you with help in the form of IntelliSense, with features such as auto-complete, list members, parameter info, and others.

In C# 3.0, Microsoft has equipped the compiler with type inference for local variables. This means that you do not have to declare a local variable's type explicitly; the variable will still be statically typed. For example, Figure 13-1 shows how the IDE correctly recognizes the variable name as a String.

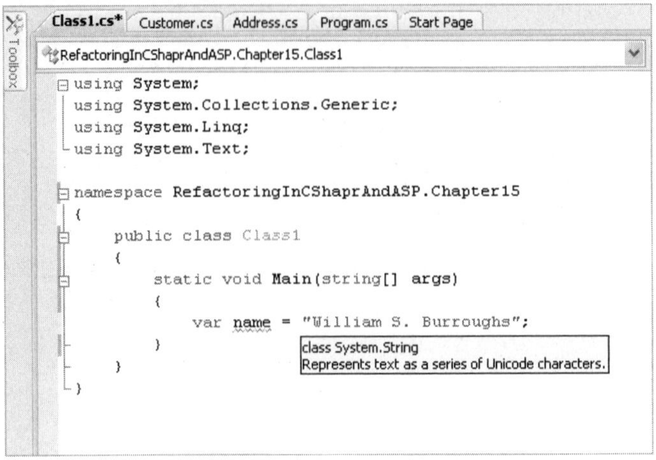

Chapter 13: LINQ and Other C# 3.0 Enhancements

Figure 13-1

By using the `var` keyword in place of type in a variable declaration, you can write more concise code and save yourself a few keystrokes. The compiler will correctly infer variable type based on the initial value, and you will be able to take advantage of all the benefits that Visual Studio IntelliSense and the C# compiler can provide. Your code will be statically checked, and auto-complete and other IntelliSense feature will be available.

Remember that you can apply type inference for local variables only. These are the variables declared inside a method or a property. If, for example, you try to declare a class variable as implicitly typed, you will receive the following error message from the compiler: "The contextual keyword 'var' may only appear within a local variable declaration."

Type inference also brings one undesirable side-effect to your code. The type of the variable is inferred based on the right side of the assignment. For example, consider the following statement:

```
var connection = new SqlConnection(Globals.ConnectionString);
```

The variable connection will be inferred as `SqlConnection`, making all `SqlConnection` class members available to the programmer. Using the standard variable declaration mechanism, you could write the following:

```
IDbConnection connection = new SqlConnection(Globals.ConnectionString);
```

This way, you access the variable through the top-level interface. Only the `IDbConnection` members can now be used inside the method. I have discussed the benefits of the "program to an abstraction design principle" in Chapter 10. Using the implementation type, as done when type inference is employed, goes against this principle.

While local variable type inference is a nice feature on its own, it was actually a necessary addition to C# 3.0 in order for it to support Language Integrated Query (LINQ). LINQ is probably the most prominent feature of the 3.0 version of C#, and is discussed in greater detail later in this chapter.

Auto-implemented Properties

When I talked about encapsulation in Chapter 9, I explained its benefits in general and how you can use Encapsulate Field refactoring to prevent direct access to fields. While Visual Studio can help you with generating field encapsulation code, you will still end up with a lot of repetitive code implementing properties that are mostly only reading from and assigning to a field. Were it not for the binary compatibility problem, you could just as well use only fields and not properties.

However, if you expose a field and later decide to encapsulate it as a property, you will break binary compatibility between versions of the class and you will have to recompile the client in order to use a property instead of a field. You will not have to change any code in the client, mind you; the syntax for property and field access in C# is the same.

Refactoring: Convert Standard Property to Auto-Implemented

Motivation

Using an auto-implemented property declaration instead of a standard property makes your code more concise and helps you eliminate superfluous, repetitive code.

When there is no additional logic in property implementation code other than field access, you will make your code simpler and easier to read if you use auto-implemented property syntax.

Related Smells

Use this refactoring to eliminate the Superfluous Code and Duplicated Code smells.

Mechanics

To convert a standard property implementation to auto-implemented, first ensure that the property implementation has no additional logic except simple field access. If so, then the property is qualified for conversion:

1. Delete the backing field declaration.
2. Delete the property's getter and setter body.

Before

```
class Client
{
    private int zip;

    public int Zip
    {
        get { return zip; }
        set { zip = value; }
    }
    //...

}
```

Continued

After

```
class Client
{
    public int Zip
    {
        get;
        set;
    }
    //...
}
```

The Microsoft C# team has realized that writing a property implementation often involves a lot of repetitive code that only provides property access to private fields. Therefore, in C# 3.0 they have added syntax that enables you to make a property declaration much simpler when no additional logic is necessary in the property implementation. With this syntax, you do not need to declare the backing field; it is created by the compiler for you automatically; and if you later need to add some additional logic to the property declaration, you can easily switch back to a standard declaration without losing binary compatibility between versions.

Refactoring: Create Property Backing Store

Motivation
When a property needs logic other than simple property access, you can convert an auto-implemented property to a standard property with an explicitly declared backing field. You can use getter and setter declarations to add the necessary logic.

Related Smells
Use this refactoring to add logic to a property implementation requiring more than simple field access.

Mechanics
To convert an auto-implemented property to a standard property, perform the following steps:

1. Declare a private backing field.

2. Implement code in setter assigning to a field and code in getter reading form field.

3. Add the necessary additional logic to the getter or setter code.

Before

```
class Client
{
    public int Zip
    {
        get;
        set;
```

```
        }
        //...
    }
```

After

```
class Client
{
    private int zip;

    public int Zip
    {
        get { return zip; }

        set {
            if (TaxGeographics.TaxableZips.Contains(zip)) {
                this.balanceCalcularor.addTaxation(zip);
            }
            zip = value;
        }
    }

    //...
}
```

Extension Methods

As already discussed in Chapter 10, C# is closed for override by default. For various reasons, this was a deliberate decision on the part of C#'s creators; but they probably realized that such a language feature might be too limiting for developers, so in C# 3.0 they opened another door for extension.

Extension methods enable you to redefine a type and add a method to a type without having to add code to the original file or recompile the type. Extension methods are a mechanism independent of subclassing, so you do not have to inherit a class in order to add a new method to it. Next, you will see how this works in practice.

> **Definition: Extension methods are static methods that you can invoke using the instance method syntax.**

Simple Extension Method Example

You are working with some textual data and you need to tokenize some strings based on a delimiter. You take a look at the System.String class and determine that a Split method with its override forms provides enough basic functionality in your case. As it happens, you also need to return delimiters, such as in a resulting array of generated tokens.

One way to go about it is to implement a static method in a new class called StringExtension. The code for this class and for a simple form that is used to invoke the SplitReturningDelimiter method is shown in Listing 13-1.

Listing 13-1: Using Static Methods to Implement New String Functionality

```
public partial class TestStringExtension : Form
{
    public TestStringExtension()
    {
        InitializeComponent();
    }

    private void button1_Click(object sender, EventArgs e)
    {
        String[] result = StringExtension.SplitReturningDelimiter(
            "123a456a789", new[] { 'a' });
        foreach (String token in result)
        {
            Console.WriteLine(token);
        }
    }
}

public static class StringExtension
{
    public static String[] SplitReturningDelimiter(String str,
        char[] delimiter)
    {
        String[] split = str.Split(delimiter,
            StringSplitOptions.None);
        String delimiterString = new String(delimiter);
        int position = 0;
        String[] result = new String[(2 * split.Length) - 1];

        foreach (String token in split)
        {
            result[position] = token;
            position++;
            if (position < result.Length - 1)
            {
                result[position] = delimiterString;
                position++;
            }
        }
        if (str.StartsWith(delimiterString))
        {
            String[] whenStartsWithDelimiter = new String[
                result.Length - 1];
            Array.ConstrainedCopy(result, 1,
                whenStartsWithDelimiter, 0, result.Length - 1);
            result = whenStartsWithDelimiter;

        }
        if (str.EndsWith(delimiterString))
        {
            String[] whenEndsWithDelimiter = new String[
```

```
                result.Length - 1];
            Array.ConstrainedCopy(result, 0,
                whenEndsWithDelimiter, 0, result.Length - 1);
            result = whenEndsWithDelimiter;

        }
        return result;

    }
}
```

Turning the static method `SplitReturningDelimiter` into an extension method is not that complicated. All you need to do is add the keyword `this` to the `str` parameter declaration before the type,
as shown here:

```
public static String[] SplitReturningDelimiter(this String str,
    char[] delimiter)
```

Now you can invoke the extension method using more natural instance method syntax. You will also get
IntelliSense help for this method. The code with the `SplitReturningDelimiter` static method converted
into an extension method is shown in Listing 13-2.

Listing 13-2: SplitReturningDelimiter Extension Method

```
public partial class TestStringExtension : Form
{
    public TestStringExtension()
    {
        InitializeComponent();
    }

    private void button1_Click(object sender, EventArgs e)
    {
        foreach (String token in "123a456a789".
            SplitReturningDelimiter(new[] { 'a' }))
        {
            Console.WriteLine(token);
        }
    }
}

public static class StringExtension
{
    public static String[] SplitReturningDelimiter(this String str,
        char[] delimiter)
    {
        String[] split = str.Split(delimiter,
            StringSplitOptions.None);
        String delimiterString = new String(delimiter);
        int position = 0;
        String[] result = new String[(2 * split.Length) - 1];
```

Continued

Listing 13-2: SplitReturningDelimiter Extension Method *(continued)*

```
            foreach (String token in split)
            {
                result[position] = token;
                position++;
                if (position < result.Length - 1)
                {
                    result[position] = delimiterString;
                    position++;
                }
            }
            if (str.StartsWith(delimiterString))
            {
                String[] whenStartsWithDelimiter = new String[
                    result.Length - 1];
                Array.ConstrainedCopy(result, 1,
                    whenStartsWithDelimiter, 0, result.Length - 1);
                result = whenStartsWithDelimiter;

            }
            if (str.EndsWith(delimiterString))
            {
                String[] whenEndsWithDelimiter = new String[
                    result.Length - 1];
                Array.ConstrainedCopy(result, 0,
                    whenEndsWithDelimiter, 0, result.Length - 1);
                result = whenEndsWithDelimiter;

            }
            return result;

        }
    }
```

Extension methods are especially useful when you don't have access to the source code of the type you wish to extend. Another situation in which you might find extension methods useful is for adding functionality to existing interfaces without breaking the binary compatibility when shipping the new version.

You can apply extension methods to interfaces as well as classes. If you define an extension method for an interface, this method will be available on any object whose class is implementing the interface in question.

Beware of excessive use of extension methods. Overuse of extension methods results in decentralized code that is harder to read and understand. When programming in C#, you are used to seeing all members of a type in the same file where the type is created, or somewhere along the type's inheritance hierarchy. After using extension methods, this is not the case anymore. This effect is propagated to the debugging process, causing types to appear with members you do not originally expect them to have. Member name collisions between type method and extension method are resolved such that an instance method hides an extension method. For this, you do not get any compiler warning. Therefore, while extension methods are useful, they are generally the option of last resort.

Replacing Extension Wrapper with Extension Method

In previous versions of C#, if you wanted to add behavior to a sealed class whose source code you did not have at your disposal, the only option available to you besides a simple static method was to create an extension wrapper class. Such a class delegates all work to the instance of the class it is extending, and implements only new functionality. If an interface is available in the wrapped class hierarchy, the wrapper can implement this interface to permit polymorphic substitution.

For example, in the previous chapter I covered enhancing Microsoft SQL Server data provider functionality and using an abstract factory to instantiate a family of classes that implement these new features. How could you go about implementing enhanced Microsoft SQL provider classes?

First, because you are only enhancing existing functionality and not implementing an entirely new provider family, you will want to reuse as much functionality already available in the data provider as possible. Second, because there are common interfaces in the System.Data namespace for all data provider implementations, you will make your classes implement appropriate interfaces.

Suppose you want to add some utility methods to the SqlConnection class that you use when performing integration tests:

❑ The DeleteAllData utility method deletes all data from the database.

❑ The RestoreDatabalseData utility method restores all data from a backup file.

❑ The DatabaseTime method returns the time as measured by the database engine.

Listing 13-3 shows the extension wrapper for the System.Data.SqlClient.SqlConnection class.

Listing 13-3: Enhanced SqlConnection

```
class EnhancedSqlConnection : IDbConnection
{
    private SqlConnection wrapped;

    public EnhancedSqlConnection() {
        this.wrapped = new SqlConnection();
    }

    public void DeleteAllData()
    {
        //... implementation
    }

    public DateTime DatabaseTime()
    {
        //... implementation
    }

    public void RestoreDatabalseData(String backupFileName)
    {
        //... implementation
    }
```

Continued

Listing 13-3: Enhanced SqlConnection *(continued)*

```
public void Open() {
    wrapped.Open();
}


// myriad of delegating members similar to method Open
}
```

The biggest problem with this solution is the huge amount of delegation code you have to write. In this case, I have shown only a single delegating method implementation, a method Open, but in a real-world scenario you would have to write similar delegating code for the rest of the members defined in the IDbConnection interface.

In another, even more complex, scenario, suppose you need to make available all methods of the SqlConnection class. In this case, the number of delegation methods has increased. In such cases, it makes sense to use extension methods instead of wrapper classes. By choosing extension methods, you can avoid writing a huge amount of the code. Take a look at the Replace Extension Wrapper with Extension Method refactoring definition for the version of enhanced SqlConnection shown in Listing 13-3, implemented using the extension method syntax.

Refactoring: Replace Extension Wrapper with Extension Method

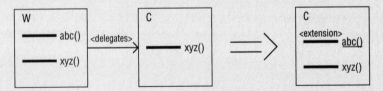

Motivation
Prior to version 3.0 of C#, writing extension wrappers was the only solution for extending the behavior of sealed classes. With extension methods in C# 3.0, you can eliminate the unnecessary delegation code and obtain the same result: added behavior to sealed classes.

Related Smells
Use this refactoring to eliminate the Superfluous Code and Duplicated Code smells.

Mechanics
In order to convert an extension wrapper class to extension methods, perform the following steps:

1. Declare new extension methods for a wrapped class that is the same as the additional method that the wrapper class provides.

2. Copy the implementation of a method from a wrapper to the newly created extension method.

3. Make a wrapper delegate call to the extension method, as shown in the following example:

```
public class EnhancedSqlConnection
{
    //...
    public void DeleteAllData()
    {
        wrapped.DeleteAllData();
    }
}
public static class EnhancedSqlConnectionExtension {

    public static void DeleteAllData(
        this SqlConnection connection)
    {
        //... implementation
    }
}
```

4. Test the method.

5. Repeat Steps 1 to 4 for all nondelegating methods in the wrapper class.

6. When the wrapper contains delegation methods only, eliminate the wrapper and make the client classes use the original type with the extension methods defined for it.

Before

```
public class EnhancedSqlConnection : IDbConnection
{
    private SqlConnection wrapped;

    public EnhancedSqlConnection() {
        this.wrapped = new SqlConnection();
    }
    public void DeleteAllData()
    {
        //... implementation
    }

    public DateTime DatabaseTime()
    {
        //... implementation
    }

    public void RestoreDatabalseData(String backupFileName)
    {
        //... implementation
    }
```

Continued

```
        public void Open() {
            wrapped.Open();
        }

        // myriad of delegating members similar to method Open
    }
```

After

```
    public static class EnhancedSqlConnectionExtension {

        public static void DeleteAllData(
            this SqlConnection connection)
        {
            //... implementation
        }

        public static DateTime DatabaseTime(
            this SqlConnection connection)
        {
            return DateTime.Now;
            //... implementation
        }

        public static void RestoreDatabalseData(
            this SqlConnection connection, String backupFileName)
        {
            //... implementation
        }
    }
```

Soon, you will see that extension methods play an important role in LINQ implementations. Before that, however, let's look at another C# 3.0 enhancement: new initializer syntax.

Object, Array, and Collection Initializers

As an object-oriented programmer, you often create and initialize objects. Those two steps often follow one another, so it makes sense to provide the language with a feature that enables you to perform these two operations in one go.

While you can often obtain a similar effect using parameterized constructors, you don't always have access to code of the type you wish to initialize, nor do you bother to write it.

Take a class Client for example:

```
class Client
{
    public String FirstName
    {
        get;
        set;
    }
```

```
    public String LastName
    {
        get;
        set;
    }

    public String Email
    {
        get;
        set;
    }
}
```

Normally, you would have to write a few lines in order to instantiate it and set values to fields:

```
Client client = new Client();
client.FirstName = "Neil";
client.LastName = "Young";
client.Email = "neil.young@rust.org"
```

In C# 3.0, you have much terser syntax at your disposal:

```
Client client = new Client
{
    FirstName = "Neil",
    LastName = "Young",
    Email = "neil.young@rust.org"
};
```

You can initialize arrays and collections in the same way. You can also combine constructor calls with this syntax, which makes this new feature especially useful for initializing larger object graphs on-the-fly, as shown here:

```
List<Client> clients = new List<Client>{
    new Client
    {
        FirstName = "Neil",
        LastName = "Young",
        Email = "neil.young@rust.org",
        Address = new Address {
            StreetAndNumber = "Harvest Street 32",
            City = "Cleveland",
            State = "Ohio", Zip = "87114"}
    },
    new Client
    {
        FirstName = "Bernard",
        LastName = "Shakey",
        Email = "bernard.shakey@ontario.org",
        Address = new Address {
            StreetAndNumber = "Cinnamon Street 32",
            City = "Buffalo",
            State = "New York", Zip = "14213"}
    }
};
```

Querying Objects with LINQ

LINQ stands for Language Integrated Query. LINQ adds native querying capabilities to C# through syntax similar to SQL. With LINQ, you can enumerate, filter, and create projections on a number of collection types, arrays, XML objects, database sources, and other objects.

Take a look at some of the benefits that LINQ brings to the C# programming language:

❑   **Querying syntax is now native to C#:** This effectively means that a number of new keywords are added to the language. Instead of complex C# code often based on iterating objects, now you can write a single query statement to locate the object you're searching for.

❑   **Universal query syntax:** Regardless of the object of your query, the query syntax is always the same. You can query a collection or an array, an XML document or a SQL database, and the code you write will always be the same. This approach is inspired by the Microsoft vision of unified data access, and should simplify the way C# programmers view data.

❑   **Full IDE support:** Now that LINQ is an integral part of the C# language, you can count on the same IDE support that your normal C# code has, with features such as syntax checking and IntelliSense working with LINQ queries as well. Remember writing embedded SQL statements inside C# code as strings and copying them over to the SQL debugger in order to test them? No more of that. This should significantly boost your productivity.

❑   **Object-relational mapping:** LINQ paves the way for implementing an object-relational mapping layer in .NET in a manner that is tightly coupled with the language itself.

Before going any further, take a look at a simple LINQ query example, so you have a better idea of how it works. Listing 13-4 shows LINQ in action.

Listing 13-4: Basic LINQ Query Example

```
using System;
using System.Linq;

namespace Linq
{
    class Author
    {
        public string FirstName;
        public string LastName;
        public Book[] Books;
    }

    class Book
    {
        public string Name;
    }


    class Program
    {
        static void Main(string[] args)
        {
            Author[] authors = {
```

```
            new Author { FirstName = "Leo" ,
                LastName = "Tolstoy",
                Books = new Book[]{
                    new Book{Name = "War and Peace"},
                    new Book{Name = "Anna Karenina"},
                    new Book{Name = "Resurrection"}
                }
            },
            new Author { FirstName = "Homer" ,
                LastName = "",
                Books = new Book[]{
                    new Book{Name = "The Iliad"},
                    new Book{Name = "Odyssey"}
                }
            },
            new Author { FirstName = "Miguel" ,
                LastName = "Cervantes",
                Books = new Book[]{
                    new Book{Name = "Don Quixote"}
                }
            }
        };

        var prolificAuthor = (
                from author in authors
                orderby author.Books.Count() descending
                select author
                ).First();

        Console.WriteLine("Author with most books: " +
            prolificAuthor.FirstName + " " +
            prolificAuthor.LastName);

        Console.ReadKey();
    }
  }
}
```

This example has two classes: Author and Book. Each Author has been assigned an array of Book. In the subroutine Main, I first created and initialized an array of authors in order to have some data to query. I used the new array initializer syntax to create a ready-to-use array of Author objects. Finally, I queried the array by first ordering descending authors by their number of books and then selecting the first author from the ordered list by means of the operator First. This way, I'm able to find the author with the most books among authors in the array.

Writing this query with LINQ was rather simple. Accomplishing the same prior to C# version 3.0 without using LINQ means iterating over elements in the array and then finding the one with the biggest book count. Several implementation details would have to be resolved. It would definitely be more verbose than the simple LINQ query. As queries become more complex, the power of LINQ becomes more evident.

LINQ is a world unto itself; numerous aggregate, grouping, restriction, partitioning, and other operators add to the expressiveness of the LINQ language. Still, LINQ can preserve the feel of SQL so that you are able to write your first LINQ queries fairly quickly. Start by writing simple queries and work your way up to more advanced LINQ features and soon you will appreciate the power of LINQ data query capabilities.

Refactoring: Replace Complex Imperative C# Query Code with LINQ

Motivation

LINQ adds powerful data querying capabilities to the C# language. The expressiveness of LINQ means that complex imperative C# query code can be replaced with compact, easy-to-understand LINQ syntax.

Related Smells

Use this refactoring to replace complex query code with the more expressive LINQ syntax.

Mechanics

If the query code is long and complex and inside a very long method, start by extracting the query code to a separate method. This way, you separate query code completely from the rest of the code in the method, and you can crystallize the intention behind the query. It is important to project the desired result of the query, because expressing it through LINQ will probably be easier than understanding the underpinnings of C# code used for the same purpose.

Before

```
decimal sum = 0;
foreach (Author author in authors)
{
    sum += author.Books.Count();
}
decimal averageBookCount = sum / authors.Count();
```

After

```
var averageBookCount =(
        from author in authors
        select author.Books.Count()).Average();
```

LINQ introduces another level of indirection to your code. For example, the query in Listing 13-4 results in ordering the `authors` collection, by means of the `orderby` command. Ordering a collection is an operation computationally more costly than simple collection traversal, an algorithm you would use to find most prolific author using traditional imperative C# code. That is why it is a good idea to understand what is going on underneath the LINQ. One tool that can help you visualize SQL code generated by a LINQ-to-SQL implementation of LINQ is the LINQ Query Visualizer. See the article "LINQ Query Visualizer Sample" at MSDN (`http://msdn.microsoft.com/en-us/library/bb629285.aspx`) for instructions on installing the LINQ Query Visualizer and integrating it with Visual Studio.

Now that you have a fairly good understanding of various features that the new version of C# provides, such as LINQ and extension methods, the following sections presents an example that brings all these features together.

Old Example in New Robes

The Calories Calculator example from Chapter 2, written in C# 2.0, has many elements of C# syntax that can be upgraded by the refactorings discussed in this chapter. I decided, however, to take another look at the application as a whole.

Patient History Display

The first thing I decided to change about Calories Calculator was the way it displays patient history data. Instead of using (rather unprofessionally, I might add) Internet Explorer to display an XML document with patient history data, I added a simple form with a `DataGridView` control to fulfill the same purpose. You can take a look at the Patient History form in Figure 13-2.

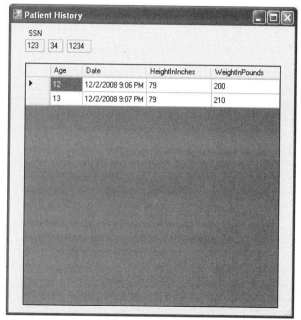

Figure 13-2

At the same time, I decided to change the data type used for measurements and calculation results from `double` to `decimal`. This way, I can round the results before displaying them on the form and avoid displaying a huge number of irrelevant decimal places in calculation results controls.

I know that it won't be difficult to make `DataGridView` display the patient data once I bind the grid to some object, but to what object should I bind the grid? Maybe I could use the XML node with the patient's measurements. Looking at the code, this looks neither straightforward nor logical.

Extracting Measurement struct

Once I drew the form, it became apparent that each patient registers a number of different measurements in time. This led me to the realization that attributes such as Height, Weight, and Age; and results of calculations such as Ideal Weight, Recommended Daily Calories Amount, and Distance from Ideal

Weight represent a snapshot of patient data at one point in time. I can use a simple structure, a struct, to represent this data. Each Patient class will contain a list of measurements.

I will add one method to a patient class called TakeSnapshot. Taking a snapshot will create a new measurement and add the measurement to the list of measurements belonging to that patient. This way, a patient object with a Measurements property will contain all the historic data for that patient.

The code for the newly created and modified domain classes is shown in Listing 13-5.

Listing 13-5: Evolved Domain Classes in the Calories Calculator Application

```
[Serializable]
public struct Measurement
{
    public Measurement(decimal heightInInches, decimal weightInPounds,
        int age, decimal dailyCaloriesRecommended, decimal idealBodyWeight,
        decimal distanceFromIdealWeight) : this()
    {
        HeightInInches = heightInInches;
        WeightInPounds = weightInPounds;
        Age = age;
        Date = DateTime.Now;
        DailyCaloriesRecommended = dailyCaloriesRecommended;
        IdealBodyWeight = idealBodyWeight;
        DistanceFromIdealWeight = distanceFromIdealWeight;
    }

    public int Age
    {
        get;
        set;
    }

    public DateTime Date
    {
        get;
        set;
    }

    public decimal HeightInInches
    {
        get;
        set;
    }

    public decimal WeightInPounds
    {
        get;
        set;
    }

    public  decimal DailyCaloriesRecommended{
        get;
```

```
            set;
        }

    public decimal IdealBodyWeight{
        get;
        set;
    }

    public decimal DistanceFromIdealWeight
    {
        get;
        set;
    }

    public override bool Equals(object obj)
    {
        if (obj == null)
        {
            return false;
        }

        if (!(obj is Measurement))
        {
            return false;
        }

        return (((Measurement)obj).Date == this.Date);

    }

    public override int GetHashCode()
    {
        return Convert.ToInt32(
            this.Date.Day.ToString() +
            this.Date.Month.ToString() +
            this.Date.Year.ToString().Substring(2) +
            this.Date.Millisecond.ToString());
    }
}


[Serializable]
public abstract class Patient
{
    protected List<Measurement> measurements =
        new List<Measurement>();

    public string SSN
    {
        get;
        set;
    }
```

Continued

Listing 13-5: Evolved Domain Classes in the Calories Calculator Application
(continued)

```csharp
    public string FirstName
    {
        get;
        set;
    }

    public string LastName
    {
        get;
        set;
    }

    public int Age
    {
        get;
        set;
    }

    public DateTime Date
    {
        get;
        set;
    }

    public decimal HeightInInches
    {
        get;
        set;
    }

    public decimal WeightInPounds
    {
        get;
        set;
    }

    public IEnumerable<Measurement> Measurements
    {
        get {
            return measurements;
        }
        protected set {
            measurements = (List<Measurement>)value;
        }
    }

    public abstract decimal DailyCaloriesRecommended();

    public abstract decimal IdealBodyWeight();

    public decimal DistanceFromIdealWeight()
```

```
        {
            return WeightInPounds - IdealBodyWeight();
        }


        public void TakeSnapshot()
        {
            Measurement measurement = new Measurement(
                    HeightInInches, WeightInPounds, Age,
                    DailyCaloriesRecommended(), IdealBodyWeight(),
                    DistanceFromIdealWeight());
            measurements.Add(measurement);
        }


        public override bool Equals(object obj)
        {
            if (obj == null)
            {
                return false;
            }

            if (!(obj is Patient))
            {
                return false;
            }

            return (((Patient)obj).SSN == this.SSN);
        }

        public override int GetHashCode()
        {
            return Convert.ToInt32(SSN);
        }
    }


[Serializable]
public class FemalePatient : Patient
{
    public override decimal DailyCaloriesRecommended()
    {
        return Decimal.Round(655m + (4.3m * WeightInPounds)
            + (4.7m * HeightInInches) - (4.7m * Age), 2);
    }

    public override decimal IdealBodyWeight()
    {
        return Decimal.Round(
            (45.5m + (2.3m * (HeightInInches - 60m))) * 2.2046m
            , 2);
    }
}


[Serializable]
```

Continued

Listing 13-5: Evolved Domain Classes in the Calories Calculator Application
(continued)

```
class MalePatient : Patient
{

    public override decimal DailyCaloriesRecommended()
    {
        return Decimal.Round(66m + (6.3m * WeightInPounds)
            + (12.9m * HeightInInches) - (6.8m * Age),2);
    }

    public override decimal IdealBodyWeight()
    {
        return Decimal.Round(
            (50m + (2.3m * (HeightInInches - 60m))) * 2.2046m
            , 2);
    }
}
```

It seems that this way, a patient's complete history is represented with a newly created object graph. This is a welcome effect of recently induced changes and will have an important repercussion on the way persistence code is implemented.

Using .NET Serialization for a Persistence Mechanism

If you look at the original PatientHistoryXmlStorage class, you will see that most of the code in it deals with creating an XML structure representing a patient's personal data and history so that this data can be restored and saved on the disk.

> **Definition: Serialization is the process of converting an object graph into a sequence of bytes so that it can be stored on a medium or transmitted across a network connection.**

Now that I am using an object structure to represent a patient's complete history, it becomes obvious that a serialization mechanism provided by the .NET Framework can be used for the purpose of persisting a patient's personal data and measurement history. Consider the PatientHistoryStorage class code that is making use of BinaryFormatter class functionality to convert the patient object graph to a stream that can be saved to disk. You can see the code for the persistence feature based on standard .NET object serialization in Listing 13-6.

Listing 13-6: Persistence Implemented Using .NET's Built-in Serialization Mechanism

```
using System;
using System.Collections.Generic;
using System.IO;
using System.Linq;
using System.Reflection;
```

```
using System.Runtime.Serialization;
using System.Runtime.Serialization.Formatters.Binary;
using System.Xml.Serialization;

namespace CaloriesCalculator
{
    class PatientHistoryStorage
    {
        private List<Patient> patients;

        public static string PatientsHistoryFileLocation
        {
            get
            {
                return Assembly.
                    GetExecutingAssembly().Location.Replace(
                    "CaloriesCalculator.exe", "PatientsHistory.bin");
            }
            private set { }
        }

        public PatientHistoryStorage()
        {
            try
            {
                LoadPatientsHistoryFile();
            }
            catch (FileNotFoundException)
            {
                patients = new List<Patient>();
            }
        }

        public void Save(Patient patient)
        {
            if (PatientIsNew(patient))
            {
                patients.Add(patient);
            }
            SaveHistory();
        }

        private bool PatientIsNew(Patient patient)
        {
            return patients.IndexOf(patient) < 0;
        }

        private void SaveHistory()
        {
            using (Stream stream = new FileStream(
                PatientsHistoryFileLocation,
                FileMode.Create, FileAccess.Write,
                FileShare.Write))
```

Continued

Listing 13-6: Persistence Implemented Using .NET's Built-in Serialization Mechanism *(continued)*

```
        {
            IFormatter formatter = new BinaryFormatter();
            formatter.Serialize(stream, patients);
            stream.Close();
        }
    }

    private void LoadPatientsHistoryFile()
    {
        using (Stream stream = new FileStream(
            PatientsHistoryFileLocation,
                FileMode.Open, FileAccess.Read,
                FileShare.Read))
        {
            IFormatter formatter = new BinaryFormatter();
            patients = (List<Patient>)
                formatter.Deserialize(stream);
            stream.Close();
        }
    }

    public Patient FindPatient(String ssn)
    {
        var found = from patient in this.patients
                    where patient.SSN == ssn
                    select patient;
        return found.FirstOrDefault();
    }
}
```

You can see that in the latest version of the Calories Calculator, many C# 2.0 and C# 3.0 features are used. For example, collections are now generic, properties are written using auto-implemented syntax, and LINQ is used to query a list of patients for a specific patient based on the patient's social security number.

LINQ has many different applications. One such application is to use LINQ for interacting with standard relational databases. The next section explores how LINQ can be used in object-relational mapping in .NET.

Object-Relational Mapping with LINQ to SQL

LINQ to SQL is Microsoft's first attempt at object-relational mapping (ORM). ORM frameworks resolve issues related to relational persistence for your Plain Old CLR Objects (POCOs) and are aimed at minimizing or eliminating the effects of object-relational impedance mismatch. (Object-relational impedance mismatch is discussed in Chapter 9).

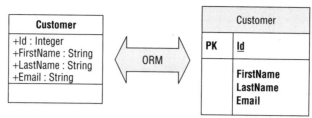

Figure 13-3

Simply put, when using an ORM framework, all you need to do is declare, in a file or through other types of metadata such as .NET attributes, how your classes are mapped to tables in the database; and then you let ORM do its magic, as depicted in Figure 13-3. ORM frameworks resolve the mismatch as follows:

❏ They are capable of generating SQL statements themselves, thus eliminating the need for programming the SQL code manually.

❏ They are capable of generating data store schemas, relieving programmers to some extent from the task of creating data store structures.

❏ They know how to interact with a data store and how to map results of queries to POCOs and back, removing any data store–related code from the view of the programmer.

❏ Some ORM frameworks know how to generate .NET classes based on the data store schema. This feature can be useful as a starting point when creating applications that use already existing data stores.

❏ Because mappings are generally declared (not programmed) in mapping files or applied in the form of mapping attributes, objects are isolated from structural changes in the data store. When the data store structure changes, it is often enough to modify the mapping, not the code of the mapped class, in order to keep the application working.

❏ Because ORM frameworks know how to generate SQL for each specific data store they support, changing from one data store product to another can be as easy as changing the ORM configuration data. This way, your code is not married to a specific data store product, successfully eliminating database vendor lock-in.

ORM frameworks are not without their share of problems, which are first and foremost related to performance issues, as many ORM skeptics will tell you. In my experience, as is generally the case where performance issues are concerned, these problems are overstated. In order to get the most from your ORM framework, you might need to tweak the mappings, generate a data store schema, and experiment with lazy loading and cache strategies.

For some expensive queries that need to retrieve and work upon huge quantities of data, you'd be better off writing your own SQL and executing it directly against the database. Most of ORM frameworks provide a back door for direct communication with your database.

LINQ to SQL at a Glance

With LINQ, Microsoft has greatly improved traditional object-relational mapping. LINQ integrates data querying and makes it an integral part of the C# (and VB.NET) programming language. Querying a database is now achieved through the same syntax you would use when querying arrays or other "queryable" objects. The syntax is part of the .NET programming language, so there is no need to learn SQL or a SQL dialect specific to a certain database in order to communicate with any database supported by LINQ to SQL. This also means that LINQ queries can count on the full support of a compiler, and IDE-like syntax checking, coloring, and IntelliSense.

> *Currently, only Microsoft SQL Server can be used with a LINQ-to-SQL database out of the box; and as Microsoft's focus shifts toward the Entity Framework, it is less likely that support for other databases will be forthcoming with the .NET Framework. Third-party provider libraries for other database engines such as Oracle and MySQL have started to appear. LINQ to SQL still represents a good example of lightweight ORM, and thanks to its POCO nature it can be supplanted by third-party ORM products.*

DataContext Class

The base class in LINQ to SQL is `DataContext`, found in the `System.Data.Linq` namespace. The `DataContext` instance functions use an underlying `Connection` object. You can instantiate `DataContext` by supplying a connection string or `IDbConnection` instance to a `DataContext` constructor. In addition to methods typical of any connection object such as `ExecuteQuery` or `ExecuteCommand`, `DataContext` boasts the `CreateDatabase` and `DeleteDatabase` methods that can be used for database schema creation and disposal, respectively.

> **Definition: The class that is being mapped to a table or tables in a database is referred to by the term *entity class*.**

The `DataContext` class contains a crucial `SubmitChanges` method that commits all changes made on entity classes to the database, synchronizing the two worlds.

Table Class

By calling a generic version of the `GetTable` method of `DataContext`, you obtain an instance of the `System.Data.Linq.Table` class, a central class for querying the database. This class is generic, and when using it you should parameterize it with the entity class you wish to map to the database. The `Table` class implements a `System.Linq.IQueryable` interface, meaning that you can write LINQ queries against this class.

System.Data.Linq.Mapping Namespace Attribute Classes

The world of relational data is represented through the `DataContext` and `Table` classes. The world of .NET entities is represented by domain classes, so you need some way to relate the two worlds. You need to tell the LINQ-to-SQL framework which property of which class maps to which column of which table in the database. The mapping information can be passed through to LINQ to SQL by the following means:

❑ **Mapping configuration file:** These files have a .dbml extension and are written in XML format. Here is a sample excerpt:

```
<Database Name="northwnd" Class="Northwnd"
xmlns="http://schemas.microsoft.com/dsltools/DLinqML">
```

```
<Table Name="Customers">
    <Type Name="Customer">
        <Column Name="CustomerID" Type="System.String"
        DbType="NChar(5) NOT NULL" IsPrimaryKey="True" CanBeNull="False" />
        <!-- ... -->
```

❑ **Attribute-based mapping:** This style of mapping is achieved by applying attribute metadata over entity classes, as shown in the following example:

```
[Table()]
class Customer
{
    private EntityRef<Address> address;

    [Column(IsPrimaryKey=true, IsDbGenerated=false)]
    public String SSN
    {
        get;
        set;
    }
//...
}
```

Using attributes means that you will have less configuration files to worry about, and it might simplify your development. Conversely, it means that any change in mapping results in recompilation of your application.

Refactoring: Replace Programmatic Data Layer with LINQ to SQL

Motivation

LINQ to SQL abstracts you from programming in database-specific language and makes your code database-neutral. You can keep your objects POCOs, without loading them with persistence-specific code. You can switch the underlying database with minimum effort, and often change the way entity classes are mapped to the database schema without any intervention in C# code.

Related Smells

Use this refactoring to simplify the persistence layer.

Mechanics

If you already have a well-defined, strongly typed data access layer, this refactoring should be fairly simple to perform:

1. Start by extracting interfaces for the data access layer classes and make your new LINQ-to-SQL data access classes implement these interfaces.

2. Once you have the new layer ready, inject the new LINQ-to-SQL data access classes instead of the traditional data access classes that communicate directly with the database.

Continued

Before

```
public class BranchData : AbstractData<Branch>
{
    //...
    private const string updateBranchSql =

        "Update Branch  Set BranchName = @Name Where BranchId = @Id";
    private const string idParameterName = "@Id";
    private const string nameParameterName = "@Name";

    public override void Update(Branch branch)
    {
        IDbCommand command = new SqlCommand();
        AddParameter(command, nameParameterName,
            DbType.String, branch.Name);
        AddParameter(command, idParameterName,
            DbType.Int32, branch.Id);
        ExecuteNonQuery(command, updateBranchSql);
    }
    //...
}
```

After

```
public class LinqData<Persisted> :
    AbstractData<Persisted>,
    IData<Persisted> where Persisted : class
{
    public DataContext Context
    {
        get
        {
            return context;
        }
        set
        {
            context = value;
            entities = Context.GetTable<Persisted>();
        }
    }
    public void Update(Persisted persisted)
    {
        Context.SubmitChanges();
    }
}
```

LINQ and the Rent-a-Wheels Application

I have managed to separate the data layer in the Rent-a-Wheels application and abstract the rest of the application from relational persistence code. However, the current implementation is far from being on the industrial level. Indeed, implementing a successful object-relational layer is not a simple feat. While the data layer will perform satisfactorily in a single-user environment, this is not the case if the assembly is placed server-side.

When placed in a highly demanding server environment with a lot of concurrent access, concurrency-related problems would certainly start to appear. Here are some problems the current version of the data persistence layer fails to address:

- ❑ **Object identity:** There is no relationship between object and database identity. At any given moment, a number of different objects in application memory can have the same database ID. This means that if one object has been changed in one place in memory, other objects with the same database ID somewhere else in memory will not be affected, and end up holding obsolete data.

- ❑ **Phantom updates and optimistic locking:** I have adopted an optimistic locking schema in the application, but there is no verification that the underlying data was not changed (by some other user, for example) from the moment it was read when committing updates.

- ❑ **Rudimentary query capabilities:** Data classes provide a few query methods that are not capable of expressing more complex query logic. As a consequence, each time a new query is necessary, the only solution is to implement a new ad hoc SQL statement.

- ❑ **Performance-related issues:** Lazy-loading, caching, and so on are typical performance features that quality ORM frameworks provide. The data layer in the Rent-a-Wheels application does not address any of these issues.

The next part of this section shows you a new data persistence layer implementation based on LINQ to SQL. However, you will not eliminate the existing layer. Because LINQ to SQL does not support any database other than Microsoft SQL out-of-the-box, you still might have a use for it.

Extracting Persistence Layer Interfaces and Restructuring the Class Hierarchy

Start by extracting common interfaces for `BranchData`, `ModelData`, `VehicleData`, and `CategoryData`. It is possible to extract a single common interface for all Data classes if a generic type is used. First, move extracted interfaces to a separate file and then to an assembly `RentAWheels.Data`.

Make your new LINQ-to-SQL persistence class implement this interface. You can call this class `LinqData`. In order to use the new LINQ data layer, and because old Data classes and the new `LinqData` implement the same interface, it is adequate to replace `BranchData`, `VehicleData`, and so on, with parameterized `LinqData<Branch>`, `LinqData<Vehicle>`, and so on, in a single place in the `Program` class. Take a look at the extracted interface shown in Listing 13-7.

Listing 13-7: IData Interface Is Implemented By All Data Classes

```
namespace RentAWheel.Data
{
    public interface IData<Persisted>
    {
        void Delete(Persisted persisted);
        IList<Persisted> GetAll();
        void Insert(Persisted persisted);
```

Continued

Listing 13-7: IData Interface Is Implemented By All Data Classes *(continued)*

```
            void Update(Persisted persisted);
    }
}
```

The IData interface now replaces the existing BranchData class and will also be implemented by the new LinqData based on LINQ-to-SQL technology. Listing 13-8 shows the original BranchData now that the IBranchData interface has been extracted.

Listing 13-8: BranchData after IData Interface Extraction

```csharp
using System;
using System.Collections.Generic;
using System.Configuration;
using System.Data;
using System.Data.SqlClient;
using RentAWheel.Business;

namespace RentAWheel.Data.Implementation
{
    public class BranchData : AbstractAdoData<Branch>, IData<Branch>
    {
        public BranchData(ConnectionStringSettings settings)
            : base(settings)
        {

        }

        private const string branchTableIdColumnName = "BranchId";
        private const string branchTableNameColumnName = "BranchName";

        private const string selectAllFromBranchSql =
            "Select BranchId as BranchId, Branch.Name as BranchName from Branch";
        private const string deleteBranchSql =
            "Delete Branch Where BranchId = @Id";
        private const string insertBranchSql =
            "Insert Into Branch (Name) Values(@Name)";
        private const string updateBranchSql =
            "Update Branch  Set Name = @Name Where BranchId = @Id";

        private const string idParameterName = "@Id";
        private const string nameParameterName = "@Name";

        private const int singleTableInDatasetIndex = 0;

        public override IList<Branch> GetAll()
        {
            IList<Branch> branches = new List<Branch>();
            IDbCommand command = new SqlCommand();
            DataSet branchesSet =
                FillDataset(command, selectAllFromBranchSql);
            DataTable branchesTable =
                branchesSet.Tables[singleTableInDatasetIndex];
```

```
        foreach(DataRow row in branchesTable.Rows){
            branches.Add(BranchFromRow(row));
        }
        return branches;
    }

    public static Branch BranchFromRow(DataRow row)
    {
        return new Branch(
            Convert.ToInt32(row[branchTableIdColumnName]),
            Convert.ToString(row[branchTableNameColumnName]));
    }

    public override void Delete(Branch branch)
    {
        IDbCommand command = new SqlCommand();
        AddParameter(command, idParameterName,
            DbType.Int32, branch.Id);
        ExecuteNonQuery(command, deleteBranchSql);
    }

    public override void Update(Branch branch)
    {
        IDbCommand command = new SqlCommand();
        AddParameter(command, nameParameterName,
            DbType.String, branch.Name);
        AddParameter(command, idParameterName,
            DbType.Int32, branch.Id);
        ExecuteNonQuery(command, updateBranchSql);
    }

    public override void Insert(Branch branch)
    {
        IDbCommand command = new SqlCommand();
        AddParameter(command, nameParameterName,
            DbType.String, branch.Name);
        ExecuteNonQuery(command, insertBranchSql);
    }
    }
}
```

You can observe that this class inherits AbstractAdoData. It used to be AbstractData, but I had to reorganize the hierarchy a bit now that SQL to LINQ has to be implemented. To view what the top of the data class hierarchy now looks like, see Listings 13-9 through 13-11.

Listing 13-9: Root Data Class: AbstractData

```
using System.Configuration;

namespace RentAWheel.Data
{
    public abstract class AbstractData<Persisted>
```

Continued

Listing 13-9: Root Data Class: AbstractData *(continued)*

```
    {
        public AbstractData(ConnectionStringSettings settings)
        {
            ConnectionStringSettings = settings;
        }

        public virtual ConnectionStringSettings ConnectionStringSettings
        {
            get;
            private set;
        }

    }
}
```

`AbstractData` does not contain a lot of functionality, but this will be enough to have all data classes injected with configuration settings (connection string and data provider information) in the same way.

Listing 13-10: Root Data Class: AbstractAdoData

```
using System.Collections.Generic;
using System.Configuration;
using System.Data;
using System.Data.Common;

namespace RentAWheel.Data
{
    public abstract class AbstractAdoData<Persisted>
        :        AbstractData<Persisted>
    {
        private DbProviderFactory databaseProviderFactory;

        public AbstractAdoData(ConnectionStringSettings settings) :base(settings)
        {
            this.DatabaseProviderFactory =
                DbProviderFactories.GetFactory(
                ConnectionStringSettings.ProviderName);
        }

        protected DbProviderFactory DatabaseProviderFactory
        {
            get { return databaseProviderFactory; }
            set { databaseProviderFactory = value; }
        }

        private IDbConnection CreateConnection()
        {
            IDbConnection connection =
                DatabaseProviderFactory.CreateConnection();
            connection.ConnectionString =
                ConnectionStringSettings.ConnectionString;
```

```
        return connection;
    }

    private IDbConnection PrepareDataObjects(IDbCommand command, string sql)
    {
        IDbConnection connection = CreateConnection();
        connection.Open();
        command.Connection = connection;
        command.CommandText = sql;
        return connection;
    }

    protected void AddParameter(IDbCommand command, string parameterName,
    DbType parameterType, object paramaterValue)
    {
        IDbDataParameter parameter = command.CreateParameter();
        parameter.ParameterName = parameterName;
        parameter.DbType = parameterType;
        parameter.Value = paramaterValue;
        command.Parameters.Add(parameter);
    }

    protected DataSet FillDataset(IDbCommand command, string sql)
    {
        IDbConnection connection = PrepareDataObjects(command, sql);
        IDbDataAdapter adapter = DatabaseProviderFactory.CreateDataAdapter();
        DataSet branches = new DataSet();
        adapter.SelectCommand = command;
        adapter.Fill(branches);
        connection.Close();
        return branches;
    }

    protected void ExecuteNonQuery(IDbCommand command, string sql)
    {
        IDbConnection connection = PrepareDataObjects(command, sql);
        command.ExecuteNonQuery();
        connection.Close();
    }

    protected IDataReader ExecuteReader(out IDbConnection connection,
        string sql)
    {
        IDbCommand command =
            DatabaseProviderFactory.CreateCommand();
        connection = PrepareDataObjects(command, sql);
        return command.ExecuteReader();
    }

    public abstract IList<Persisted> GetAll();

    public abstract void Delete(Persisted persisted);
```

Continued

423

Listing 13-10: Root Data Class: AbstractAdoData *(continued)*

```
        public abstract void Update(Persisted persisted);

        public abstract void Insert(Persisted persisted);


    }
}
```

AbstractAdoData contains the code you are already familiar with from the previous chapters. The new
class is LinqData, shown in Listing 13-11.

Listing 13-11: LinqData, the Sole Class in the LINQ Data Layer

```
using System.Collections.Generic;
using System.Configuration;
using System.Data.Linq;
using System.Linq;

namespace RentAWheel.Data
{
    public class LinqData<Persisted> :
        AbstractData<Persisted>,
        IData<Persisted> where Persisted : class
    {

        private Table<Persisted> entities;

        private ConnectionStringSettings settings;

        private DataContext context;

        public LinqData(ConnectionStringSettings settings)
            : base(settings)
        {
            this.settings = settings;
        }

        public DataContext Context
        {
            get
            {
                return context;
            }
            set
            {
                context = value;
                entities = Context.GetTable<Persisted>();
            }
        }

        public void Delete(Persisted persisted)
```

```
        {
            entities.DeleteOnSubmit(persisted);
            Context.SubmitChanges();
        }

        public IList<Persisted> GetAll()
        {
            entities = Context.GetTable<Persisted>();
            var allPersistedes =
                    from queried in entities
                    select queried;
            return allPersistedes.ToList<Persisted>();
        }

        public void Insert(Persisted persisted)
        {
            entities.InsertOnSubmit(persisted);
            Context.SubmitChanges();
        }

        public void Update(Persisted persisted)
        {
            Context.SubmitChanges();
        }

        public IQueryable<Persisted> Queryable
        {
            get {
                return entities;
            }
        }
    }
}
```

The amazing thing about this class is that it is all that is needed to replace the whole data layer written in a traditional way. And because it implements the IData interface, the replacement can be performed seamlessly.

One interesting detail is the public read-only property Queryable. It permits writing LINQ queries against LinqData, resolving the problem of complex query logic. Note, however, that this property does not belong to the IData interface, because it cannot be supported by a standard version of Data classes. In order to use this property, the client has to downcast the IData instance from IData to LinqData.

Now you are ready to start with the LINQ to SQL entity classes implementation. Entity classes are actually our POCO business layer classes. They need a few adjustments in code before they can be used as LINQ to SQL entity classes. Because you will be using attributes to implement OR mappings, you need to apply mapping attributes to classes and properties.

Applying Attributes to Entity Classes

I decided to use attribute-based mapping for LINQ to SQL. This means that classes and property attributes have to be marked by appropriate TableAttribute and ColumnAttribute classes. The good thing about metadata (attributes) is that if you do not need them, they do not stand in the way. This means that the entity classes from the RentAWheel.Business namespace work with standard data classes even with attributes applied. The only side-effect is that your classes will have to import the System.Data.Linq.Mapping namespace, but it comes with the .NET Framework so this is not a problem.

Some additional tweaking must be performed on entity classes:

❑ **Adding a default constructor:** Entity classes mapped with LINQ to SQL have to possess a default (parameterless) constructor method.

❑ **Using EntityRef for a property in a one-to-one relationship:** LINQ is capable of resolving the relationship between classes, but in order to do that, the private property value has to be changed to the EntityRef<RelatedClass> type.

❑ **Adding to classes the property to represent the Id field of related classes:** For example, the Model class has a property of type Category.CategoryId that has to be added to the Model class.

❑ **Changing the database type of columns mapping to enums from tinyint to integer.** See the README.TXT file in the source code, available for download at www.wrox.com.

The Model class illustrates well the changes performed on the entity classes. You can see the Model class code in Listing 13-12.

Listing 13-12: Entity Class Example after LINQ to SQL Adoption

```
using System.Data.Linq;
using System.Data.Linq.Mapping;

namespace RentAWheel.Business
{
    [Table]
    public class Model
    {
        private EntityRef<Category> category;

        [Column()]
        public int CategoryId;

        public Model()
        {
            //required by Linq2Sql
        }

        public Model(int id, string name, Category category)
        {
            this.Id = id;
            this.Name = name;
            this.Category = category;
        }

        [Column(IsPrimaryKey = true, IsDbGenerated = true,
            Name = "ModelId")]
        public int Id
```

```
    {
        get;
        set;
    }

    [Column(Name = "ModelName")]
    public string Name
    {
        get;
        set;
    }

    [Association(Storage="category", ThisKey="CategoryId")]
    public Category Category
    {
        get { return category.Entity; }
        set { category.Entity = value; }
    }
    }
}
```

You can see in this class an example of the use of another attribute from the `System.Data.Linq.Mapping` namespace: the `Association` attribute. It is used to map the property that holds the value of another related mapped entity class.

This completes the illustration of the most important refactorings performed on the Rent-a-Wheels application that resulted in implementation of a new data layer based on LINQ to SQL.

Summary

The future holds great promise for C#. With features such as LINQ and extension methods, 2008 should be the most productive version of C# ever. Compared to previous versions, code written in C# 3.0 is more expressive, terse, and powerful. Many new applications of LINQ and new LINQ providers are to be expected.

If you are working with code written in a previous version of C#, such code cannot take advantage of these new C# 3.0 features. In those cases, you can retrofit the code with the new features, making it more compact and expressive.

When writing code that searches for any type of data in C#, you will most probably write code that iterates some structure and has a lot of complicated implementation details. Such code, written in imperative style, can be much better expressed through declarative syntax. Replace your imperative-style query code with LINQ.

LINQ brings object-relational mapping to .NET in full swing. ORM frameworks can help you create an industrial-strength persistence layer for your objects with minimum effort. Solutions based on ORM will be more database-independent, will better insulate your C# code from database structure changes, and will help you write less code than classic solutions based on SQL. Moreover, you can replace your classic persistence layer with a new one, based on LINQ.

The space of one chapter is too small for all the novelties that version 3.0 C# brings, and by all accounts the evolution of C# is just beginning. At the time of writing, the details of C# version 4.0 are starting to trickle out. I'm really curious to see what Mr. Hejlsberg has in store for us this time.

In the next chapter we are off to the world of web development. You will first learn some typical pitfalls characteristic of web and ASP.NET applications; and then you will see how refactoring can be applied even to HTML code in order to eliminate these pitfalls.

14

A Short History of the Web for Developers and ASP.NET Tooling

For more than a decade, the Internet has been the driving force behind software application development. Many new tools and technologies have been invented in order to enable serving applications through a browser and using ubiquitous HTTP as a communication protocol.

Today, the current trend is providing a richer user experience and desktop application features and functionality through web applications, often referred to as Rich Internet Applications. With technologies such as Silverlight and by adding AJAX (asynchronous JavaScript and XML) capability to ASP.NET technology, Microsoft is right at the forefront of the game.

Because the lingua franca for different browsers on the Internet, and the underlying technology for ASP.NET applications, is HTML, this chapter covers issues related to HTML code. I will also talk about a new specification, a mixture of XML and HTML that is supposed to supersede traditional HTML, called XHTML. First, however, you will look at a free refactoring tool that you can use when refactoring your ASP.NET code.

In this chapter you will learn more about the following:

❑ Refactor! for ASP.NET, a free add-in from Developer Express

❑ Some historic aspects and evolution of important Internet technologies and standards

❑ Bad smells typically encountered in web applications and HTML

❑ The state of the relevant Internet standards, and support for those standards on the Microsoft platform

This will give you a great head start before diving into ASP.NET-related refactorings covered in the next chapter.

I feel that a few words of encouragement at the beginning of this chapter are in order. Because of the explosive evolution of the Internet, vested company interests, and the speed with which many new technologies on the Internet are produced, standardization and governing bodies are struggling to keep pace. This has resulted in a number of different, sometimes overlapping standards, with different generations of standards still being applied. While understanding these can seem daunting at first, a basic understanding of standards and their applicability is important for successful web development.

I will try to keep the discussion light and to mention only the most important standards in this chapter. If at any point you feel a bit lost, please take some time to learn about HTTP, HTML, XHTML, XML, DTD, CSS, ECMAScript, and other acronyms that comprise the basic laws governing the Internet. One good source of information is Jon Duckett's *Beginning Web Programming with HTML, XHTML, and CSS, Second Edition* (Wrox, 2008).

Refactor! for ASP.NET

Out of the box, Visual Studio does not come with extraordinary refactoring capabilities. Throughout this book you have seen some basic refactoring capabilities accessible through the Refactor menu in Visual Studio when dealing with C# code. However, thanks to its partnership with Developer Express, Microsoft has been able to offer free tools that enhance these rudimentary Visual Studio refactoring capabilities.

Refactor! for ASP.NET is a free Visual Studio add-in from Developer Express. It is a scaled-down version of Developer Express's flagship refactoring product, Refactor! Pro. It boasts a number of refactorings related to ASP.NET and C#.

Before you install and use Refactor! for ASP.NET, you should be aware of some of its limitations:

❏ Refactor! for ASP.NET will work only with 2005 and later versions of Visual Studio.

❏ Like any other Visual Studio add-in, it will not work with Express editions of Visual Studio.

❏ It is incompatible with Refactor! Pro or other free editions of the Refactor! add-in, such as Refactor! for Visual Basic or Refactor! for C++.

One interesting feature of Refactor! for ASP.NET is that, contrary to its name, can be used on C# code with other types of projects. Even when the same refactoring is available in Visual Studio, I prefer to use Refactor! over the built-in feature: For example, I prefer Refactor!'s nonmodal Extract Method to Visual Studio's modal Extract Method.

> You can download Refactor! for ASP.NET from www.devexpress.com/Products/ Visual_Studio_Add-in/RefactorASP/.

HTML refactorings available in Refactor! for ASP.NET will work only on ASP.NET pages (Web Forms). In order to use these refactorings in standard HTML pages, change the extension of your HTML page temporarily to .aspx and reopen the page, so it is opened in the Web Form Editor inside Visual Studio. The Refactor! for ASP.NET menu should then appear and enable you to perform refactorings such as Extract Style or Rename Style. After you have finished with refactoring, change the extension of your page back to its original extension (.html or .htm).

Invoking Refactor! for ASP.NET

Refactor! for ASP.NET uses Visual Studio's add-in architecture to integrate seamlessly into the Visual Studio environment. The new features become apparent once you open a C# or ASP.NET code file for editing. There is also a documentation section that is merged with the rest of Visual Studio's documentation when you install the add-in.

There are four ways to activate Refactor! and invoke the operations it provides:

- ❑ Using Smart tags
- ❑ Right-clicking the mouse
- ❑ Using the Ctrl+` keyboard shortcut
- ❑ Using cut and paste

Using Smart Tags

Smart tags appear as a small, single-character marker that underlines the first character in the identifier. When you place the caret on some identifier in your code or select the piece of code, the smart tag appears, indicating available refactoring that you can activate by opening the menu and selecting it from the list. Smart tags are context-sensitive, so you see only refactorings available for the selected code or for the identifier where the caret is placed, and the smart tag appears only if refactorings are available at the position indicated by the caret. You can see smart tag at the first line in the `ClearForm` method in Figure 14-1.

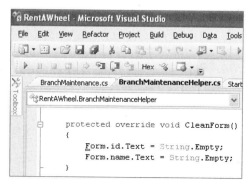

Figure 14-1

Mouse

You can make the context menu appear by right-clicking on a certain identifier or selected piece of code in your source code editor. If you have the Refactor! add-in installed, a new option called Refactor! appears in the menu. Clicking this menu item leads to a new submenu containing all the refactoring options available for that selection. Again, the submenu content is filtered such that only refactoring relevant to the selected code appears. If none are available, the menu is simply closed. You can see the context menu of the Refactor! menu item as the two last items in the menu shown in Figure 14-2.

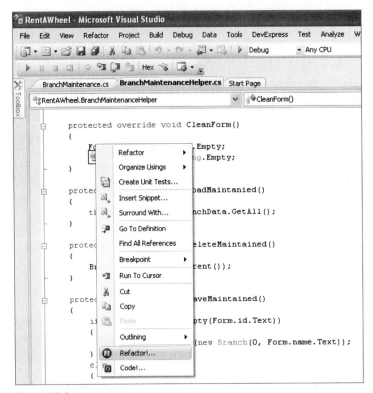

Figure 14-2

Using the Keyboard Shortcut Ctrl+ ` (One-Key Refactoring)

This key combination activates refactoring mode in Visual Studio. You first have to place the caret, or cursor, over the identifier or selected code related to the refactoring you are trying to perform. When you press Ctrl+`, a menu appears with all refactorings available for that selection or caret position. However, in one respect this mode to activate Refactor! is different. It is meant as fast access to Refactor! functionality and does not require use of a mouse, so if a single refactoring is available for the active selection or caret position, the refactoring is invoked immediately. No additional input or intermediate screen is presented. This is why it is also referred to as *one-key refactoring*. It is a good option once you become comfortable with the tool.

> *On the U.S. keyboard, the ` key is the same keyboard key as the ~ (tilde) and is generally located above the left tab key. On some European keyboards, this combination is not that easy to select, so you can reassign Refactor! to another more accessible key combination. To do this, select Tools ➤ Customize in Visual Studio and press the Keyboard button. In the Options window, define the new shortcut for the* CodeRush.Refactor *command.*

Using Cut and Paste

To use cut and paste to extract a method, just cut the code that you want for the new method and paste it inside the class in the space between methods. Refactor! will add the appropriate calling code at the cut point and build the method signature wrapper around the code you paste. You can also introduce an explaining variable with cut and paste. Just cut an expression to the clipboard and paste it on an empty line above the cut point. Refactor! will declare a new variable of the appropriate type and assign it the expression you're pasting, and add a reference to that variable at the cut point.

Now that you have seen how to invoke Refactor! for ASP.NET from the Visual Studio IDE, it's time to take a look at the basic elements of the Refactor! for ASP.NET user interface.

Exploring the Refactor! for ASP.NET User Interface

In one respect, the Refactor! for ASP.NET tool is quite different from the rest of the tools on the market. In order to help programmers always work at maximum speed and have source code in front of them at all times, the creators of Refactor! have avoided placing modal windows in front of users. Instead, they created a set of new visual features that enable users to exploit Refactor! functionality. Those features are hints, markers, linked identifiers, target pickers, and replace progress indicators. Each has a very distinctive and colorful visual appearance and some even have amusing animation effects. This section describes each of these features.

Hints

Until you really master Refactor! for ASP.NET, you will need some help finding your way around it. Hints serve exactly that purpose; they highlight all the available options and locate newly created code. There are three types of hints:

- ❏ Action hints
- ❏ Big hints
- ❏ Shortcut hints

Action Hints

Action hints appear after one-key refactoring is invoked when only one refactoring is available. Generally, they take the form of a large, red arrow pointing to the place where refactoring will take place. The arrow contains text with the name of the refactoring that is about to be applied. After a few seconds, this type of hint disappears automatically. Figure 14-3 shows an action hint.

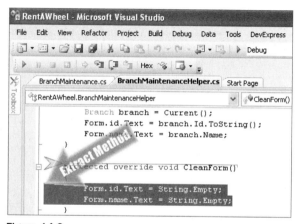

Figure 14-3

Big Hints

Big hints take the form of a tooltip window. When the refactoring menu is displayed, the content of the window provides you with a concise description of the currently selected option. As you move through the menu, the old window closes and a new one with the description of the currently selected refactoring appears. Once the option in the menu is selected and the refactoring is applied, the big hint window closes automatically. You can see the big hint for Introduce Constant refactoring in Figure 14-4.

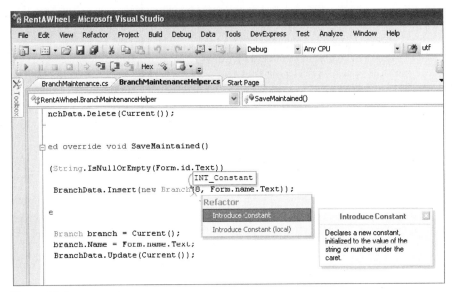

Figure 14-4

Shortcut Hints

After a certain refactoring has been selected, a *shortcut hint* lists all the available options and the keys to invoke them. It takes the form of a floating window containing a two-column table. The left column contains the key, and the right column describes the behavior that will result from pressing the selected key. The window can be moved, minimized, or closed. Shortcut hints appear for refactorings that have an interactive state, and they disappear automatically when you leave the interactive state (for example, by committing or canceling your changes). Once you're familiar with the shortcuts for a particular state, you can click the close button in the upper-right corner of the shortcut hint to suppress future appearances. Figure 14-5 shows the shortcut hints for Extract Method refactoring.

Markers

When working on large files, you might need some help getting around. For example, if you extract a piece of a method into a new method, you might wish to return to the place where the original method is located. When performing the refactoring, Refactor! will automatically place a marker in the form of a small triangle. After refactoring has been committed, you can return to the starting point by pressing the Esc key. The caret will be moved back to the place where the marker was left, followed by an animated circle to help you locate the caret inside your visual field. Once you return to the marker, it is collected and removed.

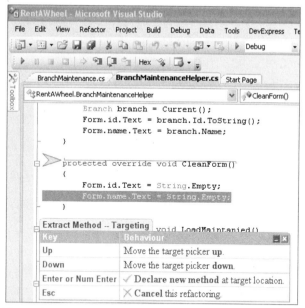

Figure 14-5

You can have multiple markers, and you can move between them in the reverse order in which they were created (*stacklike*). This functionality is similar to the bookmark functionality in Visual Studio, with the difference that markers are created automatically as you perform certain refactorings. Figure 14-6 shows a marker in place.

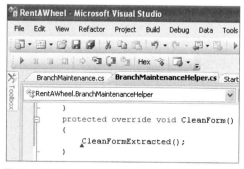

Figure 14-6

Linked Identifiers

This feature enables you to simultaneously edit all the occurrences where one identifier appears. For certain types of refactorings, it is possible to automatically identify all the instances of the identifier that need to be changed. This is the case for Rename Local refactoring, for example. Additionally, all linked items are highlighted, and it is possible to navigate through them using the Tab key. In the context menu, you can choose to break the linkage. Once the edit is finished, refactoring is committed by pressing the Enter key, and items are delinked. You can see linked identifiers activated to rename the property Form in Figure 14-7.

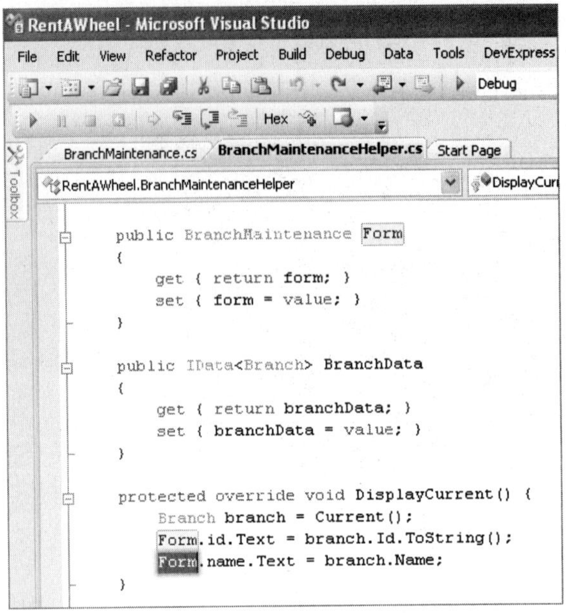

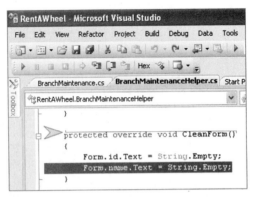

Figure 14-7

Target Pickers

Target pickers take the form of a horizontal line with an arrow. They enable you to select the location in the file for the resulting code of active refactoring. You can move the picker by using the up and down arrow keys. Once you commit the refactoring, the newly generated code is placed in the location you selected with the picker, and the picker disappears. Figure 14-8 shows a target picker.

Figure 14-8

Replace Progress Indicator

Certain refactorings cannot be executed without some user interaction. In same cases, the programmer has to decide to which items refactoring should be applied. Take an Introduce Constant refactoring, for example; the tool can identify all the appearances of a certain literal value, but it has no way of knowing which one of them you want to replace with a constant.

For example:

```
public decimal CalculateTax(int amount)
{
    //set the maximum length property of the control to 10
    telephoneInput.MaxLength = 10;
    //use 10 in tax calculation
    return amount / 100 10;
}
```

If you apply Introduce Constant refactoring on the literal 10, Refactor! for ASP.NET will search the file for all other occurrences of this number. However, only you can decide which one should be replaced with a constant. In this case, one occurrence of the number 10 is related to a tax calculation and should be replaced with an appropriate, tax-calculation–related constant, while the other is concerned with a control property and should not be replaced with the same constant, regardless of the fact that in this specific case those values coincided.

The tool uses the replace progress indicator to enable users to pick items suitable for replacement during the operation. In this mode, you can cycle through all occurrences identified by Refactor! and apply a replacement as you go along. You can see the progress indicator displayed after the literal 12 was replaced with a constant in Figure 14-9.

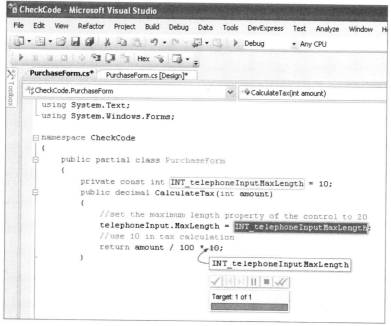

Figure 14-9

You have now seen how you can invoke and interact with Refactor! for ASP.NET, including all the major visual and interface features. As we progress, I will explain in greater detail HTML- and ASP.NET-related refactorings. For more information on C# refactoring and an updated list of available refactorings, please consult the Refactor! for ASP.NET documentation.

HTML History and Its Legacy

So far in this book, I have used the term *refactoring* in the traditional sense, as it is applied to an object-oriented programming language. HTML, conversely, is a language with quite a different purpose, that of structuring text-based information. With HTML, you won't see refactorings such as Extract Interface, Pull-Up Member or any other of the sort, but the basic premise of refactoring, whereby code is transformed while behavior is not changed in order to improve some design qualities of the code, can still be applied to HTML documents.

Some of the important problems encountered with HTML have their origins in the constant evolution of HTML as a language, driven by the growth of the Internet. Therefore, before looking at HTML smells and refactorings in detail, we will start with short descriptions of the changes and developments that occurred with HTML since its inception.

> **Definition: Most of the smells described in this chapter are often referred to by the single term *tag soup* in web development jargon. The Tag Soup super-smell puts smells such as XHTML noncompliance, using presentational elements inside the document, malformed and invalid markup, deprecated elements usage, and others under a single name. The best way to deal with tag soup is to both use CSS and make your markup XHTML compliant.**

HTML History

HTML was created as a language that would enable researchers to share, structure, and cross-reference documents. As such, it implemented the hypertext feature and was built as an application of SGML, a meta-markup language that enabled the creation of machine-readable documents.

With the rapid growth of the Internet, and with the appearance of commercial and graphical browsers, HTML was extended to incorporate tags to control the presentation and visual appearance of elements. These tags are often referred to as *presentational markup*. This was in a many ways contrary to the original purpose of HTML, to describe the structure and purpose of document elements, also known as *structural markup*.

The need to provide the user interface with more interactivity and sophistication resulted in the great popularity, and widespread adoption, of client-side scripting languages such as JavaScript and JScript.

Applications were often developed without a true understanding of the underlying communication protocol, the HTTP. This can often compromise an application's usability, scalability, and security.

Smell: Document Displays Differently in Different Browsers

Detecting the Smell

While some tools can help you check your HTML/CSS for browser compatibility, you should always check how the document is displayed in different browsers.

Related Refactorings

Use Upgrade Your HTML Markup to Valid Strict XHTML and Extract Presentational Markup to CSS in order to minimize the possible differences between the ways documents are rendered in different browsers.

Rationale

Internet Explorer's lion's share of the browser market is slowly but steadily declining. Internet sites designed to work only in a specific browser are increasingly uncommon and have no real raison d'être. Even when developing intranet applications, for which a certain type and version of browser is already known, developing web applications that can only be accessed from a single browser produces unnecessary vendor lock-in that is rarely justified by any productivity gains obtained by using proprietary browser features.

All these developments, coupled with the lack of standardization, resulted in a situation well known by web developers today:

❑   Different browsers can display the same document in different ways.

❑   In order to add behavior to a document, great care must be taken to ensure that scripts work correctly in different browsers.

❑   Information on the Internet is not easily recollected and interpreted by the machines.

These and many other problems on the Internet have their origin in the lack of standardization. Fortunately, the industry is starting to awaken from its browser slumber; and many recent initiatives, accepted to a greater or lesser extent, can help us with these issues. The following sections outline some of the more important developments in Internet-related technologies that can help us achieve a more standardized and less chaotic experience on the web.

HTML Meets XML: XHTML

In case you are not following Internet standards development very closely, you might be surprised to hear that the first XHTML recommendation was published in 2000. XHTML is meant to supersede HTML, and the current official version of XHTML is still 1.0.

XHTML is essentially HTML that also adheres to the syntax of XML. XML is much stricter than SGML (upon which HTML was supposed to be built), so documents that are written as XHTML also need to be well-formed as XML, meaning they can be processed with standard XML tools and parsers.

> Definition: A *well-formed* XML document is a document that conforms to XML *syntax*. This means, for example, that all elements must have a closing tag, that the document has to start with a root element, that attribute values have to be quoted, that elements have to be properly nested, and so on. Well-formedness is easily checked by any XML editor. If the document is not well-formed, then the XML parser should not process it. XML well-formedness should not be confused with XML *validity*.

If the document is delivered as XHTML but is not well-formed, it will be discarded by the browser. This is in a stark contrast to traditional HTML, whereby browsers did their best to display documents but still encountered various problems, including non-existing end tags, overlapping elements, and nonquoted attributes — to name just a few.

Not only the format of XHTML is checked. Content has to include a *document type declaration* informing the browser of which Document Type Definition (DTD) that document has to conform to. The exact DTD depends on the version and type of XHTML used. XHTML 1.0 specifies three formal DTDs:

❏ **Strict:** Includes all elements from the HTML 4.01 Strict specification that have not been marked as deprecated.

❏ **Frameset:** Equivalent to the HTML 4.01 Frameset specification, this includes all elements permitted by HTML 4.01 Strict, with the addition of frameset elements.

❏ **Transitional:** The least strict, equivalent to HTML 4.01 Transitional. Includes some presentational elements such as font, center, and so on.

Because both frames and presentational elements are now pretty much obsolete, you should stick with strict DTD whenever possible, especially when starting out with new documents.

> Definition: A *valid XML* document is one that both is both well-formed and follows the rules defined in the Document Type Definition or XML Schema. Schema or DTD define the *semantics* of an XML document. This means that a document should contain only elements with such attributes and in such relationships as defined in the schema or DTD. In order to be checked for validity, an XML document must declare its schema or DTD. When a browser encounters an element not defined in the DTD, it simply skips the element. Nonvalid documents are still displayed in browsers, unlike malformed documents.

At this point it is important to clarify the state of browser support for XHTML. Because XHTML is really nothing more than cleaned up HTML, browsers do not have major issues with it. However, two topics related to the Internet Explorer browser and XHTML are worth mentioning:

❏ **XML declaration:** A valid XML document should include an XML declaration. This is the line you encounter at the beginning of the XML document, generally similar to the following:

```
<?xml version="1.0" encoding="utf-8" ?>
```

Unfortunately, including this declaration inside your HTML documents might make some browsers display such a page incorrectly. Therefore, your best bet is to avoid it. On the bright side, according to the XML 1.0 specification, the XML declaration can be omitted if the encoding used is the default UTF-8 or UTF-16. Therefore, as long as your document is UTF-8 encoded, you can omit the XML declaration and your documents will still be XML 1.0 compatible.

Quirks Mode

Some browsers display pages using a proprietary interpretation of a markup and style sheet combination that does not conform to the HTML and CSS standard. This mode, often referred to as *quirks mode*, is mostly used for historical reasons, because some older versions of browsers were released without full support for HTML and CSS standards. This has resulted in a large quantity of legacy pages (and some newer ones authored by HTML developers blissfully unaware of Internet standards) written in such a way that they can be displayed in a desired way based on this proprietary interpretation of markup.

Today, most browsers use the DTD's presence in a document to determine how a page should be rendered. If the DTD is present, then the page will be rendered in *standards mode* and display elements as prescribed by HTML and CSS standards. If the DTD is not present, then the browser defaults to quirks mode.

Unfortunately, placing the XML declaration in your HTML document triggers quirks mode in Internet Explorer 6, even when the DTD is present. Both Internet Explorer 6 and Internet Explorer 7 will be placed in quirks mode if any content — such as valid XML comments, for example — precedes the DTD.

❑ **Internet Media (MIME) type):** When serving content over HTTP, your web server (typically, Internet Information Server when working with ASP.NET) has to provide media type information to the browser in form of HTTP headers. All XHTML content should be served as an XHTML media type, where the Content-Type header should have the value "application/xhtml+xml." Serving the content using this header to Internet Explorer will result in IE displaying the Save As dialog to users, instead of rendering the document. The solution is to serve your XHTML content as HTML, where Content-Type has the value "text/html." This means that IE will render your XHTML content as HTML, so many of the browser-side benefits of using XHTML are lost. However, the benefits of using the XHTML are not limited to the browser, as you will see later in the chapter.

In ASP.NET pages you can set the content type on the page level by using the `ContentType` attribute of the `@Page` directive.

Smell: XHTML Document Non-Compliance

Detecting the Smell

Use the XML authoring tool to check your document for XHTML compliance. When using Visual Studio, bear in mind that the "Target schema for validation" picker defines

Continued

the schema to be validated against for all documents in the project and does not take into account document-declared DTDs.

XHTML non-compliance can be manifested on two levels:

❑ The document is not well formed according to XML syntax rules.

❑ The document is not XHTML valid according to the XHTML Document Type Definition (DTD).

Typical errors encountered in HTML documents that are not well formed are elements such as <b>, <p>, and <li> without the ending tag, attributes whose value is missing or that are not placed inside the double quotes, elements whose tags overlap, and so on.

Invalid XHTML documents often use deprecated HTML tags eliminated from XHTML Strict, such as <font>, <center>, and <strike>, and some deprecated attributes such as background and bgcolor. Also not permitted is the use of proprietary and legacy tags, such as <marquee> or <xml> (used inside HTML in Internet Explorer's proprietary and legacy Data Island technology, made obsolete by technologies such as AJAX).

Related Refactorings

Use Upgrade Your HTML Markup to Well-Formed XML, Extract Presentational Markup to CSS, and Upgrade Your HTML Markup to Valid Strict XHTML in order to make your documents compliant with XHTML Strict.

Rationale

Using legacy HTML instead of XHTML makes your HTML code less strict. This in turn makes your document more prone to errors, may result in differences in how the document is displayed, depending on browser type and version, and may even provoke some difficult to resolve problems with ECMAScript used to manipulate such documents. It also results in slower page display inside XHTML-capable browsers, as the algorithms for displaying legacy HTML are generally more complex than those used for interpreting valid and well-formed XHTML.

When serving your documents as XHTML (using Content-Type: application/xhtml+xml) to XHTML-capable browsers, it will make the browser reject the page and display an error message instead of rendering the page.

Presentation with Cascading Style Sheets (CSS)

CSS is all about separating presentation from content. When using CSS, you define how to display certain XHTML elements. This results in moving the presentation markup out of your XHTML. Consider the following piece of CSS code:

```
p
{
text-align: left;
color: blue;
font-family: arial
}
```

This CSS segment specifies that the p tag should be displayed in blue, using the Arial font, and left-aligned. There are several ways to indicate what CSS should be applied to your XHTML document:

- As an external style sheet linked to the document using the `<link>` tag
- As an internal style sheet defined inside the `<head>` tag using the `<style>` tag
- As an inline style using the `style` attribute

The greatest flexibility and the most benefits from using CSS are obtained with external style sheets.

Smell: Presentational Elements Inside the Document

Detecting the Smell

Because XHTML Strict DTD disallows presentational elements, you can validate your XHTML document against Strict DTD, and your tool will report whether any such elements are used.

Related Refactorings

Use Extract Presentational Markup to CSS and Upgrade Your HTML Markup to Valid Strict XHTML in order to separate presentation from structure markup in your documents.

Rationale

Specifying the presentation inside your XHTML document has a number of drawbacks:

- **Duplication, leading to maintenance issues:** For example, if you change the font size for a radio button in one document, you have to perform the same change in other documents in the application and probably in more than one place in each document.

- **Loss of flexibility:** You might decide to serve different markup to different web clients (browsers or even devices) or to let users personalize the look and feel. With document-embedded presentation elements, this is not feasible.

- **More complicated development process:** You have to let both designers and developers meddle with the same files. If you use external CSS files instead, each can work on his or her own piece of the application.

- **Increased network traffic and larger document size:** Both of these are incremented when using presentational elements. Conversely, if you use an external CSS file, this file is generally transferred once and then cached inside the browsers for all the pages in that application using the same CSS file.

- **Impaired accessibility:** Not all browsers can make use of presentational elements. For example, an audio browser will not be able to interpret an `<i>` (italicized) tag.

While browser adoption of CSS varies (IE seems to be the villain yet again), it has significantly improved over time. Browser CSS compatibility issues and workarounds are generally well known to CSS developers.

ECMAScript and DOM

ECMAScript is an effort to standardize two major browser scripting language dialects: JavaScript and JScript. It can be used for browser client-side scripting, providing much-needed client-side interactivity and programmability, and it is the heart of one of the key new technologies on the Internet: AJAX.

ECMAScript standardizes the core language feature, but core libraries have different standardization. The way an XHTML document is represented and accessed in ECMAScript inside the browser is defined through the Document Object Model (DOM), a standard maintained by the World Wide Web Consortium (W3C).

The DOM representation is the direct product of HTML used when authoring the HTML document. Many bugs and problems in ECMAScript can be eliminated when using the strict form for the documents — namely, XHTML. If the XHTML you use is valid and well-formed, then you can be sure that the browser won't have any problems producing the DOM representation of the document and that ECMAScript used to manipulate it will behave as it is supposed to.

Different ECMAScript implementations build upon the standard but also provide proprietary extensions. Although you might be tempted to use them, keep in mind that this prevents accessing the application with other browsers.

> More information on non-ECMA features of Microsoft JScript can be found on MSDN:
> `http://msdn.microsoft.com/en-us/library/4tc5a343.aspx`.

The way that ECMAScript code is included inside the XHTML document is similar to CSS. It can be inlined, and functions can be defined in a single place inside the document or defined in a separate file and then included via the `src` attribute of the `<script>` tag. Again, the preferred way to organize ECMAScript is to place the code in a separate file, typically with a .js extension.

It is worth mentioning that aside from ECMAScript, with its dialects, some browsers support proprietary scripting languages. For example, IE supports the VBScript language. Even in controlled environments such as the Intranet, the use of proprietary scripting languages is discouraged, as it hampers your flexibility and promotes vendor lock-in.

> ECMAScript is a popular programming language with its own syntax, idioms, and patterns. A discussion of refactoring techniques as applied to ECMAScript is beyond the scope of this book. However, many of the refactorings described, such as Extract Method or Rename, are completely valid in the context of ECMAScript.

REST and the Web

No, REST has nothing to do with getting a good night's sleep, although describing what is actually meant by this acronym is a bit complicated. REST stands for "Representational State Transfer," an architectural style described in Roy Fielding's influential doctoral dissertation. The central theme in REST is resources (generally some kind of information) and how they are addressed — for example, using URIs on the web. For example, if you follow the URL

```
www.amazon.com/tag/refactoring
```

you will get a list of all products on amazon.com tagged with the "refactoring" tag. You can follow the link for each of the products and obtain a representation (an HTML document) of each of the products tagged under the tag refactoring. You can easily bookmark this tag, and if you decide you would like to obtain a list of all products tagged with the "CSharp" tag, you can just change the URL to the following:

```
http://www.amazon.com/tag/CSharp
```

Similarly, if you follow the link

```
http://www.amazon.com/gp/product/047043452X
```

you will obtain the document representation of the book you are currently reading. If you wish to obtain an image representation, you can follow the image link on the book's cover:

```
http://www.amazon.com/gp/product/images/047043452X
```

The browser will display a page with a large picture of the book cover. You can say that with this new representation, a browser has been transferred to a new state; you might just as well call this behavior Representational State Transfer.

Note that the server is oblivious to any previous information interchange with the client and has no need to maintain any conversation-related data (state). All the server needs in order to reply is the URL. If you decide to bookmark any of these URLs, you can easily do so and be served the same document each time you access it. If you wish to send your friend a link to any of these tags or book URLs, they will be able to see the same page you did.

Each time you access any of these resources, your browser has issued the same standard HTTP command, a GET. HTTP defines a universal interface for manipulating and accessing resources. These are known as HTTP methods, and some of the most common are GET, POST, PUT, and DELETE. A "RESTful" way to remove my book from amazon.com would be to issue an HTTP DELETE command on the book URL mentioned earlier. These commands are often compared with typical CRUD database operations.

The term (and pun) RESTful is used describe a process that operates in accordance with REST principles.

In a way, REST means using the HTTP protocol as it is supposed to be used. It can have a number of different repercussions, affecting how proxies and caching on the Internet operate, application scalability, how addressing and bookmarking are used, and so on.

Roy Fielding's doctoral dissertation is available online at www.ics.uci.edu/~fielding/pubs/ dissertation/top.htm.

Tale from the Trenches

The Unrestful.com web site's search page uses the post method to submit search key-words. The search result is kept inside the user's session on the web server. The number of items that search returns generally exceeds the number of items served on the result page. A search result pagination mechanism is in place so that only the first page result is served to the browser. As the user navigates between the result pages, the index of the page currently displayed to the user is, again, kept server-side, inside the user session. When user clicks the Next or Previous link, the server knows the state of pagination and what results to serve the user thanks to data kept in the user session.

Continued

Following are some of the drawbacks created by such a solution:

❑ Search results cannot be bookmarked or shared

❑ Keeping large amounts of data on the server adversely affects application scalability

❑ Search results are not cacheable by network intermediaries (i.e., proxy servers)

Catching Up with the Web

Many of HTML-related refactorings involve making your applications more standard and compliant with more recent specifications. Standard compliance will have the biggest implications when you work with existing, or older, legacy web applications. However, you should be aware of a few things when creating new applications. This section begins by describing how Visual Studio fares in this sense. We will be working with Visual Studio 2008, but most of the issues are applicable to Visual Studio 2005 as well.

Visual Studio and XHTML

When working on web applications with Visual Studio, many options for working with static HTML files are by default configured correctly. The situation gets a bit more complicated when working with dynamically generated pages. Therefore, you should be aware of certain issues and behavior that is probably contrary to what you would normally expect.

In order to investigate how Visual Studio performs when developing web applications, this section creates a new sample ASP.NET web application called, creatively, Sample Web Application. Next, an HTML page is added to the application. Visual Studio will add HTMLPage1.htm to the application. Listing 14-1 shows the HTML page code generated.

Listing 14-1: HTML Code Generated by VS When Adding a New HTML Page

```
<!DOCTYPE html PUBLIC "-//W3C//DTD XHTML 1.0 Transitional//EN"
"http://www.w3.org/TR/xhtml1/DTD/xhtml1-transitional.dtd">
<html xmlns="http://www.w3.org/1999/xhtml" >
<head>
    <title></title>
</head>
<body>

</body>
</html>
```

As you can see, the document starts with a DOCTYPE declaration pointing to an XHTML Transitional DTD. It means that Visual Studio is creating XHTML 1.0–compliant pages by default. The document also includes a single root tag, <html>, with a namespace correctly set to xhtml. This is quite encouraging.

Note that the XML document declaration is missing. As already mentioned, according to the XML 1.0 specification, the declaration can be omitted as long as the values defined in the declaration XML version and document encoding are the default.

In order to check the encoding for HTMLPage1, you can do the following:

- ☐ Close the editor window with HTMLPage1.
- ☐ Right-click HTMLPage1 in the Solution Explorer and select the Open With option.
- ☐ In the Open With dialog that appears, select XML Editor with encoding.
- ☐ In the second dialog window, titled "Encoding," leave the selected default Auto-Detect option.

This way, you have opened HTMLPage1 in Visual Studio for editing as an ordinary XML file. If you now take a look at the Properties window, you will see that the view has changed. One of the displayed properties is Encoding, and the value is Unicode (UTF-8).

Because this is generally the default value assumed by parsers in the absence of an XML document declaration, it means that the created document is compliant with the XHTML 1.0 specification and will be validated against the transitional DTD.

XML and Encoding

This section describes an encoding issue known to have provoked numerous headaches among developers. When I refer to encoding, I naturally refer to character encoding. *Character encoding* is the process of converting characters into a numerical representation. For example, this process takes place when you save for the first time the document you edited in Notepad. If you look at Notepad's Save dialog, you will see that the last combo enables you to select the encoding to be used for the file you are saving.

By default, the encoding offered is ASCII. When you save the file, each character is converted into a stream of bits to be recorded on your hard drive. In order for different programs and computers to be able to read the same file, some standard for representing character information has to be agreed upon. In ASCII, each character is represented with 7 or 8 bits (in Extended ASCII). For example, the letter A is represented by the number 65. Although the 256 different characters this encoding provides was once sufficient in the western world, it is not adequate on the global stage.

Today, the de facto character encoding of the Internet, and the official W3C recommendation, is Unicode. Unicode is an industry standard created to represent any of the world's writing systems in a consistent manner. Unicode can be implemented in a number of encodings, such as UTF-8, UTF-16, and UTF-32, to mention a few. Note that UTF-8 is a variable-length encoding system, not an 8-bit as you might assume based on its name, and it can represent many more than 256 characters.

When using Unicode, you can create perfectly valid documents that mix more than one alphabet. For example, the following document mixing English, Spanish, and the Serbian Cyrillic alphabet is perfectly valid:

```xml
<?xml version="1.0" encoding="utf-8" ?>
<Books>
  <Book>
    <Title>Professional Refactoring in C# and ASP.NET</Title>
    <Language>English</Language>
  </Book>
  <Book>
    <Наслов>Професионално рефакторизовање у Ц# и АСП.НЕТ</Наслов>
    <Језик>Српски<Језик>
```

```
  </Book>
  <Book>
    <Titulo>Refactorización profesional en C# y ASP.NET</Titulo>
    <Idioma>Español</Idioma>
  </Book>
</Books>
```

What I have said so far in this section is relevant for any textual file, not just XML. XML, however, requires you to explicitly declare the character encoding as a part of the XML document declaration. With XML, it is perfectly possible to save the document in one encoding, and then declare another. As a matter of fact, I have often seen developers use Windows' copy-and-paste feature when authoring XML documents, whereby the document declarations are copied with the rest of the XML text. The result of such an action is often a serious headache: Declared encoding and factual encoding do not coincide, and the XML parser will not pardon such a mistake. The problem is exasperated if an XML-unaware editor is used.

As I already mentioned, the XML document declaration can be omitted in XML 1.0, but it cannot be omitted in XML 1.1–compliant documents.

Another source of encoding-related problems can be legacy systems. In ASP.NET, HTML code served to the browser is typically generated by mixing static code written in an aspx file with the data from some kind of data source — a relational database, a legacy back end, and so on. When these two are out of sync, you can run into similar kinds of problems that are hard to debug.

Visual Studio DTD Validation for HTML

The first time you encounter the Visual Studio "Target Schema for Validation" picker, you might be puzzled by its purpose. The picker appears inside the HTML Source Editing toolbar and is enabled when you bring to the front in the editor window an HTML or ASP.NET file opened in the default editor. The Target Schema for Validation picker in Figure 14-10 shows the XHTML 1.1 standard selected for the validation target.

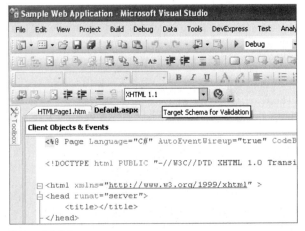

Figure 14-10

The puzzling thing about the picker is that it lets you pick the DTD you would like to validate your document against, but what about the DTD declared in the document itself? Well, when you use the picker, it ignores the declared DTD, and Visual Studio will validate the document against the one selected in the picker. Another curiosity is that the picker does not include XHTML 1.0 Strict in the list. You will find XHTML Transitional and XHTML Frameset, however, together with some legacy HTML standards.

As already mentioned, the recommended XHTML compliance today is XHTML 1.0 Strict. Because the differences between the XHTML 1.0 and XHTML 1.1 DTD are not major, and because the Target Schema for Validation picker does not include the XHTML 1.0 standard, your best bet is to validate your documents using the XHTML 1.1 option in the picker. Nevertheless, in order to let the browsers know that you are using the XHTML 1.0 Strict DTD, you should change the DOCTYPE declaration to the one shown in Listing 14-2.

Listing 14-2: XHTML 1.0 Strict DTD Declaration

```
<!DOCTYPE html PUBLIC "-//W3C//DTD XHTML 1.0 Strict//EN"
          "http://www.w3.org/TR/xhtml1/DTD/xhtml1-strict.dtd">
```

The issues regarding XHTML do not end here. Declaring DTDs in a document and validating it in Visual Studio and serving valid XHTML are two different things.

Serving Strict XHTML

As someone programming ASP.NET applications, you are well aware of how ASP.NET server controls, both web controls and HTML controls, work. These controls produce dynamic output, and some processing is performed each time a new request is sent to the server. The exact HTML that is served to the browser depends on many factors. This means that it is possible for two browsers making the same request to receive different markup as a reply. The only way for you to see the exact markup is to request the page and then take a look at the page source in the browser or some debugging proxy.

In order to turn an HTML element on an ASP.NET page into an HTML server control, just add the `runat="server"` attribute to the element definition. For example, when you place an Input(Text) control on the ASP.NET page, the following markup is created in the source view:

```
<input id="Text1" type="text" />
```

Adding the `runat` attribute, the element is transformed into an HTML control:

```
<input id="Text1" type="text" runat="server" />
```

One of the factors the ASP.NET runtime takes into account when generating the reply markup is the type and version of the browser. Browsers differ in their level of support for different standards and technologies, such as ECMAScript, CSS, DOM, and HTML. ASP.NET generally divides all browsers into two groups, *uplevel* and *downlevel*, depending on their basic capabilities.

Therefore, instead of forcing you to program different output for different browsers, ASP.NET factors out the differences for you. You are free to program the single version of the page, letting the ASP.NET runtime tweak the output for each browser accessing your web application.

The dynamic markup that the ASP.NET runtime generates by default is not strict XHTML. Fortunately, there is a configuration that you can use to tell the ASP.NET runtime to generate strict XHTML. You can accomplish this by setting the mode attribute of the xhtmlConformance configuration element to "Strict." The xhtmlConformance element should be defined under the system.web element in your Web.config file like this:

```
<system.web>
<!-- other elements -->
    <xhtmlConformance mode="Strict" />
</system.web>
```

While apparently there are some exceptions when using some optional features on some controls, this configuration should improve the XHTML Strict conformance of the generated markup significantly.

Note that if the browser accessing your application is not recognized by ASP.NET as an "uplevel" browser, this might result in the application serving legacy markup to the browser. For more information on ASP.NET browser detection and how to manually configure browser capabilities for each browser, see "ASP.NET Web Server Controls and Browser Capabilities" on MSDN: http://msdn.microsoft.com/en-us/library/x3k2ssx2.aspx.

To serve fully compliant XHTML, each page has to be accompanied by the Content-Type HTTP header with the value application/xhtml+xml. As already mentioned, Internet Explorer will not accept this Content-Type header with grace. In order to resolve this issue, several approaches are possible:

❑   Keep serving your pages as "text/html." This is the only solution that requires no effort on your side. Because XHTML is backwardly compatible with HTML, your pages can be interpreted in major browsers as legacy HTML without any problems. The downside is that you won't be reaping any XHTML benefits on the client side. If you decide to go this route, ensure that you at least test your pages, serving them as fully compliant XHTML (using the application/xhtml+xml header) in some XHTML compliant browser such as Firefox during development.

❑   Choose the correct Content-Type header to include based on browser type. This option involves some kind of programmatic implementation. Probably the best way to do this is to base your decision on the information found in the HTTP Accept header sent by the browser. The value of this header will indicate all MIME types accepted by the browser. In its raw form it may look something like this:

```
Accept: image/gif, image/x-xbitmap, image/jpeg, image/pjpeg, application/x-
shockwave-flash, application/vnd.ms-excel, application/vnd.ms-powerpoint,
application/msword, application/x-ms-application, application/x-ms-xbap,
application/vnd.ms-xpsdocument, application/xaml+xml, */*
```

You can obtain the value of this header in your ASP.NET code using the ServerVariables collection property on the Request object:

```
Request.ServerVariables["HTTP_ACCEPT"]
```

If you decide to go the path of Content-Type negotiation, you should prefer HTTP_ACCEPT to using the User-Agent header. The User-Agent header gives you the information on browser type and version and you have to maintain the list of browsers that support XHTML inside your application.

❑ Fool Internet Explorer into accepting XHTML as XML and serve your XHTML using the application/xml type. Internet Explorer will process the XML using the included style sheet and present it as if it were sent using the text/html Content-Type. For more information, check the following recommendation on the W3 consortium site: `www.w3.org/MarkUp/2004/xhtml-faq#ie`.

Although Internet Explorer dominance in the last few years has been in a slow but constant decline, it is still the leading browser on the Internet; and because it does not show any promise of accepting XHTML in the near future, it is questionable whether serving the right Content-Type header for a minority of browsers is worth the trouble. There is no doubt that you should try to make your markup compatible with XHTML Strict.

Summary

This chapter provided a lot of basic information relevant to the refactoring of web applications. In ASP.NET, when programmed in C#, a lot of techniques explained in this book so far are also applicable, as ASP.NET pages are programmed as typical C# classes. Some refactorings, however, are specific to the world of the web.

Many of these web-application-specific refactorings are a necessity that resulted from the explosive growth of the Internet, where providing users with novel features as fast as possible was more important than standardizing technologies and making different products work across vendor boundaries.

Today, the situation is improving with standards such as XHTML, ECMAScript, and CSS, but there is still a lot of existing code that is written using legacy styles of web development; and adoption of the new standards is still far from complete. This is why, when you are developing Internet applications, you have to be prepared to deal with smells such as Tag Soup or situations in which you have mixed document structure and presentation markup, the same document might display and behave differently depending on the browser, applications do not respect prescribed standards, and so on.

Such applications can be refactored into a more standards-compliant form, whereby pages will display more uniformly and the presentation and structure are clearly separated. One tool that can help you with this task is Refactor! for ASP.NET, which we will put to work in the next chapter. It sports a number of useful refactorings that can help you deal with the problems elaborated in this chapter.

15

Refactoring ASP.NET Applications

ASP.NET applications are constructed as a blend of C# (or some other .NET language) and HTML. When dealing with C# code, you can apply all the refactoring techniques we have covered in this book so far. The Web Form class used to program your ASP.NET pages (Web Forms) is your ordinary C# class that extends from System.Web.UI.Page. At this point you should have all the information necessary to deal with standard C# code, such as how to reduce duplication by extracting methods or parent classes, for example. As you should be quite familiar with standard C# refactoring by now, I will not dwell on this any further.

When refactoring your HTML code, you will primarily want to make your pages as standards-compliant as possible. I have already discussed the most important Internet standards in the previous chapter. You will also want to eliminate some general smells such as duplication from your HTML code, by extracting presentational elements to external CSS files, for example.

Finally, there are some ASP.NET-specific constructs that can make your code better structured and designed, such as Master Page and User Control. Some of the refactorings you will meet in this chapter are intended to use those constructs to make your code better organized, beginning with HTML code-related refactorings.

This chapter deals with ASP.NET-specific refactorings. You will learn the following:

- ❏ How to upgrade your legacy HTML to markup compliant with Strict XHTML

- ❏ How to separate structural markup from presentational markup using CSS

- ❏ How to leverage ASP.NET-specific mechanisms such as themes, user controls, custom ASP.NET server controls, and master pages to improve the design and reduce duplication in ASP.NET code.

Refactoring HTML

Most of HTML-related refactoring you will see in this chapter is related to making your HTML code more strict and standards compliant. Most of these standards, such as XHTML, CSS, and HTTP, have already been mentioned and are likely familiar to any web developer. However, in practice, strict compliance with these standards is seldom encountered on the Internet.

Well-Formed XHTML Documents

Well-formedness is the set of rules that all XML documents, and therefore all XHTML documents, have to abide by. You can tell if an XML document is well-formed or not just by looking at the document itself, without understanding a single thing about its content or its purpose. This is because well-formedness is established based on syntactic rules for XML. These rules can be easily checked by an XML-aware editor. Only well-formed documents are allowed to be parsed by an XML-conforming parser.

This section describes some of these XML syntax rules. You should always check for well-formedness with an XML-aware editor, which in Visual Studio means selecting at least the XHTML 1.0 Transitional schema in the Target Schema for Validation picker when editing HTML or ASP files. In order to create well-formed XML, your document should have the following:

❑ **A single root element:** When creating XHTML documents, the root element is the `<html>` tag.

❑ **A closing tag for every element:** In HTML, you often find paragraph (`<p>`), line break `<br>`, list item (`<li>`), and other tags without a closing tag.

❑ **Non-overlapping elements:** For example, the following code snippet is not valid XHTML:

```
<br><p>These tags overlap</br></p>
```

❑ **Attribute values placed inside the double or single quotes:** Omitting attribute values or omitting the quotes is not permitted.

❑ Escaped signs such as the ampersand, less-than sign, and quotation marks in attribute values

Well-formedness is the first step in making your documents XHTML conformant. Once you take care of the syntax, you should also make your document valid semantically.

Refactoring: Upgrade Your HTML Markup to Well-Formed XML

Motivation

By replacing malformed markup with valid XML, you can reap a number of benefits:

❑ Well-formed markup is easier to modify and maintain.

❑ The appearance of your pages will be more uniform across different browsers.

❑ Many rendering errors that result from malformed markup can be avoided.

❑ Valid XML can be authored by any XML authoring tool.

❑ Internet robots (search engines, etc.) will be able to better index your sites.

❏ Other applications will be able to harvest information from your pages more easily.

❏ You application will be less prone to ECMAScript and AJAX problems that originate in malformed markup.

❏ It will be easier to implement CSS in a predictable way.

❏ You will be able to process your documents using XSL Transformations and standard XML parsers.

When transforming your documents into valid XHTML, implementing well-formedness is the first step. Because some XHTML-capable browsers will not have to apply complex algorithms in order to guess the best way to display your document, the page rendering time is improved. It will be possible to render your document even on devices (e.g., mobiles and others) that do not have the computing power to perform such calculations.

Related Smells

Use this refactoring as a first step in eliminating XHTML Non-Compliance and Tag Soup smells.

Mechanics

If you are dealing with a substantial number of larger pages, begin by using a tool that helps you tidy up your HTML. One such tool is an open-source, command-line application called Tidy. It is capable of dealing with most of the problems you might encounter in malformed markup. After using Tidy, be sure to confirm that your pages are correctly rendered in the browser.

Less complicated pages can be reformatted manually, using an HTML editor such as Visual Studio. In order to check for well-formedness, select XHTML 1.0 Transitional in the Target Schema for Validation picker, and work your way toward a well-formed document by eliminating errors reported by Visual Studio in the Warnings window. Such fixes include the following:

❏ Introduce the root `<html>` element.

❏ Fix overlapping elements.

❏ Place attribute values in double quotes.

❏ Provide the ending tag for all elements.

❏ Escape ampersand, less-than, and quotation mark signs.

❏ Add namespace and DOCTYPE declarations.

Before

```
<head>
    <title>My old school HTML page</title>
</head>
<body bgcolor=aqua>
<H1>Refactoring in C# and ASP.NET
```

Continued

```
<p>
In this one-of-a-kind book, Microsoft MVP Danijel Arsenovski
shows you how to utilize the power of refactoring to improve
the design of your existing code and become more efficient and
productive.
You ll discover how to perform unit testing, refactoring to patterns,
and how to refactor your HTML code.
<BR>
As you progress through the chapters, you ll build a prototype
application
from scratch as Arsenovski walks you step-by-step
through each process while offering expert coding tips.
<p>
</body>
```

After

```
<!DOCTYPE html PUBLIC "-//W3C//DTD XHTML 1.0 Transitional//EN"
    "http://www.w3.org/TR/xhtml1/DTD/xhtml1-transitional.dtd">
<html xmlns="http://www.w3.org/1999/xhtml">
<head>
<meta name="generator" content=
"HTML Tidy for Windows (vers 7 December 2008), see www.w3.org" />
<title>My old school HTML page</title>
</head>
<body bgcolor="aqua">
<h1>Refactoring in C# and ASP.NET</h1>
<p>In this one-of-a-kind book, Microsoft MVP Danijel Arsenovski
shows you how to utilize the power of refactoring to improve the
design of your existing code and become more efficient and
productive. You ll discover how to perform unit testing,
refactoring to patterns, and how to refactor your HTML code.<br />
As you progress through the chapters, you ll build a prototype
application from scratch as Arsenovski walks you step-by-step
through each process while offering expert coding tips.</p>
</body>
</html>
```

XHTML Validity

Once you have taken care of well-formedness, you can focus on validity. The first step is choosing the compliance level, defined in the document by the DTD. Today, the most sensible choice is XHTML 1.0 Strict. You should declare the DTD in your document using the DOCTYPE declaration:

```
<!DOCTYPE html PUBLIC "-//W3C//DTD XHTML 1.0 Strict//EN"
    "http://www.w3.org/TR/xhtml1/DTD/xhtml1-strict.dtd">
```

This way, your editor will tell you what elements are valid in your document. Valid XHTML documents use only elements and attributes defined in the DTD. In order to make your document valid, you must eliminate any legacy and proprietary elements. Most of these invalid elements are presentational. In order to maintain the visual appearance, in addition to stripping your document of invalid elements you need to apply CSS to your document that reproduces the original look and feel.

In order for the browser to recognize elements inside your documents as XHTML elements, you need to include the namespace declaration. When creating XHTML documents, namespace declaration should be added to the `<html>` tag, like this:

```
<html xmlns="http://www.w3.org/1999/xhtml" >
```

By making your document XHTML valid, you achieve a more consistent interpretation across browsers. By using only defined elements, you ensure that all browsers know how to interpret all the tags you have used in your page.

Refactoring: Upgrade Your HTML Markup to Valid Strict XHTML

Motivation

Using valid XHTML ensures that a majority of browsers and devices are capable of interpreting your markup and rendering your pages correctly and uniformly.

Because Strict XHTML eliminates most presentational elements, this means that you will move most of the presentational information to CSS, achieving a separation of presentation and content in your documents.

Related Smells

Use this refactoring to avoid mixing presentational and structural markup and to eliminate deprecated and proprietary HTML elements.

Mechanics

Be sure that your documents are well-formed before embarking on this step. Next, use CSS to define presentational elements for your documents. At this point, you should be pretty close to making your documents Strict XHTML valid.

Select the XHTML 1.1 option in the Target Schema for Validation picker in Visual Studio. Eliminate all elements and attributes marked in Visual Studio as invalid. Visual Studio underlines invalid elements and attributes, and in the Warnings dialog presents messages similar to "Element 'legacy element' is not supported" or "Attribute 'legacy attribute' is not a valid attribute of element 'some element'."

Alternatively, use HTML Tidy to perform this transformation automatically, specifying the -asxhtml option. When using HTML Tidy, be sure to inspect the final result in the browser.

Before

```
<!DOCTYPE html PUBLIC "-//W3C//DTD XHTML 1.0 Transitional//EN"
    "http://www.w3.org/TR/xhtml1/DTD/xhtml1-transitional.dtd">
<html xmlns="http://www.w3.org/1999/xhtml">
<head>
<meta name="generator" content=
"HTML Tidy for Windows (vers 7 December 2008), see www.w3.org" />
<title>My old school HTML page</title>
```

Continued

```
</head>
<body bgcolor="aqua">
<h1>Refactoring in C# and ASP.NET</h1>
<p>In this one-of-a-kind book, Microsoft MVP Danijel Arsenovski
shows you how to utilize the power of refactoring to improve the
design of your existing code and become more efficient and
productive. You ll discover how to perform unit testing,
refactoring to patterns, and how to refactor your HTML code.<br />
As you progress through the chapters, you ll build a prototype
application from scratch as Arsenovski walks you step-by-step
through each process while offering expert coding tips.</p>
</body>
</html>
```

After

```
<!DOCTYPE html PUBLIC "-//W3C//DTD XHTML 1.0 Strict//EN"
    "http://www.w3.org/TR/xhtml1/DTD/xhtml1-strict.dtd">
<html xmlns="http://www.w3.org/1999/xhtml">
<head>
<meta name="generator" content=
"HTML Tidy for Windows (vers 7 December 2008), see www.w3.org" />
<title>My old school HTML page</title>
<style type="text/css">
/*<![CDATA[*/
  body {
  background-color: aqua;
  }
  /*]]>*/
</style>
</head>
<body>
<h1>Refactoring in C# and ASP.NET</h1>
<p>In this one-of-a-kind book, Microsoft MVP Danijel Arsenovski
shows you how to utilize the power of refactoring to improve the
design of your existing code and become more efficient and
productive. You ll discover how to perform unit testing,
refactoring to patterns, and how to refactor your HTML code.<br />
As you progress through the chapters, you ll build a prototype
application from scratch as Arsenovski walks you step-by-step
through each process while offering expert coding tips.</p>
</body>
</html>
```

Tool Support for Upgrading Legacy, XHTML Non-Compliant Markup

Manually transforming large quantities of legacy HTML to be well-formed and valid can be a tedious and time-consuming process, even with an XHTML-aware tool such as Visual Studio. There are some tools that take a different approach, and are capable of upgrading your HTML documents automatically and in bulk. As mentioned earlier, one such open-source tool is HTML Tidy. You can download the compiled command-line executable of HTML Tidy from SourceForge: `http://tidy.sourceforge.net`.

HTML Tidy is capable of fixing numerous common errors in your legacy HTML, such as overlapping elements, missing end tags, unquoted attributes, and so on. It can also pretty-print your documents and convert your HTML to valid XHTML when the `-asxhtml` option is specified. With the `-asxhtml` option, it will even convert your legacy presentational markup to CSS style.

See the "Upgrade Your Pages into Valid Strict XHTML" refactoring sidebar to view the new CSS style extracted, based on the legacy `bgcolor` *attribute, using HTML Tidy.*

While HTML Tidy is pretty good at tidying up your HTML code, you should still check the result of any transformation visually, inspecting the pages rendered inside the browser.

Pretty-Printing Your HTML Documents

While it will not have major repercussions on the way your markup is rendered or processed, correctly indenting and breaking the code can make your documents much more amicable to the human eye. HTML editors or tools such as HTML Tidy make it easy to pretty-print you markup.

Refactoring: Pretty-Print Your XHTML

Motivation

XHTML code that is well indented and wrapped is much easier to maintain and understand. While browsers and parsers will ignore white space, it makes any tasks for humans working with the markup much easier to perform.

Related Smells

Use this refactoring fix markup that is poorly formatted or merely ugly to the human eye.

Mechanics

This refactoring can generally be performed at the click of a button in some HTML editors, such as the one available inside Visual Studio; or multiple files can be reformatted in one go when using a command-line tool such as HTML Tidy.

Before

```
<!DOCTYPE html PUBLIC "-//W3C//DTD XHTML 1.0 Transitional//EN"
    "http://www.w3.org/TR/xhtml1/DTD/xhtml1-transitional.dtd">
<html xmlns="http://www.w3.org/1999/xhtml">
<head>
<meta name="generator" content=
"HTML Tidy for Windows (vers 7 December 2008), see www.w3.org" />
<title>My old school HTML page</title>
</head>
<body bgcolor="aqua">
<h1>Refactoring in C# and ASP.NET</h1>
<p>In this one-of-a-kind book, Microsoft MVP Danijel Arsenovski
```

Continued

```
shows you how to utilize the power of refactoring to improve the
design of your existing code and become more efficient and
productive. You 11 discover how to perform unit testing,
refactoring to patterns, and how to refactor your HTML code.<br />
As you progress through the chapters, you 11 build a prototype
application from scratch as Arsenovski walks you step-by-step
through each process while offering expert coding tips.</p>
</body>
</html>
```

After

```
<!DOCTYPE html PUBLIC "-//W3C//DTD XHTML 1.0 Strict//EN"
    "http://www.w3.org/TR/xhtml1/DTD/xhtml1-strict.dtd">
<html xmlns="http://www.w3.org/1999/xhtml">
<head>
  <meta name="generator" content=
  "HTML Tidy for Windows (vers 7 December 2008), see www.w3.org" />
  <title>My old school HTML page</title>
  <style type="text/css">
        /*<![CDATA[*/body
        {
            background-color: aqua;
        }
        /*]]>*/</style>
</head>
<body>
  <h1>Refactoring in C# and ASP.NET</h1>
  <p>In this one-of-a-kind book, Microsoft MVP Danijel
  Arsenovski shows you how to utilize the power of
  refactoring to improve the design of your existing code
  and become more efficient and productive. You 11 discover
  how to perform unit testing, refactoring to patterns, and
  how to refactor your HTML code.<br />
  As you progress through the chapters, you 11 build a
  prototype application from scratch as Arsenovski walks
  you step-by-step through each process while offering
  expert coding tips.</p>
</body>
</html>
```

Separating Structure from Presentation

Although HTML was never originally intended to describe document presentation, it ended up being used for that purpose out of necessity. Today, with other means available to define how a document should be presented, you should avoid misusing HTML.

In case you have to deal with HTML pages with embedded presentational markup, you can clean up your HTML by using CSS for presentation and eliminating all presentational markup from the HTML. While such an operation can be handled as refactoring, I find that in practice it doesn't make much sense performing this transformation in a strict manner, as you would normally transform your typical imperative code.

A better approach is to just clean the HTML and let the designer create the CSS from scratch, using the original pages more as a source of inspiration than as a strict definition. Such an occasion can even be used to update the look and feel of your website. Of course, your business needs might differ.

Refactoring: Extract Presentational Markup to CSS

Motivation

Separating presentational markup from document content reduces duplication in your code, adding flexibility to your application and enabling your document to be displayed more uniformly across different browsers, devices, and media. Because Strict XHTML should not contain presentational elements, this refactoring is a prerequisite for Upgrade Your HTML Markup to Valid Strict XHTML refactoring.

Related Smells

Use this refactoring to eliminate Document Displays Differently in Different Browsers smell, XHTML Document Non-Compliance smell, Presentational Elements Inside the Document smell, and to help reduce the Tag Soup smell.

Mechanics

Presentational elements express the web design qualities of your site. This type of design is guided by a different set of rules than software design. Qualities such as aesthetics, usability, and accessibility distinguish a web site. When extracting presentational markup, reproducing the exact appearance of each and every one of the pages in the web site might not be the best approach. It is much more practical to let the web designer construct CSS based on samples of the original pages. This approach is likely to result in a more consistent look and feel across pages, and might even represent a good occasion for a web site face-lift.

When following this more natural and less strict approach to extracting presentational markup from the web page content, do the following:

- ❑ Provide the web designer with site web pages and graphic samples and let him or her create a CSS style that mimics the original design.

- ❑ Strip the HTML pages of presentational elements and import the CSS style file created by the designer.

Alternatively, if you need to reproduce the original look and feel to the last detail, you can apply the following process:

- ❑ Apply inline style to elements that will replace all legacy markup elements. For example, replace the `<font>` element with the `font-family` and `font-size` properties in the style applied to certain elements in the document.

- ❑ Pull-up inline style to document-level style.

- ❑ Extract document-level style to external style.

Continued

Before

```
<!DOCTYPE html PUBLIC "-//W3C//DTD XHTML 1.0 Transitional//EN"
    "http://www.w3.org/TR/xhtml1/DTD/xhtml1-transitional.dtd">
<html xmlns="http://www.w3.org/1999/xhtml">
<head>
    <title>My old school HTML page</title>
</head>
<body bgcolor="aqua">
    <h1>Refactoring in C# and ASP.NET</h1>
        <p>In this one-of-a-kind book, Microsoft MVP Danijel Arsenovski
        shows you how to utilize the power of refactoring to improve
        the design of your existing code and become more efficient and
        productive. You 11 discover how to perform unit testing,
        refactoring to patterns, and how to refactor your HTML
        code.<br />
        As you progress through the chapters, you 11 build a prototype
        application fromscratch as Arsenovski walks you step-by-step
        through each process while offering expert coding tips.</p>
</body>
</html>
```

After

```
<!DOCTYPE html PUBLIC "-//W3C//DTD XHTML 1.0 Strict//EN"
    "http://www.w3.org/TR/xhtml1/DTD/xhtml11-strict.dtd">
<html xmlns="http://www.w3.org/1999/xhtml">
<head>
  <meta name="generator" content=
  "HTML Tidy for Windows (vers 7 December 2008), see www.w3.org" />
  <title>My old school HTML page</title>
  <style type="text/css">
      @import "Extracted.css";
  </style>
</head>
<body>
  <h1>Refactoring in C# and ASP.NET</h1>
  <p>In this one-of-a-kind book, Microsoft MVP Danijel
  Arsenovski shows you how to utilize the power of
  refactoring to improve the design of your existing code
  and become more efficient and productive. You 11 discover
  how to perform unit testing, refactoring to patterns, and
  how to refactor your HTML code.<br />
  As you progress through the chapters, you 11 build a
  prototype application from scratch as Arsenovski walks
  you step-by-step through each process while offering
  expert coding tips.</p>
</body>
</html>
```

Extracted.css:

```
body
{
    background-color: aqua;
}
```

Extract Style Refactoring in Refactor! for ASP.NET

In order to pull-up inline style to document-level style, you can use Extract Style refactoring. To activate this refactoring, place the cursor on the style attribute definition in the HTML tag in your ASP.NET page (Web Form). This refactoring comes in two flavors:

❑ **Extract Style (Class):** Chooses the element class as a selector in the extracted style. For example, this refactoring will transform the tag

```
<p style="font-family:Arial"></p>
```

to the following style and tag declaration:

```
<p class="pStyle1"></p>
<style type="text/css">
        p.pStyle1
        {
            font-family: Arial;
        }
</style>
```

Immediately after the refactoring, the class name is selected in rename mode, enabling you to assign a more appropriate name to the style than the name auto-generated by the tool.

❑ **Extract Style (Id):** Chooses the element id as a selector in the extracted style. If an element id is not present, it creates one. For example, this refactoring will transform the tag

```
<p style="font-family:Arial"></p>
```

to the following style and tag declaration:

```
<p id="pStyle1"></p>
<style type="text/css">
        p#pStyle1
        {
            font-family: Arial;
        }
</style>
```

Immediately after the refactoring, the id value is selected in rename mode, enabling you to assign a more appropriate value to the id attribute than the value auto-generated by the tool.

Remember that in a single document, you can have only one element with a certain id, whereas many elements can share the same class. Figure 15-1 shows the Extract Style refactoring option in the context menu.

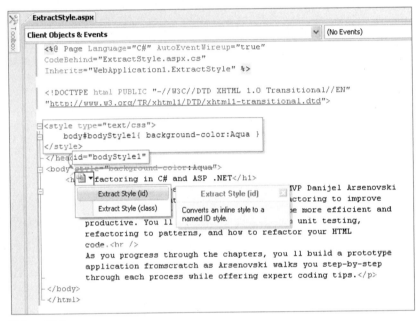

Figure 15-1

Rename Style Refactoring in Refactor! for ASP.NET

Rename Style refactoring conveniently enables you to rename the style selector and all references to this selector inside the HTML. Rename Style refactoring comes in two flavors:

❑ **Rename Style Qualified:** Takes into account both the element and the class selector. For example, the code

```
<html xmlns="http://www.w3.org/1999/xhtml" >
<head runat="server">
    <style type="text/css">
        p.pStyle1
        {
            font-family: Arial;
        }
    </style>
    <title></title>
</head>
<body>
```

```
        <h3 class="pStyle1"></h3>
        <p class="pStyle1"></p>
    </body>
    </html>
```

is transformed into the following:

```
<html xmlns="http://www.w3.org/1999/xhtml" >
<head runat="server">
    <style type="text/css">
        p.MyFunkyPStyle
        {
            font-family: Arial;
        }
    </style>
    <title></title>
</head>
<body>
    <h3 class="pStyle1"></h3>
    <p class="MyFunkyPStyle"></p>
</body>
</html>
```

❑ **Rename Style Universal:** This takes into account only the class selector. For example, the code

```
<html xmlns="http://www.w3.org/1999/xhtml" >
<head runat="server">
    <style type="text/css">
        p.pStyle1
        {
            font-family: Arial;
        }
    </style>
    <title></title>
</head>
<body>
    <h3 class="pStyle1"></h3>
    <p class="pStyle1"></p>
</body>
</html>
```

is transformed into the following:

```
<html xmlns="http://www.w3.org/1999/xhtml" >
<head runat="server">
    <style type="text/css">
        p.MyFunkyStyle
        {
            font-family: Arial;
        }
    </style>
    <title></title>
</head>
```

```
<body>
    <h3 class=" MyFunkyStyle "></h3>
    <p class="MyFunkyStyle"></p>
</body>
</html>
```

You can see Rename Style refactoring ready to be performed in Figure 15-2.

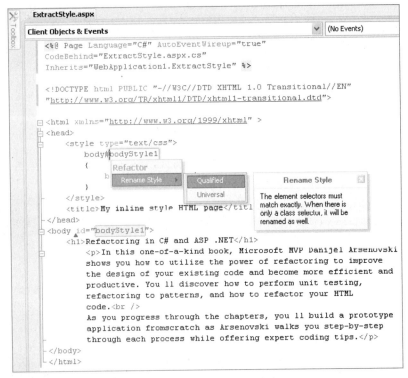

Figure 15-2

Themes and Skins

You can combine Cascading Style Sheets with the Themes and Skins feature of ASP.NET projects. A CSS file can be included inside the theme. Themes and skins help you manipulate the look and feel of your application programmatically and enable you to define the visual appearance of some properties of ASP controls that cannot be defined in CSS. One advantage of themes over pure CSS is that themes can be applied on the application level, or even globally, to all applications on web server. In order to apply a theme on the application level, set the `styleSheetTheme` attribute on the "pages" element inside the `system.web` element in the `Web.config` file:

```
<configuration>
    <system.web>
        <pages styleSheetTheme="MyThemeName" />
    </system.web>
</configuration>
```

Once you have applied the theme on the application level, there is no need to include the .css file using the standard HTML mechanism through the @Import directive inside the style element.

Using HTTP to Your Advantage with REST

The ASP.NET Framework was meant to abstract the developer away from the underlying HTTP protocol. It was created with the purpose of simplifying web application development through a familiar event-driven programming model. As such, it is not well suited for developing applications the "RESTful" way. While you can still do so, you will still have to do a lot of heavy lifting yourself.

Today, most of Microsoft's REST initiatives are geared toward the Windows Communication Foundation (WCF) framework. This is only logical, as since Rich Internet Applications, Silverlight, AJAX, and similar clients are capable of consuming web services directly. If you are interested in finding out how REST-style web services are supposed to work on the Microsoft platform, take a look at the WCF REST starter kit: http://msdn.microsoft.com/en-us/netframework/cc950529.aspx.

> **Definition:** *Rich Internet Applications* represent a new type of application on the Internet meant to provide a desktop-application–like experience to users. For example, RIAs tend to avoid complete page refreshes by repainting only a portion of a page; they might provide drag-and-drop features; they use a richer set of GUI widgets; they provide a more responsive GUI; and more. In order to achieve these features, developers leverage more recent web technologies such as AJAX, Flex, and Silverlight, to name a few.

While implementing your web site in the REST manner with ASP.NET is complicated, there are some valuable lessons that REST teaches us in regard to HTTP and the Internet that you should keep in mind when constructing ASP.NET applications.

According to the HTTP protocol specification, the GET method is used only for retrieval. A client issuing GET is not expecting the method to generate side-effects, and as such should be considered "safe." You can use GET to request a page, image, or search result, to view a location on a map, etc. Therefore, GET URLs can be cached, pre-fetched, resubmitted, repeated, spidered, and so on.

POST, however, is used for unsafe operations. Such operations are expected to have side-effects and to change the state on the server (or, in REST terms, to modify the resource). For example, you would use POST to issue a command that books a flight, checks out your shopping basket, or performs a monetary transaction. It is important that such operations are not repeated, as you do not want to book two tickets instead of one, or make two money transfers instead of one.

The entire Internet infrastructure, including browsers, proxies, firewalls, gateways, caches, and so on is built to adhere to those principles. For example, a browser will issue a warning if you try to resubmit a form using Refresh (F5). Figure 15-3 shows a warning window that is issued in Internet Explorer after an attempt is made to resubmit a form with the POST method.

If the POST and GET methods in your application are improperly used, such as when GET is used for unsafe operations and POST is used for safe operations, you can replace GET with POST and POST with GET as appropriate.

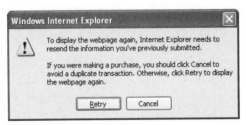

Figure 15-3

On some occasions, this can be as simple as changing the declared method in the form's HTML tag. On other occasions, transformation can be more complicated and might involve changing one type of server control with another, such as in the following sidebar. In the example for Replace GET with POST refactoring, the HyperLink control is replaced with the LinkButton control in order to enable submittal using the POST method. When rendered, the LinkButton control generates the necessary JavaScript that manipulates and submits the form when the link is clicked.

Refactoring: Replace GET with POST

Motivation

Using the GET method for unsafe operations might result in such operations being cached, repeated, resubmitted, or executed by some unwanted automated agent such as a web spider. In order to avoid this unwanted behavior, replace the GET method with the POST method.

Related Smells

Use this refactoring to eliminate misuse of the HTTP protocol in your application.

Mechanics

Sometimes changing from POST to GET can be as simple as changing the declared method in the HTTP form. More often, however, more complex changes to your code will be required, such as replacing the HyperLink control with the LinkButton control, as shown in the following example. In order to use the POST method, you have to use the HTML form element. Instead of manipulating and submitting the form with some custom JavaScript, be sure to leverage existing ASP Server controls such as the LinkButton. These controls are rendered by the server with necessary client-side JavaScript when the page is delivered to the browser.

Before

```
<%@ Page Language="C#" AutoEventWireup="true"
CodeBehind="Default.aspx.cs" Inherits="GetToPost._Default" %>
<!DOCTYPE html PUBLIC "-//W3C//DTD XHTML 1.0 Transitional//EN"
"http://www.w3.org/TR/xhtml1/DTD/xhtml1-transitional.dtd">
<html xmlns="http://www.w3.org/1999/xhtml" >
<head runat="server">
    <title>Order your coffee</title>
</head>
```

```
<body>
    <form id="form1" runat="server">
    <div>

        <asp:Repeater ID="Repeater1" runat="server"
        DataSourceID="ObjectDataSource1">
            <ItemTemplate>
                <asp:Label runat="server">Product:
                <%# Eval("Name") %></asp:Label>
                <asp:Label runat="server">Price:
                <%# Eval("Price") %></asp:Label>
                <asp:HyperLink runat="server"
                NavigateUrl=
            '<%# "~/Default.aspx?action=order&Id=" + Eval("Id") %>' >

                One Click Order</asp:HyperLink>
                <br />
            </ItemTemplate>
        </asp:Repeater>

        <br />
        <br />
        <asp:Label ID="OrderConfirmation" runat="server"
        Text="None"></asp:Label>

    </div>
    <asp:ObjectDataSource ID="ObjectDataSource1" runat="server"
        SelectMethod="ListAllProducts"
        TypeName="GetToPost._Default"></asp:ObjectDataSource>
    </form>
</body>
</html>
```

Default.aspx.cs:

```
using System;
using System.Collections.Generic;
namespace GetToPost
{
    public class Product {
        public int Id { get; set; }
        public String Name { get; set; }
        public Decimal Price { get; set; }
    }
    public partial class _Default : System.Web.UI.Page
    {
        //Create ad-hoc data model - for illustration only
        List<Product> products = new List<Product> {
            new Product {Id = 1, Name =
                "Juan Valdez Decaff",  Price = 11 },
            new Product {Id = 2, Name =
```

Continued

```
                    "Starbucks Special Blend", Price = 14 },
            new Product {Id = 3, Name =
                "Colombia Narino Supreme", Price = 12 }
        };
        public ICollection<Product> ListAllProducts() {
            return products;
        }
        protected void Page_Load(object sender, EventArgs e)
        {
            //Display order confirmation message
            if (Convert.ToInt32(Request.Params["Id"]) > 0)
            {
                this.OrderConfirmation.Text = "You ordered: " +
                    products[Convert.ToInt32(Request.Params["Id"])
                    -1 ].Name;
            }
        }
    }
}
```

After

```
<%@ Page Language="C#" AutoEventWireup="true"
CodeBehind="Default.aspx.cs" Inherits="GetToPost._Default" %>
<!DOCTYPE html PUBLIC "-//W3C//DTD XHTML 1.0 Transitional//EN"
"http://www.w3.org/TR/xhtml1/DTD/xhtml1-transitional.dtd">
<html xmlns="http://www.w3.org/1999/xhtml" >
<head runat="server">
    <title>Order your coffee</title>
</head>
<body>
    <form id="form1" runat="server">
    <div>

        <asp:Repeater ID="Repeater1" runat="server"
        DataSourceID="ObjectDataSource1">
            <ItemTemplate>
                <asp:Label runat="server">Product:
                <%# Eval("Name") %></asp:Label>
                <asp:Label runat="server">Price:
                <%# Eval("Price") %></asp:Label>
                <asp:LinkButton runat="server"
                OnCommand="LinkButton_Command"
                CommandName="Order"
                CommandArgument='<%# Eval("Id") %>' >
                One Click Order</asp:LinkButton>
                <br />
            </ItemTemplate>
        </asp:Repeater>

        <br />
```

```
            <br />
            <asp:Label ID="OrderConfirmation" runat="server"
            Text="None"></asp:Label>

     </div>
     <asp:ObjectDataSource ID="ObjectDataSource1" runat="server"
         SelectMethod="ListAllProducts"
         TypeName="GetToPost._Default"></asp:ObjectDataSource>
     </form>
</body>
</html>
```

Default.aspx.cs:

```csharp
using System;
using System.Collections.Generic;
using System.Web.UI.WebControls;
namespace GetToPost
{
    public class Product {
        public int Id { get; set; }
        public String Name { get; set; }
        public Decimal Price { get; set; }
    }
    public partial class _Default : System.Web.UI.Page
    {
        //Create ad-hoc data model - for illustration only
        List<Product> products = new List<Product> {
            new Product {Id = 1, Name =
                "Juan Valdez Decaff",  Price = 14 },
            new Product {Id = 2, Name =
                "Starbucks Special Blend", Price = 11 },
            new Product {Id = 3, Name =
                "Colombia Narino Supreme", Price = 12 }
        };
        public ICollection<Product> ListAllProducts() {
            return products;
        }
        public void LinkButton_Command(Object sender,
            CommandEventArgs command)
        {
            //Display order confirmation message
            OrderConfirmation.Text = "You ordered: " +
                    products[Convert.ToInt32(command.CommandArgument)
                    - 1].Name;
        }
    }
}
```

Sneaking a Peek at HTTP with Fiddler

While the ASP.NET Framework does a good job of hiding HTTP protocol complexities from the developer's eye, sometimes looking at what is going on at the protocol level in your application cannot be avoided. Fiddler is an HTTP debugging proxy that records all conversation between the browser and the server and presents it in a number of views. With Fiddler, you can take a look at HTTP headers, cookies, query strings and forms, HTTP body content, and so on. It also provides you with some useful statistical information such as request and response size, estimated performance, and more.

You can download Fiddler without cost at `www.fiddlertool.com`.

Refactoring ASP.NET Code

ASP.NET technology supports several mechanisms that will help you better structure and promote reuse in your application. These mechanisms are designed especially for the ASP.NET programming model, a brew of HTML markup and .NET code.

For example, master pages are useful to implement a kind of visual inheritance capacity, whereby several pages share parts of the same visual surface. User controls are great for encapsulating custom functionality that can be reused as ASP.NET server controls, and custom server controls are great for sharing such functionality between projects and distributing it in binary form.

However, before we go on to these useful ASP.NET features, let me say a few words about the ASP.NET single-file and code-behind code models.

ASP.NET Code Model: Single-file vs. Code-behind

In traditional ASP, you used to mix HTML and VB or JScript code inside the same .asp file. You would use `<%` and `%>` tags to mark the code to be processed by the server. The similar single-file (or inline) model, whereby C# code is placed inside the `<script>` tags, can be used in ASP.NET pages. Alternatively, you can separate the markup from C# code and place the C# code in a standard C# source code file. This model is called code-behind, and it resembles Windows Forms file organization whereby Visual Designer–generated code is placed in a separate file of the partial class.

Either way, the code performs and executes the same. The only considerations when choosing between code models are organizational and how they affect maintenance. In the Microsoft documentation, the recommended model is code-behind. It permits a clear, file-level separation between code and markup. Such separation can help your team be more productive, as the designer has to deal only with the markup, and the programmer only with the C# code.

The single-file model is often chosen for historic reasons. Classic ASP programmers are used to having markup and imperative code in a single file. However, classic ASP practices can often lead you down the wrong path if followed in ASP.NET, which has greatly evolved since the original ASP and requires a radically new approach to developing web applications.

Refactoring: Move Inline Code to Code-Behind in the ASP.NET Page

Motivation

Separating the ASP.NET markup from the C# code improves the readability of your code and facilitates the work of different team members on the project. Designer and analyst can work with markup without having to look at C# code, and the C# programmer can concentrate on and work with the C# source code file without having to merge changes made by other team members, and vice-versa.

Related Smells

Use this refactoring to replace the single-file model with the code-behind model in an ASP.NET application.

Mechanics

If both the code-behind (.aspx.cs) partial class and designer (aspx.designer.cs) class for your ASP.NET page are available, then this refactoring can be as simple as cutting and pasting the content of script element to the code-behind class.

If the single-file class was created from an HTML page and neither code-behind nor designer classes are present, then start by creating these classes.

1. Create the code-behind class: Add a new class to the project with the same name as your single-file aspx page, including the aspx extension. If your aspx page is named `Default.aspx`, then name the new code-behind file `Default.aspx.cs`.

2. Declare the code-behind class as partial, using the `partial` keyword in the class declaration.

3. Make the code-behind class extend the `System.Web.UI.Page` class.

4. Create the designer class: Add a new class to the project with the same name as your single-file aspx page, including the aspx extension. If your aspx page is named `Default.aspx`, then name the new code-behind file `Default.aspx.designer.cs`.

5. Declare the code-behind class as partial, using the `partial` keyword in the class declaration.

6. Add the `Inherits` attribute to the `@Page` directive in your aspx page and make it point to the code-behind class.

7. Close all files in the editor and then reopen them. Upon opening the files, Visual Studio should generate the content of the designer class.

8. Cut and paste the script element content from the aspx file to the `aspx.cs` file.

Before

```
<%@ Page Language="C#" %>
<!DOCTYPE html PUBLIC "-//W3C//DTD XHTML 1.0 Transitional//EN"
```

Continued

```
                  "http://www.w3.org/TR/xhtml1/DTD/xhtml1-transitional.dtd">
                  <script runat="server">

                      protected void Page_Load(object sender, EventArgs e)
                      {
                          Label1.Text = "Hello from C# code!";
                      }
                  </script>
                  <html xmlns="http://www.w3.org/1999/xhtml" >
                  <head runat="server">
                      <title></title>
                  </head>
                  <body>
                      <form id="form1" runat="server">
                      <div>

                          <asp:Label ID="Label1" runat="server" Text="Label"></asp:Label>

                      </div>
                      </form>
                  </body>
                  </html>
```

After

```
                  <%@ Page Language="C#" AutoEventWireup="true"
                  CodeBehind="SingleFileOrCodeBehind.aspx.cs"
                  Inherits="GetToPost.SingleFileOrCodeBehind" %>
                  <!DOCTYPE html PUBLIC "-//W3C//DTD XHTML 1.0 Transitional//EN"
                  "http://www.w3.org/TR/xhtml1/DTD/xhtml1-transitional.dtd">
                  <html xmlns="http://www.w3.org/1999/xhtml" >
                  <head runat="server">
                      <title></title>
                  </head>
                  <body>
                      <form id="form1" runat="server">
                      <div>

                          <asp:Label ID="Label1" runat="server" Text="Label"></asp:Label>

                      </div>
                      </form>
                  </body>
                  </html>
```

SingleFileOrCodeBehind.aspx.cs:

```
                  using System;
                  namespace GetToPost
                  {
```

```
        public partial class SingleFileOrCodeBehind : System.Web.UI.Page
        {
            protected void Page_Load(object sender, EventArgs e)
            {
                Label1.Text = "Hello from C# code!";
            }
        }
    }
```

SingleFileOrCodeBehind.designer.aspx.cs:

```
    //-------------------------------------------------------------------

    // <auto-generated>
    //     This code was generated by a tool.
    //     Runtime Version:2.0.50727.3053
    //
    //     Changes to this file may cause incorrect
    //     behavior and will be lost if
    //     the code is regenerated.
    // </auto-generated>
    //-------------------------------------------------------------------

    namespace GetToPost {


        public partial class SingleFileOrCodeBehind {

            /// <summary>
            /// form1 control.
            /// </summary>
            /// <remarks>
            /// Auto-generated field.
            /// To modify move field declaration from
            /// designer file to code-behind file.
            /// </remarks>
            protected global::System.Web.UI.HtmlControls.HtmlForm form1;

            /// <summary>
            /// Label1 control.
            /// </summary>
            /// <remarks>
            /// Auto-generated field.
            /// To modify move field declaration from designer
            /// file to code-behind file.
            /// </remarks>
            protected global::System.Web.UI.WebControls.Label Label1;
        }
    }
```

Move to Code-Behind Refactoring in Refactor! for ASP.NET

Be sure to create the code-behind and designer class before attempting to execute Move to Code-Behind refactoring with Refactor! for ASP.NET. If there is no code-behind class, then Refactor! for ASP.NET will not offer this refactoring in the menu; only Extract User Control refactoring will be available.

In order to perform this refactoring, click on the script tag used to mark your inline C# code. Figure 15-4 shows the `script` tag marked for Move to Code-Behind refactoring.

Figure 15-4

Master Pages

In a typical website, all pages share certain elements that do not change as you browse the site and navigate from one page to another. Usually these are the header, the footer, some type of menu that can be placed inside a header or as a sidebar, a banner, and so on.

Traditionally, there have been a number of ways you can implement this feature in your website, depending on the technology on which your site is based:

❑   **Copy-and-paste shared HTML:** You are probably guessing, correctly, that the duplication of code that results from this approach is a major shortcoming. In case you need to modify something in the header or footer, you have to edit all the pages in the site.

❑   **Using frames:** As already mentioned in a previous chapter, frames are made obsolete by the latest HTML Strict and XHTML Strict specification. Using frames makes your site counterintuitive in a number of ways: Bookmarking and linking to your site is adversely affected, it might affect the way web spiders access your site, it is relatively difficult to implement, and so on.

❑ **Using server-side includes (SSI):** This option is available only if your site is constructed in a technology intended for dynamic page generation, such as PHP, ASP, JSP, and others. You have to take care that all elements are correctly embedded and terminated, and you have to place the `include` directive inside each page, resulting in duplication of these directives across the pages.

❑ **User controls in ASP.NET pages:** You can create a user control for each common area in your website: a control that represents the header, a control for the footer, etc. You have to place these controls on each ASP.NET page on your website, resulting in duplication overhead.

❑ **Master pages in ASP.NET 2.0 and later:** This solution produces the least duplication but it is limited to ASP.NET 2.0 and later platforms. You will also be limited to using Visual Studio and editors that support this feature if you wish to preview the pages to see how they render after master and child page are merged inside the IDE.

When working in ASP.NET 2.0 and later, master pages are the best solution for maintaining common content in a single place, reducing duplication and avoiding pitfalls such as the URL and bookmarking issue present when using frames. Another nice feature of master pages is that they can be nested, created a hierarchy of master pages, and when necessary they can be manipulated programmatically.

Master Page and Web Content Form

While the master page is used to define common elements, the content of each page is defined inside another type of page, called the Web Content Form. A master page can define a number of `ContentPlaceHolders` that are replaced with Web Content Forms when the page is rendered. The URL used to display the page points to the Web Content Page; ASP.NET runtime will assure that master page template is used when rendering the web page.

The Web Content Form should have all of its content defined inside `asp:Content` element(s) and should not define any of the top-level HTML elements such as `html`, `body` or `form`. The `MasterPageFile` attribute of the `@Page` directive is used to indicate which master page should be used as a template when rendering the Web Content Form. It is possible that the page design requires more than one `ContentPlaceHolder` to be defined in the master page. In that case, you should provide the content for each of the `ContentPlaceHolders` in your Web Content Form.

Refactoring: Extract Common Content to Master Page

Motivation

Master pages are a template mechanism in ASP.NET that enables placing elements common to a number of pages into a single file without any of the side-effects characteristic of other inclusion mechanisms such as SSI or frames.

Related Smells

Use this refactoring to reduce duplication in your application and to avoid pitfalls characteristic of other inclusion mechanisms.

Mechanics

If a master page already exists in your project, then converting a Web Form to a Web Content Form is relatively easy:

1. Remove all top-level HTML from your Web Form and enclose the content of your Web Form with an `asp:Content` element. Be sure to define the

---

Continued

ContentPlaceholderID attribute for the asp:Content element; it will indicate what ContentPlaceHolder of the master page should be replaced with the Web Form.

2. Define the MasterPageFile attribute of the @Page directive so it points to a master page you wish to use for your Web Form.

In case a master page does not exist in the project, start by creating it. Move all common markup to the master page and define ContentPlaceHolder(s) on your master page. Follow Steps 1 and 2.

Before

```
<%@ Page Language="C#" AutoEventWireup="true"
CodeBehind="ContactUs.aspx.cs" Inherits="MasterPage._ContactUs" %>
<!DOCTYPE html PUBLIC "-//W3C//DTD XHTML 1.0 Transitional//EN"
"http://www.w3.org/TR/xhtml1/DTD/xhtml1-transitional.dtd">
<html xmlns="http://www.w3.org/1999/xhtml" >
<head runat="server">
    <title></title>
</head>
<body>
    <asp:Menu ID="Menu1" runat="server"
        Orientation="Vertical">
        <Items>
            <asp:MenuItem Text="About Us"
                NavigateUrl="AboutUs.aspx" />
            <asp:MenuItem Text="Products"
                NavigateUrl="Products.aspx" />
            <asp:MenuItem Text="News"
                NavigateUrl="News" />
            <asp:MenuItem Text="Contact Us"
                NavigateUrl="ContactUs.aspx" />
        </Items>
    </asp:Menu>
    <form id="form1" runat="server">

    <div>
        <asp:Label ID="Label1" runat="server"
            Text="Contact Us:" />
        <br />
        <asp:TextBox ID="TextBox1" runat="server"
            Rows="5" TextMode="MultiLine" />
        <br />
        <asp:Label ID="Label2" runat="server"
        Text="Your e-mail:" />
        <br />
        <asp:TextBox ID="TextBox2" runat="server" />
        <br />
```

```
                <asp:Button ID="Button1" runat="server"
                Text="Send Message" />
            </div>

            </form>

    </body>
    </html>
```

After

```
<%@ Page Language="C#" AutoEventWireup="true"
CodeBehind="ContactUs.aspx.cs" Inherits="MasterPage._ContactUs"
    MasterPageFile="NewMasterPageFile0.master" %>
<asp:Content ContentPlaceHolderID="NewContentPlaceHolderId" runat=
"server">
    <asp:Label ID="Label1" runat="server" Text="Contact Us:" />
    <br />
    <asp:TextBox ID="TextBox1" runat="server" Rows="5" TextMode=
"MultiLine" />
    <br />
    <asp:Label ID="Label2" runat="server" Text="Your e-mail:" />
    <br />
    <asp:TextBox ID="TextBox2" runat="server" />
    <br />
    <asp:Button ID="Button1" runat="server" Text="Send Message" />
</asp:Content>
```

MasterPage.master:

```
<%@ Master CodeFile="NewMasterPageFile0.master.cs"
Language="C#" Inherits="NewMasterPageFile0" %>
<!DOCTYPE html PUBLIC "-//W3C//DTD XHTML 1.0 Transitional//EN"
"http://www.w3.org/TR/xhtml1/DTD/xhtml1-transitional.dtd">
<html xmlns="http://www.w3.org/1999/xhtml" >
<head runat="server">
    <title></title>
</head>
<body>
    <asp:Menu ID="Menu1" runat="server"
        Orientation="Vertical">
        <Items>
            <asp:MenuItem Text="About Us"
                NavigateUrl="AboutUs.aspx" />
            <asp:MenuItem Text="Products"
                NavigateUrl="Products.aspx" />
            <asp:MenuItem Text="News"
                NavigateUrl="News" />
            <asp:MenuItem Text="Contact Us"
                NavigateUrl="ContactUs.aspx" />
        </Items>
```

Continued

```
            </asp:Menu>
            <form id="form1" runat="server">

            <div>
                <asp:ContentPlaceHolder id="NewContentPlaceHolderId"
                    runat="server" />
            </div>

            </form>

        </body>
        </html>
```

Extract ContentPlaceHolder (and Create Master Page) in Refactor! for ASP.NET

To invoke Extract ContentPlaceHolder (and Create Master Page) refactoring, select the controls you would like to keep inside your Web Form. After extraction, Refactor! will convert the current Web Form into a Web Content Form and enclose the content within the asp:Content element. It will also create a new master page based on the original Web Form and with ContentPlaceHolder for elements that are now part of the Web Content Form. Take a look at how Extract ContentPlaceHolder (and Create Master Page) can be invoked over a Web Form in Figure 15-5.

Another refactoring called Extract ContentPlaceHolder can be used over the existing master page in order to extract an area to the ContentPlaceHolder and Web Content Form. It can be useful if you realize that area on the master page is not common to each form, but depends on each Web Content Form.

Web User and Custom Server Controls

Using GUI controls for constructing views in your application by dragging them from a palette onto some WYSWYG designer area and then setting the controls' properties in a properties window is a very productive and efficient way to create a GUI. This model for GUI construction is quite familiar to programmers, going back to tools such as Visual Basic and Delphi. In ASP.NET, the same model has been applied to programming web applications.

One great productivity feature of such GUI models is that the control palette can be extended by third-party or custom controls. Creating custom controls is a great way to promote reuse and reduce duplication in your code.

Often you will find yourself in a situation where you have to add some custom behavior to built-in controls, or a few of controls are grouped and used in the same manner in different views repeatedly. In such situations, it soon becomes obvious that such duplication of code could be avoided by creating a custom control.

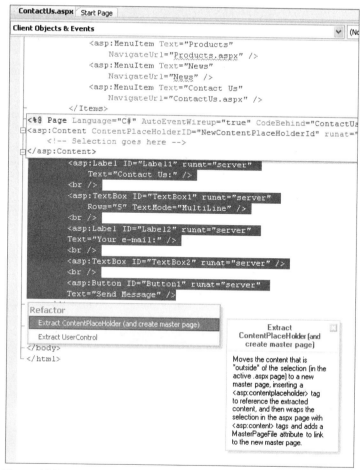

Figure 15-5

Refactoring: Extract User Control

Motivation

User controls are a great mechanism for encapsulating GUI-related functionality inside a single component. In ASP.NET, a control, in addition to C# code, can contain HTML and ASP.NET markup, JavaScript, and so on.

Related Smells

Use this refactoring to eliminate Duplicated Code smell in your application.

Continued

Mechanics

When using Extract User Control refactoring, perform the following steps:

1. Add the new user control item to the project.

2. Cut the markup from the Web Form that you wish to extract to the user control and paste it to the newly created user control.

3. Cut and paste related C# code from the Web Form to the user control.

4. Add the @Register directive to the Web Form so it points to the extracted user control.

5. Place an instance of the extracted user control on the Web Form, replacing the original extracted markup.

Before

```
<%@ Page Language="C#" AutoEventWireup="true"
CodeBehind="Login.aspx.cs" Inherits="UserControl._Default" %>
<!DOCTYPE html PUBLIC "-//W3C//DTD XHTML 1.0
Transitional//EN" "http://www.w3.org/TR/xhtml1/DTD/xhtml1-
transitional.dtd">
<html xmlns="http://www.w3.org/1999/xhtml" >
<head runat="server">
    <title>Login</title>
</head>
<body>
    <form id="form1" runat="server">
    <div>
        Enter Login Data
        <br />
        <br />
        <asp:Label ID="Label1" runat="server"
        Text="Social Security Number:" />
        <br />
        <asp:TextBox ID="SSNPart1" runat="server"
        Columns="3" MaxLength="3" />
        <asp:TextBox ID="SSNPart2" runat="server"
        Columns="4" MaxLength="2" />
        <asp:TextBox ID="SSNPart3" runat="server"
        Columns="4" MaxLength="4" />
        <asp:RegularExpressionValidator ID="validateSSNPart1"
        ControlToValidate="SsnPart1"
        Display="Dynamic" ErrorMessage="*"
        ValidationExpression="(^([0-9]*|\d*\d{1}?\d*)$)"
        Runat="server" />
        <asp:RegularExpressionValidator ID="validateSSNPart2"
        ControlToValidate="SsnPart2"
        Display="Dynamic" ErrorMessage="*"
```

```
            ValidationExpression="(^([0-9]*|\d*\d{1}?\d*)$)"
            Runat="server" />
            <asp:RegularExpressionValidator ID="validateSSNPart3"
            ControlToValidate="SsnPart3"
            Display="Dynamic" ErrorMessage="*"
            ValidationExpression="(^([0-9]*|\d*\d{1}?\d*)$)"
            Runat="server" />
            <br />
            <asp:Label ID="Label2" runat="server" Text="Password:" />
            <br />
    <asp:TextBox TextMode="Password" runat="server"/>
            <br />
            <br />
            <asp:button runat="server" text="Logins" />
        </div>
        </form>
    </body>
    </html>
```

After

```
<%@ Page Language="C#" AutoEventWireup="true"
CodeBehind="Login.aspx.cs" Inherits="UserControl._Default" %>
<%@ Register TagPrefix="user" TagName="SSN" Src="SSN.ascx" %>
<!DOCTYPE html PUBLIC "-//W3C//DTD XHTML 1.0
Transitional//EN" "http://www.w3.org/TR/xhtml1/DTD/xhtml1-
transitional.dtd">
<html xmlns="http://www.w3.org/1999/xhtml" >
<head runat="server">
    <title>Login</title>
</head>
<body>
    <form id="form1" runat="server">
    <div>
        Enter Login Data
        <br />
        <br />
        <user:SSN id="SSN" runat="server" />
        <br />
        <asp:Label ID="Label2" runat="server" Text="Password:" />
        <br />
        <asp:TextBox TextMode="Password" runat="server"/>
        <br />
        <br />
        <asp:button runat="server" text="Logins" />
    </div>
    </form>
</body>
</html>
</asp:Content>
```

Continued

SSN.ascx:

```
<%@ Control Language="C#" AutoEventWireup="true"
ClassName="SSN" %>
<asp:Label ID="Label1" runat="server"
    Text="Social Security Number:" />
<br />
<asp:TextBox ID="SSNPart1" runat="server"
    Columns="3" MaxLength="3" />
<asp:TextBox ID="SSNPart2" runat="server"
    Columns="4" MaxLength="2" />
<asp:TextBox ID="SSNPart3" runat="server"
    Columns="4" MaxLength="4" />
<asp:RegularExpressionValidator ID="validateSSNPart1"
    ControlToValidate="SsnPart1"
    Display="Dynamic" ErrorMessage="*"
    ValidationExpression="(^([0-9]*|\d*\d{1}?\d*)$)"
    runat="server" />
<asp:RegularExpressionValidator ID="validateSSNPart2"
    ControlToValidate="SsnPart2"
    Display="Dynamic" ErrorMessage="*"
    ValidationExpression="(^([0-9]*|\d*\d{1}?\d*)$)"
    runat="server" />
<asp:RegularExpressionValidator
    ID="validateSSNPart3" ControlToValidate="SsnPart3"
    Display="Dynamic" ErrorMessage="*"
    ValidationExpression="(^([0-9]*|\d*\d{1}?\d*)$)"
    runat="server" />
```

In ASP.NET, there are two types of custom controls: user controls and custom server controls. User controls are easy to create; the same WYSIWYG designer can be used to create the control. However, these controls are reusable on the source code level. The only way to reuse them across projects is to import the .ascx file to each project in which you need to use the control.

Custom server controls can be compiled into a reusable binary and can be distributed as a compiled assembly. These controls are well suited for commercial distribution of third-party controls. However, they are comparably much more difficult to construct. You won't be able to use the WYSIWYG designer and you will have to possess a much deeper understanding of ASP.NET server controls technology. Table 15-1 shows the principal differences between these two technologies for extending the built-in palette of controls in ASP.NET.

Extract to User Control Refactoring in Refactor! for ASP.NET

In order to activate this refactoring, select the markup to be extracted to the user control in some Web Form. Refactor! will create a new .ascx file for the extracted user control and will translate the selected markup to that file. It will place an @Control directive at the top of the file. In the original file, the markup will be replaced with a reference to a new user control. Figure 15-6 shows markup selected for user control extraction.

Table 15-1: Comparison of User Controls and Custom Server Controls

Factor	User Control	Custom Server Control
Distribution	Source Code	Binary
WYSWIG designer support	Yes	No
Complexity	Relatively Low	High
Appears in Toolbox	No	Yes

Figure 15-6

*It seems there is a quirk with Refactor! for ASP.NET when extracting user controls without related C#
code. Refactor! will declare the control in the @Control directive with the Inherits and CodeBehind
attributes even though there is no C# code. In order for such a user control to work, change the declaration by removing the CodeBehind and Inherits attributes and place the ClassName attribute that has
the name of the extracted user control as an attribute.*

Rent-a-Wheels and ASP.NET Refactorings

The Rent-a-Wheels application you have seen so far is a typical client-server application, with the client
implemented using the Windows Forms GUI framework. So far, you haven't seen any web or ASP.NET
code. This chapter, however, requires that we make available some of the information we have in our
database on the web.

The Requirement

The Rent-a-Wheels company has a rentawheels.com site that has some basic information about the company, such as working hours, branches and locations, contact data, and so on. It also has some fleet
information, mostly about available vehicle models.

Today, the greatest need for the company is to display the current price list. The company has a competitive pricing policy but so far has not been able to put this information on the Internet. Pricing values
change frequently and displaying outdated information is not an option. This is why a static list was
discarded from the start.

The client would like a single page that lists all vehicles and their prices: daily, weekly, and monthly
price. The data should be obtained from the same database that keeps the information administered by
the Rent-a-Wheels client-server application. This way, the data will always be current, and information
changed in the Rent-a-Wheels database will be automatically reflected on the site.

Implementation

Upon inspecting the existing client-server application, it becomes obvious that the same assemblies
used in the client-server application can be used to provide pricing list information on the web. A new
Web Application should be created that references the RentAWheel.Business, RentAWheel.Data, and
RentAWheel.Data.Implementation assemblies. The ModelData class provides a method that returns the
list of Models; Model is related with Category, which holds the price values.

All that is needed to use the existing functionality is to instantiate a new DataContext, providing it with
a database connection string configuration from the Web.config file and then inject the new ModelData
with the DataContext instance. Then, the ObjectDataSource control can be used in a Web Form to fill
controls on the form with the data obtained, calling the GetAll method on ModelData. To make things
simple, I decided to place all initialization code inside the VehiclesAndRates Web Form. Listing 15-1
shows the _VehiclesAndRates C# code.

Listing 15-1: _VehiclesAndRates Class Code

```
using System;
using System.Collections.Generic;
using System.Configuration;
using System.Data.Linq;
```

```
using System.Web.Configuration;
using System.Web.UI;
using RentAWheel.Business;
using RentAWheel.Data;
namespace RentAWheel.Web
{
    public partial class _VehiclesAndRates : Page
    {
        private static ConnectionStringSettings
            connectionStringSettings;
        private const String DbStringConfigurationSectionName
            = "RentAWheels";
        private DataContext context;
        private  LinqData<Model> modelData;
        private static void ReadConnectionSettings()
        {
            Configuration config = WebConfigurationManager.
                OpenWebConfiguration("/");
            ConnectionStringsSection connectionStringsSection =
                config.ConnectionStrings;
            connectionStringSettings = connectionStringsSection.
                ConnectionStrings[DbStringConfigurationSectionName];
        }
        void CreateDataServices()
        {
            context = new DataContext(
                connectionStringSettings.ConnectionString);
            modelData = new LinqData<Model>(connectionStringSettings)
            { Context = context };
        }
        public _VehiclesAndRates() {
            ReadConnectionSettings();
        }
        public IList<Model> GetAllModels(){
            CreateDataServices();
            return modelData.GetAll();
        }
    }
}
```

All that is left is to use the GetAllModels method as an ObjectDataSource's data source. Then, the page can be constructed whose controls will be populated with data from ObjectDataSource. The ASP markup for the VehiclesAndRates.aspx page is available in Listing 15-2.

Listing 15-2: VehiclesAndRates.aspx code

```
<%@ Page Language="C#" AutoEventWireup="true"
CodeBehind="VehiclesAndRates.aspx.cs"
Inherits="RentAWheel.Web._VehiclesAndRates" %>

<!DOCTYPE html PUBLIC "-//W3C//DTD XHTML 1.0 Transitional//EN"
```

Continued

Listing 15-2: VehiclesAndRates.aspx code *(continued)*

```
"http://www.w3.org/TR/xhtml11/DTD/xhtml11-transitional.dtd">

<html xmlns="http://www.w3.org/1999/xhtml" >
<head runat="server">
  <title>Price List of Available Vehicles </title>
</head>
<body>
    <form id="form1" runat="server">
    <div>
        <asp:Label ID="Label1" runat="server"
            Text="Vehicles and Prices:"></asp:Label>
        <br />
        <br />
        <asp:Repeater ID="Repeater1" runat="server"
            DataSourceID="ObjectDataSource1">
        <ItemTemplate>
            <asp:Label ID="Label2" runat="server">Model:
            <%# Eval("Name") %></asp:Label>
            <asp:Label ID="Label3" runat="server">Daily Price:
            <%# Eval("Category.DailyPrice") %></asp:Label>
            <asp:Label ID="Label4" runat="server">Weekly Price:
            <%# Eval("Category.WeeklyPrice") %></asp:Label>
            <asp:Label ID="Label5" runat="server">Monthly Price:
            <%# Eval("Category.MonthlyPrice") %></asp:Label>
            <br />
        </ItemTemplate>
        </asp:Repeater>
    </div>
    <asp:ObjectDataSource ID="ObjectDataSource1" runat="server"
        SelectMethod="GetAllModels"
        TypeName="RentAWheel.Web._VehiclesAndRates">
    </asp:ObjectDataSource>
    </form>
</body>
</html>
```

Implementing this functionality proved to be very simple and required a minimum amount of coding.

Refactoring in Rent-a-Wheels Benefits the New Web Application

The Rent-a-Wheels functionality was implemented in ASP.NET technology with a small amount of code, so applying any refactoring you have seen in this chapter is not really justified.

However, one much more important conclusion can be made by looking at the code in the previous two listings. Implementing new functionality proved to be simple and required a small amount of code because a high level of reuse was possible.

Thanks to the extensive refactoring that was performed on Rent-a-Wheels so far, such as separating the GUI, business and data layers, using patterns such as Dependency Injection, and organizing the code along the Reuse-Release principle guidelines, an elegant and efficient solution was possible.

What better way to conclude this book than to demonstrate the benefits of refactoring on reuse and productivity.

Summary

ASP.NET programming can be even more challenging than writing pure C# code. ASP.NET is constructed over different basic technologies such as XHTML, JavaScript, CSS, and dynamically generated output by the .NET Framework.

When developing web applications, it is all too easy to use legacy HTML elements, to mix structure and presentation elements, to write markup in non-strict form, or not to take into account HTTP protocol guidelines. Such an approach, typical of legacy web applications, has numerous downsides and can lead to a number of problems, as you have seen.

In order to fix the shortcomings typical of legacy web applications, you should transform non-strict markup into a strict form, making it XML compliant and making use of elements permitted by XHTML 1.0 Strict DTD. In order to do so, you will have to eliminate presentation-related markup from your documents, replacing it with Cascading Style Sheets definitions. You should also understand the basic premises of the HTTP protocol, the most important protocol on the web, and ensure that your applications make the best use of the features this protocol provides.

On the ASP.NET side of things, mechanisms such as user controls, custom server controls, and master pages help promote reuse and reduce duplication in your ASP.NET code. The best way to extract common web page elements such as headers, footers, menus, banners, and so on, is to make use of master pages. Instead of copying markup, using frames or SSI, extract common elements into a master page for the least duplication and the most flexible solution in ASP.NET. When you identify a repeated group of basic controls and related functionality, you will be able to reduce duplication in your application and improve maintainability by extracting these controls into a user control or custom server control.

By following the refactorings described in this chapter and avoiding the smells described in previous chapters, by improving reuse and avoiding duplication in your application, by making your application compliant with the latest standards, and with a good understanding of the underlying web protocol, HTTP, you will make your application much more robust, more maintainable, and better designed.

Rent-a-Wheels Prototype Internals and Intricacies

This appendix extends the scenario from Chapter 4 by investigating the implementation of the Rent-a-Wheels application prototype in more detail. It continues recounting the conversation between Tim, the novice C# programmer who created the first version of the prototype, and me, focusing on two main areas of the prototype application:

❑   Relevant event-handling code

❑   Relevant form class code

Remember, this code is not meant to illustrate good design principles, but quite the opposite. It is here to illustrate a non-object-oriented approach to rapid application development (RAD). Try to think about better ways to implement this application. Compare your ideas with the solutions that I offer throughout the book while refactoring and improving the Rent-a-Wheels prototype.

Hand Over Button Click Event-Handling Code

When I asked Tim about the Hand Over button click event he said, "In this case, there is no intermediate form, since no additional data is necessary for this operation. Essentially, a user can just mark a vehicle as handed over to the customer. This amounts to changing the value of the column Available for that vehicle to the number 2 in the database. Essentially, the code is quite similar to two routines we examined when looking into the Rent operation code. The only difference is that because no other form was necessary, the whole operation is performed at once, and all code is contained in the btnHandOver_Click routine in the FrmFleetView class."

To remind yourself what the code for the application's Rent operation looked like, refer to Chapter 4, or you can download the code for the whole sample application at www.wrox.com.

We turned our attention to the Receive button next.

Receive Button Click Event-Handling Code

In regard to the Receive button, Tim said, "Not too much is a surprise here. This code is quite similar to that hiding under the Rent button, too. The only difference is that the FrmRcv is displayed and not the FrmRt."

Tim showed me FrmRcv, the Receive a Vehicle form, which is shown in Figure A-1.

Figure A-1

"This form is used to enter Mileage and Tank level data after vehicle reception. The code for the Receive button click event is very similar to code for the Rent button click event: This update sets Available to 3, and Mileage and Tank level data are saved also."

I then said to Tim that it seemed he had used the same approach throughout the application. Tim said, "The similarity in code is not a pure coincidence. I was able to finish this application so quickly because I used a lot of copy-and-paste of the code."

Charge Button Click Event-Handling Code

Tim continued his thought by turning to the Charge button: "As a matter of fact, there is no need to go over the Charge button click event-handling code in detail. Again, similar to button Hand Over, the update is executed right away without displaying an intermediate form."

I said, "I guess that the SQL query code is a bit different, isn't it?"

Tim said, "Yes, the only important difference, compared to the btnHandOver_Click routine, is in the SQL code." He showed me the following code:

```
string strSql = "Update Vehicle " +
                "Set Available = 0, " +
                "Mileage = 0," +
                "Tank = 0, " +
                "CustomerFirstName = ''," +
                "CustomerLastName = ''," +
                "CustomerDocNumber = ''," +
                "CustomerDocType = '' " +
                "WHERE LicensePlate = @SelectedLP";
```

"Column Available is set to 0, so that the vehicle can again be considered available when the receptionist searches for a vehicle to rent. The rest of the data related to a previous rental is simply erased. In essence, a single update over the Vehicle table is executed."

Next, we turned our attention to the Change Branch button.

Change Branch Button Click Event-Handling Code

Tim said, "The code here is similar to the rest of the buttons for which an intermediate form is displayed first. The difference is that we need one more piece of data transferred from the grid in the main form to the intermediate form — the current branch. After that, the FrmChangeBranch is shown."

The Change Branch click event code is shown in Listing A-1.

Listing A-1: btnChangeBranch_Click from Receive Form Event Handling Routine

```
private void btnChangeBranch_Click(object sender, EventArgs e)
{
    //Check that user has made a selection
    if (dGridFleetView.SelectedRows.Count > 0)
    {
        //Read value from first cell as Vehicle Id
        string selectedLP =
        dGridFleetView.SelectedRows[0].
        Cells[0].Value.ToString();
        //set selectedLP as a value of TxtLP in FrmChangeBranch
        frmChangeBranch.txtLP.Text = selectedLP;
        frmChangeBranch.ShowDialog();
    }
    else
    {
        //Warn user if no selection made in table and exit
        MessageBox.Show("Please select vehicle first!");
    }
}
```

After we examined the event-handling code, Tim said, "The real code is in FrmChangeBranch. First, take a look at the form's appearance." He then showed me the Change Branch form, which is shown in Figure A-2.

"The form opens with the Vehicle License Plate and Current Branch values set. A new branch can be selected from the combo box in the form, so users can change the branch or close the form by pressing the Cancel button.

"In this case, I think it's best if I take you through the complete code for this class. We can start off by examining the class declaration and then look at the methods in detail." Tim then showed me the FrmChangeBranch class code, shown in Listing A-2.

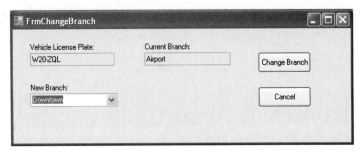

Figure A-2

Listing A-2: Class FrmChangeBranch Declaration

```csharp
using System;
using System.Collections;
using System.Collections.Generic;
using System.ComponentModel;
using System.Data;
using System.Data.SqlClient;
using System.Drawing;
using System.Linq;
using System.Text;
using System.Windows.Forms;

namespace RentAWheel
{
    public partial class FrmChangeBranch : Form
    {
        //Maintain BranchId - BranchName relation
        private Hashtable branchIdTable;
        public FrmChangeBranch()
        {
            InitializeComponent();
        }

        private void TxtCurrentBranch_TextChanged(object sender, EventArgs e)
        {

        }

        private void btnChangeBranch_Click(object sender, EventArgs e)
        {
            //see listing A-4 for method body
        }

        private void FrmChangeBranch_Load(object sender, EventArgs e)
        {
            //see listing A-3 for method body
        }
```

```
        private void btnCancel_Click(object sender, EventArgs e)
        {
            this.Close();
        }
    }
}
```

Tim noted, "Just like the rest of the classes in the project, this class imports the data provider namespaces, as observed in the import section of the class. There are three event-handling routines. `btnCancel_Click` closes the form. The Form Load event handler is used to retrieve the data and fill the Branch combo button from the Branch table. We can examine this code, and the code for the `btnChangeBranch_Click` routine, after we're done looking at the class code."

I asked Tim the purpose of the `branchIdTable` hashtable field in the form.

Tim said, "This is necessary in order to associate the name of the branch, visible to the user in the Branch combo box text, with the branch ID, necessary for the database update statement, as can be observed in the `BtnChangeBranch_Click` code. Take a look at the `frmChangeBranch_Load` code, where the combo box and the `branchIdTable` are filled with data."

In the .NET Framework, the `ComboBox` control has a `ValueMember` property that could be used for maintaining the branch Id for each item in the control.

The Load event in the Change Branch code is shown in Listing A-3.

Listing A-3: FrmChangeBranch_Load Event-Handling Routine

```
private void FrmChangeBranch_Load(object sender, EventArgs e)
{
    branchIdTable = new Hashtable();
    SqlConnection oCn = new SqlConnection(
        "Data Source=TESLATEAM;" +
        "Initial Catalog=RENTAWHEELS;" +
        "User ID=RENTAWHEELS_LOGIN;" +
        "Password=RENTAWHEELS_PASSWORD_123");
    SqlCommand oCmd;
    string strSql = "Select * from Branch";
    oCmd = new SqlCommand();
    SqlDataReader oReader;
    try
    {//open connection
        oCn.Open();
        //Set connection to command
        oCmd.Connection = oCn;
        //set Sql string to command object
        oCmd.CommandText = strSql;
        oReader = oCmd.ExecuteReader();
```

Continued

Listing A-3: FrmChangeBranch_Load Event-Handling Routine *(continued)*

```
            while (oReader.Read())
            {
                cboBranch.Items.Add(oReader[1]);
                //Add Id object to table with name as key
                branchIdTable.Add(oReader[1], oReader[0]);
            }
            cboBranch.SelectedIndex = 0;
            //close reader
            oReader.Close();
            //close connection
            oCn.Close();
        }
        catch
        {
            MessageBox.Show("A problem occurred" +
                "and the application cannot recover! " +
            "Please contact the technical support.");
        }
    }
```

Tim said, "I'm sure this `FrmChangeBranch_Load` routine code looks very familiar. It connects to the database and executes the query that retrieves the data from the Branch table, and then this data is used to fill the combo box Branch and the table that maintains the branch name-ID relationship. We'll need the ID when executing an update in the `BtnChangeBranch_Click` routine, which we can take a look at now."

Listing A-4 shows the Change Branch button click event-handling code.

Listing A-4: btnChangeBranch_Click from the FrmChangeBranch Form Event-Handling Routine

```
    private void btnChangeBranch_Click(object sender, EventArgs e)
    {
        if (MessageBox.Show("Are you sure?", "Confirm",
        MessageBoxButtons.OKCancel) == DialogResult.OK)
        {
            SqlConnection oCn = new SqlConnection(
              "Data Source=TESLATEAM;" +
              "Initial Catalog=RENTAWHEELS;" +
              "User ID=RENTAWHEELS_LOGIN;Password=RENTAWHEELS_PASSWORD_123");
            SqlCommand oCmd;
            string strSql = "Update Vehicle " +
                    "Set BranchId = @BranchId " +
                    "WHERE LicensePlate = @SelectedLP";
            oCmd = new SqlCommand();
            try
            {   //open connection
                oCn.Open();
                //Set connection to command
                oCmd.Connection = oCn;
```

```
                    //set Sql string to command object
                    oCmd.CommandText = strSql;
                    //Add parameter to command
                    oCmd.Parameters.AddWithValue(
                        "@BranchId", branchIdTable[cboBranch.Text]);
                    oCmd.Parameters.AddWithValue(
                        "@SelectedLP", txtLP.Text);
                    //exexute command
                    oCmd.ExecuteNonQuery();
                    //close connection
                    oCn.Close();
                }
            catch
            {
                MessageBox.Show("A problem occurred" +
                        "and the application cannot recover! " +
                        "Please contact the technical support.");
            }
        }
    }
}
```

Tim said, "As you can see, `btnChangeBranch_Click` contains the usual database-related code. A connection is created and opened, an SQL statement is constructed, a command and parameters are created, and the command is executed. There is the usual error-handling code. The only curiosity here is a private field, a hashtable used to maintain the relationship between the branch ID and branch name. This way, a branch ID is retrieved by using the branch name that a user selected in the Branch combo box, and the database table update can be executed."

To Maintenance and From Maintenance

The next logical items for us to examine were the two buttons left on the right-hand side, To Maintenance and From Maintenance. Tim said, "When they are pressed, the update is executed over the database directly, very much as in the Hand Over and Charge click events we already discussed. The only piece of code worth examining is the SQL command construction code." He then showed me the code for `btnToMaintenance_Click`:

```
    string strSql = "Update Vehicle " +
                        "Set Operational = 1 " +
                        "WHERE LicensePlate = @SelectedLP";
```

"Basically, for the selected vehicle, the Operational column is set to the value 1. The query for `btnFromMaintenance_Click` does exactly the opposite — it sets the value of the column Operational to 0."

```
    string strSql = "Update Vehicle " +
                        "Set Operational = 0 " +
                        "WHERE LicensePlate = @SelectedLP";
```

With the examination of code related to buttons on the right-hand side of the Fleet View form complete, we decided to next take a look at the Administration menu Tim added to the application.

Administer Fleet Form

Tim said, "The only purpose behind this menu is to display different forms used for data administration. Let's start off by taking a look at the Vehicle Fleet Administration form." The Vehicle Fleet Administration form is shown in Figure A-3.

Figure A-3

"As you can probably guess, the button strip at the bottom is used to navigate through the set of vehicles. The button with < displays the previous record, the button with > displays the next record, and the buttons << and >> display the first and last vehicle entry, respectively. Pressing buttons on the right-hand side triggers database query execution, except when the button New is pressed. The New button's only role is to erase the content of controls on the form. However, pressing Delete provokes elimination of the current record in the database. The Save button first eliminates and then saves the current record, thus performing a kind of update or insert, depending on whether this particular license plate number already exists in the database or not. If the license plate number already exists in the database, eliminating the vehicle first and then inserting the vehicle equals an update. If the vehicle is new, it means it does not exist in the database, so deleting it in a first step has no effect on the database and does not raise any exception, so this equals a simple insert. That way, I was able to simplify the user interface."

I said, "So, basically, you hold all the records from the Vehicle table in memory, and you navigate through the records with navigation buttons on the button strip. When you press the Delete or Save button, you issue a statement that synchronizes the local data in memory with the database."

Tim said, "Yes, that about sums it up. We can take a look at the code for this form in detail, starting with `btnDelete_Click`, since it is really straightforward."

Delete Button Click Event-Handling Routine

I told Tim that I thought this must be another simple SQL delete query.

Tim said, "Yes, no surprises here. This code looks very similar to a large portion of the code we have seen so far. A simple delete SQL query is executed against the Vehicle table in the database, using the vehicle license plate as a parameter."

The SQL code for the delete query is shown in Listing A-5.

Listing A-5: SQL Query Inside btnDelete_Click Event-Handling Routine

```
string strSqlDelete = "Delete From Vehicle " +
    "Where LicensePlate = @LicensePlate";
```

New Button Click Event-Handling Routine

After completing our look at the Delete button code, we moved on to the New button. Tim said, "This button is rather obvious also. Components are cleared of previous values." The code for the New button click event is shown in Listing A-6.

Listing A-6: btnNew_Click from the FrmFlt Form Event-Handling Routine

```
private void btnNew_Click(object sender, EventArgs e)
{
    txtLP.Text = "";
    cboBranch.Text = "";
    cboModel.Text = "";
}
```

Reload Button Click Event-Handling Routine

Tim indicated that another very simple routine was the one for the Reload button event handling. "All it does is call the `FrmFleet_Load` routine." The Reload Button event-handling routine is illustrated in Listing A-7.

Listing A-7: btnReload_Click from the FrmFlt Form Event-Handling Routine

```
private void btnReload_Click(object sender, EventArgs e)
{
    FrmFlt_Load(null, null);
}
```

Then Tim said, "This all leads us to the Form Load routine. It is significantly longer than the routines we have inspected so far. Let's take a look at it."

Form Load Event-Handling Routine

Tim went on, "The code in this method is again database-related code. The only real difference here is that three queries are executed instead of one. The first two queries are concerned with filling two combo boxes, Branch and Model, with data from the Branch and Model tables. Two fields of type `Hashtable` are used to maintain the relation between the text that goes into the combo boxes and what is presented to the user (Branch and Model names) and the Branch and Model IDs needed for update and delete.

"The last query is used to retrieve data from the Vehicle table joined with other, lookup tables. This data is displayed to users as they navigate through the Vehicle table records. The resulting data table is assigned to a private field `dtVehicles`."

You can see the rather long Fleet Form Load event code in Listing A-8.

Listing A-8: FrmFleet_Load Event-Handling Routine

```csharp
private void FrmFlt_Load(object sender, EventArgs e)
{
    SqlConnection oCn = new SqlConnection(
        "Data Source=TESLATEAM;" +
        "Initial Catalog=RENTAWHEELS;" +
        "User ID=RENTAWHEELS_LOGIN;" +
        "Password=RENTAWHEELS_PASSWORD_123");
    SqlCommand oCmdCombo = new SqlCommand();
    SqlDataAdapter oAdapter = new SqlDataAdapter();
    //LOAD BRANCH COMBO -->
    //Create Sql String
    string strSqlCombo = "Select * from Branch";
    try
    {
        //open connection
        oCn.Open();
        //Set connection to command
        oCmdCombo.Connection = oCn;
        //set Sql string to command object
        oCmdCombo.CommandText = strSqlCombo;
        //execute command
        SqlDataReader oReader = oCmdCombo.ExecuteReader();
        branchIdTable = new Hashtable();
        while (oReader.Read())
        {
            cboBranch.Items.Add(oReader[1]);
            //Add Id object to table with name as key
            branchIdTable.Add(oReader[1], oReader[0]);
        }
        //close reader
        oReader.Close();
        //END LOAD COMBO -->

        //LOAD MODEL COMBO -->
        //Create Sql String
        strSqlCombo = "Select * from Model";
        //Set connection to command
        oCmdCombo.Connection = oCn;
        //set Sql string to command object
        oCmdCombo.CommandText = strSqlCombo;
        //execute command
        oReader = oCmdCombo.ExecuteReader();
        modelIdTable = new Hashtable();
        while (oReader.Read())
        {
            cboModel.Items.Add(oReader[1]);
            //Add Id object to table with name as key
            modelIdTable.Add(oReader[1], oReader[0]);
        }
        //close reader
```

```
        oReader.Close();
        //END LOAD COMBO -->

        //LOAD DATASET -->
        //create data set
        DataSet dsModel = new DataSet();
        SqlCommand oCmd = new SqlCommand();
        //Create Sql String with parameter @SelectedLP
        string strSql = "Select Vehicle.LicensePlate AS LicensePlate, " +
        "Branch.Name as BranchName, " +
        "Model.Name as ModelName " +
        "from Vehicle " +
        "Inner Join Branch On " +
        "Vehicle.BranchId = Branch.BranchId " +
        "Inner Join Model On " +
        "Vehicle.ModelId = Model.ModelId";
        //Set connection to command
        oCmd.Connection = oCn;
        //set Sql string to command object
        oCmd.CommandText = strSql;
        //execute command
        oAdapter.SelectCommand = oCmd;
        //fill DataSet
        oAdapter.Fill(dsModel);
        //close connection
        oCn.Close();
        //destroy objects
        dtVehicles = dsModel.Tables[0];
        if (dtVehicles.Rows.Count > 0)
        {
            DataRow drRow = dtVehicles.Rows[0];
            txtLP.Text = drRow["LicensePlate"].ToString();
            cboBranch.Text = drRow["BranchName"].ToString();
            cboModel.Text = drRow["ModelName"].ToString();
            currentRowIndex = 0;
        }
        //END LOAD DATASET -->
    }
    catch
    {
        MessageBox.Show("A problem occurred and the application cannot recover! " +
        "Please contact the technical support.");
    }
}
```

Administer Fleet Form Class Code: Fields

Tim moved on to discuss the fields and class declaration next. "Again, this class imports SQL Data Provider namespaces. There are two hashtables, branchIdTable and modelIdTable, related to two combo boxes, Branch and Model. As you have already seen in the Change Branch form, the purpose of these two tables is to maintain the relationship between the name displayed in the combo box and the ID of the branch or model.

"A new element here is a `DataTable` named `dtVehicles`. It represents the Vehicle table from the RENTAWHEELS database. As the user navigates between vehicles on the form, a single row from the table is displayed. The integer `currentRowIndex` serves to conserve an index of the currently displayed row."

Then Tim showed me the Fleet Form class code shown in Listing A-9.

Listing A-9: Fleet Administration Form (FrmFlt) Class Fields

```
public partial class FrmFlt : Form
{
    //Maintain BranchId - BranchName relation
    private Hashtable branchIdTable;
    //Maintain ModelId - ModelName relation
    private Hashtable modelIdTable;
    //table Vehicles
    private DataTable dtVehicles;
    //Index of displayed row
    private int currentRowIndex;

    //rest of class code (methods) goes here
}
```

When we had finished looking at this code Tim said, "A look at the Left button event-handling code will show how this `currentRowIndex` number is used when users navigate through the Vehicle table records."

Navigation Buttons Click Event-Handling Routine

Tim said, "When someone presses `btnLeft` (the one with the < symbol), the current row index is decremented and then used to obtain a row from the Vehicle table. This row is then used to fill controls on the form with data. In this way, the effect of moving through the records in the table using the navigation button on the bottom of the form is achieved." The Left button click event-handling code is shown in Listing A-10.

Listing A-10: btnLeft_Click Event-Handling Routine

```
private void btnLeft_Click(object sender, EventArgs e)
{
    if (currentRowIndex - 1 >= 0 & dtVehicles.Rows.Count > 0)
    {
        currentRowIndex--;
        DataRow drRow = dtVehicles.Rows[currentRowIndex];
        txtLP.Text = drRow["LicensePlate"].ToString();
        cboBranch.Text = drRow["BranchName"].ToString();
        cboModel.Text = drRow["ModelName"].ToString();
    }
}
```

Tim then showed that similar code is present in the rest of the navigation buttons. "The Right button increments the current row index, the First button sets the current row index to zero, and the Last button sets the current row index to row count minus one."

```
private void btnRight_Click(object sender, EventArgs e)
{
    if (dtVehicles.Rows.Count > currentRowIndex + 1)
    {
        currentRowIndex++;
        DataRow drRow = dtVehicles.Rows[currentRowIndex];
        txtLP.Text = drRow["LicensePlate"].ToString();
        cboBranch.Text = drRow["BranchName"].ToString();
        cboModel.Text = drRow["ModelName"].ToString();
    }
}

private void btnFirst_Click(object sender, EventArgs e)
{
    if (dtVehicles.Rows.Count > 0)
    {
        currentRowIndex = 0;
        DataRow drRow = dtVehicles.Rows[currentRowIndex];
        txtLP.Text = drRow["LicensePlate"].ToString();
        cboBranch.Text = drRow["BranchName"].ToString();
        cboModel.Text = drRow["ModelName"].ToString();
    }
}

private void btnLast_Click(object sender, EventArgs e)
{
    if (dtVehicles.Rows.Count > 0)
    {
        currentRowIndex = dtVehicles.Rows.Count - 1;
        DataRow drRow = dtVehicles.Rows[currentRowIndex];
        txtLP.Text = drRow["LicensePlate"].ToString();
        cboBranch.Text = drRow["BranchName"].ToString();
        cboModel.Text = drRow["ModelName"].ToString();
    }
}
```

Then Tim said, "The only button left to inspect is the Save button. The code executed when this button is activated is probably the most complicated in the application so far."

Save Button Click Event-Handling Routine

Tim continued, "There is a single button to perform both insert and update. However, I am not able to distinguish between the update when a vehicle already exists in database and the insert when you are dealing with a completely new vehicle. To resolve this, two steps are always performed:

1. A record is deleted based on a primary key, license plate number.

2. A record with the same primary key (license plate number) is inserted."

The Save button click event-handling routine is shown in Listing A-11.

Listing A-11: btnSave_Click Event-Handling Routine

```
private void btnSave_Click(object sender, EventArgs e)
{
    string strSql;
    SqlConnection oCn = new SqlConnection(
        "Data Source=TESLATEAM;" +
        "Initial Catalog=RENTAWHEELS;" +
        "User ID=RENTAWHEELS_LOGIN;" +
        "Password=RENTAWHEELS_PASSWORD_123");
    SqlCommand oCmdDelete = new SqlCommand();
    SqlCommand oCmdInsert = new SqlCommand();
    string strSqlDelete = "Delete From Vehicle " +
            "Where LicensePlate = @LicensePlate";
    //Create Sql String for insert
    string strSqlInsert = "Insert Into Vehicle " +
    "(LicensePlate, ModelId,BranchId) " +
    "Values(@LicensePlate, @ModelId, @BranchId)";
    //add parameter for delete
    oCmdDelete.Parameters.AddWithValue(
    "@LicensePlate", txtLP.Text);
    //add parameters for insert
    oCmdInsert.Parameters.AddWithValue(
        "@LicensePlate", txtLP.Text);
    oCmdInsert.Parameters.AddWithValue(
    "@ModelId", modelIdTable[cboModel.Text]);
    oCmdInsert.Parameters.AddWithValue(
        "@BranchId", branchIdTable[cboBranch.Text]);
    //open connection
    oCn.Open();
    //Set connection to command
    oCmdDelete.Connection = oCn;
    oCmdInsert.Connection = oCn;
    //set Sql string to command object
    oCmdDelete.CommandText = strSqlDelete;
    oCmdInsert.CommandText = strSqlInsert;
    //start transaction
    SqlTransaction oTrx = oCn.BeginTransaction();
    //enlist commands with transaction
    oCmdDelete.Transaction = oTrx;
    oCmdInsert.Transaction = oTrx;
    //execute command: first delete and then insert record
    oCmdDelete.ExecuteNonQuery();
    oCmdInsert.ExecuteNonQuery();
    oTrx.Commit();
    //close connection
    oCn.Close();
    FrmFlt_Load(null, null);
}
```

"This, in the end, has same effect as performing an SQL update. In the case of an insert, erasing non-existing records will not provoke any problems, as I am not checking for the number of records that were affected with a delete command. And just in case some problem occurs between the executions of these two separate queries, they are executed under the same transaction, thus ensuring that a partial execution will not happen. That way, we can be confident that the record will not be deleted unless the insert is executed also.

"In the Vehicle table, the license plate number serves as the primary key. In other tables, the primary key is autogenerated by the database itself upon each insert. This makes it possible to use SQL insert and update in the rest of the administration forms, because the ID is placed in a read-only text box. If the ID is present, this means the record already exists, and we need to execute an update. If the ID is not present, then the user has already pressed the New button that cleared the form and is trying to insert a new record, meaning that an insert command should be issued to the database. The other administration forms, such as Model, Category, and Branch, are based on the same model."

Display Button Click Event-Handling Routine

Having finished our discussion about the administration forms, we returned to the last piece of functionality we needed to discuss on the application's main form, the Display button and the filtering capabilities it made available to users.

Tim said, "At the bottom of the main form, the user can set different search options and in that way filter the vehicles that are going to be displayed. The table is refreshed by pressing the Display button. Different combo boxes in the vehicle display filter group box are converted as part of a Where clause in an SQL Select query that is used to retrieve data from the RENTAWHEELS database. Additional complexity comes from the fact that certain filters can be applied, depending on the user's decision. For example, if the Category combo box is left with the value All, this means that Category should not form part of the Where clause in an SQL statement. Since there are four combo boxes, and each can form part of a Where clause or not, there is a need to dynamically construct this query."

With that, Tim showed me the event-handling code for the Display button, shown in Listing A-12.

Listing A-12: btnDisplay_Click Event-Handling Routine

```
private void btnDisplay_Click(object sender, EventArgs e)
{
    //Declare variables
    SqlConnection oCn = new SqlConnection(
      "Data Source=TESLATEAM;" +
      "Initial Catalog=RENTAWHEELS;" +
      "User ID=RENTAWHEELS_LOGIN;" +
      "Password=RENTAWHEELS_PASSWORD_123");
    SqlCommand oCmd = new SqlCommand();
    SqlDataAdapter oAdapter = new SqlDataAdapter();
    SqlDataReader oRd;
    string strSql;
    //clear grid
    this.dGridFleetView.Rows.Clear();
    //Create Sql String
    strSql = "Select Vehicle.LicensePlate as LicensePlate," +
    "Category.Name as CategoryName," +
    "Vehicle.Available as Available," +
    "Vehicle.Operational as Operational," +
```

Continued

Listing A-12: btnDisplay_Click Event-Handling Routine *(continued)*

```
"Model.Name as ModelName," +
"Branch.Name as BranchName," +
"Category.DailyPrice as DailyPrice," +
"Category.WeeklyPrice as WeeklyPrice," +
"Category.MonthlyPrice as MonthlyPrice," +
"Vehicle.Mileage as Mileage," +
"Vehicle.Tank as Tank," +
"Vehicle.CustomerFirstName as FirstName," +
"Vehicle.CustomerLastName as LastName," +
"Vehicle.CustomerDocNumber as DocNumber," +
"Vehicle.CustomerDocType as DocType " +
"from Vehicle " +
"Inner Join Model ON " +
"Vehicle.ModelId = Model.ModelId " +
"Inner Join Branch ON " +
"Vehicle.BranchId = Branch.BranchId " +
"Inner Join Category ON " +
"Model.CategoryId = Category.CategoryId";
if (cboAvailable.Text != "All" |
    cboBranch.Text != "All" |
    cboCategory.Text != "All" |
    cboOperational.Text != "All")
{
    strSql += " Where ";
    if (cboAvailable.Text != "All")
    {
        strSql += "Vehicle.Available = @Available And ";
        int available = 0;
        switch (cboAvailable.Text)
        {
            case "Available":
                available = 0;
                break;
            case "Hand Over":
                available = 1;
                break;
            case "Rented":
                available = 2;
                break;
            case "Charge":
                available = 3;
                break;
        }
        oCmd.Parameters.AddWithValue(
        "@Available", available);
    }
    if (cboBranch.Text != "All")
    {
        strSql += "Vehicle.BranchId = @BranchId And ";
        oCmd.Parameters.AddWithValue(
            "@BranchId", this.branchIdTable[cboBranch.Text]);
    }
```

```csharp
        if (cboCategory.Text != "All")
        {
            strSql += "Model.CategoryId = @CategoryId And ";
            oCmd.Parameters.AddWithValue("@CategoryId",
                this.categoryIdTable[cboCategory.Text]);
        }
        if (cboOperational.Text != "All")
        {
            strSql += "Vehicle.Operational = @Operational And ";
            int operational = 0;
            switch (cboOperational.Text)
            {
                case "In Operation":
                    operational = 0;
                    break;
                case "In Maintenance":
                    operational = 1;
                    break;
            }
            oCmd.Parameters.AddWithValue(
            "@Operational", operational);
        }
        strSql = strSql.Substring(0, strSql.Length - 5);
    }
//open connection
oCn.Open();
//Set connection to command
oCmd.Connection = oCn;
//set Sql string to command object
oCmd.CommandText = strSql;
//execute command
oRd = oCmd.ExecuteReader();
//Fill Combo Categories
while (oRd.Read())
{
    string[] row = new string[]{
        oRd["LicensePlate"].ToString(),
        oRd["CategoryName"].ToString(),
        availableText(Convert.ToInt16(oRd["Available"])),
        Convert.ToInt16(oRd["Operational"]).Equals(0) ?
        "In Operation" : "In Maintenance",
        oRd["ModelName"].ToString(),
        oRd["BranchName"].ToString(),
        oRd["DailyPrice"].ToString(),
        oRd["WeeklyPrice"].ToString(),
        oRd["MonthlyPrice"].ToString(),
        oRd["Mileage"].ToString(),
        oRd["Tank"].ToString(),
        Convert.IsDBNull(oRd["FirstName"]) ? " ": oRd["FirstName"].ToString(),
        Convert.IsDBNull(oRd["LastName"]) ? " ": oRd["LastName"].ToString(),
        Convert.IsDBNull(oRd["DocNumber"]) ? " ": oRd["DocNumber"].ToString(),
        Convert.IsDBNull(oRd["DocType"]) ? " ": oRd["DocType"].ToString()
        };
```

Continued

Listing A-12: btnDisplay_Click Event-Handling Routine *(continued)*

```
            this.dGridFleetView.Rows.Add(row);
        }
        //close reader
        oRd.Close();
        oCn.Close();

    }
```

"The user can choose not to apply filters, to apply all filters, or to apply a given number of filters. Each filter is transformed into a single condition in the Where part of an SQL query. Because of this, we need to construct the query dynamically. If no filter is applied, we do not need to add the Where keyword after the Select part of the query. If there is a single condition, we need to add Where to the SQL command. Filters are exclusive, which means they need to be concatenated using the AND keyword. Since we cannot be sure which filter is the last and so as not to add any more ANDs after constructing the query, the last AND keyword is simply removed from the SQL string."

I said, "So, while you build the Where part of the query, each time you add a condition, for example, Vehicle.Available = @Available, you always add an AND keyword to the end of the condition. That way, you always end up with one AND keyword too many."

Tim said, "Exactly. String AND plus two blank spaces amounts to a length of five, as shown in this line:

```
strSql = strSql.Substring(0, strSql.Length - 5);
```

"This way, the trailing AND is removed from the SQL query code.

"Now, since we use integers to represent the Available and Operational state in the database, we need to translate these codes to the user. In the case of Operational, this is done directly, by using the "?" operator:

```
            Convert.ToInt16(oRd["Operational"]).Equals(0) ?
            "In Operation" : "In Maintenance",
```

"Here, 0 means In Operation, and any other value means In Maintenance, but the only other value that this field can have in the database is 1. So, this corresponds to the values of the Maintenance column we examined earlier.

"With the Available column, the situation is more complicated, because this column can have more than two values. Therefore, I used a separate method called availableText to translate the integer value to a descriptive string value. The method is called using this code:

```
            availableText(Convert.ToInt16(oRd["Available"]))
```

"Now, take a look at the method itself."

Tim presented the availableText method shown in Listing A-13.

Listing A-13: AvailableText Method Used to Translate Integer Values of Available Column to Descriptive String Values

```
private string availableText(int available)
    {
        string strAvailable = "";
        switch (available)
        {
            case 0:
                strAvailable = "Available";
                break;
            case 1:
                strAvailable = "Hand Over";
                break;
            case 2:
                strAvailable = "Rented";
                break;
            case 3:
                strAvailable = "Charge";
                break;
        }
        return strAvailable;
    }
```

"That is how the dynamic search SQL query is constructed and used to help users display only the vehicles they are interested in. That way, we have provided users with an efficient tool and optimized the time used to perform each operation."

Summary

This more or less wraps up all the interesting details of the code in the prototype Rent-a-Wheels application constructed for example purposes for this book. I didn't go into the details of each and every method, but you've had a chance to inspect everything that's of major interest, and certainly all you need to see of this application in order for it to serve as a demonstration ground for the refactoring demonstrated in the book.

Again, please remember that this code is presented to illustrate a quick-and-dirty approach to programming. It is poorly designed and it does not take advantage of a majority of C# language features, but this has been done on purpose. Through the refactoring process, and throughout this book, you improve this code, and in the process discover new, better ways to design your applications.

The full code for the application is available for download at the book's website at www.wrox.com, and I definitely encourage you to download it (if you haven't already) and use it to follow along as you work through the book.

B

Unleash Refactor! for ASP.NET

Thanks to its partnership with Microsoft, Developer Express has released Refactor! for ASP.NET, a free and scaled-down version of their Refactor! Pro product. The free version comes with a limited number of available refactorings and a few options hidden from users.

The Pro version enables you to extend the capability of the tool and define your own refactorings, and it has code analysis capabilities, more refactorings, and so on.

There is one more limitation to the free version. Configuration options are visible only in the Pro version of the tool by default. However, with a little bit of tweaking, you can make a DevExpress menu item appear and obtain access to the Refactor! options window even with the scaled-down version.

The configuration options enable you to customize certain behaviors of Refactor! for ASP.NET so they better suit your personal style of programming. For example, you can change the keyboard shortcut keys used for one-key refactoring, access different visual options such as color or contrast, and, more important, customize tool behavior when performing different refactorings. Feel free to explore other options and set them to your liking.

To activate this hidden feature, you need to change a certain setting in the Windows registry. Depending on the selection you made during the installation process, this setting is located in one of two places, as listed in Table B-1.

1. Use regedit to locate this key.

2. Find the HideMenu value. This value has the DWORD type and is set to 1 when you first find it. Change this value to 0.

3. Once you apply the new setting, close Visual Studio and open it again so that the changes can take effect.

4. Open any C# source file for editing in order to load the Refactor! plug-in inside Visual Studio. The DevExpress menu item should appear now in the Visual Studio menu. If the DevExpress menu does not appear, activate DevExpress Add-in in the Tools ➤ Add-In Manager window.

Table B-1: Registry Setting Location for Configuration Options Window and DevExpress Menu Activation

Refactor! Installation Option	Windows Registry Location
Refactor! is available to any user	HKEY_LOCAL_MACHINE\SOFTWARE\Developer Express\CodeRush for VS\3.2
Refactor! is available only to the current user	HKEY_CURRENT_USER \SOFTWARE\Developer Express\CodeRush for VS\3.2

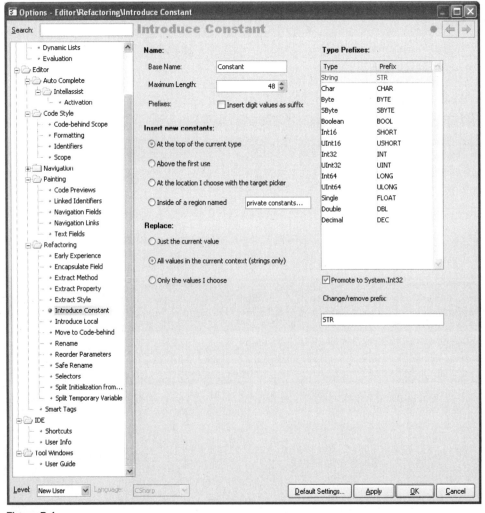

Figure B-1

The exact location of the setting might vary slightly, depending on the exact version of Refactor! you have installed on your computer.

You can open the Options window and experiment with different settings that let you further customize the tool. You can see the DevExpress top menu item inside the Visual Studio menu and the DevExpress Options window in Figure B-1.

Changes in the configuration you apply in the Options window are persisted in different .ini files. Refactor! places these files inside your User Profile folder. As another option to tweak Refactor!, these files can be edited manually. You can find these files in the folder

```
C:\Documents and Settings\YourProfile\Application Data\CodeRush for VS
.NET\1.1\Settings\
```

where `C:` is the drive on your computer where the Windows operating system is installed, and where `YourProfile` corresponds to the username under which you are logged in.

This way, you will be able to use many options that are available only in the Pro version of the tool and customize Refactor! in accordance with your personal preferences.

Index